An Economic History of Malaysia, *c.* 1800–1990

A *Modern Economic History of Southeast Asia*

The Australian National University is preparing a multivolume economic history of Southeast Asia which will for the first time place the remarkable economic changes of the late twentieth century within a broader historical framework. This series is at once a work of pioneering scholarship, since nothing remotely comparable has previously been attempted, and also a work of synthesis, since hitherto discrete literatures in several disciplines and on ten countries need to be integrated. The series will include several volumes on the economic history of the principal countries of Southeast Asia over the past 150 or so years, and a larger number of volumes integrating the whole region in terms of major themes in economic history. Each volume will be accessible to students and specialists alike, aiming to make coherent a history which has been fragmented or ignored.

The Economic History of Southeast Asia Project has been supported by the Research School of Pacific and Asian Studies of The Australian National University and by the Henry Luce Foundation.

General Editors: **Anthony Reid** (Chair), Professor of Southeast Asian History, the Research School of Pacific and Asian Studies, The Australian National University, Canberra; **Anne Booth**, Professor of Economics, School of Oriental and African Studies (SOAS), London; **Malcolm Falkus**, Professor of Economic History, University of New England, Armidale, Australia; and **Graeme Snooks**, Coghlan Professor of Economic History, Research School of the Social Sciences, The Australian National University, Canberra.

Titles include:

John H. Drabble
AN ECONOMIC HISTORY OF MALAYSIA, *c.* 1800–1990
The Transition to Modern Economic Growth

R. E. Elson
THE END OF THE PEASANTRY IN SOUTHEAST ASIA

J. Thomas Lindblad
FOREIGN INVESTMENT IN SOUTHEAST ASIA IN THE TWENTIETH CENTURY

Modern Economic History of South East Asia
Series Standing Order ISBN 0–333–71429–6
(*outside North America only*)

You can receive future titles in this series as they are published by placing a standing order. Please contact your bookseller or, in case of difficulty, write to us at the address below with your name and address, the title of the series and the ISBN quoted above.

Customer Services Department, Macmillan Distribution Ltd, Houndmills, Basingstoke, Hampshire RG21 6XS, England

An Economic History of Malaysia, *c.* 1800–1990

The Transition to Modern Economic Growth

John H. Drabble
Honorary Research Associate
University of Sydney

in association with
THE AUSTRALIAN NATIONAL UNIVERSITY
CANBERRA

First published in Great Britain 2000 by

MACMILLAN PRESS LTD

Houndmills, Basingstoke, Hampshire RG21 6XS and London
Companies and representatives throughout the world

A catalogue record for this book is available from the British Library.

ISBN 0–333–55299–7 hardcover
ISBN 0–333–55300–4 paperback

First published in the United States of America 2000 by

ST. MARTIN'S PRESS, LLC,

Scholarly and Reference Division,
175 Fifth Avenue, New York, N.Y. 10010

ISBN 0–312–23077–X

Library of Congress Cataloging-in-Publication Data
Drabble, John H.
An economic history of Malaysia, c. 1800–1990 : the transition to modern
economic growth / John H. Drabble.
p. cm. — (A modern economic history of Southeast Asia)
Includes bibliographical references and index.
ISBN 0–312–23077–X (cloth)
1. Malaysia—Economic conditions. 2. Malaysia—Economic policy. 3. Malaysia–
–Commerce—History—19th century. 4. Malaysia—Commerce—History—20th
century. 5. Social change—Malaysia. I. Title. II. Series.

HC445.5. .D7298   2000
330.9595—dc21
                                                                      99–053111

This book is printed on paper suitable for recycling and made from fully managed and sustained
forest sources.

10   9   8   7   6   5   4   3   2   1
09   08   07   06   05   04   03   02   01   00

Printed and bound in Great Britain by
Antony Rowe Ltd, Chippenham, Wiltshire

For the people of Malaysia with thanks for many years of warm friendships and an abiding academic interest

Contents

0011190

List of Tables

List of Figures and Maps

Figures

Maps

Preface

This study, in addition to meeting the need for a general economic history of Malaysia, is intended as something of a reflection on the author's personal acquaintance with the country (almost entirely in Peninsular Malaysia) extending over a period of nearly 40 years. I arrived at the end of 1958, little more than a year after *Merdeka*, as a 'mercantile assistant' with Guthrie & Company, the oldest of the British agency houses. Over the next four years I acquired a knowledge of the plantation rubber industry and an abiding interest in the country, its people and history. Few at that time, Malaysian or expatriate, could have foreseen that over the next three decades or so the Federation of Malaysia (1963) would enjoy one of the fastest rates of economic growth in the Association of Southeast Asian Nations (ASEAN) region and make substantial progress towards newly industrialised country (NIC) status by 1990. In making a change in career from business to academia following my time with Guthries I have always been extremely grateful to Professor C.D. Cowan (School of Oriental and African Studies) who suggested economic history, in particular the Malayan rubber industry, as a suitable focus for my interests, and to Professor Wang Gungwu who gave me my first academic appointment in the Department of History, University of Malaya in 1968.

After moving to the Department of Economic History, University of Sydney, in 1974 I began preliminary work on this study, but substantive progress only became possible after I received a three-year grant from the Australian Research Council in 1989, which brought me the invaluable services of Dr Janell Mills as Senior Research Assistant. She has been tireless in locating and collating materials (with assistance from Simon Gentry and Paul Kadang), and commenting on successive drafts. Shortly afterwards the Modern Economic History of Southeast Asia Project (ECHOSEA) was set up in the Research School of Pacific and Asian Studies, Australian National University (ANU). I am deeply grateful to Professor Tony Reid, the coordinator, for the opportunity to spend 1990 as a Visiting Fellow with the project (with financial assistance from the ANU). He has been the source of much valued personal and professional support at all times.

The ECHOSEA project fulfilled a crucial role for all its members through workshops which brought together scholars from Australia and overseas to discuss the various draft manuscripts. I benefited greatly from one of these in December 1994 and am indebted for helpful comments and suggestions from Amarjit Kaur, Gill Burke, Cheah Boon Kheng (who also read later drafts), Rob Cramb, Harold Crouch, Howard Dick, Peter Drake, Pierre van der Eng, Gregg Huff, Richard Leete, David Lim, Lesley Potter, Tony Reid and Peter Rimmer. At other times I received valuable assistance from Heinz Arndt, Colin Barlow, Henry S. Barlow, Philip Courtenay, Malcolm Falkus, John Gullick, Barbara and Michael Leigh, John Overton and Rodney Parker QC. Anne Booth very kindly performed the calculations underlying the export volume data in Tables 3.6 and 8.2, and Pierre van der Eng generously shared his preliminary work on Malayan/Malaysian GDP. The Malaysian International Chamber of Commerce and Industry was most helpful in obtaining a suitable photograph for the cover.

Skills on the word-processor do not come naturally to me, and I am profoundly thankful to Julie Manley, Department of Economic History, Sydney University, and to my sons Ian and Paul for continually rescuing me from the potentially disastrous results of incautious key-pressing and mouse-clicking! Ian produced the figures in the book, and another friend and colleague, Ian Metcalfe, very kindly prepared the maps.

My deep gratitude goes to my wife, Irene, for her support and forbearance with the seemingly endless preoccupation which accompanies a project of this type, and to a number of editors at Macmillan who have been generous in the number of extensions granted. Final responsibility for the form and content of this work remains with me.

Sydney   JOHN H. DRABBLE

Currency, Weights, Measures

All monetary references are in Straits dollars (later the Malayan/Malaysian dollar/*ringgit*) except where otherwise designated. Weights and measures are expressed in the metric system except where the historical figure is more appropriate.

Geographical Note

The nomenclature employed follows historical usage. Prior to 1963 'Malaysia' denotes the region comprising the territories of the current Federation. For that period also the terms 'Malay Peninsula' (or more briefly 'Peninsula') and 'Malaya' are used interchangeably. Within that unit the 'Straits Settlements' (SS) refers to Penang, Melaka and Singapore; the 'Federated Malay States' (FMS) to Perak, Selangor, Negeri Sembilan and Pahang; and the 'Unfederated Malay States' (UMS) to Perlis, Kedah, Kelantan, Terengganu and Johor. Post-Federation the terms 'Peninsula' and 'Peninsular Malaysia' are again used interchangeably.

Prior to Federation, 'British North Borneo' is abbreviated to 'North Borneo', thereafter becoming 'Sabah'. 'Sarawak' is unchanged throughout. 'East Malaysia' and the 'Borneo territories' refer to both these states.

Abbreviations

ABS	*Annual Bulletin of Statistics*
AR	*Annual Report*
ASAA	Asian Studies Association of Australia
ASEAN	Association of Southeast Asian Nations
BBTC	British Borneo Timber Company
BNB	British North Borneo
CBR	Crude birth rate
CDR	Crude death rate
EIC	English East India company
EDCC	*Economic Development and Cultural Change*
EOI	Export-oriented industrialisation
ERP	Effective rate of protection
ESCAP	(UN) Economic and Social Commission for Asia and the Pacific
FDI	Foreign Direct Investment
FEER	*Far Eastern Economic Review*
FELCRA	Federal Land Consolidation and Rehabilitation Authority
FELDA	Federal Land Development Authority
FMS	Federated Malay States
FTZ	Free Trade Zone
HICOM	Heavy Industries Corporation of Malaysia
IAHA	International Association of Historians of Asia
IBRD	International Bank for Reconstruction and Development
ICA	Industrial Coordination Act
IMF	International Monetary Fund
ISI	Import-substitution industrialisation
IRRA	International Rubber Regulation Agreement
ISEAS	Institute of Southeast Asian Studies, Singapore
JCA	*Journal of Contemporary Asia*
JMBRAS	*Journal, Malaysian Branch, Royal Asiatic Society*
JSEAS	*Journal of Southeast Asian Studies*
LDCs	Less Developed Countries
LNG	Liquified Natural Gas
MARDEC	Malaysian Rubber Development Corporation
MAS	*Modern Asian Studies*
MER/SER	*Malayan Economic Review/Singapore Economic Review*
MJES	*Malaysian Journal of Economic Studies*
MJTG	*Malayan/Malaysian Journal of Tropical Geography*
MMC	Malaysia Mining Corporation

NAP	New Agricultural Policy
NB	North Borneo
NEI	Netherlands East Indies
NEP	New Economic Policy
NICs	Newly Industrialised Countries
R and D	research and development
RCCS	Rural Cooperative Credit Society
RIDA	Rural and Industrial Development Authority
RISDA	Rubber Industry Smallholders Development Authority
RNAS	rural non-farm activities
SAB	Sabah Action Blueprint
SAFODA	Sabah Forest Development Authority
SALCRA	Sarawak Land Consolidation and Rehabilitation Authority
SLDB	Sabah/Sarawak Land Development Board
SP	Standard Production
SS	Straits Settlements
TFPG	Total Factor Productivity Growth
UMNO	United Malays National Organisation
UMS	Unfederated Malay States
VOC	Dutch East India Company

Glossary

bumiputeras	Malays and other indigenous peoples
getah	rubber
kampung	village
kedai	small shop
kerah	compulsory labour services
kerajaan	Government
ladang	shifting (dry) cultivation
kongsi	Chinese work and social cooperative
kota	fort
orang asli	aboriginals (Malay Peninsula)
orang laut	sea people
padi	unhusked rice
pasar	market
pekan	town
penghulu	district head
rakyat	common people
sawah	irrigated rice cultivation
towkay (*taukeh*)	Chinese business owner/community leader

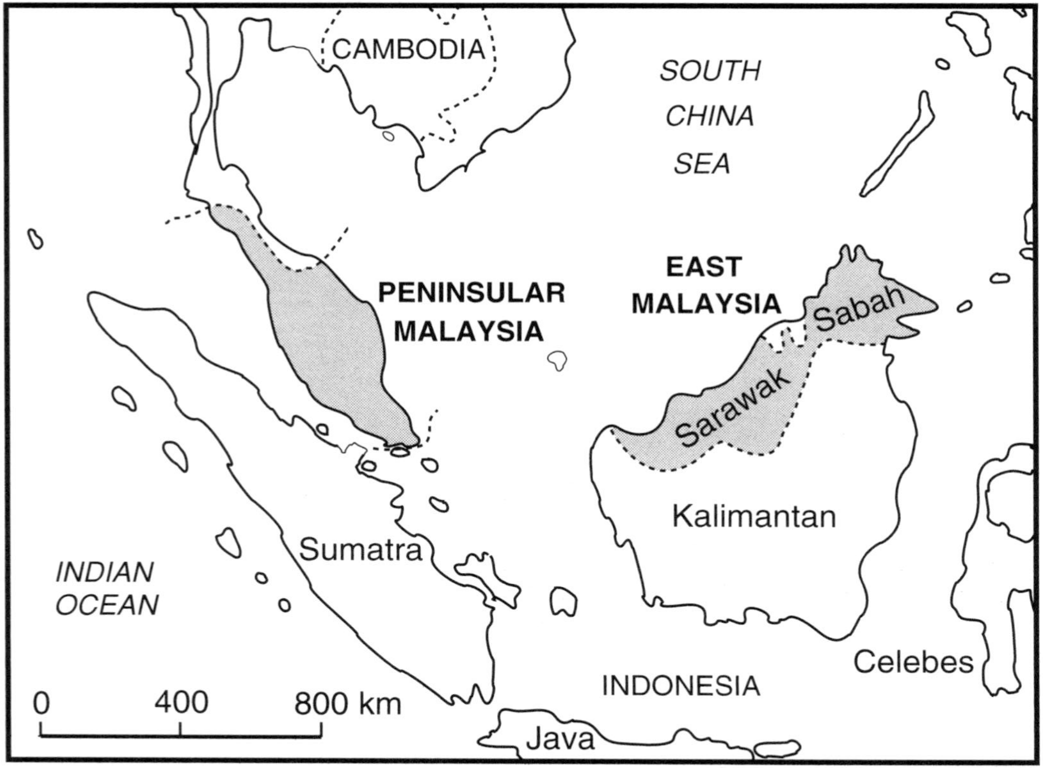

Map 1 Malaysia

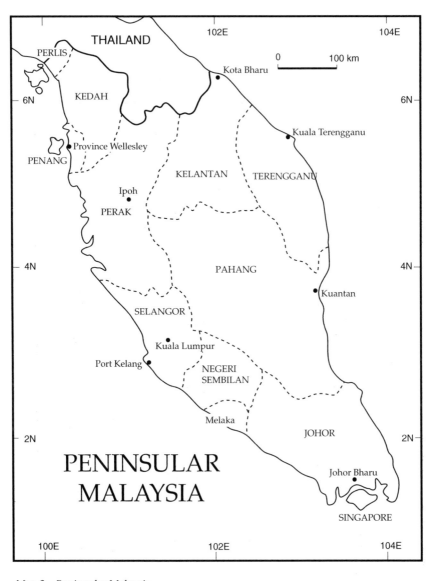

Map 2 Peninsular Malaysia

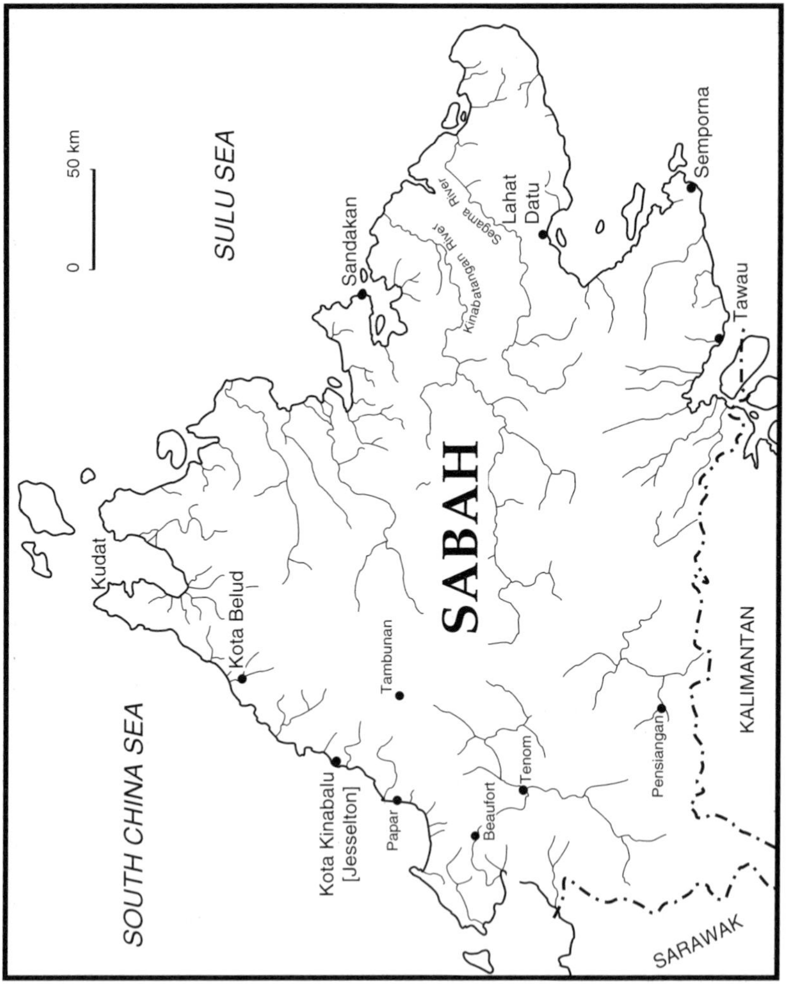
SOUTH CHINA SEA
SULU SEA
0
50 km
Kudat
Kota Belud
Sandakan
Segama River
Kinabatangan River
Lahat Datu
Semporna
Tawau
SABAH
Tambunan
Kota Kinabalu [Jesselton]
Papar
Beaufort
Tenom
Pensiangan
KALIMANTAN
SARAWAK

Map 3 Sabah

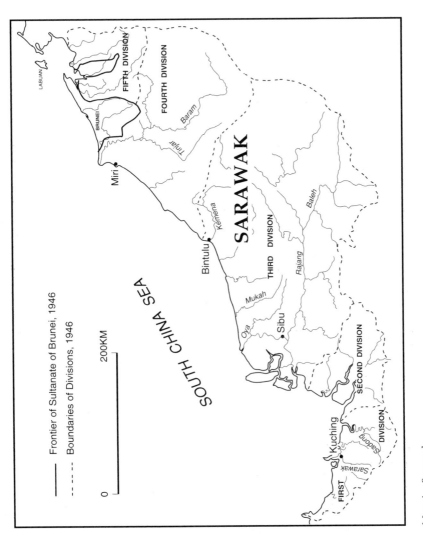

Map 4   Sarawak

1
Introduction

1.1 Theme of the study

The territories forming Malaysia have attracted considerable attention from scholars in a wide range of disciplines, especially since the formation of the federation in 1963, but relatively little work has been done on their economic history. In two bibliographical surveys (1965a, 1979) Wong Lin Ken concluded that most works in this latter category were limited in the time covered (the earlier rather than later colonial period), the geographical focus (the Peninsula rather than the Borneo territories), and the narrow sectoral coverage (the tin and rubber industries). He concluded that this literature was mainly descriptive and 'still on the frontier area of the social sciences' (1979, 23), lacking an analytical methodology grounded in economic theory. A particular need was for a study covering the entire colonial period and the post-Independence years, though Wong himself was doubtful about the practicality of constructing such an account principally because of a lack of historical statistics.

In the two decades since Wong's second survey the volume of published research has grown enormously, reflecting widespread interest in Malaysia's recent rapid economic growth approaching newly industrialised country (NIC) status. Most disciplines in the humanities and social sciences are represented. Many have adopted an analytical framework, and there are examples of long-period studies. We have, for example, a general history of Malaysia from earliest times to post-Independence (Andaya and Andaya, 1982), Melaka c.1400–1980 (Sandhu and Wheatley, 1983), colonial and postcolonial Malaya from the perspectives of dependency theory (Khor, 1983) and class analysis (Jomo, 1988). However, from the standpoint of the economic historian the situation is still to a large extent as Wong described it. Some gaps have been filled, and a notable neglect of the East Malaysian states has begun to be redressed (see, e.g., Wee, 1995; Amarjit Kaur, 1998). None the less, many political and economic studies of the recent past, whilst having

1

'Malaysia' as a title, focus on the Peninsula to the almost complete exclusion of Sabah and Sarawak.

The task for the present study, then, is to give an historical account of how the national economy of Malaysia emerged out of the geographically disparate territories in the Peninsula and northern Borneo with a small population (roughly half a million in total *c*.1800 and still only about 18 million by 1990), relatively poor soils, scattered minerals and generally difficult terrain, developing in the process labour-intensive primary and secondary industries normally associated with more heavily populated countries.

This transformation will be set in the analytical framework of the onset of 'modern economic growth' (Kuznets, 1959, 1966) a global phenomenon which, over the last two centuries or so, has seen a structural shift from 'premodern' agrarian and rural-based economies to ones which are pre-dominantly industrialised and urban-centred. This shift, often characterised by the term 'industrial revolution', has been accompanied by an 'explosion' in population growth, increasing at annual averages of up to 3 per cent (sometimes more) against only 0.5 per cent or less in premodern economies. In the latter both population and output grew at roughly the same rates with large fluctuations in the short term, permitting little increase in real per capita incomes over the long term. Modern economic growth, on the other hand, has been essentially a race to increase productivity in the various sectors of the economy at rates faster than population growth in order to sustain rising real incomes per capita. The principal means of achieving this has been the 'application of the industrial system ... of production based on increasing use of modern scientific knowledge [which] is the base of modern technology' (Kuznets, 1959, 15, 30).

The historical experience of countries which have embarked on the transition from premodern to modern economic growth has shown much variety rather than simply replicating a pattern similar to the pioneers of industrial revolution in northwest Europe. This has been because the starting point, or preconditions, for the transition (resource endowment, infrastructure, institutions, forms of government, social structure, and so on) differed greatly. Adelman and Morris (1997, 833) distinguish at least four broad historical 'development paths' to industrialised economies:

(a) 'autonomous export-led industrialization' – countries already possessing high productivity agriculture, developed market institutions and a political system which limited the power of traditional land-owning elites (minimal government intervention required);

(b) 'government-led, inward-oriented industrialisation' – countries where the preconditions in (a) were less developed, and modernisers (e.g., entrepreneurs) had to compete with landed elites for political power;

(c) 'balanced growth, open-economy, limited government intervention' – countries with few internal obstacles to growth, relatively productive agriculture, skill-intensive export industries, parliamentary government;

(d) 'agricultural, primary export-oriented, sharply dualistic' – countries with a wide range of preconditions: land ranging from scarce to abundant, population sparse to dense, varyingly productive agriculture, landed elites and modernisers powerful in some, less so in others, some domestic industry, ability of government to lead variable.

Typology (a) comprises the European pioneers such as Britain, Belgium, France, (b) Germany, Italy, Japan, Russia, (c) smaller European countries (Sweden, Denmark, Netherlands, etc.), and (d) the extra-European world, apart from Japan.

Group (d) is largely a colonial category for much of the nineteenth and twentieth centuries. During this period many regions in Africa, Asia, Australasia, Latin America and parts of North America (Canada) were integrated into the international economy as exporters of raw materials (tin, rubber, timber, petroleum) and consumables (wheat, tea, sugar, coffee, furs) to the industrialising countries in return for imports of manufactured goods.

Such economies have been categorised as 'export economies' (Levin, 1960), or 'staple economies' (Schedvin, 1990), due to the dominant role played by a small range of primary commodity exports (staples). These were capable of very rapid growth in periods of high world prices, achieving relatively high per capita incomes. Malaysia is a prime candidate for this category, having become between roughly 1870 and the 1980s one of the leading exporters of tin, rubber, palm oil and (to a lesser extent) iron ore, timber, petroleum, liquified natural gas (LNG), pepper, cocoa, and so on.

After the Second World War, and especially since gaining independence, the main aim of these 'less developed countries' (LDCs) has been to break away from the primary export structure identified with dependent colonial status, subject to strong international price instability, and to embark on a transition to industrialised economies. The principal obstacles in the way of achieving this have been a preponderance of foreign ownership with substantial remittances of profits overseas, leading to shortages of investment capital. There have been bottlenecks in the supply of labour, especially skilled workers. The enclave nature of many primary industries, with minimal processing done prior to export, has resulted in a dualistic structure with weak linkages to the domestic economy and the loss of added-value to the industrialised countries that carry out manufacture of final goods (e.g., rubber tyres in the USA). These difficulties have been compounded in numerous cases by national leaders with a high disregard for economic and technological imperatives, coupled with inefficient and often corrupt bureaucracies and domestic political instability. The result has been that countries have 'been caught in a staple trap. The tendency has been to move from one dominant staple to another [with] little export diversification ... balanced growth has been the exception rather than the rule' (Schedvin, 1990, 556–7). These comments were made with regard to countries of recent European settlement (Argentina, Australia, New Zealand), but apply equally to non-European countries. With the generally poor record of staple industries as stimuli, the successful establishment of a strong manufacturing sector has been the major economic problem confronting many LDCs in the second half of the twentieth century.

Against this gloomy general picture the recent performance of many parts of the East and Southeast Asian region, including Malaysia, has been markedly superior (see Tables 10.1, 10.2 below) at least up to the global economic crisis from mid-1997, showing a major structural shift from primary production towards manufacturing industry and services. Our object, following a survey of the precolonial economy (Chapter 2), will be to locate Malaysia within this process of global change from the advent of British colonial rule *c.* 1800 to the conclusion of the New Economic Policy (NEP) in 1990 (a convenient though arbitrary stopping point).

The study faces some practical difficulties. The first is, as Wong Lin Ken noted, the numerous gaps in the statistical sources which are compounded when the East Malaysian territories are brought into the analysis. With some of these, notably national income data for Malaya before the Second World War, only preliminary estimates are practicable (van der Eng, 1994). With others, it has proved possible to gather sufficient data to calculate export volumes and terms of trade index figures for Malaysia up to 1939 (see Chapters 3 and 8) which were previously not available.

These aspects have highlighted a very general problem in writing about Malaysia. As a geo-political entity the country is of very recent origin. Prior to federation in 1963 the component territories (apart from Sarawak) had various names (see Geographical Note) and, though under various forms of British rule for much of our period, had relatively little economic interconnection except through Singapore. It is therefore necessary to look explicitly at the historical emergence of the 'Malaysian economy' as a national unit (section 1.2). Singapore will be treated as an integral part up to the Second World War; thereafter, with its exclusion from the Federation of Malaya (1948) and pressured exit from the Malaysian Federation in 1965, attention will only be given where this affected Malaysia. Singapore's distinctive economic history from 1870 to 1990 has received comprehensive treatment in Huff (1994).

1.2 Formation of the Malaysian national economy

By way of definition, a 'national' economy constitutes an integrated system operating within a defined geographical area under the control of a central government. The various sectors, primary, secondary and tertiary, are geared in varying proportions to the domestic and international markets, with interaction between the sectors in the shape of flows of capital, labour, services, information, and so on. Productive activities are not distributed evenly within the national boundaries. Core areas develop, particularly around centres of industrial production, whilst other areas remain peripheral (following Dick, 1996). Implicit in the development of such a system is a centripetal, or 'pull', process which concentrates the economy around a centre, usually the national capital. The economy is, of course, subsumed within a *de jure* national state which further defines itself in terms of language, culture and citizenship.

In Malaysia's case the centripetal process was attenuated in time, reaching back more than a century and a half, and in some important respects earlier still. With communication and transport over land extremely difficult prior to the twentieth century, links via water assumed crucial importance. It will be the argument of this book that by the fifteenth and early sixteenth century a pattern of export-related production and exposure to international trade had emerged centring on the Malay sultanate of Melaka (see Map 2) which had commercial links throughout the region of the 'inner seas' (Fisher, 1963, 100). Position in relation to the 'inner seas' (Melaka Straits, Java Sea) was crucial in determining a commercial orientation for the Malaysian territories. The west coast of the Peninsula looks across the Melaka Straits to east Sumatra (see Map 1). The east coast, by contrast looks across the Gulf of Siam to the Southeast Asian mainland and to East Asia, as well as southwards to Borneo, Java and Bali. At the base of the Peninsula Singapore island occupies a central position in the archipelago, and in addition it lies astride the principal trade route from the Indian Ocean to East Asia. The Borneo territories have historically been oriented more towards eastern Indonesia, the Philippines and China.

The Malay Peninsula and northern Borneo have aspects of climate, geography and topography in common which underlie 'historical and geographical realities of fundamental significance' (Fisher, 1963, 99). They lie within the equatorial monsoon region of Asia, with uniform monthly temperatures and annual rainfall. The Peninsula is divided into east and west coasts by a mountainous spine along almost its whole length. On either side coastal plains rarely exceed 80 kilometres in depth, intersected by rivers whose alluvial floors allowed early human settlement and agriculture. Rivers on the east coast are longer and more susceptible to flooding, disrupting access to the coast during the northeast monsoon. The topography of the Borneo territories is on a similar but larger scale, particularly the mountains (with Mount Kinabalu, Sabah, peaking at some 4500 metres), longer flood-prone rivers and wider coastal swamps. Coastal plains, on the other hand, are narrower. Both the Peninsula and Borneo lack natural harbours, making Singapore with its ideal position astride the main sea-routes a natural focus for entrepot trade. The soils are generally poor, lacking the volcanic activity which has created the rich deposits in Java and parts of Sumatra. The situation is better in terms of mineral resources. The Peninsula has major tin deposits, and smaller ones of gold and iron ore. Gold also occurs in Sarawak and copper in Sabah, while deposits of oil and natural gas have been found off Sabah, Brunei, Sarawak and Terengganu (Fisher, 1963).

After the fall of Melaka to the Portuguese (1511) and later the Dutch (1641) the Malaysian region saw competition for commercial pre-eminence between the Dutch and English East India companies, and indigenous states (Aceh, Johor-Riau). Towards the end of the eighteenth century the foundation of Penang (1786) followed by Singapore (1819) and Melaka (1824) marked the beginning of British hegemony which, over the following century, extended to cover the Malaysian region. Economically the Straits Settlements (SS) free-trade ports acted as centripetal forces attracting a cosmopolitan mix of commercial enterprise and some early agricultural ventures (spices, pepper), especially after the swift rise of Singapore to pre-eminence and the Treaty of London (1824) which demarcated the Anglo–Dutch spheres of hegemony with a boundary down the Melaka Straits and just south of Singapore. This island-port became the centre of a trading network embracing the Peninsula, Sumatra, northern Borneo and Java/Bali, and it simply outran Dutch attempts to establish competing duty-free entrepots.

Over the course of the nineteenth century Straits trade increasingly stimulated export production in adjacent areas, notably the west coast of the Peninsula (Perak, Selangor, Negeri Sembilan), developing a dynamic which drew in more investment and immigration, leading to infrastructural growth (roads, railways). North Borneo and Sarawak, both British protectorates, participated to a lesser degree at this stage due to their relative geographical isolation. But whilst a distinctive pattern of export-oriented activity and multi-ethnic society was emerging, the Malaysian region remained politically fragmented right up to 1941. There were some administrative links between the Peninsula and Borneo territories: for example the same British official acted as Governor Straits Settlements and High Commissioner Federated Malay States (FMS), as well as Consul-General for the northern Borneo protectorates. Occasional proposals were put forward to try to achieve administrative integration. For example, in the early 1930s a customs union for the Peninsula and the incorporation of North Borneo into the Straits Settlements were mooted but discarded as impracticable, defeated by a mixture of vested political and economic interests and the financially straitened circumstances during the Great Depression (1929–32). As the economic importance of the Malaysian hinterland grew, especially the FMS with a concentration of tin and rubber production, a rivalry for centrality developed between Kuala Lumpur, 'a new type of inland administrative centre [and] in an economic sense ... a forward capital', and the 'free trade' Straits ports notably Singapore, which 'to all intents ... was the commercial capital of the [FMS]'. By the 1930s '[administratively] it was clear that the old subdivision into Straits Settlements, Federated Malay States and unfederated States had become an anachronism' (Fisher, 1956, 297, 299, 314).

Postwar, whilst economic reconstruction was a first priority, the British quickly returned to the question of a unitary administration. The first attempt in the Peninsula, the shortlived Malayan Union (1946–8), failed in the face of widespread opposition to the loss of sovereignty by the Malay rulers, and the proposed laws on citizenship for non-Malays. This was replaced by the Federation of Malaya (1948–63) which passed some powers back to the states but was still relatively centralised. Singapore was excluded from both arrangements, ostensibly on the grounds that its economic interests (the entrepot trade) were substantively separate, but in actuality the numerical preponderance of Chinese there complicated the increasingly sensitive ethnic balance. In the case of North Borneo and Sarawak it was recognised that neither the Chartered Company nor the Brookes had the resources needed for faster economic and social development, and in 1946 both were transferred to direct control by the Colonial Office.

In the remaining years of colonial rule the various administrations took more active roles in the economy. Five-Year Plans became the general framework for integrated development, which went some way to redressing the unsystematised approaches resulting from the fragmented political structure of the prewar years. A Mission from the International Bank For Reconstruction and Development in 1955 recommended that the Malayan economy be treated as an entity in its own right, not as an extension of the British economy (International Bank for Reconstruction and Development, or IBRD, 1955).

The formation of the Federation of Malaysia in 1963 was driven primarily by political considerations, namely the inclusion of Sabah and Sarawak so that their indigenous populations would help to offset the preponderance of Chinese resulting from Singapore's membership which lasted only till 1965. Brunei refused to join, principally because of disagreements over the position of its Sultan among the Malay rulers in the Peninsula, and control over oil resources. After Singapore's exit over political differences Kuala Lumpur, the 'Malay centre of gravity' (Fisher, 1963, 114), emerged as the power centre of the federation. Since that time there has been, as Fisher prophetically remarked in 1963, 'an attempt to extend the Malayan solution to the rest of the [Malaysian] area' (1963, 114). By the 'Malayan solution' he meant primarily the political system which had evolved in the Peninsula during the late 1940s and 1950s to cope with the problems of forging a nation out of the multi-ethnic society. This was based on the 'Alliance' party system (see Chapter 9 Section 2) which became the dominant factor in federal politics after 1963. As we shall see, the NEP (1970–90), which was the solution to the growing interethnic tensions in the Peninsula in the 1960s over the unequal distribution of the fruits of economic development, was also extended to the Borneo territories.

Since 1965 the federal government has exerted a strong centripetal influence over the individual states through the financial system, mainly by control of grants and allocations of development funds under the various Five-Year Plans. Coupled with the NEP, considerable progress was achieved in both primary and secondary industrialisation, with a continuing export orientation. However, by 1990 Malaysia was still some distance removed from achieving an integrated national economy. The core industrialised regions remained heavily concentrated along the west coast of the Peninsula. Relatively little industrialisation had occurred in Sabah and Sarawak which were heavily dependent on the Peninsula for imports of manufactured goods. There was only a small degree of domestic interaction in the form of flows of capital and labour between the various regions.

Whilst the term 'Malaysia' is politically applicable only post-1963, the origins of the export economy and multi-ethnic society typifying the region are sufficiently clear from the nineteenth century (with clear continuity from earlier centuries) to justify applying the term to the two centuries or so which are the main focus of this book.

2
The Premodern Economy

This chapter will range widely in time, but will focus primarily on the period between the rise of the Melaka sultanate (*c*.1400–1511) and the first permanent British footholds in the Malay Peninsula in the late eighteenth and early nineteenth century. The aim is to identify the salient features of the premodern economy, and to see to what extent these were undergoing secular change prior to the emergence of the export economy under colonial rule in the nineteenth century.

2.1 Population and settlement

The sparse data for Southeast Asia in general and Malaysia in particular indicate a low annual net rate of increase in population which was strongly typical of a premodern economy. Reid (1988, Table 2) has constructed 'the best possible estimate for 1800' and then extrapolated backwards to 1600 except 'where contemporary estimates take precedence' (1988, 13n.). In the case of the Malay Peninsula the results suggest no net growth over this period, with total population stagnating around 500 000. The entire island of Borneo went from 670 000 to 1 million, giving an annual average growth of 0.2 per cent, the same rate as Southeast Asia overall (up from approximately 22.4 million to 32.4 million). Reid's estimate of 500 000 for the Peninsula in 1800 is very close to the total of some 473 000 by the mid-1830s, arrived at by Newbold (1839, cited in Dodge, 1980). However, as we shall see in Chapter 5.1, the latter figure has been challenged by Dodge (1980) who places more weight on immigration of Minangkabau (from west Sumatra) into Negeri Sembilan from the late seventeenth century, and Bugis into Selangor in the eighteenth century. Dodge proposes a total of approximately 750 000, which represents an annual increase of a little under 0.2 per cent from 1600 to 1830, but certainly no more than the Southeast Asian average.

The major factors restraining population growth in Southeast Asia in this period were instability caused by 'constant low level warfare' (Reid, 1988,

17), diseases such as smallpox, subsistence crises and low fertility rates. The first of these was perhaps the prime cause, not so much through high casualty rates in battle (deaths were relatively few), but rather as the result of the removal of large numbers of people as captives. For example, between 1618 and 1624 several centres in the Malay Peninsula were attacked by the north Sumatran state of Aceh. Kedah lost 7000 and Pahang 11 000 in this way. Disruption of this sort had a knock-on effect through confiscation and destruction of crops which weakened the subsistence base. It also appears that fertility rates were low among animist populations, (e.g., in upland Borneo: Reid, 1988, 12–17).

All these estimates are necessarily speculative. Of more importance as indicators of economic activity were the periodic shifts in the locations of relatively large numbers of people. These can be seen in the rise and fall of various entrepot ports, notably Melaka, Brunei, Riau-Johor and Terengganu in the Malaysian region (see section 2.4 below). As their prosperity increased merchants were attracted from a wide area, together with people from the surrounding hinterland. Melaka at its foundation *c*.1400 was no more than a small fishing village, but within a decade or so the population soared to around 6000 and at the time of the Portuguese conquest (1511) was estimated at up to 100 000, though some modern scholars put it at much less, e.g. 40–50 000 (Sandhu and Wheatley, 1983, II, 206n.). Thereafter as its commercial pre-eminence declined the population fell sharply to 12 000 just before the Dutch takeover (1641), and still further to 5000 under Dutch rule (Reid, 1993, 73–5). Likewise Brunei, estimated by the Portuguese visitor Pigafetta in the 1520s to have up to 25 000 'fires' or houses (which could indicate up to 162 000 people depending on the conversion factor used), declined to about 16 000 by 1608 following attack by Manila-based Spanish in 1579 (Reid, 1993, Table 7).

The sources of population growth were natural increase, which as we have seen was held in check by several factors, and immigration. The latter was both intra- and extra-regional. Intra-regional movements occurred between Java and Melaka in the fifteenth century, west Sumatra (Minangkabau) and Negeri Sembilan from the seventeenth century, and Sulawesi (Bugis) to the west coast of the Peninsula in the eighteenth century. The main extra-regional sources of migrants were India and China. These ebbed and flowed according to the political and economic conditions in their homelands. For example, the overseas ventures of the Ming dynasty (1369–1644) in the early fifteenth century brought many Chinese to the region to trade and engage in agriculture (e.g. pepper cultivation). Travel to the Southern Seas (*Nanyang*) was later banned, but again in the later 1720s the ban was lifted and large numbers came to mine tin, among other activities, in the Peninsula and gold in west Borneo (see section 2.3 below).

The main concentrations of indigenous settlement were near the coast in the river valleys which allowed more intensive wet-rice cultivation, or *sawah* (see section 2.2 below). In the Peninsula these were principally in Perak, Kedah and Kelantan. In Borneo *sawah* cultivation developed among the population of the narrow coastal strips. In the interior the aboriginal population of the Peninsula (the *orang asli*) and the tribal groups in Borneo carried on a mixture of hunter-gatherer economy, shifting, or swidden, dry-rice cultivation (*ladang*), and in some instances wet-rice cultivation (see below).

Early urban settlement was most evident in the port-cities discussed above. Here the composition of the population clearly showed the pluralistic structure highly characteristic of Malaysia in which foreign migrants intermingled as merchants, craftsmen and so on with the indigenous people (see section 2.3 below).

2.2   The subsistence base

The principal means of subsistence was rice, along with minor food crops such as sago, millet, tubers, etc. supplemented with a range of vegetables, fruits, herbs, fish and other sea-products. As noted in the previous section rice was grown both with irrigation (*sawah*) and without (*ladang*). Both types seem to have spread throughout Southeast Asia relatively slowly, the dates of origin in particular areas being uncertain. The most recent research concludes that in the northerly parts of the Malay Peninsula *sawah* cultivation was established in the major river valleys (Kedah, Perak, Kelantan, Terengganu, Pahang) by about the fourteenth century AD. In the southern parts (Selangor, Negeri Sembilan, Melaka and much of Johor) expansion took longer due to the peat soils, brackish water and swampy terrain (Hill, 1977, 24–7). Data for Borneo are hard to gather but *sawah* may have appeared first in some highland locations (e.g., among the Kelabit in Sarawak: Reid, personal communication). The question as to whether *ladang* cultivation preceded *sawah* or whether the two occupied separate locations is debatable. A recent commentator argues that in the core areas of Malay settlement in the Peninsula the two types were often concurrent, particularly in pioneer settlements before land use patterns crystallised. By the fifteenth and sixteenth centuries *sawah* was increasingly becoming predominant in the 'traditional' Malay village economy (Zaharah Mahmud, 1992).

The level of technology in rice cultivation was generally low. *Sawah* relied for the most part on natural rainfall. In the Peninsula seeds were usually broadcast by hand, rather than established in a nursery and subsequently transplanted to the field; the latter would have obtained a more even distribution of the plants. Tools were basic. In *ladang* cultivation the main implements were the dibble-stick (*tugal*) and the short hoe (*keri*). In *sawah* the plough (*tenggala*), almost certainly Indian in origin, may have reached Kedah by the eighth or ninth century AD. Perhaps the most innovative were the Minangkabau migrants in the upper Muar valley who grew dry-rice on the hillsides, and wet-rice in rain-fed valley fields and fields irrigated from rivers by means of water wheels (Hill, 1977, 27; Zaharah Mahmud, 1992, 309). In Kedah, which was one of the few areas in Malaysia producing a marketable surplus of rice, irrigation was improved by the building of canals in the flat coastal plain, *c.*1660–1, 1738 and 1771. In the western coastal districts of Sabah by the nineteenth century seeds were transplanted, and an elaborate system of dykes, sluices and canals utilised (Ranjit Singh, 1984, 392).

Communities were not completely self-sufficient. Interchanges took place between upland and lowland peoples, the former trading forest products in return for foodstuffs, salt, cloth and so on (Dunn, 1975, 113). The port cities, with their large non-food producing populations, were dependent upon supplies from their surrounding hinterland and sometimes from much further afield. The prime example here is Melaka which drew the bulk of its food supply (mainly rice) from Java. At the time of the Portuguese conquest (1511) Pires (1515) estimated annual food imports from that source at 8000 tonnes (cited in Anderson and Vorster, 1983, 439).

Whilst the adequacy of food supplies varied over time, there do not appear to have been any prolonged subsistence crises in the region. European observers up to the eighteenth century were impressed by the generally good health and impressive physiques of Southeast Asians (Reid, 1988, 46).

2.3   Commercial production

Throughout Malaysia subsistence activities were accompanied by the production of marketable commodities to exchange for goods not procurable within a settlement (e.g., metalwares, glassware, pottery, cotton textiles). In the Peninsula one of the leading trade goods was tin, mined for export to India as early as the fifth century AD, and perhaps before that. In Borneo widely distributed deposits of iron ore enabled the development of an iron industry producing, for example, weapons for local and regional markets. One such location was at Santubong on the Sarawak river (near present-day Kuching) where the industry flourished early in the second millenium AD. Other major categories of exports from the Peninsula and Borneo were forest products (e.g., rattans, aromatic woods, camphor, birds' feathers) and sea products (e.g., tortoise shells, coral, pearls, *trepang* or sea-slugs). These two latter categories were not so much produced as collected, described by one commentator as a 'foraging export economy' (Reid, forthcoming).

As we shall see in the next section, demand from extra-regional markets played a major role in stimulating production for trade. Under the relatively liberal trade regime operated by the Ming rulers in the later fourteenth and early fifteenth centuries, demand from China sparked a major expansion in the cultivation of pepper in Sumatra, the Malay Peninsula (e.g., Kedah, Terengganu), southern and western Borneo. The supply response was aided by the introduction of black pepper plants from South India. From the sixteenth century onwards European markets took a large proportion of output. One estimate is that by the eighteenth century roughly 5 per cent of the total population of the producing areas was directly engaged in this cash crop, with many more in the ports and shipping industries indirectly involved (Reid, 1992, 469).

Exports such as tin and pepper were mainly requited by imports of manufactured goods. Some of these came from outside the region, for instance pottery from southern China and cotton textiles from eastern India, but a range of products, notably metalwares (gold, silver, tin, brass, iron), came from the local port-cities where craftsmen were concentrated. Shipbuilding also was carried on. The Malaysian region did not have many such centres in the period under review. In the Peninsula, Melaka in the fifteenth century and Kuala Terengganu in the eighteenth were the main ones, together with Brunei in northwestern Borneo.

Who were the producers of the various commodities just surveyed? The products of the forest and sea were gathered by the peoples of the interior, such as the *orang asli* of the Peninsula, and coastal and sea-dwellers (*orang laut*), such as the nomadic Bajau-Laut of what is now southeastern Sabah (Sather, 1997). Cultivation of foodstuffs, notably rice, was the staple occupation of groups such as the Malays of the river valleys in the Peninsula, the Kelabit in Sarawak and Kadazan in Sabah. Prior to the fifteenth century the relatively small volume of cash-cropping and mining came largely from indigenous peoples. After about 1400 AD, however, there was a shift to specialised crop cultivation, pepper in particular, which involved not only indigenous farmers but growing numbers of immigrants, Chinese especially. In the early eighteenth century Chinese and Bugis took up the planting of gambier (an astringent, also useful in tanning leather) in the Riau islands south of Singapore (Drabble and Mills, 1992).

There was a similar move in mining (mainly tin and gold) which began to change from being a supplement to indigenous subsistence agriculture to a year-round occupation. This was again pioneered by Chinese who, by the late eighteenth century, formed communities of gold miners in Kelantan, Terengganu, Pahang and southwest Borneo (Sambas). On the west coast of the Peninsula they were reported to be the principal miners of tin in Perak and Selangor (Dodge, 1977; Wong Lin Ken, 1965b, 17).

Manufactured goods, as already noted, came from a variety of sources. Those produced locally came largely from the coastal centres of trade. For example, silk and cotton weaving, using imported fibres, figure in Chinese records of Kelantan and Terengganu as early as the thirteenth century AD (Maznah Mohamed, 1995, 97). Metalware making, which also required imported raw materials, was similarly situated in urban centres or surrounding villages. Crafts could be restricted to certain families or guilds, with techniques kept secret as in brass-making in Brunei (Lim and Shariffuddin, 1976, 142). Local raw materials, such as clay and iron ore, were the basis of pottery and ironware production at sites such as Pengkalan Bujang (Kedah), and Santubong (Sarawak) (Christie, 1988). Trade generated other opportunities such as boatbuilding, for which Terengganu Malays were noted (Drabble, 1989, 7).

The technologies of production were labour-intensive, whether in agriculture, mining or manufacture. At the same time, given the small populations noted in section 2.1, labour was the scarce factor of production, with a division along gender lines. For example, women predominated in textile and pottery making, and men in metalworking. For much of the premodern period there was little wage labour available. Manual labour for another person was seen by indigenous people as denoting a low social status equivalent to servitude. Migrants could be hired more readily, but were relatively costly. Craftsmen in the cities were usually in a bonded relationship (e.g., through indebtedness or capture in war) to a member of the elite, and tended to produce for specific purposes, for instance weaponry (Reid, 1988, 129–36).

The growing importance of production for export towards the eighteenth century did require the ability to bring together aggregations of labour, numbering sometimes in the thousands, whether for opening up new lands for agriculture, foraging expeditions to collect sea-products organised by the chiefs (*datus*) of the Sulu sultanate region, or the more specialised mining ventures of Chinese migrants noted above.

Of the other factors of production, capital for investment in fixed assets was less important than the circulating capital required for long distance trade (see next section). Land was so relatively abundant as to constitute a free good, and thus there was little incentive to economise on its use. Cash crops such as pepper and gambier were soil-exhausting, necessitating periodic moves to virgin land. The rural population was not tied to a particular area of land. If a ruler proved unduly oppressive, local chiefs and farmers had the remedy of flight. Malay settlement and land holding exhibited a 'restless frontier spirit ... land was used rather than possessed' (Milner, 1982, 7).

Technological change was patchy because, with markets widely dispersed, the pressures to improve production methods to lower costs so that one area might gain a competitive advantage (e.g., pepper) were not strong. The situation in tin mining in the Peninsula was rather different. By *c.*1800 a competitive position was emerging in which specialised Chinese miners were beginning to displace the part-time indigenous producers. The former had better access to labour and could deal with the perennial problem of mine flooding at depths below about five metres. They also had more efficient methods of smelting the tin ore (Wong Lin Ken, 1965b, 14; Dodge, 1977, 102).

2.4   Trade and the state

As noted in section 2.2, few communities in Southeast Asia were wholly self-sufficient. Exchange through trade was thus an important activity from the earliest times, not just locally or regionally but internationally. By the early centuries of the first millennium AD the trade routes extended to China, India and the Middle East through to the Mediterranean. The principal commodities involved were gold, tin, spices and forest-products. To facilitate exchange entrepot ports, or emporia, grew up at strategic points along these routes. The Malaysian region, in particular the Peninsula, lay astride the sea-route from the Indian Ocean to the South China Sea. The alternating patterns of the northeast and southwest monsoon winds gave the west coast facing the sheltered Straits of Melaka an advantage here. The first entrepots were located in Kedah, Perak and Selangor, before the rise of Melaka (*c*.1400) which will be the major focus in this section. The east coast of the Peninsula, less well situated, had entrepots in Terengganu and Pahang, among others. In Borneo the north-west coast formed a convenient landfall for trade with China. P'o-ni, the predecessor of Brunei, was visited by Chinese as early as the fifth century AD (Andaya and Andaya, 1982, 57).

There was an integral relationship between these port-cities and the emergence of early polities in Southeast Asia. The essence of this relationship lay in the fact that control of trade facilitated the acquisition of material resources which could then be used by a ruler to build up an armed retinue of followers through whom power could be exercised over a surrounding hinterland. Trade and politics were 'indivisible' (Kathirithamby-Wells, 1993, 126). The viability of a port-polity depended on the ruler's ability to attract merchants (e.g., low taxes, efficient administration), and to control the flow of goods into and out of the surrounding area. As the 'first merchant' (i.e., the buyer to whom visiting merchants had to sell) a ruler could corner the market in imported 'prestige goods' (e.g., glassware, ceramics, ceremonial gongs), subsequently distributing these among lesser chiefs, thereby establishing a patrimonial relationship. Such a power base was inherently vulnerable to challenge from other aspiring chiefs and thus these polities were for the most part 'ephemeral, shifting and loosely structured' (Reid, forthcoming).

The prime example in the Malaysian region was Melaka, established *c*.1400 AD at a particularly favourable location athwart the Melaka Straits trade route and at a propitious point in time for trade. In the first three decades of the fifteenth century the Ming rulers of China sent out missions to establish official trade and tributary relationships with states in the Nanyang (southern) region. Melaka was a natural meeting point, and its rulers (Islamicised from about 1414) were willing to accept Chinese protection as a counterpoise to Thai pressure. Merchants flocked to the port from surrounding regions (Burma, Sumatra, Java, Borneo), and further afield (India, the Middle East, China), substantial numbers becoming domiciled there.

Melaka's rulers instituted an orderly system for administering trade: wharves, warehouses, a local coinage (though Chinese copper cash also circulated widely), standard weights and measures, prescribed rates of taxes, a law code and a hierarchy of officials. They pursued an expansive territorial policy which by the late fifteenth century had established client-relationships covering much of the Peninsula's west coast from Perak to Johor, Temasek (later Singapore), the Riau-Lingga islands to the south, Pahang and several states in East Sumatra.

During the fifteenth century the main stimulus to international trade came from the market in China where population was recovering after the depredations of the Yuan (Mongol) dynasty. The main demand was for tin, pepper, spices and forest-products which prompted the increases in production described in the previous section. Merchants had to conduct dealings with middlemen who had contacts with producers located in the port hinterland, and in the interior of the Malay Peninsula, Sumatra and so on. This in turn increased purchasing power in the region which manifested itself in heightened demand for imports, notably textiles from India. 'Melaka emerged as a key intermediary in the trade ... which had come into focus in the Straits by the fifteenth century' (Anderson and Vorster, 1983, 440).

During this period Melaka developed an exchange economy. Barter was the major instrument of trade in the entrepot, though a locally minted tin coinage probably served for everyday transactions. Silver and gold were used as units of account and measures of wealth. The rulers engaged in trade using vessels captained by a *nakhoda* who may have been Malay or Indian Muslim. However, most of their wealth came from levies on trade, tribute from client states and gifts (a certain proportion of a cargo's value). Officials also profited from trade: the Malay expression *orang kaya* (rich man) was the customary term for a noble in Melaka (Andaya and Andaya, 1982, 44, 47; McRoberts, 1991, 72).

The sixteenth century saw a new factor, external in origin, in Southeast Asian trade. This was the advent of European traders who came with the aim of establishing direct contacts with the sources of supply of goods, notably spices from eastern Indonesia (the Moluccas), which had previously reached Europe through an extended chain of mainly Asian middlemen and at high cost. The pioneers were the Portuguese and Spanish who came respectively round southern Africa and across the Indian Ocean, and across the Pacific. They were followed, and in the case of the Portuguese largely displaced, in the seventeenth and eighteenth centuries by the Dutch and the British.

In several important respects organisation of trade by Europeans resembled the indigenous structure. The basis was the entrepot port through which the aim was to channel the maximum possible volume of trade. Power was maritime rather than land-based, related directly to the number of ships employed and control over the sea routes. Europeans had a decisive advantage in ship design, armament and naval engagement tactics. By the early sixteenth century the Portuguese had established a chain of fortified ports stretching from East Africa to India, Southeast and East Asia. This involved mostly the takeover of existing ports, the most important in our context being Melaka (captured in 1511). Following this event there was a dispersal of the Melaka ruling house throughout the Peninsula (Pahang, Perak, Johor, the Riau-Lingga archipelago) and northern Borneo (Brunei). The Dutch took Melaka from the Portuguese in 1641, but their principal base was situated in northwest Java, at Batavia (1619). In face of strong Dutch competition the British found it difficult to establish a permanent foothold astride a major trade route in the region until the lease of Penang island from the Sultan of Kedah in 1786.

Each of these European groups had the backing of their home governments. In the case of Portugal the Asian trading ventures were initially financed directly by the Crown. The British and the Dutch, on the other hand, both opted for mercantile companies incorporated under charters which gave them many of the powers of governments, such as the right to negotiate with local rulers, conduct war, raise revenues and so on. The English East India Company (EIC) was established in 1600, and its Dutch counterpart (VOC) in 1602. Both were organised on the joint-stock principle, the capital being raised through sale of shares. As compensation for the dangers and high costs of long-distance trade in that era, the EIC was given a monopoly of commerce between Europe and India, and the VOC over what eventually became known as the Netherlands East Indies (NEI).

However, in each of the cases just outlined circumstances led to attempts to build a more general monopoly over trade within the Asian region. The main reason was that the Europeans lacked commodities which commanded extensive markets there (woollen textiles were climatically unsuitable). They therefore had to finance purchases of spices, pepper and so on with silver bullion from Europe, which conflicted with their mercantilist views, or else engage in intra-Asian trade to obtain supplies of local goods which did have a market (e.g., Indian cotton textiles). The latter course was taken by the Portuguese and followed by the VOC and EIC. Success in achieving monopoly varied. The Portuguese tried, through a system of passes (*cartaz*), to force Asian merchants to use ports such as Melaka. The effectiveness declined over the sixteenth century as rival ports, such as Aceh in North Sumatra, flourished outside Portuguese control.

The Dutch, with the best resources of capital and ships, had much greater success in monopolising trade between Java and the Spice Islands in the seventeenth and eighteenth centuries, with Batavia as the focal point. The

VOC was also interested in trying to control the trade in tin and pepper from Sumatra and the Malay Peninsula but was less successful since the most convenient entrepot, Melaka, was subordinated to the primacy of Batavia. Rival entrepots, such as Johor, were less amenable to VOC control.

The EIC was primarily focused on India and was least able to pursue monopoly elsewhere. Indeed, the company's trade east of India was opened to licensed private merchants known as 'country traders'. In the eighteenth century, as the resources of the VOC declined, English 'country' interests sought freer access to the trade of the archipelago. For example, shortlived trading posts were established on Balambangan and Labuan islands off the north coast of Borneo in the 1770s (Brown, 1970, 144–5).

What effects did these European mercantile activities have on production and trade during the period *c*.1500–1800? The direct links with markets in Europe heightened demand for pepper and spices. The attempts by the Portuguese to channel commerce through ports they controlled were initially disruptive to established trade routes. However, as noted above, Asian merchants were able to circumvent these controls so that competitive ports such as Aceh and Johor prospered. The result was a general boom in international trade in the sixteenth and early seventeenth centuries which saw Southeast Asian pepper exports rising between two- and threefold, and cloves as much as sixfold. The bulk of the pepper came from the Malaysian region (Sumatra and the Peninsula: Reid, 1992, 464–6). 'The maritime world of Southeast Asia [in this period] … is an example of a vigorous, clearly articulated economy that was not partitioned by political boundaries' (Dick, 1996, 28–9).

Conditions changed when the vastly more powerful VOC established its monopoly over the spice trade and, from the base in Java, gradually extended political and economic control into other areas of the Indonesian archipelago (e.g., southern Borneo, the Moluccas). Whilst ratified international boundaries did not yet exist, the VOC attempted with a high degree of success to seal off the trade within that region from outside competition (i.e., Asians and other Europeans). This helped to spark off a corresponding preference among local rulers for similar controls which were hostile to free-ranging production and commerce. At the same time, after about 1670 there was a substantial fall in prices in Europe and Asia from the high levels to which they had risen previously as a result of the inflow of silver (principally from Spanish colonies in South America).

The overall effect of these factors, coupled with adverse climatic conditions (low rainfall), was to depress levels of output and income among cash crop producers in Southeast Asia. For example the volume of pepper exports halved between the 1630s and 1670s (Reid, 1992, Figure 8.1). Pressure from the VOC led to the decline of many ports and the exclusion of indigenous merchants. Foreign Asian merchants, notably the Chinese, became largely intermediaries between the VOC and producers. These trends were less strong in the Malaysian region, but the main entrepot, Melaka, suffered the loss of its former pre-eminence (which had already begun under the Portuguese) due to VOC preference for Batavia, and also to silting up of the harbour entrance.

International trade began to revive in the second half of the eighteenth century. However, it was now based not so much on the longstanding staples of pepper and spices, but on new consumables such as coffee, tea and sugar for which a highly elastic demand was emerging in Europe. The VOC attempted to meet this demand by establishing the forced cultivation of coffee and sugar in Java. But the main source of tea at this stage was China, and European (particularly British) efforts turned towards trying to open up trade with that country using as a means of purchase first silver bullion and then, increasingly, opium. After about 1750 Batavia's central importance as an entrepot waned as the ability of the VOC to dominate trade in the outer islands of the archipelago and the Melaka Straits decreased (the company finally went into liquidation in 1799). This development, coupled with the growing importance of the China trade, refocused attention on 'what might loosely be termed the free-trade area of maritime Southeast Asia' (Bassett, 1989, 625): that is, ports bordering the Melaka Straits and the South China Sea. These included Melaka, Kedah, Aceh, Johor, Riau, Terengganu and Brunei. This situation was in many respects a revival of the more open system which had obtained prior to the coming of the Europeans.

The impact of the trade resurgence of the later eighteenth and early nine-teenth century on the regional economy was similar to that of the fifteenth and sixteenth century. The flow of commodities through the entrepot ports had linkage effects throughout the archipelago as well as the Southeast Asian mainland. There was an extension of cash-cropping and mining activity. In this later period, however, there were significant differences in the roles of the various ethnic groups involved. Whilst much of produc-tion, especially the agricultural, forest- and sea-products, remained in indigenous hands, an increasing stake was being established by newcomers, notably the Chinese whose role in particular sectors (e.g., mining), was sur-veyed in the previous section. Another dynamic group moving into the region was the Bugis, skilled navigators and traders who left their home-land in south Sulawesi to escape Dutch pressure and became a strong force in trade along the west coast of the Malay Peninsula until their military defeat by the Dutch in 1784.

Trade was a leading sector in this period. Between 1760 and 1814 the volume between Sulu and China (which involved the collecting or 'pro-curement' trade in northern Borneo) doubled, growing faster than the population of the Sultanate (Warren, 1981, 53). Total shipping arrivals at Melaka practically tripled between 1761 and 1785. The proportion of English and Portuguese vessels increased, but were far surpassed by

Chinese, 'Malay' (the boundaries of this group were fluid) and Bugis shipping. Most came from the surrounding Straits region but Melaka's trade links extended to Java, Manila, Siam, Burma and southern India. By the late eighteenth century Melaka was once again a 'Southeast Asian entrepot par excellence ... progressively less European and more Asian a town' (Reid and Fernando, 1994, 5, 10).

2.5   Overview

Is it possible to identify any secular changes in the structure of economic activity in the premodern period? The view taken in recent scholarship is that such changes did not occur to any great extent: for example, a study of the Indian Ocean region from the seventh century AD to 1750 concludes that 'examples of uninterrupted evolution from a lower form to a higher one are ... difficult to find. Historical developments in most parts of Asia seem to have been distributed in a more random temporal pattern' (Chaudhuri, 1990, 80). Economic change from 'lower' to 'higher' forms means, for instance, technological innovation or more integrated markets.

In order for secular change to occur in an economy pressure has to rise, and this can come from several sources. There are domestic factors such as increasing population pressure on land, urbanisation, exhaustion of natural resources leading to technological innovation, or capital accumulation by an entrepreneurial class seeking its own advantage. The intrusion of external influences, notably foreign trade, can be a powerful shock to the system.

We have seen that net increases in total population were small, whilst land was in ample supply. Tin and gold deposits were alluvial or mineable at relatively shallow (though in some areas gradually increasing) depths. Products gathered by foraging were relatively plentiful for the most part. In 1800 it was estimated that 4000 tonnes of rattans could be cut in the forests around Marudu bay (northern Borneo) each year without jeopardising the supply. On the other hand, though, unrestrained exploitation of the caves along the Kinabatangan river for birds' nests c.1814 led to decreasing collections (Warren, 1981, 79–80, 83).

Technological and institutional innovation in foodcrop (wet-rice) and cashcrop (pepper, gambier) production was patchy, the main shifts being towards more intensive cultivation, but with labour supply still the prime constraint.

External rather than internal influences were predominant as stimuli towards economic change because, with the difficult terrain hindering internal contacts, the prime orientation was outwards to the sea. It was commerce which underpinned the growth of the early urban centres, the port-cities such as Melaka and Brunei. As we have seen, competition between indigenous and foreign interests for control of trade intensified in the sixteenth and early seventeenth centuries, and revived in the later eighteenth century when the trade with China was a major force shaping activity in the Malaysian region (Drabble and Mills, 1991). However, this competition did not spark off major changes in the local economy, such as the emergence of a class of indigenous capitalists.

Two main explanations have been advanced for the latter phenomenon. The first is that rulers saw the accumulation of wealth and control over desirable trade goods not as ends in themselves but as the means to increase prestige and power; 'The way in which wealth was obtained, be it by force, "legitimate trade", monopoly, or even gambling or magic, was a relatively unimportant matter' (Milner, 1982, 20). Wealthy rulers were thus able, through distribution of patronage, to command support from the elites who in turn gave protection to the general population (*rakyat*) in return for compulsory labour services (*kerah*). This economic and social structure among Peninsular Malays has been characterised as feudal, for example by British colonial officials who interpreted it as essentially a version of the feudal order in medieval western Europe. More recent scholarship, however, has rejected this view largely because the hierarchy of relationships did not centre around land tenure, as in Europe. Rather, these have been described as various forms of 'psychological' feudalism, namely a mentality centring around the need of the *rakyat* for protection, an unequal relationship which demanded 'total submission and servility to the ruling class' (Shaharuddin, 1988, 5). Cheah (1994, 269) prefers to categorise the system only as 'semi-feudal'.

The second reason flows from this hierarchical system, namely a lack of fixed rules for royal succession which made rulers reluctant to see substantial concentrations of wealth in hands other than their own lest this encourage potential challengers to their power. Rulers attempted to increase controls in order to buttress their position *vis-à-vis* Europeans. 'Free market forces and security for [private] property and wealth, vital ingredients for ... profit accumulation, were not to be found within the framework of royal absolutism' (Kathirithamby-Wells, 1993, 16–17). The mercantile elements in Malay society had no autonomy and therefore did not constitute fertile soil for seeds of capitalism to flourish. Furthermore, the persistence of low-level warfare between states also contributed to the general insecurity of wealth. In 1673 raiders from Jambi (Sumatra) carried off a reported four tonnes of gold from the Johor capital, Batu Sawar (Drabble, 1989, 5).

In contrast to these internal obstacles to the development of an indigenous capitalism, the economic activities of Europeans and Chinese in Southeast Asia were following an increasingly divergent (or dualistic) path. Though Europeans performed a 'crucial role' by importing silver into Southeast Asia from Japan and South America which helped to 'lubricate ...

expanding economies' (Chaudhuri, 1990, 387; Lieberman, 1990, 83), the commercial structure and ethos of the VOC and the EIC were culturally-specific, which militated against a spread of western-style capitalist institutions beyond these organisations. Whilst the Dutch pushed the introduction of commercial crops such as sugar and coffee in Java during the eighteenth century, 'prior to 1750 agriculture throughout what would become known as Malaysia and Indonesia remained outside European direction' (Lieberman, 1990, 73). The Chinese, on the other hand, were progressively moving beyond commerce into productive ventures in mining and agriculture in the interior. In the eighteenth century the growing flow of Chinese migrants brought with them a form of organisation, the *kongsi*, which was a self-contained unit encompassing their economic activities and social order, as well as regulating relations with local rulers. By the 1770s gold mining *kongsis* in west Borneo were sufficiently strong to unite in federations over which neighbouring rulers had little power (Chew, 1990, 20–1).

By the late eighteenth century the economy of the Malaysian region, in common with the surrounding areas, was still essentially premodern in its structure. Population growth was low, and production was highly localised in small units, with little intra-regional competition. The commodities exported were largely the primary products of agriculture and mining, whilst imports were foodstuffs and manufactures (Drabble, 1989, 8). Some centres, such as Terengganu, were noted for their manufactures but

> in the area comprising modern Malaysia and Indonesia [there was] ... an inclination to import rather than manufacture [and] ... insofar as there were higher levels of skill and capitalization they were probably to be found ... in the textile and handicraft producing centres of eastern India and south China that exported goods to Southeast Asia.
>
> (Lieberman, 1990, 75, 86)

Thus an international division of labour involving the exchange of primary products for manufactures, normally identified as emerging in the nineteenth and twentieth centuries under the impact of the Industrial Revolution in the West, was in fact operating considerably earlier.

Overall the volume of output was neither quantitatively large nor quickly expandable. Together with trade, it was subject to disruption by political instability, piracy and so on. Political boundaries were still very fluid. Throughout much of the eighteenth century conditions in the Malay Peninsula were varied. Most states, excepting Kedah and Terengganu, suffered internal power struggles related to succession. In Borneo the area of influence of Brunei was declining, whilst that of the Sulu sultanate was expanding into northeast Borneo.

Whilst economic growth was thus sporadic between the fifteenth and eighteenth centuries, we can identify the presence during this period of many of the features which were to figure largely in the emergence of modern Malaysia after about 1800 (Drabble and Mills, 1991). These were the geographical position astride major international trade routes bringing openness to external influences, the growing importance of export production from specialised estates and mines, the increasing involvement of foreign capital, entrepreneurs and labour, with the concurrent growth of a plural society, and the indigenous elites who (especially in the Malay Peninsula) exercised a patrimonial power over the distribution of economic benefits. European colonial power in the nineteenth century came into a region in which export production was already long-established; it did not innovate this economy.

Part I

The Formation of a Colonial Export Economy (*c*.1800–1920)

3
The Transition to Modern Trade

3.1 World trade in transition

Over the century from 1815 to 1914 world trade underwent a profound change in both quantitative and qualitative terms. The volume of trade grew on average at between 4 and 5 per cent a year compared to 1 per cent over the preceding hundred years. This meant that a greatly increased proportion of world output entered into international exchange, as is evident from the average ratio of exports and imports to national incomes which rose from about 2–3 per cent c.1800 to approximately 30 per cent by 1913 (O'Brien, 1997, 81–2).

The principal driving force behind this unprecedented change was the Industrial Revolution which began in northwest Europe and spread to other areas, principally in the northern hemisphere. These countries constituted an industrialised centre or 'core' for the world economy. New methods of production (factories, power-driven machinery, and so on) turned out ever-increasing quantities of relatively cheap standardised goods. Whilst home markets were an important outlet for these goods, the availability of export markets enabled production to be expanded well beyond the limits of domestic demand. Pioneers such as Britain thus gained a comparative advantage which they had previously lacked in trading with areas such as Asia. This switch in position is best exemplified by the growth of cotton textile manufacture which became one of Britain's leading exports. The prime export market here was India, which had been Britain's main supplier of cotton textiles in the seventeenth and much of the eighteenth centuries. In return for their exports of manufactures the industrialising countries imported mainly primary products; foodstuffs, industrial raw materials (tin, rubber) and fuels which to a large extent came from the southern hemisphere. This interchange has since been labelled the 'Old International Division of Labour' (OIDL).

Further contrasts with trade in the premodern era were a much stronger emphasis on the exchange of low-value, high-bulk commodities against the reverse situation earlier. Modern trade was predicated on predictability: that is, that supplies adequate in quality would arrive in the required amounts at a set destination and time. The transport of goods had to be secure, for instance against piracy. Exchange via barter, though it continued for a long time in some areas, was gradually superseded by generally accepted means of payment (hard currency or various instruments of credit), and efficient channels of transmission such as an international network of banks, telegraphic communications and so on. There was also a trend, led by Britain from around 1850, to free trade, and the international mobility of capital without restrictions such as tariffs and monopolies. These developments were concurrent with, and linked to, the great surge in European colonialism in the later nineteenth century.

3.2   Colonial versus indigenous states in trade

The nineteenth century saw two types of government widely juxtaposed in the Malaysian region: the colonial state and the Malay *kerajaan* (government). In practice the colonial 'state' was not a monolithic structure which came into existence at a particular point in time. As we saw in Chapter 1.2 British hegemony in Malaysia required well over a century (from 1786 to 1919) to evolve fully, and took a variety of forms. The SS of Penang, Singapore and Melaka were 'a device for exerting power and influence with minimal force ... a new kind of trading post empire developed most effectively by Great Britain. Instead of using a chartered company ... it was even more effective ... to establish government-run entrepots' (Curtin, 1984, 241).

Given that the state had a prime involvement in trade, these settlements were not too dissimilar from the indigenous port-polities. However, a crucial difference was that they were not the personal fief of a ruler but were administered by a professional bureaucracy appointed externally (from India to 1867, and from London thereafter). The prime aim of officials was to operate a system which encouraged entrepot trade to flow with as few controls as possible; hence the free-trade status conferred on the Straits ports. Another novel aspect was that these settlements had precise political and geographical boundaries. This was a general characteristic of western colonialism in the nineteenth century; see, for example the delineation of the Anglo-Dutch spheres of interest in maritime Southeast Asia by the 1824 Treaty of London. Whereas the Dutch, behind the boundaries, tried to concentrate the trade of the Indies in the hands of their nationals, the British used their bases to attract traders from whatever source.

Singapore quickly established itself as the premier port in the SS, and the focal point for traders from a wide area of the surrounding archipelago, especially Sumatra and Borneo, as well as Chinese, Indian and private

European merchants (the EIC lost its monopoly over the China trade in 1833). The main reason for this was its unrivalled geographical position. Government did not have to take a very proactive role to achieve this, merely 'restrict[ing] itself to the maintenance of peace, stability and an atmosphere conducive to future progress' (Huff, 1994, 3–4). Singapore, and to a lesser extent Penang, also became important as gateways through which mercantile capital and immigrant labour flowed into neighbouring states, particularly those on the west coast of the Malay Peninsula from the 1830s and 1840s (see Chapter 4). Britain's formal involvement with the states in the Peninsula began in 1874, with a much wider territorial dimension than the SS, so the colonial bureaucracy there was concerned not only with trade but also the exploitation of the natural resources.

The expansion of British hegemony in northern Borneo took different forms. The Englishman James Brooke, granted a fief in Sarawak in 1841 by the Sultan of Brunei in return for assistance against domestic instability, was in many respects a commercial adventurer in the mould of the previous era. However, initially 'he saw his task in terms, not of setting up an independent raj, but of restoring legitimate government in the [weakened] sultanate of Brunei'. The prospects for this failed to materialise, and the aims of James (who ruled 1841–68) and Charles (who ruled 1868–1917) were gradually transmuted into 'an independent Sarawak ... not to reform Brunei but to replace it' (Tarling, 1992, 15, 19). The outcome was a progressive expansion of Sarawak territory and a corresponding erosion of Brunei to a fraction of its former size by 1890. Sarawak was not a colonial state in the conventional sense with internal affairs subject to regulation by a metropolitan government. It was a 'private feudal domain' of the Brooke family (Fisher, 1963, 103), though its existence was ultimately underpinned by Britain. As in the Peninsula trade was the foundation of the economy, though the Brooke rajas had an 'ideology of gradualism' (Reece, 1988, 33) which opposed rapid development by large scale foreign capital (see Chapter 4.2).

The British North Borneo Chartered Company (1881) embodied the, by then, outmoded device of the royal charter which stipulated that the company must remain British in character and accept the 'advice of the British government should the latter disagree with any dealings with the indigenous people and foreign powers' (Tregonning, 1965, Ch. 2). Subsequent territorial expansion, again at the expense of Brunei, saw British North Borneo (hereafter referred to as North Borneo) at about the size of modern Sabah by 1901 (Andaya and Andaya, 1982, 184–91). Despite being formed to earn dividends for shareholders, the Company decided almost immediately (in 1882) to operate as a 'purely administrative company' (Tregonning, 1965, 52): that is, there would be no direct involvement in trade. Development would be through attraction of further investors in concessions for mining and agriculture.

The colonial states in their various forms were expected to be self-financing through taxation. In the SS trade could not be taxed directly, and revenue had to be raised from various excises (e.g., on domestic consumption of opium), licences and property taxes. In the Malay States (Federated and Unfederated) duties on exports and imports, land rents, posts, telegraphs, and railway receipts provided the main sources. In the Borneo territories revenue came from a similar range, though the potential of the local economy for taxation was more limited. On the expenditure side, the colonial governments used revenue to provide the basics of infrastructure, for instance government buildings, roads, bridges, harbours and, initially along the west coast of the Peninsula, a network of railways and telegraphs. This expenditure on fixed capital assets was one of the most visible signs of a permanent British presence. Again, the scale of expenditure was much greater in the SS, and particularly the FMS where the booming tin industry provided the bulk of revenue (see Chapter 4.2).

By contrast, in North Borneo the Company was so pressed for funds in its first decade or so that no dividends could be paid and a bare minimum of administrative staff employed, sufficient only for a 'makeshift' form of government which left the interior regions almost untouched (Black, 1983). The position improved following booms in tobacco and rubber cultivation in the 1890s and early 1900s, but much of the Company's expenditure on infrastructure such as railways and telecommunications was 'rash and ill-conceived' (Tregonning, 1965, 54; see also Chapter 5.2 below).

The loss of autonomy by indigenous rulers took longest in what became the Unfederated Malay States (UMS), which were in the north and northeast of the Peninsula, except for Johor in the south. Some underwent periods of unsettled internal conditions in the early nineteenth century. After invasion by Siam in 1821 Kedah experienced 20 years of direct rule from Bangkok against determined local resistance. There was widespread destruction of productive resources, and large numbers of people fled, decreasing the population from about 50 000 to 21 000 (Dodge, 1980, Table 9). Droughts and floods between 1829 and 1831 worsened the situation. Kelantan and Terengganu also experienced pressure from Siam, internecine struggles over the succession and natural disasters.

The situation then changed. A common feature of these northern states from about the 1840s to the 1870s was the accession of strong rulers who were able to centralise power and effectively to control district chiefs by putting their own appointees in place. Whilst remaining traditional Malay monarchs, they adopted some western ideas and administrative practices considered useful. Economic activity recovered. A prime example is Kedah, where the Sultan had been restored in 1842, though with a reduced territory. Sultan Ahmad Tajuddin II (who ruled 1854–79) provides an instance of 'strong government and outstanding achievement … In 1850 [Kedah was] a depopulated wasteland. By … the early 1870s [it] was one of the most flourishing of the Malay states' (Gullick, 1985, 107). Roads and canals were built, helping to attract Malay immigrants (many from Patani rather than Kedah returnees) to re-open rice lands abandoned as a result of the invasion. A rudimentary system of land titles was instituted. Chinese, too, were encouraged to engage in cash cropping, such as tapioca, and tin mining. By 1884 the population had soared to 150 000, of whom 20 000 were Chinese (Dodge, 1980; Gullick, 1985, 111–4).

In Terengganu, after a disturbed period of conflict with neighbouring Kelantan (a vassal of Siam), Sultan Baginda Omar (who ruled 1839–76) exercised a strong centralised rule, providing his appointees in the districts with money and goods in the traditional patrimonial manner. Cash cropping of pepper, sugar and coffee expanded, as well as tin mining and manufacturing of woodwork, textiles, metalwares (Talib, 1990, 217–20). The British official Hugh Clifford was so impressed by the quality and variety of manufactures on a visit in 1895 that he described the state as the 'Birmingham of the Peninsula' (cited in Khoo Kay Kim, 1974, 24).

Johor state was unique in the Peninsula in that it was a nineteenth century creation which owed much to trade. Around 1800 'there was, in fact, no "state" in the area now called Johor ... [the name] referred only to a vague geographical area, much of it insular. There was nothing of great importance on the land ... The Temenggong's government was really the sea peoples' (Trocki, 1979, xv). The Temenggongs developed a close relationship with the Straits government in Singapore. They used revenue from exports, coupled with liberal grants of land, to attract population and consolidate their power for much of the century. There were no entrenched district chiefs to contend with (Gullick, 1989, 85–6). Starting with a minuscule Malay population estimated at no more than 1000 in the 1830s, the total grew to 200 000 (150 000 Chinese) by 1891 (Dodge, 1980, Table 8).

However, the states just discussed were unable to maintain this momentum. The 1890s and early 1900s saw a decline in the financial stability of government as a result of the accession of rulers of lesser calibre than their immediate predecessors. The main problem was a growing indebtedness, of which a major cause was extravagant personal expenditure by the Sultans who drew no distinction between their private means and those of the state. By 1904–5 Kedah (still under Siamese tutelage) had fallen into a state of bankruptcy, with debts totalling four times annual income. A rescue was effected by means of a loan from Siam. The Sultan had to accept the establishment of new administrative machinery, including an Adviser (of British nationality) appointed by Bangkok, and a State Council modelled on those in the FMS.

In Kelantan financial problems a few years earlier had resulted in a similar solution. In Terengganu the ruling class, especially those with royal connections, was able to appropriate the major share of the increasing wealth from production and trade. In 1909 the four northern Malay states

(Kedah, Perlis, Kelantan and Terengganu) were transferred from Siamese to British suzerainty. British Advisers were appointed in the first three, but Terengganu held out until 1919. The remaining Peninsular Malay state, Johor, was better-administered on the whole, but again the Sultan's extravagant lifestyle around the turn of the century, which was seen to threaten the future financial viability of the state, prompted British pressure culminating in the appointment of a Financial Adviser in 1909 and a General Adviser in 1914 (Andaya and Andaya, 1982, 195–200; Shaharil Talib, 1984, ch. 8; Sharom Ahmat, 1984).

By the time of the First World War, British rule, with its export-oriented economic structure, was firmly established throughout the territories of modern Malaysia. As the indigenous states saw their autonomy progressively eroded, effective control of economic resources passed into the hands of colonial officials who viewed external trade as necessary to generate the revenue necessary to pay for the cost of government, and for whom development consisted of exploiting the potential of the natural resources of the country. As we shall see, this exploitation was geographically very uneven, favouring the west coast rather than the east coast states of the Peninsula and the Borneo territories, but the following comment (originally made in the context of Terengganu) has a general validity:

> all this took place against a vanishing background. The
> Malayo-Muslim world ... was dissolving, its perspectives
> gradually narrowing, its formerly dynamic centers robbed
> of power ... The economic consequences ... as the [nineteenth]
> century wore on [were that] European competition and state
> regulations impinged ever more on their freedom to operate.
>
> (Sutherland, 1978, 38–9)

3.3   The trade in Straits products (c.1820–70)

In the early decades of the nineteenth century the patterns and content of trade in the Asian region were largely a continuation of those which had emerged since about 1760, namely the booming commerce in Chinese tea, silks and so on, and the search for commodities to exchange for these. Southeast Asia was seen as a market in which goods from India, such as textiles and opium, could be exchanged for the goods collectively known as 'Straits products' (tin, gambier, birds' nests) which could then be shipped to China.

Singapore, with its more advantageous geographical position at the foot of the Peninsula, rapidly overtook Penang and Melaka. The direction of the port's trade after 1825 can be seen in Table 3.1. These figures show the initial importance of the connections with India and China, but the impetus derived by Singapore from these trades was short-lived. Many

Table 3.1   Singapore: direction of trade, 1825–1915 (%)

Year	S.E. Asia	E. Asia	S. Asia	West
1825	48	14	20	18
1850	39	15	19	26
1870	48	13	8	30
1915	56	9	4	29

Source: Wong Lin Ken (1978), Tables 1, 8.

firms entered the market, leading to a glut of Straits products in Canton in 1827–8 and numerous bankruptcies. Opium prices were unstable, fluctuating from a peak of approximately $1800 (Spanish) a chest in the early 1820s down to $250 in 1839 (Trocki, 1990, graph, 59). After Britain's Opium War with China (1840–2), the setting-up of Hong Kong put the trade increasingly into the hands of larger merchant firms there, such as Jardine Matheson. The East Asian shares of Singapore's trade declined from about the mid-century.

The Indian connection also became progressively less important even though opium remained a significant import into Singapore for redistribution throughout Southeast Asia until the early twentieth century. A major reason for the decline was the displacement of Indian cotton piece goods in Southeast Asian markets by cheap mass-production from factories in Britain. In 1828/9 the former constituted 77 per cent of Singapore's imports in this category, but by 1840/1 the share had fallen to 30 per cent (calculated from Wong Lin Ken, 1960, 259).

Thus, the trading system which had provided much of the early impetus for the entrepot trade of the Straits ports had lost much of its force by about 1840. These ports had not been intended primarily to stimulate production in the immediate hinterlands but, as the mercantile communities grew in size and wealth, and the flows of immigrants passing through increased, there was a knock-on effect. Wong Lin Ken has remarked of Singapore that 'the trade which came [there] in the early days was not merely the result of the transfer of existing trade to new channels ... it also consisted of the traffic which the very existence of Singapore had evoked' (1960, 159). The annual average growth rates of Straits ports trade from the 1830s to the early 1870s are shown in Table 3.2. The slow rates for Penang and Melaka up to 1843 indicate the relatively low levels of activity in their hinterlands. Exports of tin from the Peninsula increased from between 500 and 1000 tonnes around 1800 to only some 2400 tonnes in the early 1840s. Thereafter the discovery of rich deposits of tin ore in Sungei Ujong, and several other districts in Selangor and Perak boosted average exports to approximately 6600 tonnes in the 1850s and 8650 tonnes in the 1860s (Dodge, 1977, Table 1). Much of this was shipped out through Penang and Melaka, which increasingly acted as feeder ports to Singapore. Melaka's position,though, was unstable. Disturbances among Chinese miners in the hinterland sent the port's trade plummeting (Turnbull, 1972, 161–2). During this period Europe, and Britain especially, emerged as the main market due to the growth of the tinplate industry.

Singapore's growth rate fluctuated, too, but the port's superiority as an entrepot for a wide area was already confirmed by the 1840s. Up to the mid-1830s the value of trade with the east coast states of the Peninsula outweighed that with the west coast. Gold (virtually all produced on the east coast) was the leading commodity, accounting for 47 per cent of total Peninsula exports to Singapore in 1835–6 (Dodge, 1977, 95). Volume data are not available for other merchandise exports, including black pepper, rattans, salt, Malay cotton textiles and so on, but aggregate values were falling at this time, suggesting declining prices.

The exports from northern Borneo were still dominated by 'indigenous, unprocessed and luxury products' (Cleary, 1996, 303) of the foraging or procurement trade, such as camphor, sandalwood, hornbill beaks and bird's nests together with more bulky items such as rattans, sago, pepper, jelutong and gutta percha (used as an insulator in electric cables). Singapore was the main outlet to the international economy by the 1830s. Though aggregate trade values rose it is difficult to establish long-term production trends for most commodities. In the case of cultivated products, such as sago and pepper, the trend was fairly certainly upwards, though shipments could fluctuate sharply in the short term due to weather conditions or localised political instability. Sarawak kept trade figures from 1849, but struggled to achieve a favourable balance in the early years. It was 1870 before an export surplus of any size, some Spanish $648 000, appeared (Wong Lin Ken, 1960, 271). The entrepot at Labuan island (from 1846) was not the hoped-for success. Efforts at coal mining to supply the growing numbers of steamships bore little fruit. Chinese were not attracted in large numbers and European

Table 3.2   Straits ports: annual average growth in total trade, 1833–73

Years	*Percentage (current prices)*		
	Singapore	*Penang*	*Melaka*
1833–43	4.00	1.66	−0.32
1843–53	1.62	5.14	12.66
1853–63	6.40	9.22	4.63
1863–73	4.30	4.20	−4.78

Note: Includes Treasure.
Source: Calculated from Chiang Hai Ding (1978), Table 1, Appendix VI.

merchants in Singapore were hostile to a potential competitor. By the late 1860s the island was increasingly being bypassed by indigenous merchants (the Taosug from Sulu) who preferred to go directly to Singapore. By that time, too, shipments of sago and antimony ore were going directly from Sarawak to Britain (Warren, 1981, 111–2; Cleary, 1996, 311).

Between about 1840 and 1870 the SS entrepots consolidated their position in the global network with trade increasingly oriented towards the West (Table 3.1). Britain was the principal customer for items such as pepper, gambier, gutta percha and sugar, especially with the progressive switch to free trade which saw substantial reductions in import duties in the 1830s and 1840s. Improvements in product quality were also significant factors in obtaining a greater market share. Straits tin gradually became known on the London market from the 1830s, suffering at first from a reputation for adulteration but overcoming this by the 1860s as smelting methods improved. Imports into Britain doubled from 9090 tonnes to 18 118 tonnes in the decade from 1856/60 to 1866/70. Those of the USA grew similarly in the late 1860s and early 1870s.

Just how important had external trade become in these economies by the mid-century? Between 1824 and 1869 Singapore's total trade value increased approximately fivefold, or a little under 4 per cent a year. The proportion of this with the Malay Peninsula rose from 15 per cent to 34 per cent by 1845, and then slipped back to 27 per cent in 1865. In absolute terms this represented an increase from $870 000 to $6.75 million (calculated from Wong Lin Ken, 1978, Tables 2 and 4). We do not have comparable figures for Borneo, but the value of trade passing through Labuan went from about $47 000 in 1855–9 to $314 000 in 1865–9 (Cleary, 1996, Table 2).

Recent scholarship has tended to downplay the importance of this trade. Drake (1979, 288) has suggested that in the Malay Peninsula 'productive activity may have been widespread and varied and with a trade component, but the economy was [still] small in scale and output and ... best characterised as stagnant rather than growing'. A study of Singapore concludes similarly that 'this was a small trade based on the export of a variety of tropical produce and a return flow of imports' (Huff, 1994, 8). In 1867 'the interior [of the Peninsula] was still almost unknown' (Turnbull, 1972, 314), a statement which applies even more strongly to northern Borneo. The present study cannot supply a definitive answer as the data are inadequate. It is possible that trade in terms of current values was increasing on average faster than population (see Chapter 6, section 6.1), which does not lend support to Drake's view of 'stagnation'. The pattern was more one of sharp fluctuations in the short term: for example, tin exports fell by half between the late 1860s and 1874 as a result of civil disturbances in Perak (Wong Lin Ken, 1965b, 246–7). On balance we can conclude that production for export in order to ensure a return flow of imports, notably cotton textiles, was becoming an increasingly vital part of the economic life of more and more communities as the networks of trade expanded (see section 3.5).

3.4   The trade in staples (1870–*c*.1920)

This period witnessed Singapore's transformation from an entrepot into a staple port: that is, from a simple collection and distribution centre to one providing processing, bulking and other facilities for primary products (tin, rubber, petroleum, coal) from the surrounding region. This change was brought about, first, by the completion of the Suez Canal in 1869 which opened East–West trade to the steamship, and second, the development in Europe and North America of major new mass-production industries, such as automobiles, with the derived demand for rubber tyres (Huff, 1994, 8). The transition in the composition of Straits trade can be seen from Table 3.3, with the proportions of premodern and modern commodities being practically reversed. The main shift occurred after 1900 with the boom in tin and rubber production (although tin had been exported for centuries, it entered the modern category as a major industrial raw material). North Borneo began slowly, with 91 per cent of its exports jungle and sea-products in the early 1880s, but by 1916 around 73 per cent consisted of cultivated products, mainly tobacco and rubber. Jungle and sea-products remained important in Sarawak, but by 1915 had declined to 21 per cent against 31 per cent for cultivated items (sago, pepper, rubber) and 22 per cent for minerals (gold: see Cleary, 1996, Tables 3, 4a, 4c).

Table 3.4 sets out the geographical distribution of Straits trade. Section (a) shows that Southeast Asia increased its dominance as the prime source of Straits imports, mainly at the expense of the West. This does not mean, though, that fewer western goods reached the region. The Straits ports were increasingly bypassed as direct shipping links with the West were established by neighbouring countries, as is evident from the fall in the proportion of exports to the NEI and 'Other Southeast Asia' in section (b)

Table 3.3   Composition of Straits trade: selected years, 1870–1915

	Percentage of total commodity trade	
Year	*Premodern*[a]	*Modern*[b]
1870	57.6	42.4
1900	58.9	41.2
1915	41.2	59.3

[a] Rice, gutta percha, opium, pepper, rattans, gambier, fish, copra, sugar, tapioca, arecanut, sago, coffee, hides, tobacco, sarongs.
[b] Coal, tin, petroleum, rubber, cotton, textiles.
Source: Calculated from Chiang Hai Ding (1978), Table XI.

of the table. Imports from 'Other Southeast Asia' (Burma, Thailand, French Indo-China) rose due to the trade in foodstuffs (rice) needed to feed the rapidly increasing immigrant population in Malaysia and the NEI. The vigorous regional trade in rice was a major factor in Singapore's primacy. Chinese merchants used rice as a unit of account in barter to obtain the export products of the archipelago, thereby economising on the still limited availability of cash (Huff, 1989).

In the export trade the outstanding change in section (a) is the increased share of the West which reflects the growth of the tin and rubber staples, reflected in imports from Malaya in section (b). The bulk of these still went out through the Straits ports, although the establishment of Port Swettenham (later re-named Port Kelang) on the west coast of the Peninsula in 1901 created competition as an outlet for rubber. The relative position of the British territories in Borneo did not change significantly, as their economies had not yet experienced an export boom on the same scale as Malaya (see Chapter 4).

A time-series of Malaysian trade from 1870 to 1915 is presented in Table 3.5. There was not much growth in either export or import values until the early 1880s, and then there was a sustained upsurge until 1900. The boom in tin production was the main constituent, though prices did not undergo a really major rise until 1899. Imports and exports grew at about the same rate for much of the first two-and-a-half decades, as the percentages in column 4 indicate. Thereafter exports pulled ahead as investment in tin and then rubber came to fruition. This was particularly evident between 1910 and 1915, with imports constrained by the outbreak of war in Europe.

Table 3.4   Geographical distribution of Straits Settlements merchandise trade: selected years, 1870–1915
(a) World

	Imports from			Exports to		
Year	S.E. Asia	Other Asia	West	S.E. Asia	Other Asia	West
1870	44.4	23.0	32.5	42.9	19.6	37.4
1900	58.0	24.2	17.8	40.2	12.0	47.7
1915	67.9	17.2	14.8	35.8	10.7	53.4

(b) Southeast Asia

	Malaya	Brit. Borneo	NEI	Other S.E. Asia	Malaya	Brit. Borneo	NEI	Other S.E. Asia
1870	10.0	1.9	16.6	16.0	4.3	1.1	18.2	19.3
1900	22.4	1.7	18.7	15.1	10.6	1.4	18.4	9.8
1915	30.0	1.5	16.3	20.0	14.2	1.0	14.9	5.7

Source: Adapted from Chiang Hai Ding (1978), Tables xix, xxi, 85–6.

This period spanned something of an hiatus in which tin output stagnated and rubber, as already noted, had only just begun to make its presence felt in trade. An increasing export surplus existed from 1870 onwards. This surplus accrued largely to the Peninsula. North Borneo ran a substantial import surplus in the 1880s as the Chartered Company had to make investments in infrastructure before the first export crop, tobacco, was established in the 1890s, but it was not until investment in rubber started around 1910 that a notable export surplus appeared. Sarawak trade values stagnated between 1870 and 1890, and only accelerated after 1900 with boosts from gold mining and some rubber.

In terms of export volume, Malaysia's performance can be seen from Table 3.6, though it should be noted that up to about 1910 this represents largely output from the Peninsula as data on quantities from the Borneo territories are difficult to find. As with trade values, the underlying factors were the surge in tin production in the Peninsula in the 1890s, followed by a decade or so in which exports did not show much net growth. During this time other crops, such as tapioca, gambier and sugar gave way virtually entirely to rubber. The impact of the latter becomes particularly marked after 1910. Exports of rubber were checked briefly by voluntary restriction among European-owned estates in Malaya in 1918, and then rebounded sharply after the war ended. Petroleum exports from Sarawak were also rising rapidly at this time (see Chapter 4.1).

Comparative work (Booth, 1991, Table 4) shows Malaysia's export volume growth rate as 4.6 per cent a year from 1895 to 1915 (the data in Table 3.6

Table 3.5   Malaysia: [a]aggregate imports and exports, 1870–1920 (current prices, nearest Str.$000)

Year	Imports[b]	Exports[b]	Total	Imports/exports (%)
1870	4 454	5 999	10 453	74
1875	4 828	5 948	10 776	81
1880	6 516	7 418	13 934	88
1885	10 568	13 059	23 627	81
1890	18 083	24 686	42 769	73
1895	27 099	44 532	71 631	61
1900	49 532	81 053	130 585	61
1905	64 303	113 606	177 909	57
1910	71 330	131 318	202 648	54
1915	85 853	202 152	294 005	42
1920	317 500	401 800	719 300	79

[a] Malay Peninsula (excluding SS), Sarawak, NB (from 1885).
[b] Imports taken as exports from Straits ports to Malay Peninsula; exports vice versa. Kedah not available 1901–9.
Sources: Calculated from SS *Blue Books,* various years; FMS (1905–15) from *Manual of Statistics Relating to the FMS 1923:* Sarawak (1870–85) from *Sarawak Gazette,* 12 May 1887; (1885–1920) from *Annual Report (AR) Dept of Customs and Trade 1925;* NB from *AR,* various years.

Table 3.6 Malaysia: growth of export volume, 1874–1919 (1913 = 100)

Year	Index[a]	Year	Index
1875	9	1900	46
1880	12	1905	54
1885	18	1910	59
1890	28	1913	100
1895	52	1915	155
		1919	339

[a] Laspeyres formula.
Sources: Calculated from data in Wong Lin Ken (1965b); Drabble (1973); Jackson (1968a); Yuen (1974); Lim Chong Yah (1967); *AR, SS* and *FMS*, various years; NB, *AR Customs Dept* 1911–40; Sarawak, *AR Treasury, Posts, Shipping Office, Customs* 1925–40.

give a slightly higher figure of 5.6 per cent), close to the NEI at 5 per cent and Thailand at 5.4 per cent, but better than Burma (3.9 per cent) and the Philippines (4.4. per cent). It was also a little better than world trade volume growth at 4.2 per cent from 1896/1900 to 1911/13 (Hanson, 1980, Table 2.1). Whereas many LDC primary exports encountered competition towards the end of the nineteenth century, in tin and rubber Malaysia possessed two industrially vital commodities for which there were as yet no close substitutes or major competing sources of supply.

The major question which arises is: to what extent were the Malaysian territories able to retain the gains from trade in this period? In terms of the ratio between imports and exports (column 4 in Table 3.5), the increasing flow of exports was substantially requited with imports throughout the 1870s and early 1880s in Malaysia overall. From 1885 the ratio declined steadily, reaching a low point in 1915 and then rebounding in 1920. The two latter years reflect the onset of war, restricting shipping space for civilian goods, and then a postwar surge as stocks were replenished.

A comparative perspective (Table 3.7) shows Malaysia approximating the NEI and Burma most closely in the pattern of a declining import ratio over time. The averages for 1871–1920, with the exception of the Philippines, all fall within a fairly narrow range, from 67 to 78 per cent. The balance constituted an export surplus of between about one-third and one-fifth of the total value of exports. The relative magnitude of these can be judged against a sample of 34 LDCs (not including Malaysia) covering the late nineteenth and early twentieth centuries. Sixteen had cumulative export surpluses ranging from 1 per cent to 37 per cent of export value (Hanson, 1980, Table 7.1). Those from Asia (excepting the Philippines) were the highest at between 25 and 35 per cent. Outside Asia only Brazil (37 per cent) was higher, and most others in Central and South America and Africa were well below 20 per cent.

Table 3.7   Southeast Asia: comparative import/export ratios, 1870–1920

Years	Percentage, decadal average				
	Malaysia	NEI	Philippines	Thailand	Burma
1871–80	81	64	92	72	92
1881–90	81	74	81	68	97
1891–1900	65	76	80	75	73
1900–10	67	65	113	70	66
1910–20	58[a]	57	101	85	62
Average	70	67	93	74	78

[a] 1910–13.
Sources: Malaysia calculated from Table 3.5, remainder from Booth (1990), Table 15. Average calculated by the author.

Whether or not a consistent export surplus is bad for a country's development depends on how it is disposed of. If the entire amount is remitted overseas as profits, dividends and savings by foreign residents, then any domestic benefit is lost and we have what has been described as a 'colonial drain' (Golay, 1976). To ascertain this we need details of the country's balance of payments. However, in the case of the Malaysian territories the data for this early period are presently insufficient to enable such calculations. With the rapid growth in foreign (largely British) investment in tin and rubber after 1900 we can be certain that substantial remittances did take place. Khor (1983, 58) estimates foreign profits from tin and rubber at one-fifth of total income from direct production in Malaya before the Second World War. However, a considerable proportion of these profits, from rubber particularly, was reinvested (see Table 4.2 and related discussion) and this, plus the large shares in these industries in the hands of locally resident Asian merchants and indigenous farmers (rubber smallholdings), makes it unlikely that the entire export surplus was lost.

Another way of analysing the gains from trade is through changes in the commodity (net barter) and income terms of trade (Figure 3.1). In the first category there was some deterioration up to 1875 as export prices stagnated while import prices rose, but over the next two decades export values pulled well ahead as a result of the booms in rubber and tin. Between 1900 and 1914 there was decline as export prices fluctuated but import prices rose steadily. Though the commodity index at 127 in 1915 was virtually the same as 1870 (124), it is clear that over this 45-year period Malaysia derived considerable benefits from external trade. The income terms of trade (i.e., the purchasing power of exports) show a continual rise throughout the period, becoming particularly marked after about 1905 as growth in the aggregate value of exports offset the decline in unit price levels.

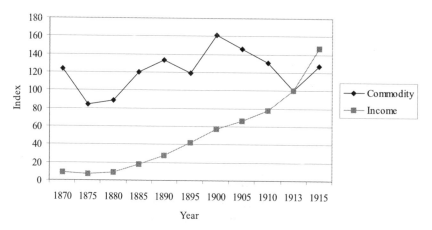

Figure 3.1 Malaysia: terms of trade, 1870–1915 (1913 = 100)
Sources: Calculated from SS *Blue Books*, various years; Chiang Hai Ding (1978); Straits Settlements Government (1926), Tables X, XII.

3.5 The structure of commercial enterprise

The system of trade which developed in the nineteenth century had three main groups of participants: (i) large-scale exporters and importers, (ii) medium-scale bazaar (*pasar*) traders, and (iii) small-scale itinerant or peddling traders. Broadly, those in (i) connected the region to the industrialised economies, and consisted of European (predominantly British) mercantile firms dealing in bulk or wholesale transactions. The bazaar trade (ii) consisted of small firms in the ports throughout the region, but strongly centred in Singapore and acting as a retail network for collection of the primary products and distribution of manufactured imports. Here Chinese, and to a lesser extent Indian, merchants predominated. Itinerant traders (iii) operated at the 'grass roots' level throughout the archipelago and up to the mainland, penetrating ever deeper and more extensively upriver and along rudimentary tracks, exchanging small quantities of imports for local products. At this level, as we shall see later, there was both indigenous and migrant (Chinese) participation early in the century, but the latter gradually established a dominant position. The Straits ports acted as centres for breaking down bulk-shipments of imports, and in return grading, processing and bulking 'Straits products', and later the major staples for shipment to international markets.

These groups constituted a three-tier structure. Their interdependence can be seen in the system of credit. European importers, using credit from manufacturers or banks, distributed goods on 60–90 day terms to the bazaar traders who in turn extended similar terms to the itinerant traders. Credit was liquidated by a return flow of products bulked up as they moved back through the system (Drabble and Drake, 1981). Over time competition for business did develop between (i) and (ii), and between (ii) and (iii). We shall now look at these interests in turn.

The European merchant firms had two main origins. Some started as branches of Calcutta agency houses active in the country trade, and others as independent concerns. As an example of the latter, Alexander Guthrie, a Scotsman, arrived at Singapore in 1821, bringing goods on account of Thomas Harrington of Capetown, and set up the company which from 1833 bore the Guthrie name alone (Cunyngham-Brown, 1971, 13ff). By 1827 there were 14 firms in Singapore holding agencies for overseas manufacturers, all but one British (Drabble and Drake, 1981, 300). This model was followed, but to a lesser extent, by Asian interests. Numbers reached a peak of 114 in 1901, of which 66 were European, 24 Chinese, 22 Indian and 2 Japanese (Chiang Hai Ding, 1970, 251). Over time European firms had acquired agencies for manufactured goods and services (insurance, banking, shipping). For much of the nineteenth century the principal form of organisation was the private partnership, and it became the practice among British firms to have an office and senior partner resident in London to acquire new agencies, liaise with manufacturers, and so on. Soon after 1900 changes in corporate structure took place, which will be discussed shortly.

In Sarawak James Brooke initially made the exploitation of mineral resources a state monopoly. However, despite his reservations about foreign capital, the Borneo Company Ltd was floated in London in 1856 with a capital of £60 000, and was given a general monopoly over production and trade in minerals. At first this covered only antimony ore and cinnabar (mercury sulphide), but by the early 1880s the company had effective control of gold mining, having bought out Chinese interests in this industry. The latter had suffered a setback after the mining *kongsi* at Bau, resentful at perceived unjust treatment, had come into armed conflict with Raja James in 1857 (Chin, 1981, 35–41). Coal and petroleum production also came within the Borneo Company's monopoly, and it was active in the trades in a variety of non-mineral products, such as sago, pepper, hides, coconuts, timber and rubber. The company derived substantial profits from these enterprises, and expanded operations to other parts of Southeast Asia, notably Siam. It has been argued that the close links with the Brooke regime enabled the company to survive 'heavy outside competition', yet the admission is made that 'evidence of competing companies has proved elusive' (Jones, 1986, 195–205).

In North Borneo the Chartered Company's policy was more open and relied on attracting private enterprise into production and trading activities. However, this did not prevent the emergence of monopolies such as the 25-year concession over all state land granted in 1920 to the British Borneo Timber Company (Tregonning, 1965, 83).

The European firms in the Straits ports, sometimes with Asian partners, did not become deeply involved in the development of the hinterland until the second half of the nineteenth century. From the 1860s stakes were taken in mining and agricultural ventures in Johor, Selangor, Perak, Pahang, and Terengganu (Drabble and Drake, 1981, 305; Khoo Kay Kim, 1972, chs 3, 4). The commercial success of these ventures was very varied (see Chapter 4.2). Agency house resources remained limited, a major constraint being that on retirement a partner withdrew funds, making capital accumulation difficult and deepening the dependence on credit from banks, manufacturers and, on occasion, wealthy Chinese (Drabble and Drake, 1981, 306).

The relationship between European and Asian mercantile interests in seeking to extend their shares in the growing volume of production and trade became more competitive in face of the successive booms in agriculture and mining (notably tin and rubber) between about the 1880s and the First World War. Chinese capital predominated in the mining of tin, but British interests made persistent attempts to break into the smelting of the ore, hitherto the preserve of small Chinese-owned smelters located near the tinfields. In 1887 a British–German partnership (Sword and Muhlinghaus) set up the Straits Trading Company Ltd in Singapore to centralise smelting and thus gain economies of scale. The company's success was virtually assured by a grant from government of the sole right to export ore from Sungei Ujong and Selangor for varying periods, giving it a share of between 30 and 54 per cent of the tin trade by 1895. The company operated smelters at Pulau Brani, Singapore, and Penang, and by the early twentieth century it was extending into southern Thailand (Wong Lin Ken, 1965b, 163–5; Cushman, 1986, 65–6).

These trends were closely linked with developments in shipping. Straits-born Chinese were particularly prominent in this field by the nineteenth century. They were responsive to technological advances, such as the introduction of the steamship, and from around 1850 set up many of the feeder links which tied in with the major western ocean-going lines at the Straits ports. By the 1880s the latter were bidding for a share in intra-regional routes to Sumatra, Borneo, Thailand: for example, Blue Funnel (British), KPM (Dutch), Norddeutscher-Lloyd (German) (Falkus, 1990).

The first major European initiative in local shipping was the Straits Steamship Company established in Singapore in 1890. However, this did not immediately mark the advent of competition with Chinese interests. Four out of the seven directors were Chinese, and several of the initial ships came from a Chinese company. None the less, the company soon became closely identified with the carriage of ores for Straits Trading. In 1914 the Ocean Steamship Company of Liverpool (Blue Funnel Line) became the largest shareholder, enabling the building of additional vessels for the Borneo trade (Tregonning, 1967, 17–19, 46–7).

In due course competitive steps were taken by Chinese interests. The Khaw family possessed major stakes in tin mining in southern Thailand (Phuket) and the tin trade with Penang. Soon after 1900 a small nucleus of ships received twelve additions to found Koe Guan, the largest shipping firm in Penang (Cushman, 1986, 67). In 1907 this company amalgamated with several others in Penang to form the Eastern Shipping Company with sixteen ships. In the previous year, 1906, the Khaws and other Chinese interests had acquired a substantial shareholding in Tongkah Harbour Tin Dredging Company, an Australian-registered concern working in southern Thailand, whose output was sent to Penang in Koe Guan ships. There it was processed in a smelting plant set up in 1898 by Lee Chin Ho (a Khaw associate), and floated as the Eastern Smelting Company in 1907. By 1910 the company accounted for 29 per cent of tin shipments from Straits ports (Cushman, 1986).

The Khaw 'group' thus possessed a vertically integrated structure (mining, smelting and shipping) similar to that pursued by European interests, but what it lacked ultimately was staying power. Eastern Smelting was sold to British interests in 1911, and Eastern Shipping to the Straits Steamship Company in 1922. The principal reason was limited sources of capital. Funds came from associated insurance and trading companies and an opium farm syndicate. This practice of financing one venture from the proceeds of another was widespread (see Chapter 4.2). There was also a decline in the quality of management, and poor maintenance of capital assets, such as ships (Cushman, 1986).

Against this lack of sustained competition, the European agency houses were able to consolidate their dominance of the Straits trade, and also in the sphere of primary production soon after the turn of the century. This was particularly the case with British firms who used their connections with the United Kingdom (Edinburgh, Glasgow and primarily London) to promote the flotation of sterling capital public joint-stock companies to acquire land for rubber and tin mining in the Peninsula, and to a lesser extent in North Borneo. The main reward for these services was appointment as Secretaries to the Board of Directors, and agents in Malaysia, which brought Board appointments and agency management fees, plus commissions on the sale of rubber, tin and supplies to the mines and estates. In this way the 'agency houses', as they became generally known, were able to tap the far greater sources of capital overseas (Drabble, 1973, 78–86).

At the same time these firms were able to expand their network of branches into the Malaysian hinterland (e.g., Kuala Lumpur, Ipoh, Melaka,

Jesselton) in the first decade or so of the century, and to stabilise their financial structure by adopting the joint-stock limited liability form though as private, not public, companies. Guthrie led the way in 1903, Adamson Gilfillan in 1904, Paterson Simons in 1907 and Harrisons & Crosfield in 1908 (Drabble and Drake, 1981, 308). Essentially this remained the basis upon which they were able to continue in business until well after Malaysian independence. A further factor explaining their long-term stability was a succession of strong, far-sighted leaders. Notable examples were Sir John Anderson and Sir John Hay of Guthrie & Company, who successively spanned the period from the mid-1870s to the early 1960s, and Arthur Lampard and Eric Macfadyen of Harrisons & Crosfield (Allen and Donnithorne, 1954, Cunyngham-Brown, 1971; Drabble, 1973, 1991). By contrast the majority of family-based Chinese firms failed to survive the death of their founder for very long, even though some (e.g., Tan Kim Seng & Company of Singapore) had structures which in many respects resembled the agency houses (Chiang Hai Ding, 1970, 257–8).

Indigenous merchants performed a function similar to that of the itinerant Chinese traders (i.e., distributing imports and collecting local products), though on a generally smaller scale and without the extensive range of family connections or the links with European agency houses. But what they lacked in individual weight was offset by their considerable numbers, at least in the first half of the nineteenth century. Shipping from the archipelago comprised 34.5 per cent of the tonnage using Singapore in 1829–30, and was still nearly 27 per cent in 1865–6 (Wong Lin Ken, 1960, Table XXXVIII).

In the Peninsula the *orang asli* were being superseded by Malays as primary collectors of forest-products as the latter pushed into the interior. At the secondary level there were opportunities for Malays as middlemen to link the interior with the coastal ports. District Malay chiefs controlled the transit trade downriver in tin (Wong Lin Ken, 1965b, 19–20; Dunn, 1975). In northern Borneo Brunei was still a notable trading power, but faced growing competition for the trade of the northeast coast (Tirun, Mangidara, Marudu, Papar) from the Sulu *datus* and other aggressive migratory groups such as the Bajau and Illanun (Warren, 1981; Ranjit Singh, 1984). The Brunei nobility (*pengiran*) controlled external trade both as actual traders and, like Peninsular Malays, as territorial chiefs taxing trade in passage (Brown, 1970, 63). Particular examples in Sarawak were the trade in sago produced by the Melanau in the Muka/Oya district (Morris, 1979, 1991), and in antimony ore discovered near Kuching in the early 1820s.

The second half of the nineteenth century saw a progressive loss by indigenous interests of control over trade. 'With the establishment of the free port of Singapore the South China Sea was awash with liberal notions that stood in stark opposition to the trading institutions of the [Malays]'

(Brown, 1970, 70). In Sarawak under the Brooke raj from 1841, as in the Peninsula after about 1874, the nobility had to forgo their customary right to control trade, receiving in return fixed annual cash payments. Chinese fanned out from Singapore in increasing numbers. The rulers of both Sarawak and Brunei welcomed them with grants of revenue farms and trade monopolies. In Sarawak every additional Chinese 'on the average increased the revenue by two pounds sterling per annum' (St John, 1899, cited in Brown, 1970, 73).

Quite apart from such privileges the Chinese proved adept in competitive trading, aiming for a low rate of profit per unit on the largest possible turnover of goods. Their clientele found that the terms of trade improved. It had been observed in the late 1820s that 'the customer pays enormously ... in the produce of his industry' (*Singapore Chronicle*, 1827, cited in Christie, 1988). In 1814 a bamboo container of high-value camphor from the Paitan river (Marudu Bay) was exchanged for an equal measure of a basic item, salt (Warren, 1981, 80). As Chinese traders extended their networks, opening shops in villages and stocking them with a diverse range of goods, they provided regular supplies in place of the periodic riverine trade of earlier decades. After the incorporation of Muka district into Sarawak in 1861 Malay merchants found themselves progressively unable to compete as they could not progress beyond their customary small-scale trading from boats (Lockard, 1987, 43–5).

Within the more confined geographical space of the Peninsula, we have already noted (section 3.3) the predominance of the east coast states in trade with Singapore up to the 1830s. Fragmentary evidence suggests that these states had the most organised and regular markets (in which women played a leading role as vendors) providing outlets for sea- and forest-products and local craftwares. The economy was already well-monetised with prices quoted in cash even in the more remote areas. Markets along the west coast were less developed, due mainly to the sparseness of the population in many areas such as Selangor and Perak. This changed as the pace of expansion picked up and communications improved (Chapter 5). Again, Chinese merchants were able to supersede Malays, though right up to the last decades of the century numbers of the latter (including migrants from Sumatra) could be found pursuing trade in the *kampungs* (villages) and the burgeoning mining settlements. In Gullick's view these constituted a nascent middle class who supplied 'the dynamism in the Malay economy' (1989, 103). Some started with inherited wealth, others operated under patronage and even direct funding from Malay nobility. As with Chinese firms in the Straits ports, however, few ventures outlasted their founder. By the early twentieth century the Malay elite, some of whom had gained considerable wealth in the mining boom of the 1870s and 80s (e.g., in the Kinta valley) were in heavily reduced circumstances (Gullick, 1989, 81), and no longer able to finance commerce.

Markets were slower to develop in Borneo than in the Peninsula due to the isolation of many of the population groups, and inter-tribal hostilities which rendered trading both difficult and dangerous. In the western coastal part of North Borneo there was the gradual spread of periodic markets (*tamu*) which provided facilities for formalised, peaceful, exchange (Ranjit Singh, 1984, 398–9).

By the beginning of the twentieth century the 'trade diaspora' (Curtin 1984, 4–5) throughout much of the Malaysian region was substantially complete. The various ethnic groups were settling into the economic relationships which were to characterise their dealings for the rest of the colonial period and some time beyond. There were, though, areas where traditional trading networks remained viable. The major example is Terengganu, where trade in many local products had not yet moved beyond longstanding routes throughout the archipelago and up to the mainland. But in general by the First World War the transition from premodern to modern trade was largely completed, at least in the Straits and western parts of the Malay Peninsula. Exports consisted principally of bulk raw materials (notably tin and rubber) while imports featured mass-produced textiles and foodstuffs. Rice had increased from around 6 per cent of SS imports in 1870 to nearly 14 per cent in 1915, since domestic production was insufficient to feed the burgeoning immigrant population (Drabble, 1989, 29–30).

3.6   International trade: 'engine' or 'handmaiden' of growth?

In the words of W. Arthur Lewis, the Industrial Revolution in the West constituted a challenge to the rest of the world: 'one challenge was to imitate it. The other challenge was to trade' (Lewis, 1978, 7). In this period most non-western countries took the latter route though, in the case of those under colonial rule, arguably not by autonomous choice.

Three differing points of view can be identified on the impact of the new structure of international exchange on the economies of primary producing countries. The first, an optimistic one, concludes that in the nineteenth century trade served as an 'engine of growth … whereby a vigorous process of economic growth came to be transmitted from the centre to the outlying areas of the world' (Nurkse, 1962, 14). The result was a large expansion in primary production through the establishment of mines, estates and so on, largely with imported capital, and a general rise in per capita incomes. The second, strongly opposed, view is that the western industrial 'core' achieved development only by consigning the 'periphery' to a dependent role as a supplier of primary products on terms of trade which were adverse to the latter in the long run. The prevalence of foreign capital, which remitted profits to the home country (the 'colonial drain'), made it impossible for countries on the periphery to accumulate domestic capital, and to pursue an autonomous path towards industrialisation (Khor, 1983, ch. 2). The third viewpoint comes somewhere in between. External trade helped to integrate most peripheral countries into the international economy by about 1860, but thereafter demand for primary products slowed as industrial countries developed alternative sources of supply for many items (for instance, rice was grown in Europe and the USA as well as in Asia). Though primary export production was undoubtedly an important influence, the size of the export sector and its local linkages were not sufficient to transform the entire structure of these economies; 'historically, trade has been more often a handmaiden of growth ... and not the engine of growth for most of the non-European world' (Hanson, 1980, 132).

The evidence indicates an orientation towards external trade in the Malaysian region long predating the nineteenth-century development. The onset of British rule did not establish any radically new departure in this respect. It greatly increased the scale, in the process entrenching an openness in these territories which was quite exceptional in the Southeast Asian region. Merchants, spreading out from the major ports were the connecting links that transmitted to the hinterland the 'pull' factor of demand emanating from the industrialising countries. They were also active in promoting and funding much of the production of primary commodities. Investment and output were highly responsive to the state of trade (see Chapter 4.2). It thus appears that Malaysia was an exception to Hanson's general finding, with trade functioning as the prime 'engine' of growth rather than a supporting 'handmaid'. In North Borneo and Sarawak, though, the impact at this time was lessened by the inadequacies of the governments and the forbidding environment, especially poor transport (see Chapter 5.2).

Owing to insufficient data it has not been possible to calculate the size of the export sector relative to national income in this early period. However, even on impressionistic grounds we can safely conclude that with the boom in tin and rubber alone the share of exports was substantial. Reference to Chapters 4 and 5 will show that the inflow of foreign capital and immigrant workers, together with the response of indigenous farmers (smallholders) to commercial crops and the provision of infrastructure by government, was of sufficient magnitude (at least in the west coast states of the Peninsula) to bring about the onset of modern economic growth. However, at the same time this induced a dependence on a relatively narrow range of export commodities and, as we shall see, vastly heightened Malaysia's exposure to the vicissitudes of the international economy.

4

The Growth of Production

4.1 Export prices and production

Malaysian production for export in the nineteenth and early twentieth century, particularly of agricultural commodities, proceeded in a 'boom and bust' cycle related directly to changes in world prices. The typical pattern (with the major exception of rubber) was a rush to extend the planted area of a particular crop in response to higher prices leading, on maturity of the trees or plants, to a sharp rise in production. Depending on the continuing strength of demand, market prices then tended to fall, sometimes very heavily, causing investment to wane. Changes in government policy (e.g., land tenure terms), together with the incidence of plant disease or insect pests, were also major factors bearing on the long-term viability of an industry.

The pattern over time was as follows. In the first half of the nineteenth century attempts were made to cultivate spices (cloves, nutmeg, mace) on Singapore and Penang islands. Prices were high in 1802–5, 1817–18 and 1841–8, and depressed in 1806–15, 1825–35 and 1850–60. By the 1860s, following widespread disease and unfavourable market conditions, planters had largely lost interest. Gambier planting became widespread from the 1820s/30s in the western and southern parts of the Peninsula. In Johor and Singapore cultivation was invariably carried on in conjunction with pepper. Prices for both products were good in the mid-1830s, but declined (particularly gambier) in the 1840s. The late 1850s and early 1860s saw some recovery, with cultivation spreading into Melaka, Negeri Sembilan and south Selangor in the 1880s/90s before prices slumped just after the turn of the century. Thereafter the planted acreage declined in the face of changes in government land tenure policy (see section 4.3) and a wholesale switch to rubber cultivation. A similar pattern showed itself in tapioca, located mainly in Melaka and Negeri Sembilan, in the second half of the century.

Sugar planting began in the SS, centred in Province Wellesley, between 1810 and 1820. Expansion was rapid from 1840 to 1870 as Straits-produced sugar qualified for the preferential import duty into Britain. Planters moved into the adjacent Krian district of Perak from the late 1870s. By the end of the century exports totalled some 36 000 tonnes, over twice those of Jamaica and a third those of British Guiana (Jackson, 1968a, 167). However, the industry was facing rising costs for labour and materials as well as competition from rice for land. As with tapioca and gambier, planters were quick to switch to rubber after 1900, and by the First World War the crop had virtually disappeared.

The last export crop to reach prominence in the Peninsula prior to 1900 was coffee. Sporadic plantings were made in Selangor and Sungei Ujong in the 1870s and early 1880s. Planters responded vigorously to soaring world prices after the abolition of slavery in Brazil, the leading producer, in 1888 temporarily dislocated the labour supply. Cultivation spread into Perak in the early 1890s, but market prices fell heavily between 1896 and 1899 as Brazilian production picked up again. The impact of this, coupled with the onset of plant disease and insect pests, sent the nascent industry into decline with planters progressively switching to rubber.

Continuous statistics of production and cultivated acreage are not available for the pre-rubber crops. It is estimated that over the century the crops involving shifting cultivation (gambier, pepper, tapioca) may have covered approximately 200 000 hectares in the Peninsula. Around 1900 their output was valued in excess of $8 million. Of the sedentary crops, sugar occupied approximately 12 000 hectares, and coffee 6000 hectares in the 1890s (Jackson, 1968a, 6, 154–6). Commercial agriculture in the FMS, though of growing importance, constituted only just over 6 per cent of total exports in 1895 against 88 per cent for tin and tin ore (calculated from Sadka, 1968, 345n.1).

The commercial crops just discussed, with the exception of pepper and to a small extent coffee and gambier, did not spread to the Borneo territories in the nineteenth century. The annexation of the Muka-Oya district by Sarawak in 1860, coupled with the stimulus of Chinese traders operating out of Singapore (but ultimately displaced by the Borneo Company), caused the Oya-Melanau people to increase the production of flour from the sago palm, a naturally occurring tree which was also cultivated. Up to the 1890s sago flour was the principal agricultural export from Sarawak; indeed 'for a number of years after 1861 the difference between solvency and insolvency depended on the sago trade' (Morris, 1991, 232). Increased immigration of Chinese in the latter part of the century stimulated the planting of pepper which, along with jungle-produce, had overtaken sago flour in export value by the early twentieth century (Morris, 1991, Tables 5, 8). Pepper production almost doubled in the 1890s, ranking Sarawak next to Indonesia in world output. In contrast to the FMS the Sarawak export economy was dominated by agricultural and jungle-products, with mining contributing around 10 per cent until the discovery of oil just prior to the First World War (Amarjit Kaur, 1998, Table 3.I).

In North Borneo the Chartered Company presided over an economy whose exports over the first decade of its existence comprised a range of sea- and forest-products (e.g., dried fish, gutta percha, cutch, camphor). An introduced plantation crop, tobacco, grew rapidly to take prime place in the early 1890s but had lost its impetus by the early twentieth century, due mainly to the imposition of the protective McKinley tariff from 1892 in the USA, the largest consumer (John and Jackson, 1973), and finally capitulated to rubber.

Alongside these cultivated crops, the production of 'natural' commodities for export continued throughout the Malaysian territories. From the forests came various timbers, resins/waxes, rattans, gums, rubbers, and so on. Production, which involved essentially foraging, was carried on by indigenous people principally in the off-season from food crop growing. None the less there was a considerable capacity for swift response to opportunities for trade as shown in the collection of gutta percha (*getah taban*). When technical advance in England revealed the usefulness of this rubber extract as insulation for undersea cables, the Temenggong of Johor promptly declared a royal monopoly and employed *orang laut* (sea-people) as collectors. Interest was sparked throughout the region. Malays, Chinese and Dayaks explored the forests of Pahang, west Borneo, Sumatra and the Riau-Lingga archipelago. By 1848 production had reached some 1200 tonnes valued at Sp\$150 000–200 000. The trade was still vigorous in the 1870s but, because it involved destroying the trees to extract the latex, the supply was inelastic in the long term (Trocki, 1979, 76–8; Gullick, 1989, 154). Indeed, the trade became a contentious issue in the 1890s in Pahang where the new British administration attempted to place the extraction of forest products in general and *getah* (rubber) in particular under official control. In 1895 a ban was placed on collection in order to protect young trees, but was lifted in 1897 as enforcement was impracticable. Malays needed cash income as the rice harvest was poor (Koch, 1982, 109–22).

Before going on to look at the introduction of rubber growing, the one commercial crop which spread to all Malaysian territories in varying degrees, we shall examine the record of the other major component of the export sector, the mining industries.

In the Peninsula the leading products throughout the nineteenth century were tin and gold. The volume of tin output showed little alteration in the first half of the century, rising from only about 1000 tonnes to 2400 tonnes by the 1840s (Dodge, 1977). Following the discovery of large ore deposits in Larut, Perak, in the late 1840s, exports rose but the precise magnitude is difficult to ascertain. Later official statistics credit Malaya with exports averaging 6500 tonnes annually in the 1850s and 8500 tonnes in the 1860s

(Yip, 1969, 392). By 1875–6 as armed conflicts over control of the production and trade in tin (involving rival Chinese mining factions and the Malay ruling elite in the major producing states like Perak) died down, output approached 10 000 tonnes, or one-quarter of the world total (Wong Lin Ken, 1965b, 30; Khoo Kay Kim, 1972, chs 5, 6). Further large ore discoveries in Perak and Selangor in the 1880s gave a sharp boost so that by the turn of the century Malayan exports reached some 52 000 tonnes, or just over half the world production (Wong Lin Ken, 1965b, 246–7). Little fresh prospecting was done thereafter and annual output dropped back to around 40 000 tonnes until a fresh burst of investment in the mid-1920s (Yip, 1969, 392).

In contrast to tin mining, which by the second half of the century was concentrated in the west coast of the Peninsula, gold production was confined to a narrow band of ore running southwards from Patani through the interior regions of Perak, Kelantan, Pahang, Negeri Sembilan and Melaka. Production was a chancy business depending very much on local political conditions. There are no continuous figures for production, but the potential for rapid fluctuations can be illustrated by Pahang with 929 troy ounces in 1890 and 17 035 ounces in 1898 (Dodge, 1977, 96). By the end of the century gold did not figure prominently in Malayan exports, but the situation was different in Sarawak where mining (antimony ore and gold) was a strong attraction at the time of the installation of Brooke rule in 1841. Despite the activities of Chinese gold miners at places such as Bau (upriver from Kuching), and investment by the Borneo Company, production did not really increase significantly until the late 1890s. By that time the reserves of antimony had been largely worked out, but with a new cyanide extraction process gold advanced to first place in mineral exports, and fourth overall by 1908–10 (Morris, 1991, Table V; Amarjit Kaur, 1998, Table 3.1). Coal, another Brooke monopoly, was mined by the Borneo Company on the Sadong river from 1874, and on Muara island (renamed Brooketon) in Brunei Bay from 1888. It enjoyed a brief lead in mineral exports in the 1890s, and though annual output was not particularly large (averaging some 26 000 tonnes up to the early 1930s) the mineral was important in local consumption, and as bunker fuel for steamers (Amarjit Kaur, 1998, 24–5).

It was not until after 1910 that Sarawak acquired the mining industry which was to prove longest-lasting (though very depressed between 1930 and the 1960s). Signs of oil had been detected as early as 1882, but exploration by a subsidiary of Royal-Dutch Shell did not begin until 1907. Production commenced in 1910–11 at 260 tonnes, rising quickly to nearly 67 000 tonnes in 1915 and 590 000 tonnes in 1924 (Amarjit Kaur, 1998, Table 3.3).

Returning to agriculture, the last decade or so of the nineteenth century was a critical period for commercial agriculture in the Malaysian territories. The boom/slump cycle of investment thus far, coupled with soil-exhausting, land-extensive crops such as tapioca and gambier was not a firm basis for growth. Apart from tin, Malaysia had no major comparative advantage with which to fuel growth. The widespread adoption of rubber cultivation from the turn of the century fundamentally altered the situation.

Rubber came from the *Hevea Brasiliensis* tree, introduced from Brazil on government initiative to British colonies (notably Ceylon and the SS) in the 1870s (see section 4.4). As the automobile industry in the west and particularly in the USA grew rapidly after 1900, the inelasticity of the supply of 'wild' rubbers (a forest product) from South America, Central Africa, and Southeast Asia became evident. Market values commenced an almost uninterrupted rise from around 4*s*. (20p) per pound in 1900 to 8*s*. 9*d*. (44p) per pound in 1910, with a peak of 12*s*. 9*d*. (64p) in the latter year (Drabble, 1973, 213). Malaysia, particularly the west coast of the Peninsula, offered large areas of suitable land and comparatively good transport facilities, so planters were quick to abandon existing crops in favour of rubber. By 1910 the Peninsula already had approximately 225 000 hectares planted, and by 1921 this had grown to 891 000 hectares (Table 4.1), or 53 per cent of the total in South and Southeast Asia. North Borneo and Sarawak, for reasons which will be elaborated later, were less

Table 4.1   Malaysia: rubber planted area, 1910–40 (thousand hectares)

	1910	1921	1930	1940
Malaya				
Estates[a]	172	522	754	848
Smallholdings[b]	53	369	476	541
Sarawak				
Estates	n.a.	1[c]	n.a	7
Smallholdings		18[c]		89
North Borneo				
Estates	6	21	47[d]	30
Smallholdings		4		24
Malaysia	231	935	n.a.	1539

[a] Holdings over 40 hectares.
[b] Holdings under 40 hectares.
[c] Author's estimate.
[d] 1933.

Sources: Figart (1925), Tables 127–8; Drabble (1991), Table 6.2; *AR N. Borneo* (1920); Amarjit Kaur (1998), Table 3.6; McFadyean (1944), Table 1.

extensively affected, having only 44 000 hectares (the bulk of which was in North Borneo) by 1922.

The expansion in rubber acreage and output (Malayan exports rose from 6500 to 204 000 tonnes) between 1910 and 1919 took place despite a declining trend in prices which averaged around 2*s*. (10p) per pound just prior to the postwar slump in 1920–22 (see Figure 8.1). It was this continued growth that distinguished rubber planting from previous crops where lower prices had stifled expansion. Despite the price fluctuations typical of primary commodities, Malaysia as the world's largest producer was able to reap pioneer profits in this period. The nearest competitors in 1919 were the NEI (85 000 tonnes) and Ceylon (45 000 tonnes: Drabble, 1973, Appendix VII). However, a signpost to future problems of productive capacity surplus to demand emerged in 1918 when America, consuming around 70 per cent of world output, imposed a quota on rubber imports, causing prices to fall heavily and European estates in Malaya to voluntarily restrict output for a short time (Drabble, 1973, 138–46).

4.2   Capital

We saw in Chapter 3.1 that the global economy which emerged in the nineteenth and early twentieth century was based on production and exchange on a greatly expanded scale. This required a corresponding increase in capital investment in physical assets (long-term fixed capital), and the financing of day-to-day operations (short-term working or circulating capital). This section will focus on private capital investment in Malaysia, leaving public investment to Chapter 5.2.

The growth of private capital investment in Malaysia in this period went through two major phases. The first, from about 1800 to the mid-1890s saw mercantile interests (migrant Asian and European) within the region as the main providers of capital, with funds accumulated largely from local trading operations. In this phase there was some complementarity and even cooperation in investment between ethnic groups, notably British and Chinese traders, with the latter playing a leading role in the sphere of export production. In the second phase, from *c*.1895 to 1920, European investment was increasingly embodied in public joint-stock companies floated and registered overseas, mainly in the United Kingdom (sterling capital), with funds coming from investors domiciled outside the region. Asian, mainly Chinese, investment on the other hand remained strongly mercantile in character, mostly in the traditional form of family firms and private partnerships. This difference in organisation was also reflected in a marked difference in the scale of operations (European firms being generally larger), and the replacement of the earlier complementarity by competition in the sphere of production in both agriculture and mining. At the same time westerners also established a dominant position in many services such as land transport, ocean-shipping and telecommunications.

Returning to the first phase, we find that much investment of mercantile resources occurred through the system of credit described in Chapter 3.5. Merchants needed an assured supply of local commodities with which to pay for the imports distributed. The former was obtained by means of cash advances or the supply of foodstuffs, tools and so on to producers who in turn were obligated to sell their output to the creditor at prices below market levels. This system was especially popular among Chinese interests. Prior to the tin boom in the 1860s/70s, European (mainly British) merchant firms ploughed back much of their retained profits into further trade rather than directing investment into production. Indirectly, though, their involvement in financing mining and agricultural ventures was considerable. In 1864 the bulk of more than $1 million that Singapore Chinese claimed to have advanced to gambier and pepper planters in Johor came from loans from British firms (Jackson, 1968a, 17; Drabble and Drake, 1981, 306).

European private, or 'proprietary', planters were another source of capital. These men were a highly mobile group who moved wherever con-ditions of climate, land and labour suited a particular crop, relying on slender capital of personal funds plus money from family or close acquain-tances. In this case they moved into sugar-growing in Province Wellesley from 1846 (after Britain granted tariff preference), having had previous experience of this crop in Mauritius and the West Indies. The move into coffee in the 1880s/90s followed a similar pattern, with planters coming from Ceylon where the tea industry had been devastated by plant disease. The slenderness of their resources is illustrated by the fact that of 4300 hectares held by the Malay Peninsula Coffee Company, only 520 hectares had been planted by 1899 (Drabble, 1973, 18).

An important contrast between European and Chinese enterprise that emerged in this first phase was that whilst the former preferred specialised investments which had to be more or less self-sustaining, for the latter agri-culture and mining were part of a complex of interrelated activities. Among Chinese entrepreneurs a highly profitable practice was the supply of food-stuffs and other needs (tobacco, liquor, clothes, opium) to labourers at mark-ups of as much as 200 to 300 per cent. This was the 'truck' system which operated up to at least the early 1890s, but the monopolistic power of the suppliers lessened thereafter. Had profits depended entirely on commodity production, the returns to investors would not have been nearly as attractive; indeed it was only the truck system which enabled smaller, marginal mines to survive during periods of low market prices. 'It was this peculiar structure of ... mining costs and profits which enabled the Chinese to complete their domination of the tin fields in the first twenty years of British rule' (Wong Lin Ken, 1965b, 81). A similar system was in use for investors in agricultural ventures such as gambier plantations in Singapore and Johor (Trocki, 1990, 69).

The discovery of new tin deposits in the 1880s and 1890s brought a challenge from direct foreign investment, mostly British, with 37 companies floated up to 1897. The challenge was unsuccessful. Many did not even start operations, and only three foreign companies were actually operating in Perak and Selangor in that year. The main reasons for this lack of success were inadequate prospecting techniques, difficulties in recruiting and retaining labour against competition from Chinese mines, and the high cost of company administration (Yip, 1969, 99–105).

The picture was different, however, in the smelting sector. Here the Europeans were able to break the practical monopoly held by the Chinese up the late 1880s. This was achieved through a combination of better technology and the official grant of a monopoly over exports of tin ore from the main producing states. In 1887 the Straits Trading Company (see Chapter 3.5) was registered in Singapore. Its furnaces obtained a much higher percentage of refined tin from the ore, and an effective network of purchasing agents was set up. By 1896 it had the capacity to smelt up to 20 per cent of world tin production (Wong Lin Ken, 1965b, 161–7).

The Chinese had a further important source of investible funds, namely revenue farming, which consisted basically of the purchase from the state by private individuals or syndicates of the right to collect taxes for a specified period. This system predated 1800, having been developed primarily by the Dutch to extract revenue, especially from foreigners, and copied by indigenous rulers and the growing Chinese community. The SS government was administratively and financially not strong for much of the nineteenth century, and farmed out to Chinese the collection of taxes on liquor, gambling and, pre-eminently, opium. The governments of the Malay States followed suit, not only for administrative convenience but also as a means of attracting Chinese capital into tin mining. For the Chinese, revenue farms were one more among a variety of resources, which reinforces the point made above that they were building an interconnected web of enterprise compared to the more specialised investments of the Europeans. However, over the first two decades of the twentieth century the colonial governments in the Peninsula felt sufficiently stable financially to abolish the various farms, replacing them with more direct forms of taxation. In the SS, for example, the trade in opium became a government monopoly from 1909 (Butcher, 1993a, 35–40).

In Sarawak revenue farms for government monopolies of opium, liquor, gambling and pawnbrokers constituted the major source of income for the Brooke raj throughout the nineteenth century: 57 per cent in 1859 declining to 36 per cent in 1896 (calculated from data in Chew, 1990, 212–3). From 1867 to 1910 the farms were held by leading Chinese merchant firms in Kuching, who were also promoters of gambier and pepper cultivation in the

First Division, and suppliers of credit to retail shops throughout the state (Chew, 1990, 212). Revenue farming came late (1907) to North Borneo owing to opposition from W.C. Cowie, Managing Director of the Chartered Company, and thus 'a fine chance of attracting private capital was lost' (Tregonning, 1965, 151).

The circumstances leading to rising world rubber prices around the turn of the century were outlined in the previous section. Between the first commercial plantings by European and Chinese interests in the Peninsula in 1895 and the First World War the planted area expanded in the surges associated with price booms, for instance 1905–6 and 1909–10. The proprietary planters lacked the capital necessary to open large properties. The British agency houses in Singapore played a crucial bridging role by bringing together planters and overseas financial interests, principally in Britain, to convert the estates into public joint-stock companies through flotation on the Stock Market, usually London. Between about 1903 and 1912 some 260 sterling capital companies were floated for Malaya alone. There were also lesser numbers of companies registered in Shanghai, Australia, Ceylon, Belgium and elsewhere, together with locally-registered companies (Straits dollar capital) in Penang and Singapore (81 in 1909–10). By the end of the 1909–10 boom the proprietary estates had mostly disappeared, though their former owners had often taken fully-paid up shares in the company as part of the sale price, and some stayed on as salaried managers (Drabble, 1973, ch. 3; Parkinson, 1996).

Chinese investment in rubber mainly followed the traditional pattern of family or private partnerships and syndicates, though a few of the Straits dollar capital companies were promoted by Chinese interests in Melaka and Singapore, who were possibly more familiar with western methods (Drabble, 1973, 67). Rubber growing was integrated into the network of interests (trade, mining, contracting and so on) which provided working capital in the manner we have seen at work in previous decades. Funds were also borrowed from Chettiars, estimated by Tan Cheng Lock at $10 million in Melaka alone by 1921 (Drabble, 1973, 191). An effective means of economising on capital expenditure and lessening the risk inherent in tropical agriculture was developed, particularly in Johor, whereby 'catch crops' such as bananas and pineapples were planted on newly cleared land along with the rubber trees. These provided revenue until shaded out by the rubber trees, with the income divided between the owner and sharecroppers, the latter cultivating both the catch crops and the trees. The cost of bringing the rubber to maturity was about one-quarter that on a European estate (Huff, 1992). The first census of rubber planting in 1921 revealed that Chinese estates (average size 140 hectares) constituted approximately 20–25 per cent of the total Malayan estate acreage, the balance being almost entirely in European hands (averaging 570 hectares: Drabble, 1973, 217–18; 1991, 2).

The Borneo territories attracted much less investment in rubber, especially of the corporate type. In North Borneo most of the tobacco estates (many started by Dutch planters from Sumatra seeking cheap land) had collapsed due to under-capitalisation. In 1905 the Chartered Company, in an effort to attract corporate investment in rubber, offered exemption from export duty for 50 years, and a government guarantee of a dividend of 4 per cent a year for the first six years, to be repaid without interest once a company earned 6 per cent on capital (Tregonning, 1965, 89). The response was poor (only twelve companies were floated from 1905 to 1910, and 20 by 1920), and the concession proved costly to government (Voon, 1976, 164).

In Sarawak the Brookes did not favour large-scale foreign enterprise, apart from the Borneo Company, but were very keen to promote Chinese immigration. The offer in 1876 of cheap land, free transport from Singapore and twelve years' freedom from export duties for pepper and gambier planters had attracted an inflow, but a major advance occurred with the arrival of 1000 Chinese from the Foochow district to establish a settlement under the supervision of the Methodist Church in 1901–2. This community was encouraged to plant rubber, despite Raja Charles' view of the boom as ephemeral, and further arrivals came as prices rose (Chew, 1990, ch. 7). By contrast applications from companies were mostly rejected, and ultimately only five estates were established, including one Japanese and two by the Borneo Company (Pringle, 1970, 138; Cramb, personal communication). Even had Brooke policy been more welcoming to large-scale enterprise it seems unlikely, given the relative isolation and poor transport facilities of Sarawak (and North Borneo), that at this stage corporate investment would have entered on a scale comparable to Malaya.

Concurrently with the boom in rubber, the tin industry in Malaya experienced a substantial inflow of investment. By the end of the nineteenth century the richest ore deposits close to the surface and mineable by labour-intensive techniques had been largely worked out. From the later 1890s the emphasis shifted to the use of more capital-intensive methods such as hydraulic power (high-pressure hose, gravel pumps) and, most costly of all, a bucket dredge, introduced by two Australian companies in southern Siam in 1906 and reaching Malaya by 1912. The dredge could work low-grade ground most profitably. Chinese miners adopted the hydraulic devices, whilst Europeans (principally British) took up the dredge. As in rubber, investment increased in surges (1906, 1911–13 and 1920), coming mainly from Britain and to a lesser extent from locally-registered (but mainly European-owned) companies. This progressively reversed the balance between Chinese and European interests in the industry. In 1900 the former accounted for 90 per cent of output from mines in the FMS (virtually the entire Malayan production). By 1920 this had decreased to 64 per cent and in 1929 would stand at 39 per cent (Yip, 1969, 141, 143, 164).

The first two decades of the twentieth century saw the largest volume of foreign direct investment (FDI) in Malaysia (mostly in the Peninsula) during the entire colonial period (there was a brief boom in 1925–7: see Chapter 8). Aggregate data for capital investment in the Peninsula during this period are very sparse. The most frequently reproduced estimates are those of Callis (1942), reproduced in Brown (1993, Table 5.5), which credit Malaya with a total of US$194 million in 1914, divided into $44 million in portfolio investment and $150 million in direct or entrepreneurial investment. No division as between European and Asian (mainly Chinese) investment was made. This was the second highest aggregate in the region after the NEI, at US$675 million.

This large inflow of FDI raises several important questions. First, can any precise conclusion be reached as to whether the domestic economy gained or lost in net terms (i.e., did capital inflows exceed profits remitted overseas or vice versa)? Second (and this applies mainly to rubber), why did estate owners continue to deepen their investment in the face of declining rubber prices after 1910? Third, how did the developments in rubber and tin production affect the respective positions of European and Asian capitalists?

No categorical answer is possible on the first question, since it is not currently feasible to calculate overall balance of payment figures. The most that can be done is to bring together some estimates for the two main industries involved (see Table 4.2). In each instance the profits up to 1922 substantially exceeded the issued share capital, thus creating the potential for a large outflow of funds. However, the issued capital is only a partial indicator of investment magnitude. Sterling capital companies in both tin and rubber used retained profits and the proceeds of shares issued at a premium (above par value) at times of high commodity prices, notably 1909–10. Together these could have amounted to around 30 per cent of capital expenditure in rubber (Drake, 1972, 960–1; Drabble and Drake, 1974, 111). Thoburn (1977, 64) suggests that in boom years such as 1910, 1915 and 1920 profits possibly exceeded capital formation, whilst reinvested profits could 'in principle' have financed between a third and a half of these outlays in other years. Drake (1972, 960) points out that such reinvested capital arose from profitable past production in Malaya and therefore did not constitute a fresh transfer of resources from abroad. The data on tin cannot be analysed in this way, but on balance the evidence suggests that in these two industries Malaya was a net exporter of funds in this formative period, but perhaps less so in the case of rubber.

The reasons for the continued investment in rubber are not hard to find. Despite the wide fluctuations and generally downward trend in prices after 1910 Malaysia had a comparative advantage as the world's major supplier of rubber (the Peninsula alone produced about half). Estate owners had

Table 4.2   Malaya: rubber and tin company capital and net profits (£ million)

	Capital	Net profits
Rubber		
Voon	35.0[a]	47.22 (to 1922)
Drabble	11.85[b]	18.39 (1912–22)
Tin		
Yip/Khor	5.35[c]	11.09[d] (1913–20)

[a] All sterling capital companies.
[b] Sample of 56 sterling capital companies.
[c] Includes foreign- and locally-registered companies.
[d] Probably gross profits.
Sources: Calculated from data in Voon (1976), 164–5; Drabble (1991), 34; Yip (1969), 141–3; Khor (1983), Table 5.1.

committed large funds during the boom years and needed to bring their plantings to maturity in order to increase output and lower costs of production to earn a satisfactory return on investment. Some pioneer British companies were able to pay annual dividends of several hundred per cent, but these were abnormal and the average for such companies between 1912 and 1922 was around 12 per cent (Drabble, 1991, 35), which was not unreasonably high for tropical agriculture.

By 1920, as noted above, European capital had far outdistanced Chinese in the rubber industry and was on the way to predominance in tin mining. How can this shift be explained? Were the Chinese unable to compete in the realms of finance or technology, or were they simply culturally averse to rapid modernisation?

In rubber the Chinese slightly predated the earliest commercial ventures by Europeans in the 1890s. The basic technology of production was relatively simple. The trees planted were grown from unselected seeds, available to all comers, and were tappable with a variety of implements. Europeans had no technological edge at this stage, and neither did their generally larger properties generate major economies of scale in cultivation. The vital differences were ones of access to long-term low-cost finance and corporate organisation. As the pace of investment quickened after 1900 rubber growing was incorporated into the network of Chinese activities in the same way as the earlier crops (gambier, pepper and so on). Funds were moved between enterprises as relative returns shifted. In contrast European capital came specifically for rubber and was highly immobile in this period. The public joint-stock companies floated in London had access to far wider sources of funds, and whilst the quality of management (under agency house supervision) varied, in general there was greater continuity and stability among these firms (Drabble, 1991; Brown, 1994, ch. 6).

Many of these arguments also apply to the tin industry, but in this case the factor of technology was paramount. As the labour-intensive phase moved towards its end Chinese miners took up the hydraulic techniques because these were the least costly of the advances. Bucket dredges, which could do the daily work of 2000 labourers, cost £12 000 and required at least 160 hectares of land to operate economically (Yip, 1969, 134; Hennart, 1986, 136). This in turn led to British-based mining interests turning to financial markets, as had the rubber growers. There were other changes emanating from government policy which adversely affected the position of Chinese capital at this time. Secret societies, intimately linked to control of mining labour, were proscribed from 1891 and the truck system a little later. Opium smoking declined, and the revenue farming system was progressively eliminated between 1909 and 1912 (Wong Lin Ken, 1965b, 219–23). All these changes constricted the sources of investment funds for mining, which furthermore now had to compete with rubber.

However, it would be wrong to conclude from this that Chinese capital in Malaysia was in both relative and absolute decline. The booms in tin and rubber, coupled with trade and revenue farming, had brought considerable wealth to this community between c.1875 and 1920. Loke Yew is an outstanding example, arriving as a migrant, free but without wealth, in 1858. By the early 1900s he had amassed a fortune, estimated at $20 million on his death in 1917, from a variety of sources; shopkeeping, mining, revenue farms, contracting, rubber and, not least, real estate which he used as security for bank loans (Butcher, 1993b). In Sarawak the Chinese community grew greatly from the organised immigration of groups of settlers after 1898 who set up colonies in the First and Third Divisions. These included Foochow, Hakka, Cantonese and Henghua. Among these the Foochow were to build on their success in rubber to play a leading economic role in later years (Chin, 1981, ch. 6; Chew, 1990, ch. 7).

Thus far in this section our concern has been with the investment of financial capital in production for export. But indigenous farmers were also responsive to opportunities for increased production for the market. For much of the nineteenth century this involved simply the extension of longstanding activities in mining, foodstuffs and foraging for sea- and forest-products. A notable example of the latter was the boom in gutta percha collection from the 1840s. As population grew, and communities became more settled, land was opened up for the cultivation of tobacco, coconuts, nutmeg, pepper, coffee and so on. By the 1870s/80s, for example, the Kelang Valley in Selangor was becoming a focus for both large- and small-scale commercial development (Shamsul, 1986, 15–23; Lee Boon Thong, 1994). In such regions a peasantry was emerging which was becoming increasingly dependent on cash incomes for subsistence, and therefore exposed to the same vicissitudes from price fluctuations (such as the 1890s coffee slump) as the capitalistic enterprises.

It was rubber which proved the crop *par excellence* for the small farmers. They faced no technical barriers (section 4.4), and there was no high capital threshold restricting entry to the industry. Rubber fitted readily into the existing pattern of village agriculture. The main inputs required were land and household labour, and the product, known as smallholder rubber in Malaysia and 'native' rubber in the NEI, was readily saleable on world markets through the network of Chinese dealers in rural areas and ports such as Singapore (Huff, 1989). These dealers encouraged the spread of rubber growing by distributing seeds to peasants, including those returning from pilgrimage to Mecca (the *haj*). In Sarawak Christian missions performed a similar facilitating role among Chinese migrants and the Iban in districts such as Saribas. However, animist groups, such as the Balleh Iban, were reluctant at this stage to take up the crop, fearing that the tree spirit would drive away the *padi* (unhusked rice) spirit (Pringle, 1970, 203–5; Cramb, personal communication). In North Borneo, where the Chartered Company favoured capitalist enterprise, the proportion of smallholdings was low (Table 4.1). Smallholding rubber took hold most widely in the west coast states of the Peninsula, coextensive with estates and drawn there by the relatively good transportation network (Chapter 5.2). Like the larger owners, peasants continued to plant rubber in the face of declining average prices after 1910. In the most densely planted areas, such as Selangor, they had become dependent on cash crops for subsistence and had largely abandoned rice cultivation. Rubber, as a perennial crop, provided a year-round source of income, and required less intense physical effort to produce than rice (Seavoy, 1980, 62).

Whilst rubber gave indigenous groups the opportunity to expand their role in export production, the trend in mining was the reverse. This was particularly so in the tin industry in which Malay participation had largely disappeared by the late nineteenth century. Up to the 1860s/70s district chiefs used their control over access to tin-bearing land and riverine trade to accumulate sufficient resources to exercise personal independence. Long Jaafar discovered the rich tinfield at Larut (Perak) in the late 1840s and invited Chinese miners to work there, gaining further revenue by supplying them with opium (Khoo Kay Kim, 1972, 69–73).

The balance shifted in the unstable political conditions of the late 1860s/early 1870s, followed by the advent of British control in the west coast states and the disempowering of the Malay elites. Burns (1982) argues that this choked off an incipient growth of indigenous capitalism, as it resulted in large-scale losses of mines to Chinese. However, Wong Lin Ken (1965b, 46, 91) makes the fundamental point that the small scale of Malay mining, and the inflation of costs by traditional practices such as payments to a magician (*pawang*), made it uncompetitive with Chinese and later European mines. The decline in Malay ownership was rapid. In 1885, 350 out of 500 mines registered in Kinta (Perak) were classified as 'ancestral', but only three years later the number had fallen to 215.

4.3 Land and labour

As we saw in Chapter 2, at the beginning of the nineteenth century Malaysia was a region with abundant land and sparse population. In the indigenous societies control over people (and their labour) was more important than property rights in land, though this was not so much the case among shifting cultivators in northern Borneo (Cramb, personal communication). By the early twentieth century a general reversal in these relationships had occurred.

Demand for land for agriculture and mining increased throughout the nineteenth century, with a distinct acceleration over the last two or three decades and continuing into the early 1900s as people of all races responded to the stimulus from export production. The colonial governments introduced a new departure in a system of individual ownership based on western legal principles. These prescribed rights and obligations, such as precise delineation of boundaries by survey, and annual cash rentals. Overall these created a permanency of ownership quite different to the precolonial era. Land, from being a 'free' good, became a commercial commodity which could be traded and, just as importantly, used as security for loans. At the same time the new governments attempted to reconcile the demands of capitalist enterprise for plentiful cheap land with a custodial policy towards the 'ancestral' land rights of the indigenous peoples.

Up to the 1890s the rules of tenure differed between states, but in 1897 a (still imperfect) Federal Land Enactment was passed in the FMS, based on the Torrens system from South Australia. This provided for grants or leases up to 999 years on large blocks (over 40 hectares or 100 acres). On smallholdings (not over 40 hectares) survey was replaced by a more approximate demarcation, with each owner receiving an Extract from the Mukim Register (EMR) as evidence of title. Some earlier legislation (e.g., the Selangor Rules of 1891) had decreed that a Muslim holding land under 'customary' tenure could not transfer this to a non-Muslim, but this distinction was not enshrined in the Federal Enactment (T.G. Lim, 1976, 184; Sadka, 1968, 342–4). Malay rulers in other states took up some of these innovations well in advance of formal British control: for example, Kelantan registered occupation rights from 1881 (Gullick, 1989, 114).

The new form of tenure was initially unwelcome among the Malay peasantry who, having been relieved of the burden of *kerah*, resented having to pay rentals. In Selangor collections had to be suspended between 1884 and 1886 but, as land gained in commercial value, there was gradual acceptance. By the end of the century the cumulative effect on the growing Malay population was that 'what had been an unstable settlement, subject to the demands of *kerah*, had become a more settled comunity, aware of the value of its land but subject to a tax upon those rights of ownership. In this situation lay the origins of the smallholder rubber economy' (Gullick, 1989, 116).

Colonial policy, especially in the FMS where much of the early rubber planting was concentrated, aimed at keeping estates and smallholdings as far as possible in separate locations, with the best-situated land (road frontage) earmarked for the former. Officials regarded rubber as too speculative a crop for Malays, and from 1905 applications from Europeans were in principle to receive priority. However, the pace of expansion during the 1909–10 boom in rubber investment rendered it administratively impracticable to enforce such a policy. Applications 'conflict like a fretwork puzzle' wrote the District Officer, Ulu Langat, in 1910 (Drabble, 1973, 75). Malays, locally-born and immigrant, speculated in selling rubber land to such an extent that officials feared major losses of 'ancestral' land, integral to village life, to non-Malay interests. The outcome was the FMS Malay Reservations Enactment 1913, restricting land sales in areas designated as reservations to those between Malays (with three-year leases to non-Malays permitted). Lower rentals were offered as inducement to owners who would accept a limiting condition, such as no rubber to be planted. In 1917 the FMS Rice Lands Enactment prohibited rubber on land suitable for wet-rice cultivation. There was a good deal of evasion of this legislation, but gradually it became more difficult for smallholders to obtain fresh land for rubber legally as the application books in the most popular districts were closed for varying periods of time from 1916–17 onwards (Drabble, 1973, 101–2, 133, 150).

In the Borneo territories both the Brookes and the Chartered Company were concerned from the outset of their rule to protect indigenous land-holders from commercial pressures. As early as 1842 James Brooke had decreed that no immigrants could settle on land already occupied by native people. But policy was not consistent, since Land Orders of 1863, 1875 and 1899 placed limitations on native access to fresh land under customary tenure, thus failing to appreciate the significance of shifting cultivation (Hong, 1987, 38–41). During the rubber boom Charles Brooke followed the Malayan example by prohibiting sales of land in the Lower Rajang from Malays and natives to Chinese, and subsequently extended this to sales by any non-European to a European (Pringle, 1970, 138, 310–14). None the less, these rules did not prevent conflicts breaking out over land demarcation between Foochow Chinese settlers and Iban virtually from the time the former arrived in Sarawak (Chew, 1990, 162).

In North Borneo the Chartered company barred direct dealings in land between natives and Europeans. From 1889 no title could be issued without prior notification to the local chief, who had a right of appeal. Documents of title were available from 1903 but, as in Malaya, there was an initial reluctance to take them out until the rubber boom led to a rise in land values (Tregonning, 1965, 120–2).

In the Malaysian territories, until about 1920 the frontiers of cultivation and mining were continually being extended, with the main constraint on the availability of new areas being transport and communications (Chapter 5.2).

Turning to labour supply, an outstanding characteristic of this period was the fact that by far the greater part of the wage-labour force was composed of migrants from India, China and neighbouring parts of the archipelago, notably Sumatra and Java. Malays (locally-born and migrant) and other indigenous peoples were largely self-employed and, apart from purely short-term wage-work such as tree-felling on newly-opened estates, carried on their subsistence and commercial activities within the village economy.

Among foreign entrepreneurs the Chinese were successful for most of the nineteenth century in building up a labour force over which they exercised a strong control that amounted to a *de facto* property right, rather than the customary rights over persons, notably the right to extract *kerah*, which existed in Malay *adat* (tradition). Chinese employers, for ethnic and cultural as well as economic reasons, preferred to import their own workforce for the business of production. Workers came either as *sinkhehs* under the credit-ticket system, with recruiting costs having to be repaid, or as *laukhehs*, 'paid immigrants' who had met their own passage costs. In both mining and agriculture there existed the *kongsi* system of employment under which a labourer received a fixed wage, but in the former industry an alternative form of organisation was the *hun* or tribute system (also known as *chabut*) where remuneration depended directly on the success or failure of the mine. In the first the worker had some assurance of income, but in the second, none, apart from subsistence whilst working. Whether their workers were *sinkhehs* or paid immigrants, employers wanted to maintain the maximum possible control over them in order to keep down costs and limit freedom of movement. The principal instrument of control was the secret society which the Chinese brought with them and which, in the tin industry, enabled employers to '[rule] their labourers with an iron hand' (Wong Lin Ken, 1965b, 40).

Generally employers in the Peninsula enjoyed a virtually unchallenged ascendancy over labour until the great expansion in tin and rubber production in the late nineteenth and early twentieth centuries. There are no annual figures for Chinese immigration before the 1880s but up to then supply seems to have kept up with demand. Thereafter a conjunction of factors led to a shift in advantage to the workers and an improvement in their bargaining position. Demand began to outstrip supply as Malaya faced competition from Dutch planters in Sumatra, and in North Borneo where the tobacco boom was getting under way. The greater difficulty in obtaining labour in the 1890s was compounded by periodical bans on emigration imposed by the Chinese government, and a steep fall in tin prices between 1896 and 1898 which deterred intending migrants. The policies of the British colonial administration also placed growing constraints on Chinese mining employers. Secret societies were declared illegal in the Malay States in 1888 and 1889, followed by prohibition in the SS in 1890. Government also tightened the requirements as to the minimum numbers of workers to be retained for each block of mining land held. The Discharge Ticket System, without which a worker could not change employers, was replaced in the Labour Code 1895 by written contracts for specified periods.

The cumulative results were evident in a sharp rise in wages; daily rates in Perak went from 33 cents to 70/80 cents (1896–9). Workers showed an increasing preference for the tribute system (60 to 70 per cent by 1901), with mine owners pressured to accept a lower share in the profits, from 10 per cent to 8 per cent or less in Perak (Wong Lin Ken, 1965b, 172–7). This shift in advantage continued into the new century. Priority was given to wages owed to workers in cases of insolvency (1899). In 1908 the truck system was limited by law, though in practice it continued to flourish. Very little non-Chinese labour was used. In 1911 Chinese constituted 96 per cent of mining labour in the FMS, with 2.4 per cent Indian and 1.3 per cent Malay (Yip, 1969, Table V-19). The rubber boom generated further competition so that by 1911 Chinese formed 25 per cent of the estate workforce (Wong Lin Ken, 1965b, 180–7, 203–5). By the First World War workers were freer to choose a mode of employment to suit their own economic preferences, leaving employers with far less of the *de facto* property rights which they had contrived to exercise throughout the nineteenth century.

European employers were precluded from significant access to Chinese labour before the end of the century, due to the controls just outlined, and therefore had to depend principally on workers from India. As with Chinese employers, the dominant motive was to retain the greatest degree of control possible over the workforce. In the early years of the SS there was an assortment of slaves (abolished in the first decade), convicts (until the 1860s) and increasingly from the 1830s indentured or contract labourers. Only very approximate estimates are available on Indian immigration prior to the 1870s, but it appears that there was a perennial shortage relative to the needs of planters and government. Consequently the freedom of movement of workers was hedged around with legal constraints carrying fines (which added to constant indebtedness) and imprisonment (Sandhu, 1969, 84–5). The economic viability of estates, notably the sugar industry in Province Wellesley, depended to a large extent on keeping wage rates low. In 1886 indentured sugar workers received 14 cents a day against 18–20 cents for free Indian labourers and 24 cents for Javanese, who also cost two to three times as much to recruit. Expenditure on worker's accommodation and health facilities was woefully inadequate. The inevitable consequences were very high incidences of death and desertion. The latter averaged

18 per cent a year between 1885 and 1888 (Chanderbali, 1983, 53, 272), notwithstanding periodic attempts by the government of India to regulate recruitment under indentures.

Towards the end of the century a freer market for Indian immigrant labour began to emerge in Malaya as demand was increased sharply by the expansion in mining and agriculture (coffee), coupled with government's needs for road and railway building. Employers outside the sugar industry developed an alternative system of recruiting through the *kangani* (foreman) system under which migrants arrived in Malaya relatively free of debts. This had the backing of government which had subsidised steamship fares from India between 1887 and 1892, and then in 1907 established the Indian Immigration Committee with an accompanying Fund, financed by a quarterly levy on all employers of Indians to increase the flow of free labourers. By that time rubber cultivation was entering the boom period and the average number of arrivals rose to 61 000 a year between 1900 and 1920 against only 15 000 a year in 1884–99 (calculated from Sandhu, 1969, 304–5). In the FMS Indians constituted between two-thirds and three-quarters of the rubber estate labour force up to 1920 (calculated from Parmer, 1960, 273, Table 4). Indentured labour in Malaya was abolished for Indians in 1910 and Chinese in 1914.

A third stream of migrants came from the NEI, mainly from Java, Sumatra and Sulawesi. Many of these settled in the west coast states, principally Selangor, Negeri Sembilan and Johor, after their contracts had expired and took up land for cultivation, though still available for wage work and forming a 'floating labour reserve' (Houben, 1992, 13). By 1930 Java-born residents in Malaya totalled 90 000 and local-born ethnic Javanese a further 170 000 (Hugo, 1993, 37).

In North Borneo the growth of a wage-labour force also depended on immigration, but the Chartered Company was less successful in attracting sufficient numbers at the requisite times; hence there was a perennial labour shortage. Initially the Company looked to China as the prime source, but encountered continual difficulties due in no small measure to the indifferent abilities of the British recruiting commissioners appointed as the Company's representatives in Hong Kong. The contract system of recruitment was adopted, on the Straits pattern, but emigrants were deterred by reports of bad treatment on the early tobacco estates. The imposition of a heavy tax on rice was a further disincentive. The inadequate inflow was compounded by the attitude of Cowie, the Company's Chairman, who refused to import any labour between 1895 and 1905 as he believed, quite erroneously, that an ample supply existed in the interior. The policy was moderated as the rubber boom got under way, with improved arrangements for supervision of conditions on estates. Groups of Christian Chinese arrived fleeing persecution in the Boxer rebellion. Another source of labour was Java from where 10 000 came between 1914 and 1932 under an agreement with the Dutch government. There was also immigration from the Philippines and neighbouring Sarawak. The general labour laws followed the Malayan model except that the contract was retained as the basis of employment long after it had been abolished in the Peninsula, until 1932 in fact, the reasoning being that labour could not be attracted to this relatively isolated area without a firm promise of employment. However, during the 1920s unattached or free labour started to arrive in increasing numbers for work on the rubber estates (Tregonning, 1965, ch. 7). By 1928–9 the ethnic composition of the wage labour force was approximately 42 per cent Javanese, 38 per cent Chinese and 20 per cent indigenous (calculated from Houben, 1992, Table 4).

In Sarawak the need for wage-labour did not loom quite so large. The main requirements were for workers in the mines and the oilfields, and to some extent pepper and rubber plantations, along with public works and surveys. These were sourced from Chinese and Indian immigration respectively, and to a lesser extent Java. Restrictions on freedom of movement remained tighter than in Malaya, and labour conditions were less closely supervised by government. A Labour Department was not set up until 1928 (Amarjit Kaur, 1998, 94–111).

For indigenous peoples the removal of traditional constraints on their labour, coupled with the new system of landholding, presented them with opportunities for a redistribution of work-effort between subsistence, export commodity production, and wage employment. The main constraints had been slavery, debt-bondage and forced labour (among Malays). The process went furthest in the Peninsula where these institutions were extinguished by British officials in the western Malay states at various times in the 1880s and 1890s (Sadka, 1968). In North Borneo and Sarawak the trade in slaves and bonded-dependence (found mainly among the Malays and other Muslim peoples) were banned from around the same time. In the former, slavery as an institution was outlawed in 1902. However, obligatory labour service to government was retained until the 1930s (Amarjit Kaur, personal communication).

We saw in section 4.2 that the response to commercial stimulus was rather patchy during the nineteenth century, and it was not until the advent of rubber that a shift of major proportions occurred in indigenous labour patterns. This, as we have seen, took the form of a massive investment of family labour in rubber smallholdings. Those with insufficient land offered themselves as share croppers (*bagi dua*) on the larger holdings (above 4–5 hectares), rather than as permanent wage labour on estates. This raises the question of the extent to which smallholding production represented an outlet for resources (land and labour) previously unemployed or under-employed.

Myint (1977, 29ff) formulated the 'vent-for-surplus' theory to explain the way in which a sparsely populated country entered export markets through increased output by indigenous farmers (who had surplus labour capacity over and above minimum subsistence needs), and/or by an influx of foreign capital, enterprise and labour. In both instances work-effort was applied to an abundance of unused or virgin land. Clearly, both processes were at work, but it is misleading to regard Peninsular Malay 'society' in this period as a 'unitary cultural, much less social, reality' (Nonini, 1992, 19–21). In common with the other ethnic communities in this emerging 'plural society' (see Chapter 6.2) it was in a state of considerable flux. New settlements were springing up, particularly along the west coast, which were populated by locally-born Malays, those migrating from elsewhere in the Peninsula (for instance, fleeing floods in Kelantan in the 1880s) or from Java, Sumatra, Sulawesi and so on.

In general settlers were 'footloose' (Gullick, 1989, 132), but there were notable concentrations of NEI migrants, reportedly comprising two-thirds of the Selangor population in 1886 (Sadka, 1968, 328n.). These cannot be classified analytically as part of the *domestic* stock of resources at the outset of growth. They, and all migrant workers, represented a net addition to the workforce. The 'vent-for-surplus' model, therefore, does not explain the Malayan circumstances fully in this respect, since there is little evidence to suggest a substantial surplus of indigenous labour. Agricultural production was only part of a spectrum of year-round activities for the peasant household (fishing, forest-product, coconut, fruit collection and so on) which added up to full employment, indicating that the opportunity cost of labour was not zero (van der Eng, personal communication). It was India, southern China and the NEI which were the sources of surplus labour.

A similar picture emerges from North Borneo where the Chartered Company found it difficult to hire labour on a permanent basis, either locally or from Sarawak. It is possible, though, that vent-for-surplus is more applicable where shifting cultivators, such as the Sarawak Iban, combined dry-rice growing with rubber smallholdings as the boom took hold. Clearly, too, there were other factors at work in the general unwillingness to take up permanent wage employment, such as a reluctance to work for an alien employer, the unhealthy conditions on many estates, and the relative abundance of land (despite the official constraints noted earlier).

We have noted that Burns (1982) has attempted to account for the lack of an indigenous proletariat as due to British intervention at the time of the tin boom in the 1870s/80s, resulting in the transfer of all but proven 'ancestral' mines to Chinese entrepreneurs. Gullick, however, makes the case that none of the customary ways of extracting peasant labour available to the Malay elite (i.e., *kerah*, debt bondage or slavery) was adaptable as a basis for the creation of a wage-labour force engaged in capitalistic production. The amount of *kerah* which could be demanded had to be limited in time and numbers of men to avoid disrupting the subsistence base of the village economy. Debt bondage and slavery were unsuitable; the former 'yielded to the creditor not an economic return but higher social standing. The services of the debtor were regarded as of "scarcely more than nominal value"' (Gullick, 1989, 213; see also Sadka, 1968, 85).

4.4   Technology

As the Malaysian economy was progressively drawn into a trading relationship with industrialised countries, what was required was a secular increase in the output of raw materials of consistent quality at prices which, though subject to the vagaries of supply and demand, would not exhibit a marginal propensity to rise due to resource bottlenecks. This necessitated the application of new technology to the production process, and it is the prime aim in this section to examine the extent to which such technology was imported as against developed locally.

In the tin mining sector traditional Malay technology had generated little division of labour. Chinese miners coming to the Peninsula imported most of their technology. Along with the labour-intensive methods which dominated that industry until practically the end of the nineteenth century they brought a number of techniques used in operations in Banka (NEI) since the early eighteenth century. These included the open-cast technique of using a relatively large number of workers to excavate a pit to remove the top-soil to expose the ore stratum, multi-purpose hand tools such as the hoe (*changkol*), the chain-pump (*chin chia*), a wooden sluice-box (*lanchut)* with fixed and portable versions, and several types of furnace for smelting the ore, thus generating economies of scale. These innovations were spread over a considerable period of time since, apart from instances such as the furnace just noted, there was no strong pressure to change as labour supply was generally sufficient up to the 1890s, and most ore deposits lay near the surface. Between 1875 and 1895 a notable advance was the adoption of the steam-powered pump, a western product, which lessened the necessity to locate mines near a reliable water supply. However, the pump cost sixteen times as much to install and eighteen times as much to operate, and thus it by no means displaced the water-driven *chin chia*, and neither did it significantly lower the depths at which mining could be carried out (Wong Lin Ken, 1965b, 57).

By the end of the century Chinese miners had exploited much of the readily-accessible deposits of ore, and no major new finds were in prospect. Tin production in the FMS dropped from approximately 49 000 tonnes in 1895 to 39 000 tonnes in 1899. Output per worker was dropping whilst wages rose due to labour scarcity, exerting pressure to find more efficient methods of production. Chinese miners, facing a 'technical crisis' (Wong Lin Ken, 1965b, 199), looked primarily for means of economising on the use of labour, such as a change from open-cast pits to lines of shafts (*ta lung*; whether of local or foreign origin is uncertain). European entrepreneurs found in machinery a means of overcoming the labour problems which had effectively kept them out of the industry thus far.

During the 1890s hydraulic methods (high-pressure hoses using a directed water flow) were introduced from California and were taken up by both Chinese and Europeans. These were followed quickly by the steam- or electric-driven gravel pump. The most capital-intensive innovation was the bucket dredge introduced to Malaya in 1912. By 1920 there were 20 dredges in use, all European-owned, with 39 out of 51 British mining companies committed to this method. Despite the capacity of the dredge to re-mine profitably ground already worked, no Chinese entrepreneurs invested in this device. The main reason adduced is an unwillingness to adopt the western corporate organisation which was needed to raise capital on the appropriate scale (Wong Lin Ken, 1965b, 218), rather than an absolute shortage of funds.

The very large reductions in the cost of treating ore-bearing ground resulting from the innovations just discussed are set out in Table 4.3. Between 1911 and 1920 the total labour force fell by some 37 per cent, from 198 000 to 122 000, mostly from the open-cast sector, whilst output per worker (which had stagnated around 0.25 tonnes up to 1911–15) rose to 0.32 tonnes (28 per cent) from 1916–1920 (Yip, 1969, Tables V-17, 18).

These advances, and many smaller ones, caused a major shift in the sources of power used in the industry from manual, and natural water flow, to artificially generated power (steam and electricity) by 1914. At the same time the Malayan Railways were moving away from wood fuel and, coupled with the needs of the tin industry and electricity generation, stimulated the establishment of a new local industry, Malayan Collieries Ltd in 1913 (Thoburn, 1977, 126; Tate, 1989). However, the overall effect of technological change on Malayan tin exports was relatively modest, with a recovery from 39 000 tonnes in 1899 to 52 000 tonnes by 1905, followed by a decline to 36 000 tonnes by 1920. This reflected the lack of new ore discoveries.

In the mining sector in Sarawak, antimony and gold were the main items produced by Chinese and the Borneo Company operating in the Bau

Table 4.3   Malaya: sample costs of treatment of tin-bearing ground, 1912–15

	Average \$ per cubic yard
(1) Open-cast	0.61–0.94
(2) Gravel pump	0.57
(3) Hydraulic	0.13
(4) Dredge	0.106

Source: (1–3) from Yip (1969), 131; (4) calculated from data in Yip (1969), Table II-1, 135.

district. In the case of gold the company introduced machinery in the 1880s which was hired out to Chinese whose labour-intensive methods had been pushed to their limits. Then in 1898 the company imported the cyanide extraction process which was used to great effect in its new mines at Tai Parit and Bidi. These operated until 1921 and accounted for the bulk of production, 983 000 troy ounces valued at practically $26 million. The other major industry, coal, was produced by government-owned concerns at Labuan since the mid-century, and at Brooketon and Sadong from the 1870s/80s. Antimony mining does not seem to have undergone any technical changes and shrank to insignificance by the end of the century. The next major boost came from the commencement of petroleum production in the Miri district in 1910–11 using imported technology. Within two decades the area became a 'foreign enclave with oil derricks, refineries, electric stations, machine shops, telephone wireless and sawmills' (Amarjit Kaur, 1998, 26). In North Borneo on the other hand mining played a very minor role at this stage.

Whilst much of the mining sector in Malaysia developed through successive technological changes, few similarities can be found in agriculture where, as we have seen, the boom/slump cycle militated against continuous investment. There were few large economies of scale in cultivation. As Lewis (1970, 19) has commented, 'of the crops then prominent in international trade, only two – sugar and tea – required large scale processing immediately after harvesting'.

The relationship between raw material supply and processing capacity is well illustrated by the sugar industry in Malaya. Chinese planters played a pioneering role here, using labour-intensive methods of cultivation and processing with poor quality control using a local variety of cane (*tebu kapor* or 'Selangor cane'). When European planters arrived from Mauritius and the West Indies in the 1830s/40s they brought improved varieties of cane from overseas, together with improved management practices, which were used to open up estates larger than those of the Chinese. Cultivation practices were not dissimilar, but in processing the Europeans used their greater capital resources to install steam-powered machinery (centrifuges) which gave a significant cost advantage over the buffalo-powered crushing mills used by the Chinese. The latter began to switch to steam to some extent after the 1860s, but the processing of cane became largely a European preserve whilst the Chinese supplied cane under contract. By the late nineteenth century the industry was short of labour, whilst an increasing scarcity of timber pushed up the price of firewood for factory fuel. Fresh land became more difficult to obtain in the 1890s, and the advent of rubber completed the demise of what had always been, despite technological advance, an economically insecure industry (Jackson, 1968a, chs 7, 8).

In the case of plantation rubber the British aim was to grow the trees on monocultural estates, but the central technical problem was how to extract the latex without quickly damaging or destroying the tree. A solution was found locally in the 1880s/90s by H.N. Ridley, Director of the Singapore Botanic Gardens, who developed the technique of tapping (removing) the outer bark to a controlled depth with a special knife. But when planters began commercial growing from the 1890s they still had only a very limited fund of technical knowledge, assisted by some sketchy government trials and the establishment of the FMS Department of Agriculture in 1905 (Drabble, 1973, 42–7).

Concurrently with the boom in corporate investment in rubber, the crop was also taken up by smallholders. This was both technically feasible and economically attractive because, as Barlow and Jayasuriya (1986, 639–40) point out, '[at] the stage in which [peasant] agriculture begins its transition to a cash economy ... the real prices for land and labour are low, whilst that of capital is very high ... [technology is] divisible, scale neutral, and robust to poor treatment'. As we have seen, smallholders were able to get access to land despite official constraints (mainly in Malaya), and family labour was readily available. Seeds could be collected from neighbouring estates. Tools such as latex cups and coagulating trays could be fashioned at no cost from cigarette- and kerosene tins, and the rubber sheets sun-dried.

Whilst peasants were successful in adapting the basic technology of rubber production to their particular circumstances, smallholdings represented specialisation by product rather than by process of production (Drake, 1979, 266); that is there was no division of labour leading to higher productivity because the same workers carried out the cultivation, collection and processing functions which on estates were assigned to different groups of labourers. Thus, peasants 'took full advantage of the *market opportunities* available to them; but ... not ... full advantage of the *technical opportunities* to improve their productivity' (Myint, 1977, 39; italics original).

4.5   The domestic economy

The expansion in exports of primary commodities had generally weak long-term effects on other areas of production in the Malaysian economy. We will look at trends in rice-growing and manufactures.

In Chapter 2.2 we saw that in the Peninsula the regions best suited to *sawah* were the river valleys of the northern states (Kedah, Kelantan, Terengganu). The establishment of the Straits ports, with their large migrant populations, created a demand for foodstuffs from the hinterland. This is well exemplified by the rice trade from Kedah to Penang after 1786, the volume of which had nearly doubled by the time of the invasion by Siam in 1821 (calculated from Hill, 1977, 51). The ensuing instability disrupted production for several decades, but by the 1870s/80s the Kedah economy had recovered. Perak and Province Wellesley were also producing marketable surpluses of rice. By 1911–12 these northern regions contained just over three-quarters of the estimated 250 000 hectares under rice in the Peninsula (calculated from Courtenay, personal communication).

The rice industry remained almost completely in Malay hands. For example, in 1911 Malays (including Siamese) constituted 98.7 per cent of rice growers in Kedah and Perlis, the remainder being Chinese (calculated from Hill, 1977, Table 2). This situation continued throughout the rest of the colonial period. It has been argued that the division of labour along ethnic lines was mainly the result of government policies which sought to channel immigrant workers into the capitalist sector, and to direct Malays towards less profitable subsistence activities such as rice-growing (see T.G. Lim, 1977, 187). True, officials disapproved of Malays taking up rubber cultivation, though enforcement of this policy fell far short in practice. Paternalistic though it was, government regarded Malays as the only permanent agricultural population in the Peninsula and best suited to subsistence crops. Kratoska (1982, 314) has pointed out that non-Malays were not attracted to rice-growing as the returns were relatively low. This latter point was evident well before British rule had spread throughout the Malay States. By 1889 in Kedah 'the rice growing peasantry was already ... a relatively depressed class' (Hill, 1977, 55). But this did not deter Malays (except in the most popular areas for rubber such as Selangor); the importance of owning land under rice was as much cultural as economic.

In any case, the heavy influx of immigrants (Chapter 6.1) rapidly outstripped the rice-producing capacity of the Peninsula despite measures such as the FMS Rice Lands Enactment of 1917 which sought to prohibit suitable land going under any other crop. There was no major increase in productivity despite government initiatives to improve the unreliable water supply. The main initiative was the Krian (Perak) irrigation scheme constructed between 1898 and 1906 to serve 20 000 hectares of land. This smoothed out fluctuations in total output but has been judged a failure 'because that very stability consigned the scheme and its farmers to set production parameters – a stable but stagnant economy when the rest of the country was growing' (Overton, 1989b, 14). The large deficiency against demand was made good with imports of rice principally from Burma, Thailand and French Indo-China, which supplied about two-thirds of total annual consumption in the Peninsula prior to the Second World War (Cheng, 1973, Appendix IX). A similar situation existed in North Borneo and Sarawak, both of which were dependent on rice imports before the end of the nineteenth century.

The impetus to the growth of secondary industry in Malaysia was very limited during this period. The new industries were primarily connected with the major export industries, tin and rubber, for which they provided basic processing, such as tin ore smelting, and various grades of sheet rubber (mostly from smallholder output) prior to shipment. Other processing industries dealt in rice, sugar, sago and pineapples. There was some degree of import-substitution manufacture: woodworking, furniture, clothing, building materials (bricks, cement) and foodstuffs (bread, biscuits, drinks), all final consumption goods with a high ratio of weight to cost. Intermediate goods were represented by a small engineering industry which produced and serviced equipment for tin mines, rubber estates, car and cycle repair and so on. With the great bulk of European capital tied up in trade and primary production, this sector became largely a Chinese preserve with a heavy concentration in Singapore due to its central geographical location (Huff, 1994, ch. 7).

As noted in Chapter 2.3, the precolonial centres of indigenous manufacturing (notably textiles) lay on the east coast of the Peninsula. The decline of the cotton textile industry in India (a traditional source of competitive imports) in the nineteenth century initially presented an opportunity for Malay handicraft producers to increase output not only for the domestic market but also for export to neighbouring countries. However, by about the turn of the century competition from imports of cheap factory-made textiles from Britain placed Malay producers under growing pressure, and the weaving centres in Kelantan and Terengganu (along with other local handicrafts in similar situations) were showing clear signs of decline by the early twentieth century (Maznah Mohamad, 1996, chs 1, 4).

5
The Infrastructure

5.1 The development of money, banking and credit

For most of the nineteenth century monetary conditions in the Malaysian territories, in common with the Southeast Asian region as a whole, were irregular and disorganised. Drake characterises the period to 1867 as the 'casual money stage' (1969, 13). The primary need was for coinage as a medium of exchange and this was met from a variety of sources, mainly silver dollars (Spanish, East India Company, Rix, Mexican, British and American trade dollars) and Japanese yen which exchanged according to metal content by weight. In the SS, between 1837 and 1857, the government in India attempted unsuccessfully to enforce the Indian silver rupee as the sole legal tender. Thereafter the other coins became legal tender at various times, but government had no control over the supply of precious metals and therefore over the money supply. The ensuing problems were exemplified over the period 1870–93 by a decrease in the supply of Mexican dollars and Japanese yen causing an acute shortage of currency for trading deals and a net outflow of mainly silver bullion from the Straits totalling $54 million (Drake, 1969, 15).

The metal coinage was supplemented to a minor extent by note issues from the early foreign exchange banks (see below). Persistent requests from Straits merchants for a British trade dollar were rejected as too costly until 1893 when the Bombay mint was allowed to produce this coin. Shortly thereafter the Straits government established a Board of Commissioners of Currency which issued notes from 1899, swiftly replacing banknotes. The initial issues had two-thirds backing in silver, reduced to one-half (1902), and finally one-third (1909). By 1910 these notes had overtaken coins as the major circulating medium. However, there remained a need for a silver Straits dollar whose issue government could control (Drake, 1969, 16; S.Y. Lee, 1974, 10).

Straits mercantile interests were split over whether such a dollar should be linked to the gold standard or remain silver-based. European groups,

Table 5.1   Malaya: Currency Board assets, 1920–38 ($000, selected years)

Year	Total assets	As % of total currency liabilities
1920	54 229[a]	110
1925	168 538	140
1930	123 625	155
1934	138 293	197
1938	147 915	110

[a] Incomplete.
Source: Adapted from S.Y. Lee (1974), Appendix 3.3.

(e.g., the Chambers of Commerce and Planters Associations), whose business lay mainly with gold standard countries, preferred the former in order to minimise fluctuations in the exchange rate and slow the rising costs of imports from the west. Most Asian interests, on the other hand, wanted to stay on a silver standard, arguing that the long-term devaluation of silver against gold (about 50 per cent between 1870 and 1900) made Straits exports cheap, and that any change would adversely affect trade with neighbouring countries still on silver. A Straits Currency Committee reported in 1903 in favour of a silver dollar linked to gold at a fixed rate of exchange. The change required another three years, till 1906, to implement with the rate fixed at 2*s.* 4*d.* sterling (12p), a value maintained until 1967. All other coins were demonetised.

A local gold standard soon proved unsustainable. From 1908–1909 the metropolitan government insisted that all gold reserves should be held in London, together with holdings of sterling securities to a total value of 110 per cent of all issues of Straits currency. The Straits currency was thus on a gold exchange standard (a fixed parity against an external gold-standard currency, sterling) which lasted until 1931, when Britain finally abandoned the gold standard, and thereafter a sterling exchange standard to 1967 (Drake, 1969, 20–7; S.Y. Lee, 1974, 10–14; Chiang Hai Ding, 1978, 178; Narsey, 1988, 210–32). North Borneo and Sarawak had domestically-issued currencies, which also enjoyed wide circulation outside those states and had been linked to Straits dollar parities since the late nineteenth century (Pridmore, 1956; Tregonning, 1965, 70).

How did these currency reforms affect the economies of the Malaysian territories?

The major advantages attributed were (i) that the territories were spared the expense of setting up and operating an independent monetary system; (ii) the link to a world currency, sterling, gave stability to the exchange rate which benefited trade and increased the region's attraction to external investors, and (iii) it provided a built-in mechanism to control inflation, since any increase in the money supply had to be matched by additions to the London reserves, whilst any balance of payments deficit would be corrected immediately through a decrease in these reserves with a corresponding contraction in local money supply, credit and national income (S.Y. Lee, 1974, 29–30).

Disadvantages were (i) the colonial government was left without an independent means of using monetary policy to stabilise the economy in times of slump or boom (ii) the requirement to maintain London assets well in excess of 100 per cent backing for currency issues (see Table 5.1) tied up funds which might have been utilised to further social development (e.g., in education or health); and (iii) colonies such as the SS were obliged to raise external loans at interest rates higher than the returns earned on the assets tied up (S.Y. Lee, 1974, 31–7).

It is difficult to separate out the net effects of exchange stabilisation from other contributory factors. Empirical research by Chiang Hai Ding found the effect on Straits trade was 'minimal' (1978, 164), whilst van der Eng concludes that it 'did not necessarily retard export growth' and 'may have contributed positively to the increase of foreign investment' (1993, 19, 20). Hanson (1975) takes a wider approach, arguing that the rapid growth of Malayan trade in this period was due more probably to the general impact of colonial 'law and order', and the fact that the 'opening-up process' had begun from a relatively low point. Narsey, in a general critique of monetary reforms in British colonies, demonstrates that policy was manipulated by the metropolitan government to maximise imperial benefits whilst stopping short of full integration with the British monetary system; 'the [SS] colony, for currency purposes, was effectively treated as a foreign state, although all ... policy decisions were made by Britain' (1988, 3).

The structure of commercial transactions which developed during the nineteenth and early twentieth century required not only an expanded and formalised medium of exchange, but also institutions capable of facilitating dealings between the people of the region, as both producers of exports and consumers of imports, and the predominantly overseas markets. Exports took considerable time to reach their final markets, but producers needed to realise the value of their output as quickly as possible, either through barter, straighforward monetary payment, or some form of credit. Merchants similarly needed to liquidate goods into money with the least delay, which often involved dealing in different currencies, as well as having some means of access to funds or credit in centres in different parts of the world.

What we see in the Malaysian region between about the middle of the nineteenth and early twentieth century is a gradual (though by no means complete) contraction of barter in face of progressive monetisation, and the development of a banking system to facilitate the commercial dealings outlined above. This was the formal financial sector, and in addition there developed an informal sector which comprised moneylenders (notably the

Chettiars), and local credit providers (shopkeepers and produce dealers) who catered to the needs of small farmers, amongst others.

Prior to the establishment of the first exchange banks after 1840, the limited supply of currency obliged European and Asian merchants to operate on a system of barter and credit (see Chapter 3.5), with the former carrying the considerable risk of default (Drabble and Drake, 1981). The Union Bank of Calcutta was the first to open in the SS in 1840, followed over the next decade by the Oriental Bank, the Asiatic Banking Corporation and the Commercial Bank of India. Three major British-owned banks, the Mercantile, the Chartered, and the Hong Kong and Shanghai Bank, established branches in the Straits between 1856 and 1877. All were mainly engaged in exchange banking (dealing in different currencies), and in the provision of short-term credit to merchants principally through an acceptance business in sterling bills of exchange drawn on London. Sharp exchange rate fluctuations made the period one of uncertainty. In a financial crisis in 1866 two of the firstcomers, the Asiatic and the Commercial Bank of India, failed (Drake, 1969, 103–7; S.Y. Lee, 1974, 66–7). None the less, most survived which meant that a banking network with international connections was already well in place prior to the major surge in export production towards the end of the century. Because of the fact that investment in production was financed to a considerable extent from the local proceeds of trade prior to the corporate boom in tin and rubber after 1900, the banks were not called upon to act as providers of funds for long-term investment. Thereafter it was the British mercantile agency houses in Singapore which constituted the link with external sources of capital (see Chapter 4.2).

The role of the exchange banks in the colonial era has been seen as catering mainly for the requirements of European-owned businesses, due to rigid and conservative bank policies as to the criteria for credit worthiness (Myint, 1977, 57). However, this was certainly not the case in the Straits and the Peninsula in the late nineteenth and early twentieth centuries. The banks were conservative in that they sought business which was a good risk, but the number of western customers in this category was relatively small thus forcing banks to compete strongly, and to deal with Chinese and Indian merchants in the more risky bazaar trade, together with other financial intermediaries such as the Chettiar moneylenders. Indeed it is possible that up to at least 1905 Asian customers were the 'backbone of banking business', and there does not appear to have been any discrimination in the rates of interest charged (Drake, personal communication). There was a widening of business from the 1880s when the newly established British administrations in the Malay States started to use the system.

Besides using the western banks Asian interests, the Chinese in particular developed a variety of methods of financing their trade and production activities. We have seen (Chapter 4.2) how the system of advances by Straits merchants operated in the mining and planting industries. In trade, barter remained an important element; 'bookkeeping barter ... a halfway house between pure barter and a money economy' (Huff, 1989, 171) helped Chinese merchants over the problems associated with a limited supply of coin and its fluctuating exchange value. The system was based on the trade in rice between the surplus-producing areas, Burma, Thailand, Indo-China and the consuming areas, Malaysia and the NEI. Pure barter between these areas would have been difficult because of the need to ensure a coincidence of wants. Chinese merchants in Singapore utilised the entrepot function of that port as a clearing house in which rice exports were essentially bartered against primary products, with rice itself, the 'pecunia of the East' (SS Committee on Profiteering, 1920, cited in Huff, 1989, 171), functioning as the unit of account. In some respects rice was a preferable medium since its purchasing power stayed more constant relative to gold or commodities than did that of the silver coinage (Huff, 1989, 172).

It was not until the beginning of the twentieth century that the first Chinese-owned deposit banks appeared, modelled on their western predecessors in the Straits. One possible reason for this later emergence is that there was a need for established and wealthy businessmen, some having spent time gaining experience as compradores for the western banks, to provide the necessary financial backing and social standing in the Chinese community (Huff, unpublished). There was no similar requirement in the case of the European banks because these were branches enjoying the backing of their (mainly London-based) head offices. Chinese banks also needed a pool of English-educated staff to draw on for management. In the first two decades seven banks were established, mostly incorporated in Singapore: Kwong Yik (1903), Sze Hai Tong (1906), Chinese Commercial (1912), Ho Hong (1917), Oversea Chinese (1919), Lee Wah and the Batu Pahat (1920), together with a branch of the Bank of Communication (Peking) (Drake, 1969, 111–12, 114n). These flotations mostly had strong links with the dialect group of the founders: for example, Kwong Yik (Cantonese), Sze Hai Tong (Teochew).

The banks attracted deposits from the Chinese community, but the banking 'habit' took some time to develop to any great extent. Short (1971) contends that the attitude to holding deposits did not undergo a significant positive shift until the boom of 1926 (see Chapter 8.1). The conditions of business showed much volatility in the early years. The Kwong Yik bank collapsed in 1913 because of unsafe loans granted to its directors, though 88 per cent of the debts had been paid off by 1922. At the outbreak of war in 1914 Chinese importers in the Straits held off settling their debts, leading to a run on the Sze Hai Tong Bank which only survived with a large injection of funds by its principal shareholder. The Chinese Commercial Bank lost one-third of its deposits and suspended business for two weeks, only reopening when the

Governor issued a statement of support. In the slump of 1922 local banks suffered heavy withdrawals which reached 60 per cent in one case (the newly formed Batu Pahat Bank) as depositors needed liquid funds. However, there were no collapses (Short, 1971, 70).

In general the Chinese banks performed a complementary rather than a competitive function alongside the western ones, as they catered predominantly to the local needs of small traders as against the international exchange transactions, advances to European firms and Government business secured by the latter. Their growth was limited by the fact that 'in contrast to the British banks, they lacked capital funds and drawing rights in London' (Drake, 1969, 113).

Formal banking activities were much slower to develop in the Borneo territories. As we saw in Chapter 3.5, the network of barter and credit linked to Singapore through Chinese merchants penetrated the interior in the second half of the nineteenth century. The Borneo Company leased plots of land and advanced money to Chinese pepper and gambier growers in Sarawak (Amarjit Kaur, 1998, 46). We may safely assume, from the activities of the Borneo Company and other capitalistic enterprises in Sarawak, together with the Chartered Company in North Borneo, that some access to exchange banking facilities was available in this period. The major British exchange banks, Hong Kong & Shanghai and the Chartered Bank, together with several Singapore Chinese banks, did not set up branch offices in North Borneo until after the Second World War (Tregonning, 1965, 232), but the wealth generated by the rubber boom created the basis for the emergence of domestic banks among the various Chinese dialect groups, such as the Foochow in Sarawak (Cramb, personal communication).

Apart from the institutional sector, the informal financial network in Malaysia expanded to cater for the credit and loan needs of the large numbers of people, particularly small businesses and farmers, as monetisation spread. The response here was rapid both in the Peninsula and those parts of Borneo where contact with foreign enterprise was close, (e.g., in wage employment). Track workers on the construction of the railway through the Padas gorge in North Borneo in the 1890s were paid at first in lengths of cloth, but within twelve months were expressing a preference for silver coins or, if unavailable, the Company's notes (*British North Borneo Herald*, 16 January 1896). Among the Malaysian peasantry in general there was need for currency for use in paying taxes (land rent, door and capitation taxes and so on). For normal household expenditure, including imported goods, the main need was for short-term credit (usually one crop season). This was usually provided by the local (Chinese) shopkeeper as the *kedai* (small shop) network spread throughout the villages. For major items of expenditure, such as housebuilding, purchase of cattle, jewellery, performance of the pilgrimage (*haj*) to Mecca, larger aggregations of funds were necessary. By the early twentieth century peasants, especially in the areas most extensively drawn into rubber production, were turning to moneylenders to fulfil these needs, and principally to the Chettiars who in turn drew their finance both from sources in India and from the western banks (Drabble, 1973, 61).

Borrowing was heavy during the years when rubber enjoyed relatively high prices, 1909–10, 1915–17 and 1919–20. Chettiar rates of interest were high relative to those in the formal sector. In Kuala Lumpur and Ulu Langat districts (Selangor) they ranged between 12 and 36 per cent per annum (Drabble, 1973, 190–1), whilst in neighbouring Semenyih valley the range was from around 10 to over 40 per cent (Voon, 1987, 50). Borrowing spread across all ethnic groups, but proportionately the heaviest in terms of both the number and average size of loans were among the Chinese. In Melaka state by 1920–1 Chettiars had advanced approximately $10 million, mostly on the security of Chinese rubber land (Drabble, 1973, 191).

However, government in Malaya was primarily concerned about the extent to which Malays had become indebted to Chettiars. As early as 1911 a committee was set up to investigate why Malays in Perak had made little use of an official scheme for small loans for productive purposes at interest of 0.5 per cent monthly or 6 per cent annually. The conclusion was that the Chettiars were preferred as lenders because they were prepared to lend a higher proportion of the value of the security pledged, and to place few restrictions on the use to which the loan was put, though one government official took the view that the limitation of the Planters Loans Fund FMS mainly to European planters had helped to 'drive [small farmers] into the hands of Chetties' (Selangor Secretariat file 4504/1917 cited in Voon, 1987, 31). Apprehension among officials that indebtedness would lead to heavy loss of 'ancestral' land by Malays came to the forefront during slumps, as in 1918 when rubber prices fell, and a moratorium was placed for three months on payments due and court orders made against lands under 20 hectares (Drabble, 1973, 141). There were no parallels to this in Sarawak, as debts to shopkeepers were more of the nature of seasonal credit (Cramb, personal communication), normally extinguished at the time of harvest.

5.2   Transport, urbanisation, communications and power

Transport and communications were 'overwhelmingly important' factors (Myint, 1977, 32) underlying economic development at the regional, country and international levels. At each of these levels the period from *c*.1850 saw the introduction of 'modern transport technology, a product of the Industrial Revolution in Northern Europe and North America' (Dick and Rimmer, 1989). The second half of the nineteenth and early twentieth century was a transitional period in which the new modes of transport and communication (metalled roads, railways, motorised vehicles, steamships, telegraphs and so on) gradually displaced the preceding modes consisting mainly of costly carriage by manpower or pack animals along narrow footpaths or elephant tracks, manually propelled river craft, sailing ships, slow-moving mail and so on. The intra- and inter-country networks which developed were hinged around a hierarchy of towns, cities and ports, or 'nodes', through which the flows of goods, services, information and people passed. In the Asian region the principal components of this 'urban hierarchy' were the port cities. In the Malaysian region the major node was Singapore, with Kuala Lumpur and Penang as minor ones (Dick and Rimmer, 1989, Map 2). These ports built up links with hinterlands in north Sumatra, southern Thailand, Malaya, Riau, Borneo.

These links have been described by Evers (1983, 326) as 'urban circuits' defined as a 'system of exchange in which capital in its various forms, including labour commodities and money, is circulated and a consonant system of social interaction takes place'. These circuits had their origins in the early nineteenth century. In the Peninsula there were initially two, a 'northern circuit' centred on Penang and extending to Kedah, Taiping and Ipoh in Perak, and a 'southern circuit' based on Melaka and encompassing Seremban, Kuala Lumpur and Singapore. In Chapter 4.2 we saw how the Straits ports acted as sources of enterprise and capital, and as conduits for labour for production ventures in the interior with return flows of export commodities. Penang attracted people from Kedah, Perak and southern Thailand. There was considerable movement of Chinese between Melaka and Singapore, whilst Malays moved from Melaka to the Kuala Lumpur region early in the nineteenth century (Evers, 1983, 326–7; Gullick, 1990, 15–16). In the second half of the nineteenth century Melaka was in relative decline, though its economy received a brief boost from rubber in the early 1900s (Drabble, 1983), and the leading position in the 'southern circuit' passed to Kuala Lumpur (Evers, 1983, 331). This schema appears to relegate Singapore to a subordinate position. However, it can be argued that the Island's 'circuit' in this period was much broader than just the southern Peninsula, extending to the surrounding archipelago.

The first phase of urban growth in the interior of the Peninsula was based on the tin mining industry which produced a new type of settlement, the mining camp. Many of these were shortlived, but some gained permanence as collecting and distribution centres for exports and imports, together with shops and other trading facilities (Lim, Heng Kow, 1978, 78, 185). Prime examples in Selangor were Petaling, Ampang and Kuala Lumpur itself (Gullick, 1990, 16–17). The stable conditions under British administration from the 1870s brought in a flood of miners and traders with a concomitant increase in the number of urban centres. The years up to about 1911 were ones of 'phenomenal growth', and can be divided into two sub-periods.

The first, to roughly 1890, saw a relatively uncontrolled 'mushrooming' in which towns appeared quickly, much building was temporary and living conditions were extremely basic. The second, *c.*1890–1911, saw a reduction in the number of new centres, and a slowing, perhaps even relative decline, in the position of some of the early leaders as the tempo of local economic activity slowed: for example, Taiping, Perak, in the 1890s (Khoo Kay Kim, 1991, 26).

In most cases, however, there was redevelopment along more permanent and consciously planned lines. In the largest towns, such as Melaka, Kuala Lumpur and Penang, suburbs began to appear as wealthy Chinese merchants built substantial houses for themselves. Government helped to confer urban status by selecting administrative capitals in each state. As some of the impetus went out of tin mining in the first decade of the twentieth century the rubber industry took over as the stimulus to further growth in communications and urbanisation (Lim Heng Kow, 1978, 188–9; Evers, 1983, 328–30). We must note, though, that this rapid development was largely confined to the west coast of the Peninsula. The east coast failed to attract much population and investment during the tin and rubber booms. As a result there was little urban growth in the interior, and the major eastern coastal towns, Pekan (Pahang), Kuala Terengganu and Kota Bahru (Kelantan), were 'sub-systems' which retained far more of a traditional Malay *'kota* and *pekan'* character (Evers, 1983, 330).

By about 1920 infrastructural and urban development in western Malaya had achieved 'a structure comparable in scale and efficiency with that existing in the advanced countries of the West ... out of the returns from rubber and tin' (Emerson, 1937, 156). The importance of the period up to 1911 for the initial spurt of urbanisation is clear from the proportion of 25 per cent of the population of 'British Malaya' who were town dwellers. Over the next decade this rose only slightly to 27.7 per cent. The regional incidence was highly uneven: 59.5 per cent in the SS, 22.4 per cent in the FMS. There are no aggregate figures for the UMS, but the proportion there was much smaller: for instance, only 4.2 per cent in Kelantan in 1921 (Lim Heng Kow, 1978, 126, 190). This imbalance was also evident in the ethnic composition of the urban population as between migrants and Malays. In 1921, outside the SS, the most highly urbanised states were Selangor and Perak with 31 per cent and 22.5 per cent respectively overall, but with Malays forming only 9–10 per cent against 63–66 per cent Chinese and 21–24 per cent Indian. On the east coast, Kelantan and Terengganu towns had 80–87 per cent Malays, 11–15 per cent Chinese and very few Indians (Lim Heng Kow, 1978, Table 45). Between 1911 and 1921 the proportion of urban Malays actually fell in every state.

In the 1870s and 1880s the main need in the Peninsula was for improved transport facilities to ensure that the increasing output of tin found its way to the ports with least delay. In the leading mining states the British administration gave early attention by upgrading footpaths and bridlepaths into bullock cart tracks, resulting in large reductions in carrying costs, in the case of tin down from $2.50 to $1 per slab from Kuala Pilah (Negeri Sembilan) to Melaka (Gullick, 1989, 159–60). This advance was shortlived as track surfaces frequently broke up under heavy usage and rain. The availability of draught animals was affected by disease and their carrying capacity was low.

Increasing volumes of both goods and people led quickly to the next innovation, railways. The pioneer lines were short, simply connecting the mining centres to the nearest port. The first, opened in 1885, linked Port Weld with Taiping, a distance of some 13 kilometres. Over the next 25 years this and similar east–west lines were joined by a north–south trunk line from Prai to Johor Bahru at a total cost of $46 million (Jackson, 1968a, 236; Amarjit Kaur, 1985). Between 1910 and the early 1920s extensions were made across the Peninsula to Pahang, northwards to link up with Siamese railway system, and finally the causeway to Singapore island. At the same time a closely corresponding road network was built, under the rationale that roads would act as feeders to the railways. In addition the domestic extension of the international communications system (in 1870 the Straits ports were linked by submarine cable to Madras and thence to Europe) was provided through postal, telephone and telegraph services, again with heavy concentration on the west coast. The total wire mileage grew from approximately 2900 to 26 450 kilometres between 1903 and 1925 (Amarjit Kaur, 1985, 136).

The finance for this infrastructure came almost entirely from government revenue, principally Selangor and Perak. The tin industry, through direct duty on exports and indirectly on opium, made the largest contribution. Export duty alone provided an annual average of some 38 per cent of FMS revenue between 1889 and 1900, totalling about $38.5 million. In years of peak constructional activity, such as 1898, expenditure on roads, railways and bridges absorbed 58 per cent of revenue (Yip, 1969, 114–15). Selangor and Perak were sufficiently wealthy to be able to assist the less well-endowed states such as Negeri Sembilan, whilst the FMS provided a loan of £4.75 million pounds sterling ($40.7 million) to the Siamese government to build a line to Bangkok on which construction began in 1912 (Amarjit Kaur, 1985, 64–5).

The interactive relationship between the growth of urban centres, the transport network and the opening up of fresh resources such as land was already evident in the Kelang valley region encompassing the area from Kuala Lumpur to the coast where Port Swettenham was opened in 1901. Not only was there a concentration of estates and mines here, but the valley acted as channel along which flowed export products from neighbouring regions in Selangor. 'By the 1910s, the interior of Selangor had a well-developed system of settlements connected by good road and rail networks. The foundations were distinctively laid ... for the Klang [*sic*] Valley to become the spatial foci upon which ... present-day metropolization and mega-urbanization are taking place' (Lee Boon Thong, 1994, 112, 114). Generating equipment, variously-powered (coal, hydro, gas, oil), provided Kuala Lumpur with a public electricity supply in 1905, shortly after Penang in 1904. The spread of the power grid thereafter was slow and patchy, reaching only eleven more west-coast towns by 1925. The suppliers were a mixture of government and private enterprise bodies (Tate, 1989, 284).

Compared to the changes in the Peninsula, the growth of urbanisation and communications in the Borneo territories, though not without highlights, was very limited in this period. As late as the 1960s a geographer could write that 'in British Borneo ... the urbanization process has not yet advanced to a stage when the large urban units provide a striking contrast to the pioneer and rural settlements' (Y.L. Lee, 1962b, 82).

In Sarawak, Kuching was founded by a Brunei Malay aristocrat sometime in the 1820s as an administrative centre and port for the export of antimony ore. In 1841 with the Brooke takeover it became a royal settlement, continuing as a port as well as 'the political, social and economic capital of a much larger region' (Lockard, 1976, 110). With the early struggles of James Brooke to impose his authority, together with Kuching's pre-eminence, the initial impact on other areas was negative: for example, the highly destructive clash with the Chinese mining settlement at Bau in 1857. The restoration of peace and the expansion of the Brooke territories helped to enlarge Kuching's population, attracting Chinese and some Indian immigrants, though up to about 1900 it remained predominantly a Malay settlement.

Rajah Charles Brooke promoted Chinese immigration into Sarawak which, along with the internal migrations of the Dayak peoples, helped to open up the interior. This resulted in the establishment of administrative and 'bazaar' trading centres in the latter part of the nineteenth century, particularly in the First, Second and Third Divisions. Examples were Simanggang in the Batang Lupar district, and Kanowit in the Rajang river basin (Chew, 1990, 69). The continuing dependence on trade on this riverine network meant that the centres of export-oriented activity were focused towards the coast. Eight out of the ten largest towns in Sarawak and Brunei after the Second World War were ports (Y.L. Lee, 1962b, 86). There was thus little of the interaction between districts which was such a strong impetus behind urbanisation along the west coast of the Peninsula. Neither James nor Charles Brooke placed much importance on improving internal transport facilities apart from what was considered necessary for administrative purposes, and so roads were short and unconnected, even those built by the Borneo Company and Sarawak Oilfields Ltd. Railway building was confined to a mere 16 kilometre stretch out of Kuching built between 1911 and 1915, but this was totally uneconomic once a parallel road was constructed (Amarjit Kaur, 1998, 82). Whilst the surge in rubber and oil production after 1910 increased government revenues, neither provided the volume of funds over a fairly short space of time to finance the construction of an infrastructure of transport and communications comparable to that in Malaya (Reece, 1988, 27).

In North Borneo the Chartered Company started operations with little more than bases in Labuan and Sandakan on opposite sides of the northern coast (see Maps 3 and 4). It was the latter, established in 1879, which soon took precedence and grew rapidly in the 1880s (Bhar, 1980). The territory was divided into East and West Coast Residencies. As in Sarawak, the nature of the terrain made rivers the most important means of transport, especially for the two export industries, tobacco and timber.

W.C. Cowie, a director dominant in the affairs of the Chartered Company between 1894 and 1910 and influenced by the swift progress in Malaya, made early and ambitious plans for trans-Bornean rail and tele-graphic links. The first of these proved impracticable, and the second was completed by 1897, but only at a very high cost of nearly £20 000 against an original estimate of £5000 (Tregonning, 1965, 54–5). Such railway build-ing as took place was confined to the west coast, linking Jesselton, Papar, Kimanis, Beaufort and Tenom by 1905, a total of 172 kilometres costing £500 000. Construction suffered badly from misconceived planning and severe technical shortcomings which from 1912 onwards required the rebuilding of much of the track and several bridges. The railway incurred a consistent operating loss up to 1923 amounting to approximately $517 000 against a cumulative capital cost of £800 000 (Amarjit Kaur, 1998, 86–7), or $6.86 million. None the less, the project did open up land along the lines which attracted companies during the rubber boom.

The development of paths and roads was similarly very circumscribed and confined largely to the west-coast regions. Such development posed major problems on the east coast due to the swampy environment near the sea and the mountainous interior. The Company's limited financial resources did not permit much beyond the development of a network of bridle paths in the Western and Interior Residencies to link up administrative posts and to act as feeders to the railway. This totalled only 1024 kilometres by 1929, one 400 kilometre stretch having taken 22 years to complete (Amarjit Kaur, 1998, 90). Given the difficulties of internal communications coastal shipping was of prime importance: for example, to get the tobacco and timber from the east coast to external markets. As in Sarawak, urbanisation was mainly a coastal phenomenon, six out of nine towns by the 1960s being ports (Y.L. Lee, 1962b, 86).

As the volume of export produce coming out of the Peninsula and Borneo grew, along with a return flow of imports, there was a prime need for more shipping ranging from the smallest craft for river and coastal transport, to larger vessels to connect with ocean-going ships at the Straits ports. This sector showed a three-tier structure similar to the structure of commerce in the region described in Chapter 3.5. Indigenous people were concentrated at the first level, though there was some overlap with the ubiquitous Chinese traders. The latter retained a premier position in coastal and regional shipping largely unchallenged until the late nineteenth century. By that time Europe-based companies, too, wanted to enter regional networks in order to secure more cargo. A major example was the Ocean Steamship Company of Liverpool (the Blue Funnel Line) which in the 1880s and 1890s gained a good share in the Bangkok–Singapore rice trade, and the shipment of tobacco from Deli (East Sumatra) and North Borneo. The advent of steamships in the last third or so of the century, together with the opening of the Suez Canal in 1869, brought freight rates down heavily and quickly: for instance, Blue Funnel rates on gutta percha and general goods fell by 40–45 per cent between 1875 and 1879 (Falkus, 1990, 40–1, 123).

6
The Growth of a Plural Society

6.1 Population growth

In Chapter 2.1 we noted estimates which put Malaysia's population growth rate over the two centuries prior to 1800 at between zero (in the Peninsula) and 0.2 per cent a year, with the latter figure posited also for Southeast Asia as a whole.

In the nineteenth and early twentieth centuries there was a general acceleration in growth rates. Data from Reid (1988, Table 2) give annual averages of 1.56 per cent for Malaya (excluding Patani), 0.83 per cent for Borneo and 0.84 per cent for Southeast Asia (the last figure my calculation). However, these magnitudes remain open to debate because, whilst we have growing numbers of official censuses c.1900, there are few reliable contemporary benchmarks for the early nineteenth century to use as a starting point for calculations.

In the case of the Malay Peninsula Newbold's estimates for the mid-1830s aggregating 473 000 are the most-used basis but have been criticised as far too low, especially as regards the indigenous Malays. Dodge (1980) argues for a substantially higher total of around 750 000 at that date. When placed against the first pan-Malayan census (1911), this gives an annual increase of roughly 1.7 per cent (quite close to Reid's figure) compared to 2.3 per cent if Newbold's figure is used. The growth rates for the Malay/Malaysian component were 1.8 per cent (following Newbold) and 0.84 per cent (Dodge). The case for the lower rate is based on the grounds that prior to British administration there were no widespread improvements in nutrition or public health, and no consistent political stability throughout the Peninsula, to provide a 'likely environment for a [natural] population explosion' (Dodge, 1980, 452). However, Maznah Mohamad (1996, 42, n.54) argues that the east coast states, principally Terengganu where handicraft industries flourished in the nineteenth century, could have supported much denser populations.

None the less, although the Peninsula as a whole was still relatively sparsely populated at some 2.34 million in 1911 (Table 6.1), by that date fundamental changes had occurred in the ethnic composition and spatial distribution of the population. In the first category the main driving force was the surge in immigration associated with the tin and rubber booms. Malaya experienced 'a far higher volume ... than any other part of South-East Asia' (Fisher, 1964, 52). Net immigration of Chinese more than doubled from about 90 000 in 1881 to 214 000 in 1893. Assisted Indian migrants soared from approximately 22 000 in 1908 to 91 000 by 1913 (Saw, 1988, Tables 2.2, 2.6). There were also substantial inflows from the NEI, though annual data are hard to obtain for this period.

The result was a major shift in ethnic composition with the proportion of Malays and other Malaysians falling from 84 per cent *c.*1835 to about 53 per cent by 1911, whilst Chinese rose from 9 per cent to 35 per cent, and Indians from 3 per cent to 10 per cent (calculated from Dodge, 1980).

In spatial terms immigrants were concentrated most heavily in the west-coast states of the Peninsula, drawn there by the Straits ports, the concentration of investment in mines and estates, and the network of

Table 6.1   Malaysia: population growth, 1911–90 (thousands)

Year	Peninsular Malaysia[a]	Sabah	Sarawak	Malaysia
1911	2 338	208	421	2 967
1921	2 910	263	444	3 618
1931	3 766	277	469	4 130
1947	4 908	331	546	5 786
1960	7 017	454	745	8 216
1970	8 775	649	976	10 400
1980	11 442	1 013	1 309	13 764
1990	14 670	1 480	1 674	17 824
Annual growth rate (per cent)				
1911–21	2.21	2.74	0.53	2.00
1921–31	2.61	0.52	0.53	2.23
1931–47	1.67	1.12	0.95	1.57
1947–60	2.79	2.46	2.42	2.73
1960–70	2.26	3.64	2.74	2.38
1970–80	2.64	4.55	2.98	2.84
1980–90	2.52	3.86	2.49	2.62
Average				
1911–90	2.35	2.51	1.83	2.30

[a] Excludes Singapore. If Singapore is included, the average is 2.82 per cent.
Source: Population data from personal communication, Pierre van der Eng. Annual percentage growth rates author's calculation.

urban centres. Chinese and Indians were in the majority (59 per cent and 76.5 per cent) in Perak and Selangor. Locally-born Malays were a minority (32 and 15 per cent respectively) in these states, compared to 94 and 97 per cent in the earlier population centres on the east coast, Kelantan and Terengganu (Dodge, 1980, Table A).

There is even less certainty about nineteenth-century population growth rates in the Borneo territories. Valid intertemporal comparisons are virtually impossible due to the boundary changes as fresh territories were annexed. For example, Sarawak as ceded to James Brooke in 1841 contained some 10 500 people, 150 000 in the area covered by 1857, and 222 000 by 1877 (Jackson, 1968b; Pringle, 1970, 106; Amarjit Kaur, 1998, 18). It would be reasonable to conclude that the annual rate of growth prior to 1900 was lower than the Peninsula, probably about 1 per cent or less, since immigration was not a really significant factor before the beginning of the twentieth century. Chinese migration jumped sharply in the first decade, reaching 10–12 per cent of the total population by 1909–11. Growth rates among the indigenous peoples, particularly the swidden cultivators, were very slow. For example, in absolute terms the Iban, the major group in Sarawak, increased their numbers by only just over one-third between 1848 and 1939 (Tate, 1979, 270). Population densities in a region were affected by the internal migrations during the nineteenth century. Again, the Iban form a prime example. Between the 1850s and 1880s they moved into the middle and upper Rajang river, the Entabai river, Sibu and the Muka and Oya rivers, coming into armed conflict over land with the Kayan and Kenyah peoples (Tate, 1979, 271).

There is little that can be said about early trends in North Borneo as the first three censuses (1891, 1901, 1911) were all incomplete. In both this state and Sarawak the indigenous peoples were in substantial majorities; 77 per cent in North Borneo and 74 per cent in Sarawak (calculated from Y.L. Lee, 1962a, 230).

Up to the early twentieth century the population growth of the Malaysian region had not yet assumed a normal demographic pattern: that is, one primarily driven by natural increase. This was so because of predominantly male immigration, resulting in a completely unbalanced gender ratio in the rapidly expanding migrant communities. In the Peninsula the ratios among Chinese and Indians in 1911 were respectively 215 and 320 females per thousand males (Hirschman, 1975b, Table 2.3).

6.2   The structure of society

The economic and social changes in this period were inseparable. The increased volume and variety of production required, and in turn was further facilitated by, new forms of occupational specialisation, administrative and social organisation.

Though the Malay elite in the Peninsula lost its occupational specialisation, namely the power to rule, under the restructuring of government by the British, it nevertheless retained a collective identity at the apex of indigenous society. For a time in the late nineteenth century this group was, as Gullick (1989, ch. 4) terms it, 'a ruling class in search of an occupation'. The British met this need for continued status and income in the case of the Sultan and the more prominent families by creating honorific positions such as appointment to the newly created State Councils (*Majlis Negeri*), and the payment of official pensions related to the holder's previous income. The pensions, by virtue of being fixed, set limits to aristocratic incomes, but at the same time the progressive banning of the carriage of arms and the abolition of debt bondage and *kerah* meant that large household retinues no longer needed to be maintained (Gullick, 1989, 75).

A greater measure of financial independence was attainable where, in addition, title could be proved to 'ancestral' resources. A notable example was the 400 or so owners of ancestral tin mines in Kinta valley who in the 1880s received royalties of between $500 and $1000 a month. Others held land within the new urban settlements such as Ipoh which could be sold off as shop lots. Cash incomes of this type were used in commercial ventures such as elephant hire to miners for transport, and the construction of dams to supply water to rice farmers. However, these were not successful in the long run (the hire charges for elephants were set too high compared to labour to push wheelbarrows: Gullick, 1989, 80, 199). A generally reduced financial position by the turn of the century, coupled with the severance of their administrative control over districts, meant that the elite was no longer able to perform the traditional function of leadership and assistance in economic activities to village communities. Whilst a few aristocrats built impressive town houses alongside those of the immigrant elites, they were not permanently involved in the increasingly urban-based commercial networks. That such connections were transient can be illustrated by the case of the Datuk Panglima Kinta, at his death in 1902 the richest Malay in Perak, whose opulent house in Ipoh was then sold to be used as a court house (Gullick, 1989, 81). 'There was no structural group of indigenous origin that could integrate itself effectively with the urban centres founded on modern capitalism' (Tham, 1980, 12).

Lesser members of the elite found salaried employment in government posts such as Native or Malay Magistrates, and *penghulus* (now in charge of the *mukim* or sub-district rather than a village). A meeting of the Selangor State Council in 1883 appointed 24 *penghulus* of whom thirteen were of the royal (*raja*) class (Sadka, 1968, 276). Others sought minor government positions; forest rangers, village school teachers, office messengers (*peons*), whilst some could even be found working as road labourers (Gullick, 1989, 77).

Whilst the Sultans found their titular, and even real, social status enhanced under British control, the traditional elite as a group found itself increasingly marginalised in relation to the growing scale and complexity of government, especially after the formation of the FMS in 1896. The British, looking for fresh means to associate upper-class Malays with government, decided upon English-medium education as the major way forward. In 1905 the Malay College, Kuala Kangsar, was established to provide this for the sons of the elite, followed in 1910 by creation of the Malay Administrative Service as their principal career path. A start with the admission of commoners was not made until the 1920s (Stevenson, 1975, ch. VIII). A critical study sees the Malay elite as generally cooperative with the colonial government, with little attempt to '[champion] the rights and interests of the masses' (Shaharuddin, 1988, 47).

The changes just described were mainly characteristic of the FMS which experienced the deepest impact of British administrative control. In the UMS the Malay elites retained a more vital connection with government. In Johor the Malay bureaucratic elite was a new one in terms of personnel as many were recruited from among the middle class of Singapore Malays. However, they were given prominent titles and took precedence over the handful of those with hereditary minor titles (Gullick, 1989, 86). In the northern states the traditional elites were able to maintain an independent economic base in Terengganu into the twentieth century through the royal grants of revenue collection rights, land concessions and so on, but even here its role was 'merely as a consuming class rather than a genuinely entrepreneurial class' (Talib, 1984, 221). It was not until the interwar decades that tightened British controls led to the incorporation of this elite in the manner that had occurred in the FMS. In Kelantan the elite retained particular influence over the administration of religious affairs, whilst in Kedah the British, at the handover of suzerainty in 1909, found the Malay elite already well entrenched in the bureaucracy (Gullick, 1989, 85–7), doubtless as a result of the reconstituted administration following the state's bankruptcy a few years earlier (see Chapter 3.2).

For the *rakyat* of the Peninsula, especially along the west coast, the period between about 1880 and 1910 was one of considerable population mobility as new settlements were established by migrants from within the country (Kelantan, Terengganu) and from the NEI. This movement was accompanied by new economic opportunities ranging from short-term wage employment to the cultivation of cash crops and small-scale trade. Gullick (1989, 101, 119n.) suggests that an embryonic Malay middle class had begun to emerge in the villages by the late nineteenth century. The composition of this group cannot be identified with precision, but possible candidates were the traders whose relatively wide experience made them alive to commercial possibilities and ready to move into areas of endeavour such as land development. Another group were the *penghulus* whose office, though restructured by the British, provided a channel of continuity through which some Malays were able to gain for themselves, their families and close asssociates such as other founding families of the village, an advantageous position with access to economically valuable resources. In Mukim Mawar (a pseudonym for a sub-district in Selangor) the *penghulu* group obtained title to lands they already occupied, plus fresh grants of land (with exemption from survey charges, annual rental and so on), interest-free house loans and cash advances from government among other privileges. These facilities were particularly valuable as the boom in rubber intensified after 1905. *Penghulus* were able to convert existing holdings from coffee and coconut cultivation to the new crop, and obtain new land at a time when official policy did not favour alienation to smallholders for this purpose (see Chapter 4.3). Small loans from government also assisted them to buy up holdings abandoned by less fortunate villagers.

In addition to accumulating assets, the status of *penghulus* was enhanced by the intermediary role which they exercised between the *rakyat* and the government, which in practice enabled them to dispense patronage (Shamsul, 1986, 16–29). A trend observable over time was for such families to consolidate their hold over the office. In the district of Temerloh, Pahang, the appointment 'remained within the immediate family of the initial appointee for all but five of the fifteen mukims' (Koch, 1982, 87). Holders of other official appointments in the village which carried status as well as a regular cash income, such as the school teacher, were also in a position to use social connections to build up their holdings of land. For most Malays, however, the basic economic and social unit continued to be the family whose total labour power was the main determinant of the extent of the assets such as land which could be acquired and operated.

Despite the rapidity of change, especially as it diminished the power of the elite, Malay society retained a cohesiveness which centred around hierarchy based on rank, adherence to the Islamic faith and location of the mass of the people (including migrants from the NEI) in the *kampungs*. In terms of influence over the economy, however, Malays were progressively marginalised as the important linkages with the export economy (shopkeepers, produce dealers) were largely monopolised by non-Malays. Malays were generally reluctant to take up work for wages outside the villages on a permanent basis since, with land relatively easily available at this stage, there was no economic imperative to do so.

The indigenous peoples of northern Borneo present an enormous range of differences in this period which make generalisations a hazardous undertaking. Broadly, researchers have concluded that though Borneo peoples have similarities in physique, material culture and languages of the Malayo-Polynesian group, 'Bornean societies are ... characterised by instability, shifting residence and impermanence in social groups' (Lingenfelter, 1990, 2–3). Group membership through kinship is complicated because societies are of the 'cognatic' or 'bilateral' type in which descent can be traced equally through the male or female line. The formation of descent groups with 'strong corporate characteristics' for long-term tasks such as the management of property from one generation to the next has thus been extremely difficult (e.g., among the Melanau of Sarawak: Morris, 1978, 45–6). The social organisation of groups varies from stratified (Kenyah) to more egalitarian (Iban) structures. As a reflection of these, relationships in exchange transactions have ranged from superior/inferior to more balanced, negotiating types with elements of reciprocity (survey based on Appell, 1977; King, 1978; Lingenfelter, 1990; Sellato, 1994).

Contact with external influences (other indigenous groups, migrants and governments) has been a major determinant of the pace and direction of change in northern Borneo. As the flow of Chinese migrants increased around the turn of the century these moved into trade, commercial agriculture (pepper, gambier, rubber) and some food cropping. Along the lower Rajang river (Sarawak) the demonstration effect was not lost on the Iban who took up rubber and wet-rice in suitable locations (Sutlive, 1978, 129). In the Tenom valley (North Borneo) the Timugon Murut offered themselves for wage work after the railway reached the district in the early 1900s and two foreign-owned rubber estates were established (Brewis in Lingenfelter, 1990, 15–18).

The Brooke and Company governments in northern Borneo devoted much of their efforts towards the pacification and settlement of the various tribal groups whilst maintaining their traditional cultures. In Sarawak the Iban were slowly persuaded to abandon headhunting, though their warlike skills were utilised by the Brookes in the police and small armed force. P.M. Kedit, himself an Iban, sees the principal modernising influence of the Brookes as creating for that group 'a new sense of identity … transcending their traditional parochial loyalties by way of loyalty to a strong central government' (1980, 58). In North Borneo the Company gradually weaned nomadic groups such as the Sama-Bajau and Bajau Laut away from their involvement in the 'foraging' or 'procurement economy' of the northeast coast (see Chapter 2.3) by the establishment of permanent trading centres such as Semporna, Lahad Datu and Tawau (Sather, 1997, 44–51).

The social groupings created by Chinese migrants to Malaysia from the late eighteenth century onwards derived the basic form and structure from their country of origin, but were not identical. Out of the three major social classes in Ch'ing China, the governing scholar elite (*shih*), the merchants (*shang*), and the artisan/labourer (*kung*), only the two latter were clearly reproduced overseas, though Yen (1986) argues that there was a functional equivalent of the *shih* in the literate group employed in clerical posts or in the colonial administration. The creation of a 'normal' social structure was extremely difficult. For most of the nineteenth century the male:female ratio among migrants was heavily unbalanced, as shown in the previous section. Kinship connections were certainly used by the predominantly male migrants to bring over more relatives, but it was to various social organisations that they had to turn primarily for support in an alien environment. As Edwin Lee has commented: 'the Chinese did not view economic pursuits as something to be fought over in an impersonal marketplace governed by values of efficiency and productivity. Instead, they applied values pertaining to social and kinship behaviour ... in order that economic pursuits might become less impersonal, and more familiar and predictable' (E. Lee, 1991, 250). We shall, however, see that this did not preclude strong social antagonisms from developing.

The Chinese community established a range of associations to regulate internal affairs as well as relations with external political authority, whether that of a local Malay ruler or the British colonial government. The main associations which appeared in Malaysia in the nineteenth century were based on clan (an extension of kinship), dialect, and regional ties. At a more general level the *pangs* combined dialect, regional and occupational groupings. A close connection emerged from the outset between the first two and the third because of a natural tendency for people established in a job or trade to recruit others of the same clan or speech group background. Thus, by the mid-nineteenth century the Teochews dominated plantation agriculture, the Hokkiens commerce, the Cantonese and Hakkas were tradesmen, and the Hainanese provided services (Yen, 1986, 117–18). A further most important organisation was that of the triads or secret societies (*hui*). It has been argued that all these associations can be classified under the general category of the *kongsi,* 'a generic Chinese term ... that includes everything from business partnerships to clan and regional associations to secret triad societies' (Trocki, 1990, 11). Yen (1986) also adopts a wide perspective to include the maintenance of social control (law and order) at the grass roots and, in association with the temples, the preservation of Chinese cultural identity through ancestor worship, traditional festivals, promotion of vernacular education and so on.

The *kongsis* also provided a basis for the emergence of leadership (the *taukehs*). As we have seen (Chapter 2.3) for the Chinese mining communities in western Borneo in the unsettled conditions of the late eighteenth and early nineteenth century these associations were 'resilient frontier organisations' (Chew, 1990, 220). Under the aegis of British rule there was no question of political autonomy for the Chinese, who none the less maintained a desire to minimise outside interference in the community's affairs. Throughout the nineteenth century the *taukehs* needed the associations, particularly the secret societies, as power bases to further extend their political and economic interests. This in turn involved working with the colonial government which, as we have seen, had only limited administrative capacity and was thus willing to rely to a large extent on the Chinese leadership to maintain social control.

A notable example of this collaboration was through the revenue farms (Chapter 4.2). The British continued the practice, inherited from the Dutch, of appointing a *Kapitan Cina* to act as the community intermediary. The *Kapitans* came from among association leaders, often with strong triad links, popularly elected largely on the basis of their wealth.

Chinese society in Malaysia had considerable social dynamism and internal tensions during the nineteenth century. Trocki (1990) argues that for much of this period the viability of the economy and society of Singapore and its environs, notably southern Johor, rested on a complex interrelationship of control embracing the British administration, the Chinese leadership and the mass of the largely Chinese working population. The crucial element in this was the revenue farm system, and in particular the opium farm. Right up to the 1880s the dynamic within Chinese society took the form of power struggles among the *kongsi* leadership, grouped into syndicates, for control of the revenue farms. From time to time riots ensued, as in 1846, 1851 and 1854. There appears to have been a growing popular resentment against the *taukeh* leadership. Towards the end of the century the Straits government moved to ban secret societies, and began the process of dismantling the revenue farm system.

This general pattern over time fits in well with trends elsewhere in the Peninsula. As the Chinese mining communities flourished along the west coast from around the mid-century, they adopted a social structure of associations and leadership very similar to that in Singapore. Power struggles between secret societies ensued for control of productive resources, notably tin mines in the Kelang valley and Larut in the 1860s (Khoo Kay Kim 1988, 185). In the early decades of British control a mutualistic relationship developed with the Chinese leadership, mediated through the revenue farms. In 1890 nearly 90 per cent of government revenue came from economic activities associated with the Chinese. Strong leaders such as Yap Ah Loy (*Kapitan Cina*) in Kuala Lumpur possessed near absolute control over their districts in the 1870s and early 1880s. There was a fair degree of social interaction between the British and Chinese elites, but this phase was relatively short. By the 1890s secret societies had been banned, and the degree of control possessed by the mining *kongsi* leaders over the workers lessened as the latter's bargaining power was improved by the strong demand for labour. The power of the *Kapitan Cina* diminished and the office was abolished in 1902. Wealth became more dispersed throughout Chinese society. The advent of British capital for rubber growing and tin mining brought a new commercial elite alongside the Chinese.

The dynamic economic performance of the Chinese in the Straits ports and the western Peninsula in the nineteenth century was based on a social system which allowed full rein to 'their ability to organise systematically and effectively' (Khoo Kay Kim 1988, 188). They did not lose this ability as the twentieth century dawned, but the congruence between the labour-intensive methods of production and the leadership structure of society was no longer as strong as it had been. Competition had to be faced from Europeans who now possessed both capital and a (largely Indian) labour supply, together with new forms of corporate association. The traditional *kongsi* lost much of its efficacy; 'only those ... successfully established family kongsis stayed on top ... [who] kept their wealth concentrated' (Trocki, 1990, 217) through careful marriages, small partnerships and so on. Loke Yew, for example, accomplished a successful transition because, by the time the farms were abolished, he had already diversified his wealth into other areas, real estate, moneylending and rubber planting, among others. At his death in 1917 his assets in the FMS were estimated at $10 million, and as much as $20 million in total (Butcher, 1993b). In some organisational respects Chinese business interests paralleled those of the Europeans in the formation of associations such as Chinese Chambers of Commerce (Singapore 1906, Penang 1903, and later in the FMS).

The social organisation of the Chinese in northern Borneo shows many similarities to that in Malaya, especially the importance of voluntary association groups. A characteristic feature was for groups of immigrants to arrive in response to some particular arrangement with government: for example, Hakkas in North Borneo in 1883 and Foochows in Sarawak in 1901. But in addition to dialect and clan ties, they arrived with a further strong unifying element in the form of Christianity. In the case of the Foochows this was the Methodist church, whose ministers served as community leaders. The group settled along the Lower Rajang river, and after failing to cultivate wet-rice (the government had hoped to lessen dependence on imported foodstuffs) they took up pepper and rubber growing with considerable success. They formed a tightly-knit community whose relative social isolation was increased by the grant in 1909 of a land concession from which Iban were excluded (Chew, 1990, ch. 7). In Kuching 'speech-group particularism was the overriding feature of Chinese society' (Lockard, 1987, 65), with the first dialect association established in 1853. As in Malaya, a close correlation developed between dialect groups and particular occupations, a very relevant point here being that the vocabulary used in a trade was that of the dominant group, which served to exclude others (Tien Ju-K'ang, 1953, cited in Leigh, 1988, 183).

The structure of leadership within the Chinese community again approximated that in Malaya, though one important difference was a lack of secret societies. Many of the first generation of leaders were China-born, but by the 1890s a growing proportion were locally-born and more formally educated, some in English-language mission schools. Overall, the Chinese community did not possess a strong social unity in the late nineteenth century, due to the dialect divisions noted above, but it is possible to see the beginnings of a new grouping in Kuching around this time, mostly locally born and combining Chinese and western cultural traits (the latter through education). The emergence of new organisations such as the Chinese Chamber of Commerce in Kuching (founded probably in 1897 and the oldest in the region) 'represented the beginnings of a social and economic structure that might transcend dialect divisions because of their pan-community scope' (Lockard, 1987, 74).

The community of Indians, mainly southern Tamils but with an admixture of other groups such as the northern Sikhs, had some similarities with the Chinese, but also some significant differences. In demographic terms it was predominantly male until well into the twentieth century, and was vertically divided along various lines. Linguistic and regional affiliations existed, comparable to those among the Chinese, but there were in addition religious divisions (Hindu, Muslim, Sikh) as well as the horizontal lines of caste differences. The conditions under which Indians established themselves in Malaysia, principally in the Peninsula, differed from those affecting the Chinese. Whereas the latter had come almost entirely of their own volition and through a migration network organised very largely by fellow Chinese who also provided the employment, Indian immigration was officially controlled right from the outset. Many of the early arrivals were convicts sent to work in the Straits, along with soldiers, seamen, and so on. Employment was with the colonial government or, as the indenture and *kangani* systems developed (see Chapter 4.3), with British planters who practised tight control of labour. As a result Indians did not develop an autonomous leadership structure comparable to the *Kapitan Cina*.

Indians were also slower than the Chinese to transmute from a community of transients to one of permanent residents (in 1921 the respective proportions locally born were 12 per cent and 22 per cent). They were a predominantly rural, agricultural people living on estates where life in workers' quarters reproduced that in the home villages. It proved extremely difficult for them to break out of this environment, and ethnically separate mining and fishing villages, such as characterise the Chinese and Malay communities, did not emerge to any extent. Indians were well represented in many other occupational groups, such as public works, the services sector, commerce and the professions (Sandhu, 1969, chs. 6, 7). Some of these, the Chettiars for example, were noted for their comparative wealth, but this did not place them in any position of leadership since they were 'highly communal in outlook [and] possessed few organic ties with the rest of "Indian" society' (Stenson, 1980, 28). Up to the interwar years there was a high degree of social fragmentation among Indians, reflected in the lack of a clearly identifiable elite and a paucity of voluntary associations. A similar pattern is evident in the much smaller community in Kuching, Sarawak (Lockard, 1987, 74–5), whilst very few

Indians were attracted to North Borneo due to the better opportunities available in Malaya (Tregonning, 1965, 134).

The European (roughly 90 per cent British in the FMS) section of the community was numerically the smallest, largely male, and socially the most narrowly based. Most came to perform one of two functions, either to play a role in government, or in the organisation of export production and trade. In broad terms they were divided into the officials and unofficials. In the early years of British rule there was some interchangeability between these spheres. Men joined government and then, after a few years, left to seek their fortunes as, for example, proprietary planters (in some cases they speculated in land whilst still officials). Pioneer planters and miners were a mixed collection ranging from younger sons of the aristocracy down through the social scale, and often with an itinerant, relatively unspecialised life behind them. For example, sugar, coffee and rubber planting attracted men from the West Indies, Mauritius and Ceylon, whilst miners had been in Australia and the USA.

From about the turn of the century, however, this flexibility disappeared. Well before this date recruits for administrative posts in the Straits and Malayan Civil Service (MCS) were selected by the Colonial Office on criteria based on superior social background and education (major public school, Oxford or Cambridge degree for preference), allied with good sporting abilities. As the functions of the bureaucracy multiplied there was a need for technically and professionally qualified men, such as doctors, engineers and research scientists. In the mining and planting industries the influx of corporate investment saw the replacement of the footloose pioneer by a class of salaried managers. During the boom periods demand for staff outran supply and posts were given to men of more modest social origins and without formal training in agriculture. This phase soon passed and by the interwar years employers had become more selective on both social and educational grounds. Managers themselves set up the Incorporated Society of Planters (1919) to improve their professional skills and standing through recognised courses in planting techniques, vernacular languages and so on. Recruitment was not completely impersonal, though, as personal contacts and introductions continued to play an important role especially in the larger agency houses and the banks (Drabble, 1973; Butcher, 1979; Parkinson, 1996).

From early in the nineteenth century the European community in Malaysia displayed a marked predilection for the formation of voluntary associations, partly for the maintenance of ethnic and social solidarity like the Chinese, but also for the promotion of economic interests. Thus we find the ubiquitous 'Club' in the towns and in the mining and planting districts, together with European Chambers of Commerce (Singapore, Penang, Sarawak, the FMS and so on.), planters' associations at district, state and federal level, with counterparts in the United Kingdom, notably the Straits Settlements Association, the

Rubber Growers' Association, Rubber Shareholders' Association, and so forth. In the official sphere the Straits Settlements Legislative Council (1867) and the FMS Federal Council (1909) provided unofficials (Europeans and fewer Asians) with a channel to represent their views to government (Drabble, 1973; Butcher, 1979).

The European community in Malaysia prior to the Second World War possessed a greater homogeneity in social terms and in its prevailing set of values than other ethnic groups. Another important characteristic was its transience. Very few ever came to regard the country as 'home', and after about 1900 social contacts with the Asian community in Malaya became much less frequent (Butcher, 1979, 49, 225–6). The situation was not fundamentally different in the much smaller European communities in the Borneo territories, although in Sarawak the Brooke family did have a permanent attachment, but Charles Brooke discouraged Europeans from bringing in wives, which led inevitably to local liaisons and the emergence of a Eurasian community (Lockard, 1987, 78–9).

The capacity of the Europeans as an elite likely to foster broad-based economic and social development in the longer term was inherently limited because the composition of the group was in a constant state of change (retirement to the home country was normally at the age of 55) and its function was confined within fairly inflexible roles. The officials came out to administer policies many of which were increasingly determined externally by the Colonial Office, whilst most of the mercantile, planting and mining personnel were employed by companies subject to direction from the metropolitan country (see Chapter 8).

6.3   Government and society

By the beginning of the twentieth century there had emerged in Malaysia a plural society in which the various ethnic groups occupied increasingly separate social and cultural spheres, and performed different economic functions. The latter is evinced in the distribution of occupations. In the first pan-Malayan census of 1911 just over half the economically active Malays are recorded as rice planters, whilst the leading occupation for Chinese was mining labourers (41 per cent), and for Indians agricultural labourers (56 per cent). Subsidiary occupations for Malays were coconut cultivation, fishing, atap-making, weaving and so on. Chinese grew fruit and vegetables, and provided carpenters, gardeners, domestic servants and traders to cater to the expanding urban population. Indians worked for the government on railways, road-making, cartage, watchmen (Snodgrass, 1980, Tables 2.3–2.5).

Similar data is not available for North Borneo and Sarawak, but on impressionistic grounds we can say that a broadly similar specialisation by race developed, with the indigenous peoples very largely engaged in subsistence agriculture, whilst the Chinese and Javanese migrants provided the workforce for export production and urban services, though some overlapping occurred as Iban and other indigenous groups moved into rubber cultivation.

Was this plural society and workforce in Malaya the outcome of conscious government policies ascribing roles and capitalising on ethnic separation to make overall control easier and to promote British economic interests? Such a viewpoint is expressed by Missen (1986, 74): 'the deliberate segregation of labour along racial lines by the British colonial government, support[ed] British capital, where different tasks were allotted to different groups within wage labour sectors'. British attempts to direct Malays towards subsistence agriculture (preferably rice cultivation) rather than rubber have also been interpreted similarly (T.G. Lim, 1977, 187, and 1984). Kratoska, on the other hand, argues that 'while the administration may have wished to ... manipulate the structure of the economy and the composition of the workforce, it did not have the capacity to do so' (1982, 314).

Both interpretations can be supported with historical evidence, but the debate has been affected to some degree by hindsight. Whilst government undoubtedly thought in terms of immigrant labour for the capitalist sector, and Malays for the subsistence sector, this distinction arose primarily out of a paternalistic desire to conserve the economic and social structures of the indigenous peoples against the full impact of commercial forces, rather than to serve only the narrow interests of foreign capital. We have seen (Chapter 2) that division of labour along ethnic lines had some of its origins prior to colonial rule. This can be seen in the growth of the mining industries, tin especially, which, having been increasingly undertaken by Chinese enterprise and labour, continued (almost inevitably it might be said) to draw workers of the same ethnic origin. Similarly the preference of European employers for Indian labour (regarded as more amenable to control) came from planters who had already formed this predilection from their experiences elsewhere (Mauritius, the West Indies).

As part and parcel of the bureaucratic system of government introduced by the British came the need to provide for health and education. Health came first in the utilitarian order of priorities as the pace of land development quickened from the 1870s. 'In the nineteenth century the Peninsula was one of the unhealthiest areas in the tropics' (Tate, 1979, 251). The principal diseases were malaria and beri-beri, together with smallpox, dysentery, typhus and pneumonia. The incidence of the first two soared as the large areas of cleared jungle created breeding grounds for the malarial mosquito, and immigrants from India and China lacked natural immunity. A preference for polished rice coupled with a generally poor diet, particularly among Chinese mineworkers, helped to create vitamin deficiency which heightened vulnerability to beri-beri. The worst period for malaria was roughly the decade c.1910–20, in which over 200 000 died in the FMS alone (Parmer, 1990, 181).

Particular years such as 1909 saw death rates among Indian labourers of 77.5 per thousand (nearly 8 per cent) in Perak, and 201.4 (20 per cent) in unhealthy Pahang. Periodic epidemics of other diseases were also highly destructive to human life: for example, a major influenza outbreak in 1918 pushed the death rate among FMS labourers in general to 48.3 per thousand (nearly 5 per cent: Houben, 1992, 22–3).

Government built the first hospital in the Malay states in 1878 (Taiping, Perak), followed shortly by Kuala Lumpur, Selangor. By 1895 these two states had 29 hospitals between them, but Negeri Sembilan and Pahang had five only. In addition to government buildings, hospitals were provided through private philanthropy, for example by Yap Ah Loy, Yap Kwan Seng, Loke Yew. Malays generally avoided seeking hospital treatment owing to religious restrictions on food. Town Sanitary Boards were established from the 1890s. As the numbers of estates multiplied rapidly in the early 1900s, employers provided rudimentary medical and hospital treatment (Chai, 1964, 198–200; C.Y. Lim, 1967, 309).

In 1900 the Institute for Medical Research was established in Kuala Lumpur. The Institute, originally intended to be independent, suffered from bureaucratic interference and from 1906 operated as a branch of the FMS Medical Department. One of the officers, Malcolm Watson, whose work was to lead by 1918 to the control of malaria through efficient drainage of pools and swamps, left the Institute in 1907 to work for European rubber estate interests who had a vital interest here. The FMS Government set up a Malaria Advisory Board in 1911, and then Malaria Destruction Boards. By 1920 death rates among FMS labourers were down to around 24 per thousand (2.4 per cent) (Chai, 1964, 201–3, 220–1; Houben, 1992, Table 6), which was less than one-third of the peak levels of the previous decade, though there was to be a resurgence as rubber planting picked up in the second half of the 1920s.

In relative terms, despite the programmes described above, government expenditure on health programmes did not rank very highly. Even in the SS which had an early start, the proportion rose only slightly from 7.1 per cent of total outlays in 1909 to 10.8 per cent in 1919, compared to 20.3 per cent up to 55.7 per cent for military purposes in the same period. Exactly comparable figures for the UMS are not available, but in Kedah in 1906 the share was 2.2 per cent, whilst in Kelantan and Terengganu no amounts were listed (Li, 1982, Tables 2.9, 2.12).

Neither Sarawak nor North Borneo achieved improvements in public health at all comparable to those in the most developed states in the Peninsula. In the former 'the role of the Brooke adminstration was limited by the vastness of the country, the poorness of communications, and above all by the scarcity of funds' (Tate, 1979, 277). Christian missionary organisations took the lead before about 1900. Very little was done outside Kuching. Sibu, the next largest town, had merely a 'converted shack' to serve as a hospital in 1913, without a modern drainage system until 1928. An epidemic of cholera in 1903 killed over 1000 people in the Second Division. In the rural areas medical care simply devolved onto the district officers (Tate, 1979, 278).

Health in North Borneo was, if anything, worse than in Sarawak, at least up to about 1913, reflecting the shaky condition of the Company's finances and also disinterest on the part of W.C. Cowie, Chairman until 1910. Conditions of 'wanton neglect' on the early estates led to death rates of up to 40 per cent, though self-interest on the part of employers and some pressure from government reduced these to 2.5 per cent by about 1910. Sir West Ridgeway, Cowie's successor, commissioned a report in 1912 after which a more systematic programme was undertaken (Tate, 1979, 301–2; Black, 1983, 113).

As the British established themselves in the SS, the first steps in education were of a mixed nature. The Penang Free School (1816) was set up mainly to produce an English-educated class for employment in government. The Anglo–Chinese College in Melaka (1818) was sponsored by the British Protestant Mission to China to spread Christianity, and to foster study of English and Chinese language and literature. The Singapore (or Raffles) Institute (1823) was founded by public subscription on the initiative of Raffles, who saw the school as a regional centre for education combining the study of local languages, culture and so on with western civilization, hopefully attracting the sons of the indigenous elites. Also in the 1820s Chinese dialect groups (Cantonese, Hokkien) set up vernacular schools in Singapore (Turnbull, 1972, 222–4; Andaya and Andaya, 1982, 226–7).

The results of these various activities were extremely modest. The Straits government kept a tight purse where education was concerned. The Malay elites were reluctant to send their sons to a foreign institution. Vernacular education, for example in a Chinese dialect, brought no social or economic advancement, whilst English-language instruction was wanted simply to gain employment with the European mercantile firms. Tamil schools in the Straits ports also proved unsuccessful. Orfeur Cavenagh, Governor of the SS 1859–67, was very disappointed over the 'entire apathy' exhibited by all classes towards education (cited in Turnbull, 1972, 232).

As British hegemony spread in the Peninsula the provision of education was complicated by the fact that only the Malay population had a normal age distribution. The school age cohort in other ethnic groups was small: for instance, in Selangor in 1901 only 7.5 per cent of all Chinese children were below fifteen years of age, in Perak 4.2 per cent (Chinese) and a somewhat higher 12.7 per cent for the Indian population (Chai, 1964, 228). English-language education was confined largely to the towns, but here Government efforts starting in the mid-1880s were less successful than Christian missionary schools up to about 1900. In vernacular education particular difficulty was encountered in persuading Malay parents to send their children to school, a major reason being the lack of Islamic instruction. Selangor and Negeri Sembilan passed laws in 1891 and 1900 respectively requiring all Malay males between 7 and 14 to attend, but Perak (which had the best record) did not do this until 1916. Total school attendance in the FMS in 1901 was only about 13 per cent of those eligible (calculated from Chai, 1964, 228).

The quality of the education, particularly in the vernacular schools, was poor. The supply of adequately trained teachers fell far short of the needs. The transience of Chinese society meant a scarcity of resident scholars. Rote learning was the dominant method. After the fall of the Ch'ing imperial dynasty in 1911, and the establishment of the Nationalist Republic in China, Mandarin (*kuo yu*) became the standard medium of instruction in Chinese vernacular schools which thus acquired a nationalistic ethos. Education in Tamil for the Indian workforce on European estates was rudimentary. In many cases teaching was done by one of the estate foremen (*kanganis*) or clerks, and pupils rarely stayed beyond about ten years of age as they could then earn wages to contribute to the family budget (Andaya and Andaya, 1982, 222–4). Many migrants, and some Malay parents, would have preferred English-medium education to be more widely available, but government policy was against this. As early as 1890 Swettenham, then Resident of Perak, warned that teaching English 'indiscriminately [to Malays] ... would only unfit them for the duties of life and make them discontented with anything like manual labour' (cited in Chai, 1964, 239). On a selective basis the Malay College at Kuala Kangsar, opened in 1905, was run along English public school lines to train the sons from elite families for employment in the Malay Administrative Service. Some upward mobility for non-Malays was provided through technical and industrial education in the Teacher Technical School set up in Kuala Lumpur (1905), but opportunities in this direction were as yet limited since the main areas of employment were in commerce (clerks, bookkeepers, typists: Chai, 1964, 258–60; Andaya and Andaya, 1982, 229).

The emerging Malayan educational system lacked unity of purpose, and the capacity to perform a leading function in economic development (Stevenson, 1975, 199). In the SS expenditure on education accounted for only 4.7 per cent of the total in 1909, and dropped to 3.8 per cent in 1920.

In Sarawak 'the Brookes ... stimulated more by example than by any policy or program, and this was certainly true with regard to education' (Pringle, 1971, 71). Raja Charles considered English-medium education to be destructive of the self-respect of the 'native'. Prior to the twentieth century formal education was left entirely to the Christian missions and to the initiative of the Chinese communities, with very small grants-in-aid from government. Chinese education was based entirely on the traditional Confucian system imported, along with teachers, from China, but most vernacular schools of the period were shortlived. The arrival of the Foochow migrants in 1901 brought some changes, representing a fusion of Christian missionary English and vernacular education, with each school having a small rubber garden to assist with running costs (Ooi, 1994, 519). Charles Brooke left the education of indigenous people entirely to mission schools, but these had little impact. 'In 1913, after sixty years of effort in the Second Division, SPG [Society for the Propagation of the Gospel] schools there had an enrolment of only thirty-three students. Yet this was the only province ... where Ibans enjoyed any regular access to education' (Pringle, 1971, 73).

7

Overview: The Colonial Export Economy *c*.1920

By about 1920 the structure of the colonial export economy was fully in place in terms of the leading commodities, the types of production (estates, mines, smallholdings), the basic infrastructure and the ethnic division of labour. The aim in the present chapter is to consider some central analytical issues, drawing together materials from Chapters 3 to 6.

7.1   A turning point for the economy

In the literature on economic growth there is considerable interest in the concept of a 'turning point' in a country's economic history, in the sense of a transition from a generally long period of extensive, mainly labour-intensive, growth to one of intensive growth in which output enters on a rising trend. In the period of extensive growth, output per capita and population increase at about the same annual rate, and in intensive growth output starts to outstrip population on a sustained basis, accompanied by 'systematic changes in the composition and uses of national output'. In the case of Malaysia (referring only to the Peninsula) Reynolds has designated 1850 as the turning point, though this is meant to cover the 'decade or so' on either side in order to indicate that growth was sustained (1986, 8, 32, 34). The principal indicator adopted was the upsurge in tin mining output from about the mid-century.

Table 7.1 presents two sets of estimates for the per capita output of tin in the Peninsula from 1835 onwards. A similar picture emerges from both. Production was declining or at best stagnant between 1835 and 1850, but grew some threefold to 1870. The latter period thus saw an annual average increase of about 6 per cent which was well ahead of population growth. The next 20 years to 1891 saw a slowing to 4.2 per cent, 1.64 per cent to 1901 and then a sharp drop to 1911 as the early deposits were worked out whilst population surged through immigration.

These data provide some support for Reynolds' criterion of rising per capita output after about 1850, but this did not mark intensive develop-

Table 7.1   Malaya: per capita output of tin; selected years (kg)

Year	A	B
1835	2.79	2.80
1850	1.67	3.06
1870	5.39	9.88
1891		23.56
1901		27.73
1911		20.67

Sources: Col. A: Tin production calculated from Wong Lin Ken (1965b, 30); population, mid-point figures from Dodge (1980, Table D).
Col B: Tin Production, 1835–70, Dodge (1977, Table 1); 1891–1911, Wong Lin Ken (1965b, 246); population, 1891, Dodge (1980); 1901, 1911, Lim Chong Yah (1967, 181–2).

ment on a very wide front. The significance of mining and the various agricultural industries at this point in time was as pathbreakers, stimulating infrastructural growth and preparing the way for the major expansion in rubber after the turn of the century.

As we have argued (Chapter 4.2), the advent of rubber cultivation restored the impetus to growth. Had tin remained the principal export, then, in default of further major ore discoveries, the economy could well have done into decline. Rubber, on the other hand, was a renewable resource. The initial expansion of the industry was extensive (rapid growth in planted acreage) rather than intensive, but the impact in terms of new forms of enterprise, investment by all ethnic groups, and the dispersal throughout so many regions of Malaysia, marked an irreversible step in the emergence of the export economy. In these decades, too, tin production staved off decreasing returns through the adoption of more capital-intensive techniques such as the dredge. The first two decades of the twentieth century, therefore, have a stronger claim to be regarded as a turning point for the economy of the Peninsula.

This rapid expansion was, however, a two-sided phenomenon. It brought rises in investment, employment and earnings to private and public interests, but at the same time tied the economy to a growth path which would take about half a century (up to the 1960s) to work through before another turning point, industrialisation, was reached. During that period the economy would be exposed to wide fluctuations in international primary commodity prices which 'created a divergence between *private* risk and *social* risk, with private risk-taking creating a social risk for the whole economy ... Colonial governments, however, generally did not concern themselves with this social risk' (Snodgrass, 1966, 67; italics original).

The foregoing argument applies to the Borneo territories to a lesser extent, since we have shown how North Borneo and Sarawak did not experience an export boom on the same scale as Malaya (Chapter 4.1), whilst in the latter state the Brookes were concerned about possible adverse economic and social consequences of large-scale capitalist enterprise. North Borneo had a very patchy growth record. Tobacco faded away after 1900, and neither rubber nor timber grew very rapidly. In Sarawak the long-term trends in the production of pepper, sago, gambier, rubber and so on were upwards but, again, not in really large volumes. The establishment of a petroleum industry just before the First World War was a high-bulk, low-value commodity which was a prime example of an enclave activity with few linkage effects.

7.2 A segmented economy

A paradigm widely used to describe the export economies which developed under colonial rule is that of a segmented, or unintegrated, structure. The usual model is that of a dual (or dualistic) economy in which a 'modern' sector with large, capital-intensive, specialised units of production, wage labour and advanced technology exists alongside a 'traditional' sector of small-scale, unspecialised producers (largely peasant farmers) using mainly household, non-wage, labour and low-level technology. The modern sector is dominated by foreign interests, whilst the traditional sector contains mostly indigenous farmers. Similar dichotomies have been discerned in the financial sector, the markets for labour, the administrative and fiscal system of government, and a 'sociological dualism' which contrasts 'rational' profit-maximising behaviour of (western) capitalist enterprises with 'irrational', non-profit oriented behaviour of indigenous producers (Myint, 1985, 24–5).

Several aspects of this paradigm were reflected in the structure of the Malaysian economy by the early twentieth century. There was a clear division into the foreign-owned, capital-intensive estates and mines sector, and the indigenous, labour-intensive, farming sector. In finance the modern sector had access to capital and credit at relatively low interest rates through the institutionalised system of banking and capital markets: for example, in the corporate flotation boom in tin and rubber. Indigenous producers had to rely on a network of moneylenders (principally the Chettiars), and local (usually Chinese) shopkeepers for loans and credit at high rates of interest. The market in labour for capitalist employers operated largely through the flows of migrants, whilst indigenous farmers used the labour of family members, supplemented by sharecroppers often from the same locality. In fiscal and administrative policies Governments distinguished between large-scale (foreign) enterprise, seen as the main driving force in commercial development, and the indigenous population, viewed primarily as subsistence agriculturalists. An example of the latter was the Malay Reservations Enactment (1913) in the FMS aimed at discouraging speculation by Malays in land planted with rubber trees (Chapter 4.3). The 'sociological' aspects of dualism can best be considered in the next chapter (8.2).

However, the dualism paradigm, whilst useful as an analytical device, tends to draw distinctions sharper than those observable in the historical situation in Malaysia at this time. The factor making a two-sector analysis unrealistic was the presence of immigrant Asian communities which, though foreign in origin, were becoming increasingly domesticated, and which constituted a layer between the unquestionably foreign western interests, whose ownership lay outside the country, and the indigenous population. In the rubber industry, for example, there was a continuum of holdings from the larger estates over 400 hectares (mostly European-owned), down through the medium-size estates (40–400 hectares) and the medium smallholdings (10–40 hectares) with Chinese predominant in both, and the 'true' smallholdings under 10 hectares, again with substantial Chinese ownership, but with Malays heavily in the majority under 2 hectares (Drabble, 1991, 2). Despite the difference in scale between the largest and smallest holdings (with the latter using more labour per hectare) there was no pronounced technological dualism in the industry at this stage. All producers used the same basic production technique (tapping, collection, coagulation, processing), and unselected (gathered at random) seeds for planting (Drabble, 1973, 208–10).

'Dualistic' is also an inappropriate way of describing the financial infrastructure (see Chapter 5.1), a mixture of foreign and local (Chinese) banks 'with its remarkable range of makeshifts [and] adaptations to need' (Huff, unpublished, 8). Again, the evidence is more suggestive of a continuum, through intermediaries such as the Chettiars, rather than a sharp separation.

There is a stronger case for technological dualism in tin mining, dating from the introduction of the dredge by British interests which created a distinct differentiation from the more labour-intensive Chinese mines, although 'technical change in both tin sectors has done little to alter their basic economic characteristics' (Thoburn, 1977, 209).

In another version of a segmented model, Silcock (1963, 1) describes colonial Malaya as 'not one economy but three'. This schema is based on differences in kind, and in geographical location: the mercantile sector centred on the Straits ports, the plantation and mining sector in the west coast states of the Peninsula, and the 'modified subsistence' (rice, fish, mixed farming) economy operated mainly in the northern and east coast states. The economies of North Borneo and Sarawak were not dissimilar, with the mercantile economies of the ports (Jesselton, Sandakan, Kuching), the export industries of the coastal regions and the subsistence-based groups in the interior, although in Sarawak's case the distinctions were perhaps less marked owing to the limited presence of large-scale capitalist enterprises in agricultural production.

Though the segmented models tend to over-emphasise the discontinuities, there is no doubt that the various sectors of the Malaysian economy of the early twentieth century were not interactive to any great extent. This was due principally to the orientation of much of the productive activity towards overseas markets, and the external (migrant) origins of a large proportion of the population. Overall, there was no strong domestic competition for resources, except perhaps for land in areas where export production was most heavily concentrated (e.g., Perak and Selangor).

7.3   The impact of colonial rule

The origins of some structural characteristics, as we saw in Chapter 2, had their origins before 1800, so that the growth of Malaysia's export economy cannot be seen simply as a consequence of colonial rule. In order to demonstrate the effect of the latter, we must show in what ways and, if possible, at what point in time this growth began to take on colonial characteristics: that is to say, the ways in which the major parameters in the economic affairs of these territories came to be determined by an extraneous political power, Britain, in the light of metropolitan interests which were not necessarily the same as local ones.

This process did not really commence in the Peninsula until after the SS came under direct rule from London in 1867, and the residential system was established in the Malay states from 1874 onwards. Chartered Company rule in North Borneo, and Brooke rule in Sarawak, as we saw in Chapter 3.2, are hard to categorise in the same sense in this period. Though both were subordinate to the metropolitan government in foreign relations, in economic respects the Company and the Brookes acted essentially like traditional rulers in generating income for their own use.

Imperial rule impinged in the SS in the form of a contribution to the costs of local defence. In the Peninsular Malay States the official view that the Malay sultans still ruled, but subject to British 'advice', proved largely a fiction. The establishment of the FMS in 1896 brought new layers of bureaucracy which removed the Malay rulers further from any real exercise of power (Sadka, 1968, xiv, 379). The leading edge of economic change can be seen in the new system of land tenure (Chapter 4.3) imposed to meet the needs of outside investors, British capital in particular, at long-term cost to Malay interests (T.G. Lim, 1976, 156–7).

Until about the turn of the century the Colonial Office in London left a good deal of discretion to the local administrations as far as the economy was concerned. This attitude began to alter with the currency reforms of 1906 (Chapter 5.1), and even more so with the rush of corporate investment in rubber (which can be seen as the most 'colonial' of the export industries, having been founded with planting material introduced by government) and tin in the first decade of the new century. The outbreak of the First World War in August 1914 found Malaysia with a crucial position in the world economy as the principal supplier of these products which, in the hostilities, assumed strategic significance. All such commodities were placed under the control of a Tin and Rubber Exports Committee sitting in London which issued an export licence only when satisfied that there was no possibility of a consignment reaching enemy hands. Furthermore, to conserve funds for the war effort United Kingdom-registered Malayan companies were barred from raising any fresh capital without Treasury permission (Drabble, 1973, 125–6).

In the later years of the war the British Cabinet instructed that in Malaya from July 1917 no further grants of land for rubber cultivation over 20 hectares should be given to non-British nationals apart from subjects of the Malay rulers and others resident locally for at least seven years. This resulted from fears that American manufacturing interests were trying to obtain large tracts of rubber land in the Peninsula which, if not checked, might ultimately threaten British dominance in the industry. Shortly afterwards, when in May 1918 America imposed a quota on imports of raw rubber (to conserve increasingly scarce shipping space), the British government – urged on by corporate interests – considered the imposition of compulsory restriction of rubber exports by all producers in order to reverse the resulting drop in prices. However, the end of hostilities in November 1918 rendered the proposal superfluous (Drabble, 1973, 134–46).

These episodes show that the economic interests of Malaya in particular were subordinated to metropolitan ones, though (as will be argued in the next chapter) this did not mean that the colonial government was simply a tool of business groups with investments in the region. The fact that the bulk of tin and rubber went to the USA made Malaya an increasingly valuable dollar earner for the sterling area, and tax revenue from Malayan companies registered in the United Kingdom was important to the Treasury. This value was also underlined by contributions to the Imperial war effort totalling £15 million from the SS, and £13 million from the FMS, plus the gift of a battleship, HMS *Malaya*, costing £2.25 million (Li, 1982, 30).

7.4   The material benefits

What were the results of the growth of the colonial export economy in terms of the distribution of benefits in society? It is not possible with data currently available to construct an annual time series for Malaysian national income (GDP) in this early period. However, van der Eng (1994) has made some preliminary calculations for the Asian region which are presented in Table 7.2. Given that the starting figure for 1900 (for Malaya only) is merely a 'guesstimate', the growth over the next three decades at 4.1 per cent a year on average was well above population growth at roughly 2.5. per cent (Table 6.1) and carried the country well clear of the rest of the region.

Table 7.2 GDP per capita: selected Asian countries, 1900–90 (1985 international dollars)

	1900		1929		1950		1973		1990
Burma	523		651		304		446		562
(Annual per cent)		0.8		3.6		1.7		1.4	
Thailand	594		623		652		1559		3694
		0.2		0.2		3.8		5.2	
Malaya/M'ysia[a]	600[b]		1910		1828		3088		5775
		4.1		−0.2		2.2		3.8	
Singapore	–		–		2276[c]		5372		14 441
						7.1[d]		6.0	
Indonesia	617		1009		727		1253		2118
		1.7		−1.5		2.4		3.4	
Philippines	735		1106		943		1629		1934
		1.4		−0.8		2.4		1.0	
South Korea	568		945		565		1782		6012
		1.8		−2.4		5.1		7.4	
Japan	724		1192		1208		7133		13 197
		1.7		0.1		8.0		3.7	

[a] Malaya to 1973.
[b] Guesstimate.
[c] 1960.
[d] 1960–73.
Source: van der Eng (1994), adapted from Tables 3, 4.

However, per capita GDP is not an entirely reliable guide to changes in the standard of living, especially for a country which has a high ratio of exports to GDP. In Malaya's case rubber and tin accounted for nearly 38 per cent of GDP in 1920 (calculated from data supplied by van der Eng). Burma had a ratio of 47 per cent, and the NEI 24 per cent in 1921–2 (Booth, 1990, Table 13). The average for OECD countries in 1913 was 21.2 per cent (Maddison, 1989, Table D-6). Changes in the terms of trade can have a correspondingly large effect on the international purchasing power of a country's exports. As we saw in Figure 3.1, Malaysia's commodity (or net barter) terms of trade had deteriorated substantially by the end of the war. Rubber, which had surpassed tin in value as the main export commodity from Malaya in 1916, was one of the few raw materials whose price deflated over the war period, with an index of 73.2 in 1920 (1913 = 100) (SS Government, 1926, Table X). But this unit price fall was offset by the very large expansion in output from 6500 tonnes in 1910 to 204 000 tonnes in 1919 (Drabble, 1973, Appendix VII) with a corresponding jump in export earnings; thus the income terms of trade improved slightly.

The increase in commercial activity and expansion in production presented three main types of opportunity for income growth: (i) the acquisition of commercially valuable assets (e.g., land, real estate) which could be disposed of for windfall profits or retained to produce an income stream which would enable further asset accumulation; (ii) wage-earning occupations; (iii) a range of ancillary activities (e.g., supply of foodstuffs, local transport, general contracting and retail businesses). How well placed were the various groups in society to capture some of the benefits?

We saw in Chapter 4.1 that prior to the tin and rubber boom export production was relatively small in quantity. The mercantile economy of the Straits ports was the main centre of income growth. As tin production increased in the Peninsular Malay states from around the mid-century, district chiefs were the principal indigenous beneficiaries from levying taxes on goods in transit. Soltow (1983) and Gullick (1989) have argued that substantial material inequality existed in Malay society at this time between the elite and the *rakyat*, and among the latter, between freemen and slaves. 'Debt bondage was born of the desperate financial need of the peasant class ... yet, for good or ill, it was a personal, not an economic relationship, based on political status' (Gullick, 1989, 212–13). The progressive abolition of debt slavery by the colonial administrators from the 1880s actually worsened the immediate economic position of those released, as their former owners no longer had the obligation to house and feed them, they had no land, and wage employment was still relatively scarce. The former district chiefs, too, lost much of their former income by the end of the century. In general, though, 'the real wage from subsistence farming was relatively good, and rural life was not unpleasant' (Drake, 1979, 284).

It was the rush to take up, and in many cases then sell, rubber land which brought commercialism into the heart of village society. This proved such a remunerative activity that in many areas along the west coast of the Peninsula, Malays (local and immigrant) shifted much of their work effort away from subsistence crops such as rice. Even those who lacked sufficient land for subsistence could fare significantly better as sharecroppers on rubber smallholdings than as estate wage workers. In 1920 a sharecropper on a 2 hectare holding receiving 50 per cent of the output (*bagi dua*) averaged $31 per month against $17 for an estate tapper. Owner-operators of holdings 'would have earned at least 150 per cent of the sharetappers return' (Barlow, 1990, 31, 34), as well as enjoying living and health conditions superior to those on estates.

Some Malay rulers had had personal ventures in agriculture (tea, coffee, cocoa, coconuts, for instance) and mining prior to the rubber boom, and several (e.g., in Negeri Sembilan and Johor) took up the new crop, though their properties were not managed very efficiently. As accumulators of wealth their success varied greatly. Two extremes in 1918 were the Sultan of Selangor who had a bank overdraft of $167 000, and the Sultan of Perak whose assets at his death totalled $950 000. It was difficult to keep such estates together, since Islamic law required division among surviving heirs, in the latter case six sons, seven daughters and three widows (Gullick, 1992, 212–13).

Data are sparse on the income-earning capacity of Malays living outside the main rubber-growing regions, for example in Perlis, the interior of Kelantan, and Terengganu, but it would appear to have been relatively low. Evidence from Perlis in the 1930s indicated poverty and undernourishment in families with cash incomes of only $3–6 per month (Drabble, 1991, 137).

Profitable though rubber growing was, it was not a total gain to indigenous Malays since there was an offsetting effect from previous activities given up either voluntarily (rice growing), or largely discontinued due to competition from new sources of goods. The major example of the latter was traditional handicrafts such as textiles which were undercut by cheaper imports.

On the basis of respective shares in production, the bulk of the proceeds from export production in Malaya both prior to and following the advent of rubber went to non-indigenous groups. The principal gainers were those who had control of productive assets, mines and estates, and here the outstanding factor was the increasing element of foreign ownership which in turn employed the growing force of wage labour.

In neither the tin nor the rubber industry were workers able to share proportionately in the big rises in labour productivity, especially in the second decade of the twentieth century. Between 1910 and 1920 annual tin output per worker rose from 0.25 tonnes to 0.32 tonnes (Yip, 1969, 383), or 28 per cent, but the monthly money wage per capita fell from $13.37 in 1913 to $9.56 in 1915, recovering to $14.40 in 1918 and falling heavily to $7.25 in 1920 (calculated from Yip, 1969, Table V-18, 384; Thoburn, 1977, Table 5.18). Estate rubber production remained more labour-intensive than tin mining. Annual output per worker soared from a mere 0.05 tonnes in 1910 to 0.84 tonnes in 1920 (calculated from Drabble, 1973, 220–1, 226). This resulted from higher yields as the trees increased in age, and not from major technological change. The average monthly wage showed a sharp rise from $6 in 1910 to $10.30 in 1911 when competition for labour for newly opened estates was strong, followed by fluctuations peaking at $13.90 in 1918 and dipping slightly to $12.40 in 1920. In addition, the imputed value of labour benefits such as free housing added a further $2–2.50 per month (Thoburn, 1977, 285). Thus, estate labour seems to have maintained and possibly slightly improved its position, but in no way proportional to the rise in productivity. The ready supply of fresh workers from India and China undoubtedly acted to keep upward pressure on money wages in check.

The discussion thus far has been about nominal wages/incomes. The unit cost of rice imported into the FMS showed no major increase after 1900 until after the end of the war when poor harvests and speculative buying in the countries from which most supplies came (notably Burma) caused costs to triple in 1920, though government subsidised the market price to lessen popular discontent, leading to a loss of $21 million (Drabble, 1973, 170n.; Kratoska, 1990, 139). Unit costs of cotton piece goods went from $3.18 in 1916 to $7.34 in 1919 and $12.76 in 1920 (calculated from Abdullah Azmi, 1981, Table 1.8). The Controller of Labour, Penang, estimated that the general cost of living had risen more in 1919 than in the previous four years whilst wages were only 30 to 40 per cent above 1914 levels (cited in Drabble, 1973, 159). In Singapore the cost of living index on the 'Asiatic Standard' had more than doubled (100 to 209) between 1914 and 1920, and somewhat less (100 to 180) on the 'European Standard' (Malaya, 1930, Table XXIII).

The share of export production going to capital in the shape of profits and dividends rose during the second decade. Using data from Khor (1983, 56–7), and Thoburn (1977, 108) it appears that between 1913 and 1920 the share of foreign (i.e., mainly sterling capital) company profits in the total value of tin exports from the FMS increased from 11.96 to 22.62 per cent. Dividends paid on issued capital rose from 9 to 17 per cent (Yip, 1969, 141). Among rubber companies dividend levels had declined from the spectacularly high rates paid by some of the pioneer flotations during the 1909–10 boom. However, the bulk of profits was still absorbed in this way. A sample of 56 sterling companies paid out just over 77 per cent of net profits on average over the decade 1912–22 (Drabble, 1973, 63; 1991, Table 2.3).

The overall picture which emerges is one of considerable elasticity in the proportion of export income going to foreign interests, and thus available for remittance overseas, as against a stickiness in the share going to labour (whose savings remitted to homelands were also a source of 'leakage'). However, Thoburn (1977, 250–1), in an analysis stretching from the late nineteenth century to the early 1970s, has found that both the Malayan tin and rubber industries were characterised by a high 'retained value' (the proportion of export revenue remaining in the country) in excess of 70 per cent for foreign-owned sectors, higher still for domestically-owned (principally Chinese) ventures, and highest of all for indigenous smallholdings.

It is not possible to construct a similar quantitative analysis of North Borneo and Sarawak in this period. However, it is not unreasonable to infer that their experience was broadly similar to Malaya, though not on the same scale or at the same magnitude of growth. There was no comparably large mining sector, but foreign-owned estates in North Borneo followed a low wage policy, and there was a dependence on imported foodstuffs (principally rice) and manufactures (textiles). Given that the production of items such as forest products, pepper, gambier, sago and much of the rubber was in the hands of locally-domiciled producers, we may conclude that a substantial proportion of the export value (with the exception of the oil industry in Sarawak) was retained in the country.

How far this was translated into a general improvement in living standards is difficult to quantify. For the indigenous peoples this would have depended very much on the extent of their contacts with the commercial economy. In Borneo these were strongest along the coastal regions, as manifest in rubber cultivation (and lesser crops such as pepper, coconuts and sago), and more marginal in the interior where subsistence agriculture and the collection of forest products still went hand in hand. Health conditions, as we have seen, were generally poor. In both these territories economic development had not so far penetrated the interior to any great extent, and in North Borneo's case replicated the contrast between the east and west coasts of the Malay Peninsula.

In the Peninsula the main impact of expanded production and improved infrastructure was felt on the west coast. The east coast had relatively isolated pockets of export activity, small scale for the most part (apart from the large Duff Company concession in Kelantan), and traditional industries (metalwares, textiles, prawn paste and so on), though as noted above the latter had lost much of their former vigour. All of this was a considerable range of activity, but it represented a truncated role in the economy for indigenous groups, with the supra-village linkages very largely in the hands of other ethnic groups.

Part II

Depression, War and the Advent of Independence (1920–63)

8
The Interwar Years (1920–41)

8.1 Malaysian trade and the international economy

> Between 1913 and 1950 the tropics passed through a long depression,
> associated with world wars and adverse terms of trade. The rate of growth
> of tropical trade [volume] fell to 2.2 per cent per annum between 1913
> and 1955 [compared to 3.6 per cent between 1883 and 1913].
>
> (Lewis, 1969, 8)

Whereas for much of the nineteenth and early twentieth centuries these
countries had experienced the external stimulus of rising demand for
primary commodities, engendering a major expansion in productive
potential, they now entered a period in which demand fluctuated very
strongly, leading to extended periods of slump (1920–22, 1929–32) which
revealed substantial excess in supply capacity. However, the situation in
the interwar years was not continually adverse. There was a recovery
following the 1920–22 downturn, led by the US economy, which created
boom conditions in the mid-1920s.

During the war the loss of markets in Europe for primary commodities
was more than offset by growing demand in North America. When the war
ended, industrial production in both Europe and the USA (which had
entered the war in 1917) was quickly switched from military to peacetime
goods, which helped to employ millions of demobilised soldiers, but
consumer demand outran supply and by March 1919 'a boom of astonish-
ing dimensions' (Lewis, 1966, 18) had developed. The effects of this on
Malaysia's leading exports, tin and rubber, in terms of market prices were
muted. In the case of rubber average prices actually fell slightly in 1919
(Figure 8.1), but with the lifting of wartime restrictions on shipping space,
output and exports from Malaya nearly doubled over 1918 so that
aggregate earnings were much higher.

By the early part of 1920 adverse factors were beginning to affect the
boom. The international situation was unsettled by the overhanging

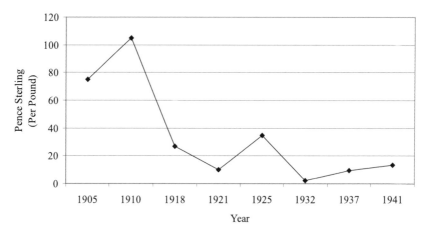

Figure 8.1   Average London rubber prices, 1905–41
Sources: Drabble (1973; 1991, Appendix I).

question of the war reparations settlement to be imposed on Germany by the victorious allies (Britain, France, USA). In April 1920 a conference of the allied governments decided on deflationary policies, namely a rise in interest rates and restriction of credit to check inflation. The boom quickly dissipated, with manufacturers cutting back on output and employment. Purchase orders for raw materials dwindled, with a resultant fall in prices. Rubber, for example, slumped from an average of approximately 25 *d.* (10p) per pound in 1919 to 9.5*d.* (4p) in 1922 (Figure 8.1). The price of tin also dropped heavily from $151 per picul (60.6 kilograms) to $81 in the same period.

Primary producing countries, such as Malaysia, were faced with a situation in which export earnings not only fell heavily in the short term (see Figure 8.2), but their major industries, which had expanded with varying degrees of rapidity in the previous two decades, appeared now to have productive capacities quite out of line with foreseeable demand in the industrialised countries. At the same time the prices of imported goods stood at relatively high levels. This was particularly marked for foodstuffs such as rice, which accounted for approximately 28 per cent of Malaysian imports by value in 1919. As a result both the commodity and income terms of trade showed a steep fall, the former by nearly 75 per cent and the latter 51 per cent between 1919 and 1921 (see Figure 8.3).

Due to the widespread geographical distribution of production for export, particularly rubber, the slump had a much more extensive effect than the earlier fluctuations. The most general characteristic of the slump

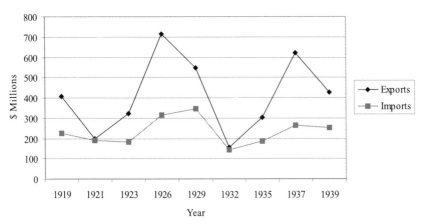

Figure 8.2   Malaysia: exports and imports values, 1919–39 (current values)
Sources: SS *Blue Books; AR FMS; AR UMS; AR North Borneo Customs Dept; AR Sarawak Treasury, Post, Shipping and Customs Office; AR Sarawak Dept of Trade and Customs,* various years.

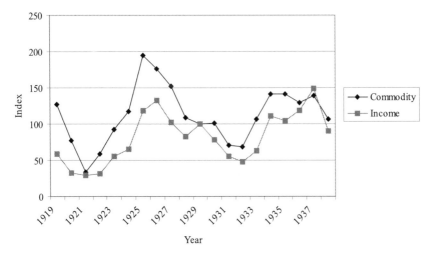

Figure 8.3   Malaysia: terms of trade, 1919–39 (1929 = 100)
Sources: SS *Blue Book 1920–39; AR FMS 1920–39; AR UMS 1928–39; Statistical Abstracts for Brit. Overseas Dominions, No. 57 (1926); Statistical Abstracts for Brit. Empire No. 60 (1929); 68 (1938), 70 (1946); AR North Borneo Customs Dept 1920–30; AR Sarawak Dept of Trade and Customs 1925–40; SS Average Prices and Declared Trade Volume 1925; Malaya: Av. Prices Declared Trade Values, Exchange, Currency 1930, 1939.*

was a slowing down in the circulation of money and goods, as the channels along which these moved became clogged. The British agency houses had ordered heavily from their suppliers in Europe with the result that large shipments were arriving in 1920 as market values started to decline under the deflationary policies. The firms were thus caught with substantial quantities of goods already out in the market in the hands of dealers who found them increasingly difficult to dispose of within the normal period of credit. Producers of primary products found it difficult to reduce output and exports, and thus world markets were dampened by a build-up of stocks: for example, rubber stocks in 1922 were estimated as equivalent to twelve months' consumption as against the eight months considered normally sufficient for the requirements of the trade. The colonial government's response to the economic problems was to adopt a more interventionist role in the economy, notably in the restriction of rubber exports from November 1922–October 1928 (see section 8.2).

After 1922 the international economy experienced a resurgence. The USA, the main customer for Malaysian rubber and tin, recovered quite quickly and entered an extended period of prosperity which lasted until late 1929. World commodity prices rose to peaks in 1925–6 (Figure 8.1), generating record levels of export earnings (Figure 8.2). Imports were slower to increase, doubtless due to the need to clear existing stocks accumulated during the slump, leading very probably to the adoption of a cautious policy by importers.

The effects of this boom on patterns of investment and general living conditions in Malaysia are dealt with later in this chapter, but in the present context of trade benefits there appears to have been a substantial increase in general levels of liquidity particularly in Malaya, where the value of currency in circulation went from $85.4 million at the beginning of 1925 to $153.4 million by the year end, climbing to just over $163 million in 1926 (Straits Settlements, 1926, Table XIV). An estimated $10 million to $50 million in 'idle money', awaiting some form of permanent investment, was thought to be in mainly Chinese hands by the end of 1926 (Whittlesey, 1931, 117).

The onset of the Great Depression from October 1929 brought to a close a period of overall growth in Malaysian export volumes at an annual average rate well above that of its Southeast Asian neighbours, and for tropical trade as a whole (Table 8.1). The depression began with the collapse of speculative activity in stocks and shares (though this was not the sole cause) which had been gathering pace in the USA since 1926, creating a false impression of lasting prosperity. By 1932 the US national income had contracted by 38 per cent. Because of the importance of America as a producer of manufactured goods and consumer of primary commodities the effects spread rapidly through the international trading system. Production of raw materials continued at rather higher levels, but this

Table 8.1   Southeast Asia: comparative rates of export volume growth, 1915–40

| | *Per cent per annum* | |
	1915–30	1930–40
Burma	2.3	3.0
Indochina	n.a.	3.4
Indonesia	6.9	0.1
Malaysia	8.6	1.9
Philippines	6.9	2.7
Thailand	3.0	2.0
All tropical trade	3.1 (1913–29)	1.6 (1929–37)

n.a. = not available
Note: 5-year averages.
Sources: Southeast Asia, Booth (1991), Table 4; Tropical trade, calculated from Lewis (1969), Table 11.

meant that supply in many instances constantly tended to outstrip demand, with resultant lower prices.

Malaysia's high degree of exposure to the US industrial economy (which took approximately 43 per cent by value of gross merchandise exports from Malaya in 1929), meant that the depression struck with particular force (Figure 8.2). Between 1929 and 1932 Malaya's export earnings plummeted from $546 million to $157 million, or 73 per cent, those of Sarawak from $35 million to $14 million (60 per cent), and North Borneo from $12 million to $6 million (50 per cent). However, the Malaysian export volume index (Table 8.2) declined by only 22 per cent as producers were reluctant to cut output.

The aggregate value of Malaysian imports also fell heavily between 1929 and 1932 by an average of roughly 60 per cent. Though these falls were proportionately less than for exports, the balance of visible trade remained positive, Malaya having a small import surplus only in 1931, offset by continuing Sarawak/North Borneo export surpluses (data from Figure 8.2).

In the face of increasing surplus stocks of tin and rubber on the world markets, official policy in Malaysia once again opted for control through restriction of exports of tin (from 1931) and rubber (from June 1934), as the remedy for the problem of excess capacity in these industries (section 8.2).

World trade recovered from 1933 onwards, but more slowly than world production. Total tropical trade volume grew at only 1.62 per cent a year between 1929 and 1937 (Table 8.1). None the less, the higher market prices resulting from the controls just mentioned certainly assisted a recovery in Malaysian export earnings, which more than tripled between 1933 and 1937 (Figure 8.2). The terms of trade, too, showed a recovery from 1933 (Figure 8.3). As a foretaste of future trends, though, industrial consumers were constantly developing ways of economising on the use of natural raw

Table 8.2   Malaysia: Export volume, 1919–40 (1929 = 100)

Year	Index	Year	Index
1919	45	1930	97
1920	42	1931	89
1921	38	1932	78
1922	48	1933	83
1923	46	1934	92
1924	45	1935	80
1925	54	1936	88
1926	66	1937	113
1927	62	1938	79
1928	74	1939	80
1929	100	1940	124

Sources: Calculated from Abdullah Azmi (1981), Tables 2.5, 2.6; Jomo (1988), 158–9; Barlow (1978), 444; McFadyean (1944), 226–9; *AR North Borneo Customs Dept*, various years; *AR Sarawak Customs Dept*, various years; *UN Statistical Yearbook*, 1948; Yuen (1974); Lim Chong Yah (1967), Appendix 5.2.

materials (e.g., a rayon-cord tyre with up to 50 per cent longer life) thus raising doubts about continuing expansion in long-term demand. The decade ended with the outbreak of war in Europe in 1939 which caused a rush to build up stocks of strategic raw materials, boosting export output and earnings, though still well short of the peaks in the 1925–6 boom (Figure 8.2). Both the net barter and income terms of trade showed marked recovery from 1933 onwards, with import prices remaining relatively stable (Figure 8.3).

The commodity composition of imports is usually a fair guide to domestic activity within a country. In the case of the FMS the principal change during the interwar years was a switch in the relative importance of foodstuffs (including drink and tobacco) and manufactures. In 1920 the first group constituted approximately 55 per cent of total imports, and the second 36 per cent. In 1940 the proportions were practically reversed at approximately 42 and 53 per cent respectively. This reflects a slower rate of population growth after the Great Depression, increased domestic food production, and some capital expansion in the tin and rubber industries in the 1920s leading to increased imports of machinery and other capital items which peaked at $14.6 million, or roughly 7.8 per cent of total FMS imports in 1928 (Abdullah Azmi, 1981, 326–7).

Imports in the Borneo territories showed a similar trend, though North Borneo remained more dependent on imported foodstuffs and did not receive much developmental stimulus by way of trade.

Singapore remained the prime focus of Malaysian trade during this period. Commerce in many of the region's earlier products (e.g., gambier, gutta percha, rattans) stagnated or declined between about 1910 and 1940, but was more than replaced by rubber and petroleum which accounted for nearly 57 per cent of Singapore merchandise exports in 1937/8 (Huff, 1994, Tables 3.1, 3.3).

The dominance of the predominantly British, business houses over Malaysia's international trade (Chapter 3.5) remained generally undiminished during the interwar decades, but some developments indicated that this might not continue indefinitely. A major new element consisted of growing competition from lower-priced Japanese goods, notably cotton textiles which soared from 18 per cent of Malayan imports in 1925 to 69 per cent in 1933. British cottons declined from 58 per cent to 20 per cent in the same period (Jomo, 1988, 146). There was also increased competition from Japanese shippers for a larger share of oceanic trade, principally the carriage of rubber to the USA.

Some mercantile interests pressed for the imposition of import quotas, but leading firms were firmly of the view that the traditional free-trade status of the Straits ports must be maintained. For the same reason they also opposed an official proposal in the early 1930s for a customs union covering the entire Malay Peninsula. However, in 1933 the metropolitan British government imposed quotas on Japanese goods in most colonies, including Singapore. By 1937 their share in textiles had fallen back to 36 per cent. Thereafter Japanese commercial interests were adversely affected by boycotts following the outbreak of war in China.

An important consequence of Japanese competition was that Asian merchant firms were able to order directly through an agency in Singapore, thus bypassing the intermediary role of the European agency houses. Another development which contributed towards the changes in the commercial scene at this time was the establishment of local sales offices by major western manufacturers, such as Firestone, Pirelli (tyres), Ford and Fiat (cars), Kodak (films) and Singer (sewing machines) (Huff, 1994, 267–70).

Courtenay (1972, 133) makes the point that in the interwar years Malaya (and *pari passu* the Borneo territories) was 'governed as part of a much wider trading empire rather than as an independent unit'. We shall now look at the major instances of this policy in the export restriction schemes imposed on the rubber and tin industries.

8.2 Commodity control schemes

There were two ways in which export producers could attempt to cope with the major economic fluctuations described in the previous section. First, they could maximise output, take the prices determined by open market forces, and hope to cover at least fixed operating costs until supply and demand came back into balance. Second, they might seek to manipulate the market through collective action to reduce output so that surplus stocks could be absorbed more rapidly, with prices rising as consumers placed fresh orders.

The problem for capitalist enterprises was that restriction of output led to increased unit costs. If these rises were not more than offset by higher market prices, restriction would be counter-productive. Smallholders had low cash costs of production and few fixed overheads, but reduced output would cut incomes, causing difficulty in paying off credit or loans.

For these reasons a sufficiently wide measure of voluntary agreement to restrict output proved extremely difficult to obtain. This had been attempted by European rubber estate interests in 1918 (see Chapter 4.1), but virtually no support was forthcoming from Asian estate owners or smallholders.

Voluntary restriction of output was again attempted in the 1920–2 slump, but once more European interests failed to elicit sufficient support. A decision to impose export restriction on all producers in Ceylon and Malaya (together accounting for 65 per cent of world output) was not announced by the metropolitan British government until late in 1922. This was made not in the narrow interests of British capital, but from a wider imperial perspective. As Winston Churchill (Secretary of State for the Colonies) minuted, 'by making the Americans pay' higher rubber prices, the sterling–US dollar exchange rate could be stabilised (cited in Drabble, 1973, 193). The Dutch government declined to restrict NEI rubber exports, most probably due to fears that the rapidly expanding 'native' rubber producers (as NEI smallholders were known) in the Outer Islands could not readily be controlled. Thus the Stevenson restriction scheme (named for its originator) was implemented in Ceylon and Malaya from 1 November 1922, with British-owned estates in the NEI and North Borneo volunteering to observe similar restraints.

The central principle underlying export restriction was, first, to determine a country's aggregate output, or Standard Production (SP), under open market conditions. This was then distributed among individual producers according to an official formula. Each quarter (three months) government announced the percentage of SP which could be produced and exported. The deterrent to producing in excess of this quota was a prohibitive rate of export duty. Changes in the level of quota were linked to market prices; a rise would permit a higher quota in the following quarter, and a fall the reverse. The aim of the Stevenson scheme was to stabilise prices at a 'pivotal' level, set initially at 1s. 3d. (6p) per pound, raised later to 1s. 9d. (9p), a level thought sufficient to allow a 'reasonable' margin of profit. Over the six years of operation exports were restricted to an average of about two-thirds of SP.

The scheme was successful in raising price levels to near the desired level in the first two years, but due to administrative inflexibility failed to release enough rubber to meet a sudden expansion in American demand in 1924–5. This led to a buying 'panic' which pushed prices to high levels (see Figure 8.1). The boom brought new British corporate investment into Malaya, and also attracted strong interest from smallholders there as well as in northern Borneo, and in particular the NEI where swidden cultivators in southern Sumatra and southwest Borneo put hundreds of thousands of hectares under rubber.

The second half of the scheme (1926–8) was decreasingly effective, with prices falling back to near prerestriction levels (Figure 8.1). By 1928 Malaya and Ceylon were losing their comparative advantage, with their share of world output down to 53 per cent. The British government, increasingly apprehensive that restriction was locking these territories into heavily reduced output whilst others (notably the NEI) were free to produce unrestricted, decided to end the scheme from 1 November 1928 (Drabble, 1991, 13–18).

Freed from controls, Malaysian rubber exports surged from approximately 315 000 tonnes in 1928 to 480 000 tonnes (96 per cent from Malaya) in 1929. But, as we saw in the previous section, conditions deteriorated quickly from the end of that year as the Great Depression took hold. As rubber prices crashed even more disastrously than in 1920–22 (Figure 8.1), European estate interests urgently requested the reimposition of compulsory export restriction, this time with NEI participation as essential for success. Governments were reluctant to become involved again, but by 1932–33 there was a growing awareness that the vast expansion of smallholder interests from about 32 per cent of the world planted area in 1922 to nearly 47 per cent by 1929 was altering the balance in the industry. European owners feared that any price recovery would be choked off by a flood of smallholder output well before a level profitable to most estates could be reached. There was widespread apprehension that the industry might 'go native' (Drabble, 1991, ch. 6).

The intergovernmental negotiations which resulted in the International Rubber Regulation Agreement (IRRA) took over four years partly because of the need to involve all producing territories of any note (Malaysia, Ceylon, India, Burma, NEI, French Indo-China, Thailand), and partly because of the enormous difficulties which the Dutch faced in working out a means of controlling smallholder production (there was no system of registered land titles, or accurate details of planted areas, in much of the Outer Islands).

The first IRRA covered the period 1 June 1934–31 December 1938, and was renewed for five years to 1943. The basic export quota system of the Stevenson scheme was retained, but no specific price level was targeted (to minimise vulnerability to American criticism). Another major difference was that no new planting of rubber (apart from a small amount in 1939–40) was permitted, to prevent any recurrence of the 1925–6 planting explosion, and replanting was limited under the first IRRA. Overall, the scheme was more successful in raising prices without the extremes which had marred its predecessor (Figure 8.1). Export quotas over the $7\frac{1}{2}$ years up to the outbreak of war in the Pacific averaged about 75 per cent of SP, though Allied stockpiling during the final year (1941) brought the *de facto* removal of restriction with quotas raised to 120 per cent in the last quarter (Drabble, 1991, 21–4). Malaysia's major industry, rubber, was thus under official control for 13 1/2 years, or well over half the two interwar decades.

Events in the Malayan tin industry followed a slightly different pattern in that the 1920–2 slump did not lead to restricted exports. Official intervention took the form of purchases of tin at a price sufficient to enable marginal (mainly Chinese) mines to stay in production and obviate any possibility of discontent among the workforce. The FMS government bought up some 10 000 tonnes at a cost of nearly $19 million. The NEI government took similar action, and the two administrations jointly formed the Bandoeng Pool to hold these stocks until prices improved. When sales were effected in 1924 the FMS government reaped a profit of over half a million dollars. Tin prices, like rubber, soared in the mid-1920s and brought an influx of capital, mostly British, much of which went into the dredging sector where numbers operating went from 20 in 1920 to 105 in 1929, which gave Europeans the major share (61 per cent) in production (Yip, 1969, 154, 157; Baldwin, 1983, 65–7).

As the Great Depression arrived, it appeared that much of the new investment in tin during the 1920s, not only in Malaya but also in the NEI, Nigeria and Bolivia, had resulted in surplus productive capacity. As with rubber, miners turned to output control. Because there were far fewer tin producers and ownership was much more concentrated, especially among European mines with large interlocking groups (in Malaya the Anglo-Oriental Mining Corporation was formed in 1928), combined measures were relatively easy to organise. None the less, a voluntary restriction scheme in 1930 failed for lack of support. The next step was to request government intervention to formulate a scheme for international control somewhat like the IRRA. The negotiation period was much shorter, a matter only of months, so that the scheme began in March 1931 (Yip, 1969; Baldwin, 1983).

There were three successive international agreements to control output and exports of tin during the 1930s: 1931–3, 1934–6, 1937–41. As with rubber, each one allotted the signatory countries (Malaya, NEI, Thailand, Nigeria, Bolivia) a standard tonnage on which export quotas were based. The overall results were satisfactory for producers. Excessive price fluctuations were avoided, and over the period 1932–41 the London tin price averaged £217 per long ton against £155 from 1929 to 1931. However, Malaya was considerably under-assessed by possibly 20 per cent in its basic tonnage because this was based on production in 1929 when many of the newly installed dredges had not reached full operation. The shortfall impinged particularly severely on small, labour-intensive mines, mostly Chinese-owned, of which at least 14 per cent had to close down in these years (Yip, 1969, 208). This did not lead to reduced productive capacity for the industry. The closed mines sold their quota share to larger ones. Many were also re-equipped with machinery and re-opened. Chinese interests particularly increased their stake in gravel pump mines which rose from 260 in 1931–3 to 733 in 1940, but the average mine size remained small. The industry's large rise in total output from 35 000 tonnes in 1931–3 to 82 000 tonnes in 1940 (with restriction effectively removed) was largely achieved by bringing to full capacity the dredges installed in the 1920s. In 1940–1 European mines accounted for 72 per cent of output (Yip, 1969, 208, 257–60).

The restriction schemes in both rubber and tin were extensively criticised both at the time and subsequently. The US government depicted rubber restriction as a blatant attempt by the western colonial powers to wrest monopoly profits from control of most of the producing territories. However, a total monopoly was never in prospect. In the 1920s the non-adherence of the NEI effectively undercut the Stevenson scheme. In the 1930s the IRRA, when fixing export-quotas, had to take account of the strong pressure from America manufacturers for an adequate supply of rubber at reasonable prices (Drabble, 1991, ch. 6).

Another trenchant criticism was that by raising prices above the open market equilibrium level, restriction precluded a competitive 'shakeout' in which the least efficient producers would have been forced out of these industries and surplus capacity thus eliminated. This point had particular resonance because the structural divide into estates and smallholdings, and large and small mines, largely coincided with the pattern of ethnic owner-ship, broadly European and Asian respectively (Chapter 4.2). This was given further force by complaints that the formulas by which SP was calculated discriminated against Asian producers with the result that their export quotas were inequitably low relative to those allotted to European enterprises. Furthermore, since production of these commodities was spread over several countries, restriction prevented low-cost producers, such as Malayan tin mines, rubber smallholders and NEI 'native' rubber, from maximising their competitive advantage (see Yip, 1969, 264–84; T.G. Lim, 1977).

These criticisms have considerable force. Without compulsory restriction some proportion of producers in all categories would undoubtedly have been eliminated. In rubber the smallholding sector would probably have gained ground at the expense of estates, and in tin the low-cost dredging sector over gravel-pump and open-cast mines, but the likely magnitude of such structural shifts remains speculative. Under-assessment of rubber smallholding SPs in both schemes is indisputable, though the author argues elsewhere (Drabble, 1991, ch. 5) that this was not as proportionately severe as other scholars have suggested.

Did the Borneo territories have different interests from Malaya under rubber restriction? The arguments are hypothetical but Sarawak in particular, with its high proportion of smallholdings (see Table 4.1) which suffered severely from under-assessment, could perhaps have survived rather better at lower average prices for rubber, but ultimately would have faced the need for progressive replanting. However, North Borneo and Sarawak, which together exported only 53 000 tonnes of rubber in 1940, carried no weight against the major producers, Malaya (553 000 tonnes) and the NEI (547 000 tonnes), in the deliberations leading up to the IRRA.

In the short term, restriction helped to alleviate some economic and social distress in Malaysia (see section 8.7), but in the longer term it lessened pressure on producers to adopt new cost-reducing technologies. This was most evident in the rubber industry in Malaya where, by 1941, a large proportion of the trees were nearing the end of their economic life, but only about 14 per cent of the estate acreage and a mere 2 per cent of smallholdings had been planted with specially-developed trees capable of yields per hectare three to four times that of the unselected types planted in the early 1900s (Drabble, 1991, 24). The artificially higher prices under restriction generated economic rents which enabled investors, foreign ones in particular, to stay in primary industries and thus reinforced the general immobility of capital within the colonial economy.

8.3   Other products

Timber

Exports of this commodity assumed greater importance, especially in North Borneo after the decline of the tobacco industry from about 1913 (Chapter 3.4). In order to attract investment the Chartered Company decided to concentrate timber exploitation within a single company. In 1920 the British Borneo Timber Company (BBTC) was formed, owned jointly by the Chartered Company and a British agency house, Harrisons & Crosfield, and granted a 25-year monopoly over all unalienated state land. Previous operators, two European and two Chinese companies, became sub-licencees. The BBTC introduced mechanical methods of extraction, but operations were hampered by transport difficulties which limited activity to within a few kilometres from water or rail facilities. In Sarawak timber exports remained largely under Borneo Company control. Much of the product was for consumption locally or in neighbouring areas (Labuan, Brunei, Singapore), though exports to the United Kingdom increased after 1932. As in North Borneo the physical growth of the industry was constrained by transport difficulties (Amarjit Kaur, 1998, 62ff).

Iron ore

This industry was established in Malaya by Japanese capital during the 1920s to supply the needs of the rapidly expanding iron and steel production in Japan. The colonial government saw no conflict between between this investment and British rubber and tin interests. The location of the mines in Johor, Terengganu and Kelantan was a welcome addition to the economy of these less-developed states. However, the impetus was relatively shortlived. Output rose from 75 000 tonnes in 1921 to nearly 1.7 million tonnes in 1936, but by the latter date existing deposits were nearing exhaustion and further development was more difficult and costly due to the poor transport infrastructure (Yuen, 1974).

Other export products

Brief reviews will be given of copra, sago, palm oil and petroleum. The first two both showed growth in output volume in the interwar years, but in relative terms remained minor products in the hands of small farmers. Copra, principally from the Peninsula and North Borneo, rose from 28 000 tonnes in 1920 to 142 000 tonnes in 1940. As with the larger industries there was the problem of surplus capacity which came to the forefront during the Great Depression. Planting had been extended especially during the boom years of the mid-1920s. As a result of an official review committee in 1934, land rents and drainage rates were reduced, but government did little to tackle major problems in the industry such as poor drainage (T.G. Lim, 1977, 196–8, 255). Sago production in Sarawak was some 16 000 tonnes in 1920 and reached a peak of 25 000 tonnes in 1933 before falling back to around the 1920 level by the late 1930s. The only technical innovation up to 1945 was the substitution of a nail-studded plank in place of the adze formerly used to strip the trunks of the sago palms to produce the flour (Morris, 1979, 232).

Oil palms had been introduced to the Peninsula from West Africa in the 1870s, about the same time as rubber, but planters showed no interest in commercial cultivation until about 1917. Plantings grew rapidly in the 1920s as there were fears that Malaya had become too dependent on rubber, but by 1930 there were still only 23 000 hectares, mostly in Johor, Selangor and Perak. Planting slowed during the 1930s to reach 32 000 hectares by 1941. Thus far the industry in Malaya was confined to estates (almost entirely European-owned), principally because of the expensive technology necessary to process the fruit quickly after harvesting to prevent the build-up of free-fatty acid (FFA). The growth of the industry was helped by the good transport connections to Port Swettenham and Singapore, and cheapened freight costs due to the pioneering of bulk-shipment techniques (Lim Chong Yah, 1967, 128–43).

The boost to the Sarawak economy from petroleum production proved shortlived. After a peak output of 15 000 barrels a day in 1929, the Miri oilfield declined to a mere 3000 barrels a day by 1941 with operations ceasing at the end of that year as reserves were exhausted. Only the opening of the Seria oilfield in adjacent Brunei in the early 1930s provided throughput for the Miri processing facilities, though the benefits to Sarawak do not seem very substantial. The contribution of mineral exports, mainly oil, to government revenue dropped from roughly $771 000 in 1928 to $388 000 in 1938 (Amarjit Kaur, 1998, 23, 27).

Rice

The interwar period began with the crisis in rice imports which saw the governments in the Peninsula having to intervene to ensure supplies at highly subsidised prices (see Chapter 4.5). This episode highlighted the question implicit since the emergence of the major export industries, namely, the wisdom of heavy dependency on imports (then running at around 60 per cent) of a basic foodstuff, which had to be paid for out of fluctuating export earnings. The High Commissioner FMS, Sir Laurence Guillemard, viewed the crisis as a 'pretty severe lesson' which pointed to the desirability of steps to lessen this dependence (cited in Kratoska, 1982, 297). There was some increase in domestic rice production during the lean years. Malayan output from 1920 to 1924 averaged 224 000 tonnes a year against 191 000 tonnes in 1918–19, but this proved shortlived. Once the emergency was past and rubber prices improved under restriction, peasant interest waned and annual production dropped back to 206 000 tonnes between 1925 and 1929. In the same period imports averaged over 70 per cent of consumption (calculated from Cheng, 1973, Table 10).

The problem resurfaced during the Great Depression, due to the precipitous fall in export earnings. The FMS government set up the Rice Cultivation Committee whose brief was to make recommendations on ways of improving the country's performance. Foremost among these was the establishment of a Drainage and Irrigation Department, implemented in 1932 at a time when administrative retrenchment was the general trend in official policy. The Committee also urged that the potentialities of large-scale irrigated rice cultivation be investigated. Two such schemes were established in the 1930s, Sungei Manik in Lower Perak and Panchang Bedina (now known as Tanjong Karang) in Kuala Selangor, totalling 6000 planted hectares by 1939 (T.G. Lim, 1977, 184–5).

The effects of these projects, and related technical work on water control, types of seeds, manuring, and so on, were quickly evident in an increase in production of approximately 75 per cent in Malayan rice production to 337 000 tonnes during the 1930s, but in relative terms imports still remained very high, running at upwards of two-thirds of consumption.

Government expenditure on infrastructure, especially water control, for the rice industry up to the Second World War achieved a more stable environment in terms of protection from the vagaries of weather. Attempts were also made to provide low interest loans for farmers and, in the 1920s, the establishment of a cooperative movement (section 8.6). Before 1914 government had encouraged Chinese entrepreneurs to build processing mills in the Krian district to provide better prices to farmers. A little later government entered the sector, building a mill at Bagan Serai in 1918. However, these initiatives were spasmodic rather than consistent policy.

The Borneo territories faced the same problem as Malaya; a high dependence on imported rice for the immigrant communities. Up to the Second World War Sarawak imported an average of 60 per cent of its needs, and whilst the Brookes gave general encouragement to rice growing, there was no expenditure comparable to Malaya on improved irrigation facilities or cultivation techniques (Amarjit Kaur, 1998, 35–6). Among both immigrants, such as the Foochow Chinese, and the indigenous peoples there was movement between rubber and rice-growing according to relative prices. During the 1920–1 rice crisis officials tried to attract Foochows to grow more rice by offering land at nominal rentals. Land in the Rajang could be taken up with only an 'occupation ticket' (no prior survey necessary), but when rubber prices improved there was the same move as in Malaya to drop rice growing (Chew, 1990, 156).

The Great Depression intensified the problem. In the most commercialised areas, such as the Saribas region, officials speculated that the time might be approaching for more intensive practices to be adopted in rice cultivation. Iban complained that rubber planting had extended so widely that little land was available for rice. Not until the late 1930s did the Brookes begin to develop a policy on rice, with the secondment of an Agricultural Officer from Malaya, and several partially-completed drainage and irrigation and colonisation schemes (Cramb, 1988, 114–15, and personal information).

8.4   Industry

There was little by way of industrial development in Malaysia prior to the Second World War. Such secondary industries as had appeared were processing facilities mostly linked to the growth of the export industries. These were largely located in the leading ports, Penang and Singapore, the rationale being the need to process raw materials, notably smallholder rubber sheet and tin ore, as near to the source of supply as possible since impurities (for instance, moisture in rubber sheet) made transport over extended distances uneconomic due to loss in weight. In addition there were firms catering to the domestic market for some consumer items, notably foodstuffs (bread, biscuits), beverages, building materials (bricks, cement) and some metal goods (iron pipes) which had a high weight-to-cost ratio, and which again were uneconomic to import from distant sources (Huff, 1994, 212–14).

For the most part these activities were undertaken by Chinese entre-preneurs. Huff has focused attention on those who amassed considerable fortunes from the cultivation of rubber and pineapples (the 'rubber-pineapple complex') in Singapore and southern Johor, especially in the more prosperous years of the 1920s: Tan Kah Kee, Lim Nee Soon, Lee Kong Chian and others. Tan Kah Kee, for example, expanded his interests beyond rubber-pineapple cultivation into shipping, rubber milling, sweets, medicines and so on, and, from 1923, rubber goods (notably canvas shoes with rubber soles which were exported in large quantities throughout Southeast Asia and China). However, during the Great Depression Tan's business was unable to maintain repayments on heavy borrowings from British banks during the 1920s, and in 1934 the company went into liquidation. Chinese banks in the SS, heavily involved in rubber business, also faced financial difficulties in the 1930s. These events may well have deterred Chinese entrepreneurs from further extension of manufacturing interests (Huff, 1994, 226–34). Another commentator concludes that 'the reasons ... seem to lie more with the Chinese than with the restraints placed upon them' (Brown, 1994, 232).

There were other more general reasons why industrialisation remained at a low level, with few moves towards import-substitution during these years when Malaysia's capacity to finance imports was greatly reduced. The domestic market was still relatively small, even had the colonial government been willing to give tariff protection to infant industry. Straits mercantile interests generally opposed any modification of the traditional free-port status, whilst the British metropolitan government regarded 'the development of local manufactures in the Colonies ... [as] undesirable except where the industry can be regarded as natural to the colony concerned' (cited in Huff, 1994, 214). One import-substituting industry which might have offered some prospect of success was textiles which commanded good markets not only in Malaysia but also in the NEI (which had no protective tariffs against Singapore). However, this industry was relatively labour-intensive, whilst wages were high compared to other competing countries such as Japan, India, Hong Kong and China. Huff (1994, 215) points to this as the most probable reason for the lack of development in this direction. We have noted in Chapter 4.5 the decline of the indigenous textile industry in the east-coast states of the Peninsula.

European capitalists, too, failed to play a leading role in extending the manufacturing industrial sector at this time. The main problem here seems to have been a blinkered outlook: Huff terms it an 'entrepot mentality' (1994, 215), whilst Wheelwright coins the phrase, 'rubber-tin mentality' (1963, 71). A similar view prevailed in the 1930s in the Colonial Office where it was thought that sheer 'inertia' would tend to keep the capital in rubber and tin companies locked up in those sectors (Drabble, 1991, 73). Silcock points out a structural problem in that when primary product prices and profits were high, available capital and labour were fully employed in those industries, whereas in times of slump when workers were laid-off, the owners of capital (who generally took a short-term view) were reluctant to make fresh investments; 'it is a difficult task to create the conditions in which new enterprises can be established when labour is available and the level of prosperity low' (1959,119).

Whilst it can be said that some foundations for future industrialisation were laid during the interwar years, the still-small weight of industry in the economy can be seen from the 1931 Malayan census which revealed overall 12.7 per cent of the economically active population in the secondary sector (highest at 28 per cent in the SS, 10.3 per cent in the FMS, and 6.9 per cent UMS). Comparative figures were 12.1 per cent (Dutch East Indies), 3.9 per cent (Thailand), and 8.7 per cent (Philippines) (Brown, 1994, Table 12.4).

8.5   Infrastructure

During the interwar period the only major extension to the rail network in Malaya was the completion of the line to Kota Bharu by 1931. Cumulative capital expenditure on railways went from $192 million by 1923 to $229 million by 1938 (Li, 1982, 27). The road system provided increasing competition to railways as imports of vehicles increased rapidly. In the FMS the number of cars registered rose from 4521 in 1923 to 11 597 by 1925, and lorries from 371 to 1844 (Amarjit Kaur, 1985, 99). Roads were also extended into areas where railways had not penetrated in the FMS, other west coast states Johor and Kedah and, in the 1930s, to a lesser extent in the east coast states (Courtenay, 1972, 135). The general outcome of this competition was improved and cheaper transport services for the domestic economy (Amarjit Kaur, 1985, 117). More ample supplies of electricity for industrial users such as tin mines and urban areas became available from the later 1920s. Suppliers were a mixture of government and private enterprise, such as the Perak River Hydro-Electric Power Company (Lim Chong Yah, 1967, 290–1).

In North Borneo the major capital work undertaken was a road-building programme from 1928 which saw the total of metalled and earth roads increase from approximately 158 to 386 kilometres by 1940 (Amarjit Kaur, 1998, Table 4.2).

In Sarawak road building was done only near towns in short stretches with no interconnections, the sole exception by 1940 being a 64 kilometre stretch from Kuching to Seria. The minuscule railway (Chapter 5.2) was closed to regular traffic from 1931 with an accumulated loss of just over

$1 million. Poor land communications were not compensated for by good waterborne links, either along the coast or between major towns (Kuching, Miri) and Singapore, although the latter improved during the 1930s. The net result was higher costs to the general populace in Sarawak due to more frequent handling of goods in transit (Amarjit Kaur, 1998, 82).

8.6 Land, credit and cooperatives

Throughout the generally prosperous conditions obtaining up to the onset of prolonged depressions in the interwar years, the agricultural frontier for both large and small producers in Malaysia had expanded fairly continuously. Closely allied with this there had emerged a system of loans and credit based on the value of land and its products which involved a sizeable proportion of the population. No major problems had developed to cause any serious questioning of the extent to which economic well-being had become dependent on a small range of products. The situation began to change during the 1920–22 depression. This section will focus on various initiatives in official policies which put a brake on agricultural expansion, and which attempted to strengthen what was seen as the weak position of the indigenous small farmers relative to other groups.

The availability of land, and the conditions governing its use, became the subjects of debate between government and private interests. In 1921 European planting interests in the FMS Federal Council requested a three-year moratorium on further grants of land for rubber, to which government gave a negative response on the grounds that the downturn was only temporary. Even had it been complied with, the situation of most larger estates would not have been adversely affected, since they already possessed unplanted reserves of land acquired at, or soon after, flotation.

Asian estate owners were in a more difficult position since many had borrowed money on the security of their holdings at high rates of interest (12 to 36 per cent per annum) in better times. Foremost among the lenders were the Chettiars who held mortgages over approximately 28 000 hectares of land in the FMS in 1919 (Ampalavanar, 1971/2, 76). As long as borrowers could maintain the interest payments, Chettiars were customarily reluctant to foreclose because it burdened them with an illiquid asset whose realisable value was low. However, many were in their turn subject to pressure as borrowers from western banks, and by 1922 they had foreclosed on an estimated 8000 hectares of Chinese-owned rubber holdings.

Malays, too, were borrowers from Chettiars and credit-takers from local produce dealers and shopkeepers (usually Chinese). Some officials expressed concern over the potential which existed for expropriation of Malay land. Non-Malays could gain an effective permanent interest therein through mortgage, promissory note or power of attorney even over Malay reservation land. Foreclosure could be achieved with sanction from the appropriate State Council. The immediate remedy was sought through the extension of Malay reservations which totalled approximately 1.1 million hectares in the FMS by 1923, or nearly 16 per cent of the total land area (T.G. Lim, 1977, 165).

As rubber prices boomed in the mid-1920s, there was a corresponding revival in applications for land. Government tried to dampen down demand by charging much higher premiums. But at the same time increasing evidence came to light of quite extensive unauthorised plantings, frequently on land originally granted for some other use such as rice or fruit trees, and carrying a cultivation condition specifying no rubber. Officials finally decided that this condition was not sufficiently watertight legally to warrant resuming the land, and retrospective conversion to rubber was permitted at a higher rental and premiums.

Concurrently, government was also considering ways of moderating what was seen as the undesirable dominance held by middlemen over Malay farmers leading to excessive credit rates, low buying prices and outright exploitation through incorrect weights, measures, and so on. This was particularly prevalent in the rice and rubber industries. From the early 1920s policy became more interventionist. In the Krian rice growing district a government mill was set up at Kuala Kurau to supplement one started in 1918 at Bagan Serai. Neither was particularly successful, though officials claimed that the monopoly of the Chinese mills had been broken (T.G. Lim, 1977, 155–6). A more general remedy was sought through the introduction of the cooperative movement in the FMS from 1922 onwards. The aim here was to offset the individual weakness of farmers through collective strength. Rural Cooperative Credit Societies (RCCSs) were established whose members contributed regular savings and in return were eligible for loans at rates well below those in the informal sector. The movement expanded in the SS and FMS under favourable economic conditions of the later 1920s but, with a maximum of 99 societies with 3648 members, still affected only a minority of farmers.

The impact of the Great Depression brought the expansion of the movement to a halt. Some societies had to be liquidated, for instance two out of four cooperative processing centres among rubber smallholders (Drabble, 1991, 124–5). Besides this there were some fundamental problems such as a lack of trained staff to operate the societies, lax repayment of loans by borrowers, difficulty for peasants whose cash income was irregular to save regularly, conflict between cooperative principles and religious prohibitions on interest (*riba*). RCCS numbers and membership recovered slightly in the later 1930s, but not to peak levels.

The interwar RCCS movement has been described as a premature attempt to superimpose a capitalistic-type of institution on a 'traditional-feudal society' (Fredericks, 1973, 161). The notions of social democracy implicit in voluntary membership of an RCCS (collective ownership of the share capital, autonomous decision-making, and so on) were in tension with the authoritarian elements in Malay society (as when local chiefs were asked to 'persuade' villagers of the value of membership), and in the colonial administration (notably the District Officers: Fredericks, 1973, 163–5).

The Great Depression brought the question of Malay land holdings to the forefront of official attention again. In the late 1920s an additional 183 000 hectares were gazetted in the FMS as reservations, bringing the total to approximately 1.3 million hectares. Over two-thirds of this was as yet unappropriated for private use, but was known to contain extensive areas unsuited to settlement and agriculture. As a short-term measure to guard against widespread expropriation of Malays, the FMS government passed the Smallholdings (Restriction of Sale) Enactment in 1931 which granted a twelve-month stay of execution of a court order for sale, provided that payment of at least 75 per cent of the interest owing was maintained. A new Malay Reservations Enactment in 1933 prohibited leases or mortgages to non-Malays, and gave exemption from attachment under court order. This did not prevent non-Malays from continuing to gain beneficial interests in reservation land through devices such as Malay proxies. However, since all but 108 000 hectares of Malay-owned rural land in the FMS was within reservations 'the economic future of the rural Malays would necessarily be worked out within Malay Reservations' (Kratoska, 1983, 166).

The implication of these measures, as noted in the report of a Committee on Malay Reservations in 1930, was ideally to aim at the creation of 'self-supporting Malay communities' with 'internal facilities for credit' parallel to the economy dominated by non-Malay interests (cited in Kratoska, 1983, 166). However, with Malay access to outside sources of loans so heavily circumscribed and, as we have just seen, the failure of the rural cooperative movement to achieve much magnitude, this community faced a real short-age of funds for productive investment. But, as Kratoska comments, 'the choice, particularly in the 1930s, may not have been between development and stagnation, but between stagnation with indebtedness and stagnation without it' (1983, 168).

Other official initiatives directed towards Malay smallholders, primarily rubber growers, in this period were pilot programmes in the 1930s to get them to improve the quality of their product whilst concurrently urging dealers to offer better prices. At a more general level Malays were urged towards self-improvement through the formation of General Purpose Societies, Better Living Societies coupled with weekly fairs, exhibiting at agricultural shows and provision of a Rural Lecture Caravan to help raise the standard of farming. Again, these reached only limited numbers of people. However, leading officials remained pessimistic about the economic prospects for Malays. In 1935 the Director of Cooperation FMS stated his view that few owners with only a single holding (often less than two hectares) could hope to enjoy a 'reasonable standard of living' (cited in Drabble, 1991, 129).

The increasing confinement of Malays to holdings whose size and output were under pressure to support growing numbers of people (the more so as the Islamic law of inheritance led to fragmentation and increasing joint ownership) assumed even greater importance in the light of the decision of the FMS government in September 1930 not to make any further grants of land for rubber growing. Then, under the IRRA, new planting of rubber was prohibited with effect from June 1934, so that along with financial difficulty in replanting (loss of income for up to seven years), the Malay peasantry in the 1930s faced the prospect that unless government did take major initiatives, their principal cash crop, rubber, would gradually atrophy.

The decreasing availability of land bore heavily on Asian owners who possessed much smaller reserves, both financial and land, than European interests. The impact of the 1930 ban on land grants for rubber became clear during a temporary lifting in 1939–40 when Asian estate owners figured prominently among applicants for land for new planting compared to requests to replant existing areas (Drabble, 1991, 80–1). Another category of land tenure, the Temporary Occupation Lease (TOL), to which many unemployed Chinese mine workers resorted during the Great Depression to grow foodstuffs and cash crops such as tobacco and groundnuts, was increasingly restricted by government. The possibility of granting land to non-Malays to grow rice to augment domestic production, raised several times during the 1930s, encountered strong opposition from Malays who viewed this as a threat to their rightful heritage (Kratoska, 1982, 304–8; Loh, 1990).

Land use in the Borneo states faced few comparable constraints. In North Borneo the cultivated area totalled only just over 127 000 hectares by 1939, a mere 1.7 per cent of the state's area (Tregonning, 1965, 101). From the Chartered Company's coastal bases, such as Jesselton, Kudat and Sandakan, settled development spread inland in the form of territorial enclaves: Beaufort, Keningau, Tambunan, Marudu and others on the west coast, and Labuk, Sugut and Kinabatangan (among others) on the east. There were also some isolated developments further into the interior (the fringes of the Central High Plains), but for the most part the population in these latter regions remained shifting subsistence cultivators (Mustapha, 1990, 228–33). It would appear, therefore, that contact between the indigenous population and foreign enterprise was very limited, with no extensive scope for conflicts of interest to arise.

In Sarawak the regulation of land matters had been prominent since the inception of Brooke rule. As rubber cultivation began to be more widely taken up from about the time of the First World War, the government attempted to introduce more system into land administration. Land Orders VIII and IX of 1920 provided for two categories of rural land: Country Lands and Native Holdings. Among the latter, 'Native Land Reserves' could be created in which 1.2 hectare blocks were available to all 'native born subjects', which included those of immigrant stock (Hong, 1987, 41). The rubber boom of the 1920s led to the expansion of the Foochow Chinese community along the Rajang river to other parts of the state. This led to an intensification of the friction with the Iban over land which had been occurring since the Foochows first arrived at the turn of the century. A new concession area opened up in Binatang was a particular focus of discontent as the land was claimed by Iban who were dismayed at the rapid influx of Foochows, who swiftly cleared the land and planted half a million rubber trees. Physical clashes occurred in 1926 (Chew, 1990, 167–8).

In an attempt to separate the interests of Iban and migrants, further Land and Land Settlement Orders in 1931 and 1933 decreed a division into 'Native Areas' (for indigenes only), and 'Mixed Zones' (for non-natives). Land within Native Reservations was not to be sub-divided, and no individual titles were to be issued, thus preventing mortgage, sale or any form of transfer other than inheritance. Only crops such as rice, vegetables and fruits could be planted (Hong, 1987, 42–3; Chew, 1990, 169). Sarawak was clearly following, and even getting ahead of the Peninsula in these respects. Finally, in 1939 a circular laid out selective procedures for defining native customary law in such a way that community boundaries could be more precisely defined, and hence population movement in pursuit of shifting agriculture controlled more readily (Hong, 1987, 43–4).

Neither the North Borneo nor the Sarawak government appears to have considered the introduction of a cooperative movement in this period.

8.7   Population and welfare

The Malaysian population grew more rapidly in the 1920s (2.23 per cent per annum) than in the previous decade, but slowed to 1.57 per cent in the 1930s. The bulk of this increase occurred in Malaya where growth was not far short of 3 per cent per annum in the 1920s, but fell sharply in the 1930s. Paradoxically the trend in the Borneo territories was the reverse: a drop to around 0.5 per cent (premodern levels) in the 1920s and a relatively strong recovery in the 1930s (see Table 6.1).

Immigration remained the major factor in population growth, certainly up to the Great Depression. The last major inflow prior to the Second World War came during the boom of the mid-1920s. In Malaya the number of Chinese went from 856 000 in 1921 to 1 285 000 in 1931, an annual growth rate of 4.15 per cent, and in relative terms from approximately 29 to 34 per cent of the total population. Indians increased at 2.66 per cent a year, but their share remained steady at 15–16 per cent. The Malay population, including immigrants from the NEI, rose more slowly at 1.74 per cent (calculated from Lim Chong Yah, 1967, Appendix 7.1). The 1920s marked a significant stage in the growth of a plural society. By 1931 the Chinese and

Indians together constituted practically 49 per cent of the population, outnumbering local-born Malays and virtually equalling the aggregate (49.2 per cent) if Malays of immigrant descent were included.

The volume of migration into the Borneo territories in the 1920s was much smaller. As in Malaya, Chinese comprised the majority of arrivals. They were attracted to North Borneo by a free pass system under which a male immigrant could bring in a spouse or relative without cost, and numbers increased by nearly 28 per cent between 1921 and 1931. Substantial numbers of Javanese contract labourers also came (Tregonning, 1965, 150–1; Y.L. Lee, 1962a, 230). Continuous data on Foochow arrivals in Sarawak is not available, but their numbers were directly related to rubber prices, peaking in 1926–7 (Chew, 1990, Table 8.1).

The Great Depression marked the end of a long period of almost completely unrestricted immigration. The contraction of wage employment in estates, mines and so on led to a heavy return flow to countries of origin. In Malaya, for example, total Chinese and Indian departures exceeded arrivals by some 360 000 from 1931 to 1933 (calculated from Sandhu, 1969, Appendix 4; Li, 1982, 115). Not all departures were voluntary, however. Governments attempted to provide some temporary employment on public works, but ultimately resorted to repatriation of labourers unable to support themselves. Private philanthropy by wealthy members of the Chinese community also helped to mitigate hardship and destitution. The numbers of migrants arriving, males in particular, were kept down by official controls. For example, in Malaya the Aliens Ordinance 1932 applied a quota system to all adult males other than British nationals or British-protected persons. In Sarawak aliens had to possess an official passport or landing permit, and to pay a deposit before being allowed to enter. In North Borneo the number of registered labourers fell by nearly 55 per cent between 1929 and 1932 (Li, 1982, 115; Chew, 1990, 173; Amarjit Kaur, 1998, Table 4.5).

After the depression eased in 1932–3 governments placed more emphasis on promoting unrestricted immigration of women to reduce the long-standing gender imbalance and promote the formation of locally-domiciled families. In 1937 Chinese new arrivals comprised 948 women for every 1000 men. The 1931 Malayan census revealed that about 30 per cent of Chinese and 21.5 per cent of Indians were locally born (Hirschman, 1975b, Tables 2.2 and 2.3; Li, 1982, Table 6.4). These proportions continued to rise in the 1930s, especially after the British government of India banned assisted emigration to Malaya from 1938 (due to dissatisfaction over wage levels on estates), and the Malayan government placed restrictions on both male and female Chinese immigration from the same year (Lim Chong Yah, 1967, 188; Sandhu, 1969, 113). From this decade natural increase became the prime factor in Malayan population growth.

The situation in the Borneo territories (Sarawak especially) is less clear due to inadequate statistics, but again the Chinese appear as the most rapidly increasing group. In North Borneo their annual growth rate was 3.37 per cent in the 1920s and 2.52 per cent in the 1930s. Only the Bajau, themselves a migratory group, approached these rates with 3.24 per cent and 2.84 per cent respectively (calculated from Sabah Government, *Annual Bulletin of Statistics* (*ABS*), 1966, Table 2.3).

Another feature common to all the Malaysian territories was the relatively slow natural increase of the indigenous groups. In Malaya the Malays (including NEI migrants) rose at only 1.74 per cent in the 1920s, and even slower at 1.66 per cent from 1931 to 1947 (calculated from Lim Chong Yah, 1967, Table 7.1). The principal reason for this was high death rates in the rural areas where the bulk of the Malay population lived, and where the incidence of endemic diseases such as malaria, smallpox and cholera was heavy.

In North Borneo between 1921 and 1951 the indigenous growth rate was only 0.6 per cent a year (calculated from Y.L. Lee, 1962a, 230). Child survival rates up to the age of 29 (70 per cent) were well below those of the Chinese (93 per cent). In Sarawak it was virtually impossible to know the trends among all the tribal peoples but some, such as the Muruts, were certainly declining. Here too, Chinese had much higher survival rates (Y.L. Lee, 1962a, 232; Jones, 1966, 22). The poor state of internal communications and inadequate expenditure on health were responsible for high tribal death rates.

The geographical distribution of population did not change greatly in Malaya, where urbanisation proceeded slowly in the interwar decades at an annual growth rate of 0.76 per cent (1921–31) and 1.4 per cent (1931–47), comprising nearly 19 per cent of the total population by 1947. This process was even slower in the Borneo territories, accounting for only 12.9 per cent by 1957 (UN, 1982, Tables 10, 19; McGee, 1986, Table 2.8). At the same time the population in North Borneo and Sarawak was relatively fluid, with a general movement from the interior to the more developed coastal regions. The driving force here was a search for wage employment in the rubber, timber and oil industries. In North Borneo, for example, in 1921 some 26 per cent of the Dusun (Kadazan) and Murut groups lived in four districts in the interior. By 1960 the proportion had fallen to 16 per cent (Jones, 1966, 237).

In welfare terms the interwar period saw extremes of prosperity and depression. The 1920s were the last decade of a 30-year burst of rapid growth in which Malayan per capita GDP averaged about 4 per cent increase annually (Table 7.2). The next two decades, spanning the 1930s, war and reconstruction witnessed a marginally negative (–0.2 per cent a year) trend.

A closer picture of the impact of the fluctuations can be gained from the net annual returns per acre from rubber for Malayan smallholders who were plainly on a switchback. Returns soared from approximately $85 in

1922 to nearly $214 in 1925, crashed to around $19 in 1932 recovering to $88 in 1937, then fell back to $52 in 1939 (Drabble, 1990, Table 3.3). Import prices remained relatively stable throughout the 1920s, and it appears highly probable that the decade saw increases in real incomes. During the Great Depression (1929–32) incomes fell much more heavily than import prices. The IRRA scheme brought some recovery in incomes, with import prices again remaining reasonably steady until the outbreak of war in Europe. However, the Borneo territories were heavily under-assessed in the IRRA. Tapping had to be suspended in Sarawak for 44 days in 1935 and 114 days in 1936 to keep the state within its export quota (Chew, 1990, 173). In 1938 there were fears that government there could have difficulty in maintaining control over 'turbulent smallholders' (cited in Drabble, 1991, 190). This evidence suggests very limited, if any, gains in real incomes in the 1930s until the outbreak of war in Europe caused primary product prices to soar.

The situation for wage labourers was no better, and probably worse at times. In the 1920s both Indian and Chinese tappers on Malayan rubber estates did relatively well from 1925 to 1929, but during the slump rates of pay tumbled to around half those of a decade earlier (Barlow, 1990, 37). Wages were very slow to recover, especially those of the Chinese (who previously had earned two to three times the Indian rate) with an index of 46 (1929 = 100) as late as 1935 (calculated from Parmer, 1960, Table 8). Strikes and violent confrontations with employers by Chinese workers in 1936, and by Indians from 1939 to 1941, extracted some grudging concessions but wages did not return to 1929 levels. Rates for unskilled labour in Sarawak in 1935 were around $10–20 a month, similar to those in Malaya.

Whilst the depression undoubtedly caused a great deal of human distress, the subsistence base of the Malaysian territories does not seem to have been seriously threatened. Per capita availability of rice in Malaya dropped from an average of 181 kg in 1926–30, to 170 kg in 1931–5 (a 6 per cent fall), and recovered to 184 kg from 1936 to 1940 (Booth, 1990, Table 7). In both Sarawak and North Borneo the quantities imported (the bulk of requirements) at the trough in 1932 decreased by approximately 45 per cent as against 1928, compared to 22 per cent in Malaya, which suggests some fall in per capita availability. However, by 1935 Sarawak was importing 126 per cent of the 1928 quantity, whilst North Borneo had recovered to nearly 87 per cent (calculated from *Statistical Abstract for the British Empire*, No. 68; Cheng, 1973, Appendix IX).

Expenditure on social services, notably education and health, did not receive anything approaching the priority accorded to transport. In the SS education took just under 4 per cent in 1919 and 1929, rising to 6.1 per cent in 1938. Health, arguably the best in Malaya, did somewhat better, averaging around 10 per cent between 1919 and 1938 (Li, 1982, 33–4). The FMS government spent roughly 6–8 per cent on health services and 3–6 per cent on education (calculated from Lim Chong Yah, 1967, 340n.). Li (1982, 127), however, argues that the poorest and least-developed states (such as Kelantan which had one of the lowest death rates) contained some of the healthiest sections of the population. Possibly this reflected the sparse population and smaller disturbances to natural conditions from agriculture and mining, with concomitantly less risk of widespread disease.

The educational system in Malaya underwent little change interwar. The bulk of government expenditure went on English-medium schools: 48.3 per cent in the FMS in 1938, against 41.5 per cent on Malay vernacular schools, 6 per cent on Chinese and 4.2 per cent on Indian (Lim Chong Yah, 1967, 298). Neither the Malay or Tamil streams led on to a general secondary education which was available only to the English and Chinese streams, and tertiary education (in Singapore) to the former alone. The establishment of the Sultan Idris Training College at Tanjong Malim, Perak, in 1922 was designed to provide some secondary education for Malays from the villages, primarily in vocational subjects related to agriculture but with an increasing content of Malay language, literature and history. Least catered for were the children of the Indian estate workforce. Under the Labour Code of 1923 estate managements were required to provide schools where there were ten or more pupils, but few had qualified teachers and attendance was not compulsory.

Prior to the Second World War Malaya (the FMS in particular) enjoyed the reputation of being extremely well-endowed in terms of public revenue and the provision of services. The initial rapid growth of the tin and rubber industries funded large outlays on public works and contributions to the Imperial war effort, but the 1920–22 slump saw a substantial drop in FMS revenue and big budget deficits ($60 million in 1921). Loans in both local and sterling currency had to be raised to ease the pressure. The 1925–6 boom brought a recovery in revenue, but the strengthening trend throughout the 1920s and 1930s was towards achieving economies in administrative costs, with budgets as nearly balanced as possible. Overall, after the recovery of the economy in the 1930s most states in Malaya were in a reasonably sound financial position. Around 1935 their surpluses aggregated approximately $260 million, but much of this was not immediately available locally due to the Currency Board system which required a large proportion to be held in sterling securities or as loans to metropolitan agencies (e.g., Crown Agents). In 1934 around 41 per cent of FMS funds were thus disposed, about the same for Johor, and a massive 94 per cent for Kedah (Khor, 1983, 50).

In North Borneo the finances were never adequate to meet both the needs of the Chartered Company to pay a return to shareholders, and the provision of a remotely satisfactory infrastructure for the country. We have seen that the rubber boom came relatively late in the 1920s and 1930s. During the First World War, though economies were made in the administration, dividends were paid at up to 5 per cent in 1919 and continued throughout the slump. The Company had also taken loans (in the form of debenture issues) for development expenses, including railways, roads and its investment in the British Borneo Timber Company. By 1941 a large part of the debenture loans had been redeemed, and the Company possessed adequate cash and general reserves. However, this was only accomplished with highly conservative financial policies which minimised capital expenditure and kept recurrent outlays well within revenue. In social services the Company's record was little other than pitiful: a mere 1 per cent at most spent on health, and only 1 in 30 people reached by primary education. A slightly brighter side can be found in the death rate on estates which, after a law in 1922 required the provision of health facilities, dropped from 26.5 to 4.4 per thousand by 1940 (Tan et al., 1987, 7; Amarjit Kaur, 1998, 112).

As with North Borneo, Sarawak's relatively late entry into major export industries was reflected in rather slow revenue growth up to the First World War. Thereafter rubber and petroleum underpinned a major expansion in the 1920s and again in the late 1930s. The Brookes maintained throughout a conservative policy on expenditure (the state had no public debt after 1905) with no deficits except for a minuscule $10 241 in 1938. Over the period 1897–1940 revenue grew at an annual average of about 6 per cent against expenditure at 5.5 per cent (calculated from Amarjit Kaur, 1998, Table 4.6). Public works were the largest outlay but, as noted in section 8.5, these did not result in any well-developed system of communications.

In these same years education and health in Sarawak received 3–4 per cent and 4–7 per cent respectively. Though comparable in proportionate terms with Malaya, in actuality the provision was sparse in the extreme. At the end of the Brooke period primary education had reached one in 26 persons. In public health no concerted action was taken after epidemics such as cholera (over 1000 deaths in the Second Division alone in 1903) or smallpox (Kuching in 1925). By the interwar period there were only three medical officers in the state, and two hospitals with 300 beds (Amarjit Kaur, 1998, 112).

8.8   Overview

For much of the interwar period the Malaysian economy basically continued the pattern of extensive growth, especially in agriculture. The fastest annual rates of growth in output came for the most part from the newer industries (oil palm, iron ore, petroleum to about 1930), or smaller ones (tea, pineapples, timber) which did not have much weight in the economy. Older industries such as pepper, sago, cutch and gold had mixed records, but none showed significant development.

Productivity in the major export industries, tin and rubber, certainly improved in these decades. Annual output per estate worker in rubber doubled from 0.56 to 1.16 tonnes between 1920 and 1930, and in tin from 0.3 to 0.87 tonnes, but these gains came largely from economies in the use of labour rather than the introduction of major new technology. The tin mining labour force decreased by about 57 per cent (calculated from Yip, 1969, Table V-18; Barlow, 1978, Special Annex, Table 2.5).

However, constraints upon expansion of the agricultural frontier materialised in the shape of government policies (restriction of exports, no new planting of rubber, reduced availability of new land). These policies, especially in Malaya, were custodial rather than developmental and effectively constrained technological progress. After the boom of the mid-1920s there were no major infusions of new capital. Malaysia effectively lived on the existing capital stock for about the next quarter century.

Official resources were too limited for government to play a very positive role in social development (education, health and welfare). The revenue base remained narrow (import/export duties, land rents and so on). Residents and companies whose permanent domicile was overseas paid no local taxes on incomes or profits.

9

War, Reconstruction and the Advent of Independence (1942–63)

9.1   Japanese occupation 1942–5

The military subjugation of Southeast Asia by Japan at the end of 1941 and early 1942 was in large measure driven by the aim to gain direct control over the raw material resources of the region vital to the Japanese economy. The period 1942–5 saw a military administration centring on Singapore (renamed Syonan), which imposed a command economy. In external trade the former integral link between exports and imports (the one financing the other) was severed. Exports were now to consist only of what was required for the Japanese economy, whilst on the import side Malaysia was to become as self-sufficient as possible, especially in foodstuffs.

The principal controls on economic activity were restrictions on trade, the movement and settlement of population, distribution of labour and the rationing of foodstuffs. These were allied to a system in which the existing structure of production and trade was dismantled, with major assets (such as former European tin mines) handed over to Japanese firms. At the retail level the myriad small, largely Chinese, shopkeepers were replaced as far as possible by Japanese nationals. Monopolistic associations (*kumai*) controlled the supplies and prices of essential foodsuffs and commodities such as tyres (Horner, 1973).

Chronologically, 1942 saw repairs and reconstruction after the damage of the invasion, aimed at getting the major export industries and food production going again. The following year, 1943, represented the peak of achievements here, after which conditions rapidly degenerated in 1944 and 1945 with shortages of all commodities and of labour, coupled with soaring inflation, black marketeering, declining living standards, increased incidence of disease and so on.

The extent to which export production was restored was, in most cases, modest. Iron ore output quickly peaked at about 92 000 tonnes in 1942, dropping to 50 000 tonnes in 1943 and a mere 11–14 000 tonnes in

1944–5. Coal production (for domestic use) peaked at 490 000 tonnes in 1943, dropping to 204 000 tonnes by 1945. Rehabilitation in the tin industry took longer due to the scorched-earth policy adopted by the retreating Europeans and a growing shortage of spare parts. Production achieved at most one-third of the 1940 level by 1943, falling back to a mere 3000 tonnes in 1945 (Yip, 1969, 291, 295). Oil output in Borneo did rather better, recovering to nearly half the prewar level following the drilling of new wells in the Seria and Miri fields (Cramb, 1993b).

For the Malaysian rubber industry the occupation period represented 'years of disaster' (Barlow, 1978, 75). Japan could only consume a small proportion of the potential production. Between 1942 and 1945 a total of some 168 000 tonnes were shipped from the Peninsula, equivalent to about 30 per cent of output in 1940 alone. Estate upkeep was allowed to lapse, and the resident labour force remaining turned to food production which involved cutting down large areas of rubber trees. Smallholders behaved similarly, though to a lesser extent as the trees represented their personal assets. In total roughly 4 per cent of the total area of rubber in Malaya was excised. The Borneo territories were affected in a similar way. In Sarawak most rubber holdings (along with pepper and sago plantings) closed down and became overgrown, though some were switched over to food cultivation (Cramb, 1993b).

On the import side Malayan imports of rice in 1942–3 averaged only 180 000 tonnes a year against 600 000 tonnes prewar. Areas producing a rice surplus (such as Kedah and Kelantan) were prohibited from exporting to other parts of the country, and people in the rice deficit areas (the southern states) were similarly forbidden to move northwards. The Japanese were particularly anxious to increase the level of food production in Johor, due to its proximity to Singapore (Syonan). To this end resettlement projects, mainly of urban Chinese, were implemented, and the area under foodcrops (rice, tapioca, vegetables and so on) in that state grew to a reported 68 000 hectares against 11 000 hectares prewar (Office of Strategic Services, 1944).

This period saw a widespread redistribution of labour according to official priorities. It appears that, in Malaya, there was no great shortage of labour up to about mid-1944. As food shortages mounted, however, there began an exodus to the countryside, particularly as the resettlement schemes already referred to took hold. The lack of work for labourers on rubber estates made them a convenient reservoir for the authorities, and about 80 000 Indians were drafted to work on the Burma–Thai railway, of whom perhaps half survived (Stenson, 1980, 90). Chinese mineworkers were also drafted. In North Borneo and Sarawak workers were conscripted to build roads and airstrips.

The war period saw a steady deterioration in the conditions of living. This was the result of a growing scarcity of goods, and inflation caused by the demonetisation of the colonial currency. It was replaced by the so-called *duit pisang* ('banana currency' after the emblem it bore) which rapidly lost value after vast quantities flooded the market. Workers with scarce skills fared relatively better, but overall real incomes dropped heavily. By 1943–4 the shortfall of food supplies against the official allowances drove people into the flourishing black market. The incidence of beri-beri rose steeply, and cases of starvation occurred, for instance in parts of Johor (Office of Strategic Services, 1944).

Japanese rule had two contrary effects on the ethnic divisions in society. On the one hand, these divisions were perpetuated through the compulsory grouping of Malays, Indians and Chinese into associations which were vehicles for controlling the population for taxation, distribution of goods, requisitioning labour services and so forth. On the other hand, the increasing scarcity of labour in the later years started to blur ethnic divides, as in the 'Free Labour Service Corps' in Singapore which comprised Malays, Indians, Eurasians and Arabs. Some jobs, for example, the Dungun iron ore mines in Terengganu, were open to all races. The gender balance, too, changed with a large expansion in jobs for women (officework, telephonists) in towns (Office of Strategic Services, 1944; Horner, 1973). Against this, inter-ethnic tensions were heightened by the brutal treatment meted out disproportionately to some groups, notably the Chinese, whilst the Japanese were more concerned to maintain better relations with the indigenous peoples.

As we noted at the beginning of this section, the Japanese occupation period marked the practical dislocation of the former export economies. Operation through the allocation of resources and the distribution of goods according to market prices was seriously distorted by the imposition of military rule combined with preferential treatment for Japanese firms. Labour was directed according to the dictates of the military administration towards jobs not related to economic production, such as digging trenches or building the Thai–Burma railway. The various categories of export producer were not able to respond on the basis of their normal production schedules, but rather were bound by the arbitrary needs of the Japanese. The cutting-off of imports of manufactures coupled with the emphasis on local production for self-sufficiency could in principle have provided Malaysia with an opportunity to develop domestic industries, but again this was vitiated by the lack of raw materials, machinery and spare parts.

In the short term the losses to the Malaysian economy vastly outweighed any gains. There are no figures to indicate how much was extracted from the country in the form of profits by Japanese companies and individuals. The wealth of the communities of migrant descent was heavily reduced, especially that of the Chinese through forced 'contributions' or 'gifts' to the Japanese. Virtually all the Chinese and Indian-owned banks were compulsorily liquidated and their assets appropriated by Japanese banks.

Throughout Malaysia there was a major deterioration in the condition of physical capital in production and infrastructure. Standards of public health also fell badly.

9.2   The late colonial state 1945–63

The principal trend in this period was towards centralisation of authority which, as we have seen, had its origins prewar. This was most evident in the Federation (1948) which has been called 'the anvil of modern Malayan political development' (Rudner, 1976, 495). Centralisation took the form of financial and legislative authority over the individual states. Control of excise revenues was ceded to the Federal government, which could legislate in 144 areas leaving only ten to the states (mainly land, agriculture, primary and secondary education).

Concurrently colonial policy was subject to the general commitment of the postwar Labour government in Britain to eventual independence. In the case of Malaya this involved steps towards the creation of a more cohesive society out of the increasingly locally-born ethnic groups. In 1947 approximately 50 per cent of Indians, 63 per cent of Chinese and 95 of Peninsular Malays were locally born (Sandhu, 1969, Table 8b). A core issue was the creation of Malayan citizenship and the terms on which this could be acquired by non-Malays. It also required the construction of a framework within which the various groups could conduct political, economic and social relations. In other words, what was needed was provision for a distinctively Malayan system of politics.

The bases of this framework came into being with the formation of communal political parties: the United Malays National Organisation (UMNO) in 1946, the Malayan Chinese Association (MCA) and the Malayan Indian Congress (MIC), both in 1949, which constituted themselves as the Alliance in 1952. In 1954–5 municipal, state and Federal elections were held, the Alliance gaining a majority of elected members in the Federal one, giving Malaya effective home rule. At this stage these parties were elite- rather than mass-based (Rudner, 1976, 505). Between 1955 and formal independence (*Merdeka*) for Malaya in August 1957 the Alliance adopted a stance of moderate nationalism which was to characterise its policies in the first decade or so post-Independence: for instance, an assured place for foreign capital. Another central element in the political platform was the *Merdeka* 'bargain' between the parties noted above. In return for conceding Malay political paramountcy, the incontestable position of the Malay sultans, the Islamic religion and Malay as the national language, qualified non-Malays gained Federal citizenship, freedom to pursue their economic interests and some concessions on the continued use of their vernacular languages.

In its final years the colonial state had to withstand an armed threat from within the country. In 1948 the Malayan Communist Party (MCP), largely Chinese in membership, took to the jungles to conduct guerrilla warfare with the aim of forcing the British to leave, and subsequently establishing a Malayan Peoples' Republic inclusive of all races. The military campaign, which ultimately failed, was largely over by the mid-1950s, though the Emergency was not officially declared at an end until 1960.

The Borneo territories were well behind Malaya in acquiring the rudiments of political and social organisation. Indeed, after decades of paternalistic Chartered Company and Brooke rule they were 'almost apolitical' (Ongkili, 1986, 137). The transfer to direct rule from the Colonial Office in London in 1946 was the outcome of a growing recognition that neither of these regimes possessed the resources to achieve major progress in development. This unpoliticised condition persisted into the 1950s, especially in North Borneo. The handover to Britain did provoke some strong, even violent, sentiment in Sarawak, and prompted the formation of the Malay National Union and the Dayak Association of Sarawak. There was also some development in the associational structure within the various communities, led by economic elites. In North Borneo newly-rich timber entrepreneurs (the 'timber *towkays*') played a leading role in reviving the *huay kuans* (dialect associations) and Chinese Chambers of Commerce, whilst the Foochow community led the formation of the Sarawak Chinese Association (E. Lee, 1976, 37–8; Leigh, 1988, 187–9).

The 1950s saw further discussion of possible merger between British territories in the Malaysian region. However, the process of negotiation which led to the Federation of Malaysia in 1963 seems to have arisen directly out of the political-strategic situation which existed *c.* 1960. Despite the ending of the Emergency, the Malayan Federal government considered communism to be far from a spent force in the area. Singapore, which had its own internal Communist Party, had gained internal self-government in 1959 and contemplated a merger with Malaya for both economic (long standing trade links) and political (security) reasons. The prospects for union were complicated by the delicate ethnic balance. The Chinese majority in Singapore together with Chinese Malayans would outweigh Peninsular Malays, but if the Borneo territories (including Brunei) were included, the total of *bumiputeras* (Malays and other indigenous peoples) would have numerical superiority over the Chinese.

The Malayan Prime Minister, Tengku Abdul Rahman, made a proposal in May 1961 for a 'closer understanding' between these territories. Negotiations proceeded quickly thereafter and the Federation of Malaysia was formed in September 1963. Brunei declined to join, principally because no agreement could be reached on control of the revenue from its oil resources. North Borneo (renamed Sabah) and Sarawak agreed subject to certain safeguards, known as the Twenty Points, to guard against undue dominance from the Malayan Federation. These covered control over all immigration (from within as well as outside Malaysia), special rights for the indigenous peoples analogous to those enjoyed by the Peninsular Malays, education, the status of the English language, and specific guidelines for the division of functions and revenues between the state and Federal governments (Luping in Kitingan and Ongkili, 1989). The economic rationale underlying the Federation is examined in section 9.4.

During these final years the colonial state in Malaysia (which overlapped with the first years of Malayan independence) presided over the emergence of some of the basic characteristics of the polity within which the economy and society would develop over the next three decades or so.

9.3   Last years of the colonial export economy

The title of this section should not be taken to infer that the advent of political independence brought about an immediate change in the structure of the Malaysian economy. As we shall see in succeeding chapters, this transition stretched over several decades. What independence did bring was an end to external controls exerted by Britain through, for example, the colonial monetary system and the commodity control schemes. It opened the way for the building of a national, though still strongly export-oriented, economy.

The years leading up to independence were ones of wide fluctuations in the rates of economic growth, as can be seen from the case of Malaya (Table 9.1).

Table 9.1   Malaya: growth phases of GDP, 1947–63

Years	Annual average (%)[a]	Per capita (%)[a]
Phase 1		
1948–58 Fluctuating growth	2.8	0.3
Sub-periods		
1948–50 Reconstruction	6.4	3.7
1951–3 Stagnation	–0.2	–2.6
1954–58 Slow growth	2.5	–0.1
Phase II		
1959–63[b] Stable growth	6.8[c]	3.4[c]

[a] GDP (1959 prices).
[b] This phase extended to 1971 with annual average growth of 6.4 per cent, and 3.4 per cent per capita.
[c] Calculated from source data.
Source: Bhanoji Rao (1980), Table 7, 8.

Population growth

Due to the disturbed conditions of the 1930s, but more especially the war period, Malaysia's overall population growth rate between 1931 and 1947 was a low 1.57 per cent a year; it was 1.67 per cent in Malaya, 1.12 per cent in North Borneo and 0.95 per cent in Sarawak (Table 6.1). The Indian community in Malaya had actually fallen by about 40 000 due to repatriation in the depression, and high death-rates among labourers conscripted by the Japanese army (Saw, 1988, Table 3.3).

Between 1947 and 1960 the Malaysian growth rate accelerated to 2.73 per cent a year, with Malaya at nearly 2.8 per cent, North Borneo 2.46 per cent and Sarawak an unprecedented 2.42 per cent. In the case of Malaya the increase was the result of natural growth, since there was a net migration deficit of 254 137 from 1947 to 1957. This represented mostly an exodus of Chinese to China, and a rural–urban drift of Malays attracted principally to Singapore. The restoration and further improvement of health facilities, especially in the rural areas, brought about a sharp fall in the death rate. This was most evident among Malays where it fell by 54 per cent (1947–60), Chinese (45 per cent), and Indians (43 per cent) (calculated from Tan *et al.*, 1987, Table 1).

In the Borneo territories the growth rates among indigenous peoples continued to be low. Immigration remained important, particularly in labour-short North Borneo where from 1951 to 1960 there was a net gain of nearly 21 000, mainly Indonesians. Sarawak gained just over 10 000 immigrants, mostly Chinese, between 1948 and 1960 (Jones, 1966, 28).

The result of this surge in growth rates was to skew the Malaysian population further towards the younger age groups. Between 1931 and 1947 the proportion of the 5–19 years age-group in the total male population of Malaya increased from approximately 25 per cent to 34 per cent (calculated from Smith, 1952, Table VIII). This in turn had major implications for long-term demand for employment and social services.

Reconstruction of the economy 1946–9

The resumption of international trade restored, almost overnight as it were, the markets for the region's primary products. The sooner producers could get their enterprises restarted, the quicker their cash flows would recommence, wage employment would revive and social reconstruction could get under way. The first priority, however, was the restoration of the basis of civilian life (food supplies, health, law and order, stable currency, and so on). From August 1945 to March 1946 this was the task of the British Military Administration (BMA) in both Malaya and the Borneo territories.

The Administration proved unable to grapple with these problems in an even-handed way as between large and small producers, or European and Asian interests. Smuggling and the black market undermined efforts at price control, and attempts to increase the output of foodstuffs were a 'dismal failure' (Kratoska, 1988, 37). Domestic rice production did not regain the prewar (1941) level until 1948. The international trade in rice was controlled, but even so the shipments reaching Malaya fell behind schedule and the daily rice ration was much less than half the minimum requirement. The Japanese 'banana' currency was quickly demonetised but inflation continued as the BMA put into circulation notes amounting to 80 per cent above the prewar issue.

In the major export industries government faced the need to provide financial assistance to enable tin miners to restart operations, and in rubber to direct the flow of labour and the availability of supplies such as acid coagulant. Despite the disbursement of $78.5 million in loans to mines, some three-quarters of which went to European companies, the dredging sector recovered slowly, By 1949 the aggregate production of tin was only about two-thirds that in 1940 (Yip, 1969, 297–309).

The rubber industry recovered relatively quickly, surpassing the 1940 output by 1947 despite initial shortages of labour and supplies. Malayan smallholders, who could call on household labour, were swifter than estates, reaching 63 per cent of capacity compared to 32 per cent as early as May 1946. The prewar restrictions on exports were not reimposed, although the bans on new land grants and new planting were maintained (the latter was lifted in 1947: Rudner, 1970, 28–34). In 1948 earnings from rubber totalled $754 million, the highest since 1926. However, natural rubber now faced very different market conditions. During the war the USA, deprived of much of its supplies, had developed a synthetic (petroleum-based) rubber which, though not yet a perfect technical substitute, presented strong potential competition.

Whilst the Borneo territories participated in the recovery of rubber exports, their other products had a patchy record. Pepper and sago flour output fluctuated strongly from year to year. Timber extraction in North Borneo remained subject to the monopoly of the BBTC (see Chapter 8.3) which was valid until 1954. Domestic oil production in Sarawak declined, and much of the throughput at the Lutong refinery was from Brunei's Seria field.

By 1949 the Malaysian economy had been reconstructed in its prewar form, and substantially on the basis of its prewar technology. Labour was used more economically. In rubber the Malayan estate workforce in 1949 was about 20 per cent below the 1940 level, and output per worker stood at 1.44 tonnes against 0.96 tonnes (calculated from Barlow, 1978, Appendix 3.2 and special Annex 2.5). The yield per acre showed some benefits from the enforced rest, and the effects of the replantings during the 1930s with high-yielding trees were starting to show up. Overall though, these gains were quickly exploited; the record production in 1948 was not to be surpassed until 1961. All the Malaysian territories had comfortable export surpluses between 1947 and 1949 (see Figure 9.1), though North Borneo had the smallest margin.

Apart from measures to assist in the reconstruction of specific industries, the overall financial contribution from government was limited by a number of circumstance. This was particularly so in the case of Malaya. In both monetary and fiscal policy the interests of the country were subordinated to those of Britain and the sterling currency area. Britain ran a substantial trade deficit postwar, and thus the gold-dollar earnings of the most profitable colonies, among which Malaya was the leader, were of particular importance in balancing sterling area accounts. As hard-currency export earnings increased from 1946 to 1948 the Malayan government was unable to get open access to these for domestic use. Indeed the country made an involuntary contribution to the gold-dollar 'pool' amounting to £63.6 million in 1946–7. Additionally, the extent of the sterling cover required for the expanded Malayan note issue was increased, from 110 per cent to over 115 per cent in 1946. The Malayan Union was refused permission by the British Capital Issues Committee to raise a $200 million loan on the London capital market to fund reconstruction, so a $60 million loan had to be floated locally, putting additional pressure on domestic resources. The restricted access to gold-dollar funds also curbed Malaya's purchases of hard-currency imports (Rudner, 1994, ch. 1).

The Malayan government was thus forced to rely largely on domestic resources. Between 1946 and 1949 the principal sources of government revenue remained the indirect taxes on exports and imports. In 1947, in

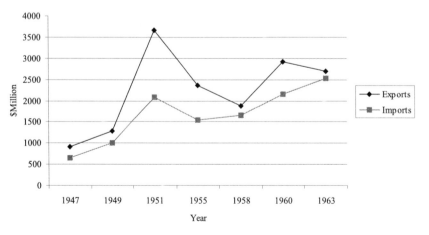

Figure 9.1   Malaysia: foreign trade values, 1947–63
Sources: International (IMF), *International Financial Statistics,* various years; Mitchell (1982), Table F1; Malaysia, *ABS,* various years.

the face of strong opposition from business and professional interests, a tax on incomes was legislated, but due to generous allowances this affected only about 56 per cent of the assessable income of individuals, and in the first two years of operation provided only a small proportion of total revenue: 11 per cent in 1949 (S.A. Lee, 1974, 83, 86). Even with such new sources, current revenue proved insufficient for expenditure, and budget deficits were incurred with a consequent drain on reserve funds.

On the current expenditure side general services, defence (especially during the height of the Emergency) and economic services absorbed the great bulk of outlays. Community and social services (mainly public health and education) received only 4 and 7 per cent respectively in 1948. Capital expenditure was a similarly small proportion at between 5 and 6 per cent of total expenditure (S.A. Lee, 1974, Tables 6.1, 6.3).

Malaya's major export industries, rubber and tin, had to find much of the finance for rehabilitation, apart from the government loans previously noted. Between 1947 and 1949 reinvestment of profits became a prime means of finance here, as it had been in the early years of the century. This shows up in the fact that the amount of net factor income paid abroad ranged between only 0.5 per cent and 1.3 per cent of GDP (this figure includes Singapore: S.A. Lee, 1974, Table 2.2). Conditions thus made it difficult for the government to develop consistent and systematic policies during these years, but we shall see a change as we move into the 1950s.

An important point to bring out here is that during the immediate postwar years there was a growing notion of Malaya as having an intrinsic economic interest which was not necessarily congruent with that of Britain. The fact that Malaya had no voice in the disposition of its substantial sterling balances was not lost, even on the colonial government, which remarked that: 'the extent of Malaya's contribution to the recovery of the Commonwealth and other countries of the world would seem to qualify her for a right to be represented in the ... negotiations that take place for the disposal of the products in which she is interested' (AR *Federation of Malaya*, 1948, cited in Rudner, 1976, 508). In the late 1940s just on half of Malaya's GDP came from the primary sector, 44 per cent from the tertiary or services sector, and a minuscule 6 per cent from the secondary manufacturing sector (Bhanoji Rao, 1980, 35). Whilst the productive capacity of the economy had been restored relatively swiftly, with a very respectable growth in per capita income (see Table 9.1), this was a shaky foundation on which to base plans for future development. With rubber in particular, as we shall see, the question of the growing obsolescence of the trees on both estates and smallholdings could not be shelved much longer.

For the Borneo territories, the reconstruction phase was much lengthier. Tregonning (1965, 223) uses very graphic terms to describe the condition of North Borneo postwar: 'no other part of the British Commonwealth, not even Burma, had been so utterly devastated. In some respects the country was back to pre-1881 standards'. Destruction was particularly bad in the towns and in the very limited communications infrastructure. Over 60 per cent of railway rolling stock was unusable and major bridges, for instance over the Papar river, required complete rebuilding. North Borneo was short of just about everything: capital, labour, raw material supplies, trained and educated manpower (much reduced under the Japanese). A full range of government departments (some reconstituted, such as agriculture, forests, posts and telegraphs, and others new, such as geological survey and social welfare) was necessary before any systematic development plan could be implemented. Sarawak presented a similar picture, although it was not as extensively bomb-damaged as North Borneo. The technical branches of government were weak, and there was a dearth of basic data upon which to draw up development plans.

Both colonies were visited late in 1946 by H.S. McFadzean, Economic Adviser to the Malayan Union, to assess the immediate needs. His reports brought out the severe shortcomings in all the respects mentioned above. In Sarawak, for example, the assets totalled just over $19 million, but only $8.6 million was available for purposes of rehabilitation and development. The annual revenue stood at the level of 1929, having been characterised in the interim by quick expansion and contraction, periodic retrenchments and resuscitation of key posts such as those of the Directors of Agriculture and Education which made for lack of continuity at the highest levels; 'This is a history that cannot be allowed to repeat itself' (McFadzean, 1946). McFadzean proposed a development plan involving the expenditure of $13 million over five years, 1947–52, subsequently extended to 1956, and the expenditure increased to $23.56 million (Morrison in Cramb and Reece, 1988, 38). In North Borneo a Plan for Reconstruction and Development covered the period 1948–55 costing just over $52 million (Gudgeon, 1981, 205). The details of these plans will be examined in due course along with the Draft Plan for Malaya 1950–5, but for the moment we will just note that the transition to colonial status put these two territories on a course of economic and social development which had already begun in Malaya in the 1920s and 1930s, though not in a very systematic fashion. So much remained to be done, notably in the infrastructure, that rehabilitation continued for much of the 1950s (see next section).

An underlying problem which was becoming increasingly apparent in these postwar years was the disparity in incomes between the main Asian communities in Malaya. Some approximations of annual income per capita by ethnic group are set out in Table 9.2, along with figures showing the proportions of income drawn from different sources. The latter reflected very clearly the outcomes of the ethnic division of labour which had emerged over the preceding half century or so. Malays were predominantly self-employed in the primary sector. Conversely, the great majority of Indians were in wage and salary employment (estates and government service). The Chinese were evenly distributed between these two sources, but derived a much larger proportion of income from business profits.

Once the economy had come through the unsettled conditions of 1945–7 living costs, though undoubtedly inflated over prewar levels, seem to have been fairly stable in the late 1940s. The retail price index for the Peninsula (1959=100) dropped from 89 in 1947 to 79 in 1949, rising to 85 in 1950 following the devaluation of the pound sterling by 30 per cent in 1949, and with the onset of the Korean war (Bhanoji Rao, 1974, 353; S.A. Lee, 1974, 10).

Table 9.2   Malaya: incomes by ethnic group, 1947 (%)

	Wages/salaries (%)	*Own account (%)*	*Profits (%)*	*Income per capita ($)*
Malays	28.35	68.60	3.05	258
Chinese	36.93	36.81	26.25	656
Indians	64.69	26.41	8.90	560
Overall				519

Source: Columns 1–3 calculated from Silcock and Fisk (1963), Table A3. Column 4 from Table 1.1 (ibid.).

Growth resumes 1950–63

The period from 1930 to 1950 had seen per capita GDP in Malaya experience negative growth at –0.2 per cent a year (Table 7.2). None the less, in 1950 Malayan per capita GDP at $1828 (in 1985 international dollars) was easily the highest in the Asian region. Japan was well behind at $1208, with the rest of East and Southeast Asia (excluding China) ranging between $565 and $943 per capita (van der Eng, 1994, Table 4). Malaya's leading position on this measure was owed primarily to its high level of export earnings relative to the still small absolute size of the population.

The 1950s witnessed the start of a period of nearly a quarter of a century in which world trade emerged from the long spell of stagnation which had lasted from the interwar decades, and entered a 'golden age' of unprecedented rates of growth. Between 1950 and 1973 the industrialised (OECD) countries recorded an annual increase in export volume of 8.6 per cent, the Asian region 7.1 per cent and Latin America only 4 per cent. In a sample of 32 OECD and developing countries, GDP grew at 5.1 per cent a year and per capita income at 3.3 per cent (Maddison, 1989, 65, Table 6.1).

The Malaysian growth record, as is evident from the Malayan data in Table 9.1, was patchy. The high rate in the reconstruction period was boosted by the Korean War (1950–1), which caused a rush to stockpile raw materials. Rubber and tin prices soared from index values (1958=100) of

48 and 80 respectively in 1949 to 211 and 144 in 1951 (IMF, 1966/7). The effect, however, was shortlived. Malaysia's export earnings similarly peaked and slumped (Figure 9.1), though the impact was muted in the Borneo territories, Sarawak especially, as these had other exports (oil, timber, sago) whose values were more stable. For the remainder of the 1950s Malayan exports stagnated until rubber prices picked up in 1959–60. Sarawak showed little net growth, except in 1959, but North Borneo began to show the effects of booming timber exports ($6.5 million in 1950, $90.7 million in 1960) with aggregate trade expanding at 22 per cent a year between 1947 and 1960 (Gudgeon, 1981, Table 8, 213).

All the Malaysian territories maintained surpluses on visible trade until the early 1960s, but the experience during this period brought to the forefront the question of the balance of payments. Under the Currency Board system operating since the early part of the century (Chapter 5.1) a fall in export earnings led automatically to a contraction in domestic money supply, decreased incomes and a lessened demand for imports, thus obviating a balance of payments problem. In 1955 a mission from the IBRD had visited Malaya and concluded that this system operated to constrain the growth of counter-cyclical domestic activities by restricting credit and making long-term capital difficult to raise in the face of the dominant role played by fluctuating export earnings. The Mission concluded that, 'Although many of the prewar economic features remain, Malaya ... is now a distinct national economy ... which must cope with Malayan economic problems from a Malayan viewpoint ... above all ... not in terms of outside ... capital ... [but] primarily ... domestic financial facilities' (IBRD, 1955, 475).

A report by T.H. Silcock on the Sarawak economy in 1956 reached much the same conclusions. '[It] is like a car which has no brakes or gears and ... therefore ... [needs] ... a reliable system of varying the amount of fuel that reaches the engine' (Silcock, 1956, 6). In the latter half of the 1950s the expansionary forces in the Sarawak economy slowed, due primarily to stagnation in aggregate export earnings (about 50 per cent of GDP). Up to 1955 expansion had been based largely on funds accumulated from the Korean war boom. Between 1950 and 1955 ordinary government expenditure (excluding development of posts and telegraphs) had roughly doubled while national income had risen only about 10 per cent (Silcock, 1956). By 1957–8 Sarawak's revenue reserves were practically exhausted, with a budget deficit up from $0.26 million in 1955 to approximately $19 million in 1957 (*AR* Colombo Plan, 1957–8). North Borneo, too, had a public debt totalling $8.7 million by the mid-1950s (Baker, 1962, 63–4).

In sum, as independence arrived for the Federation of Malaya and came on to the horizon for the Borneo territories, the drawbacks of reliance on a limited range of primary export commodities, and the constraining effects of the colonial monetary and financial system on the domestic economy, were becoming very clear.

Sources of growth

In this section we shall review the role of government, the private sector (capital, entrepreneurship and labour), technical and educational change.

The postwar years saw government adopting a broadly interventionist role in the economy (as opposed to the more specific measures of the inter-war period such as the export restriction schemes). This was most evident in the formulation of development plans, mainly covering five-year time spans. These are set out in Table 9.3. It is clear that throughout the territories, except for North Borneo's 1947–55 plan, infrastructure received the largest allocation of funds. In Malaya there was a need for a network of

Table 9.3   Malaysia: development plans, 1947–63

	Planned sectoral allocation (per cent)		
	Economic projects	*Infrastructure*	*Social services*
Malaya			
Draft Devel. Plan (1950–5):			
Initial	10.3	63.8	25.7
Revised	18.5	72.3	9.2
1st Malaya Plan (1956–60)	24.5	46.1	18.1
2nd Malaya Plan (1961–5)	23.4	47.9	17.0
North Borneo			
Reconstruction and Devel. (1947–55)	8.2	26.05	65.75[a]
Development (1955–60)	[details n.a.]		
Development (1959–64):			
Initial	7.7	48.6	13.80[a]
Revised	14.9	44.8	17.50[a]
Sarawak			
Plan 1947–56	[Details n.a., but emphasis on raising exports, foodstuffs and infrastructure]		
Plan 1951–7:			
Initial	4.0 (agr. only)	63.0	21.3
Revised	10.0	55.0	25.0
Plan 1955–60:			
Initial	14.0	55.0	25.0
Revised	20.0	40.0	31.0
Plan 1959–63	[Details n.a., but emphasis on infrastructure]		

n.a.= not available.
[a] General allocation to administration, internal security not included.
Sources: Malaya, Draft Development Plan, S.A. Lee (1974), Table 4.3; remainder Bhanoji Rao (1980), Tables 59, 60; North Borneo, Gudgeon (1981), Tables 3, 12; Sarawak, Morrison in Cramb and Reece (1988), *Report on Development* (1956), AR Sarawak (1957).

minor roads in the country areas to facilitate connection with market centres. The electricity network required corresponding development. In the Borneo territories much reconstruction was necessary before new developments could be undertaken. Roads, railways, ports and airfields required restoration, the latter being of particular importance as a means of overcoming the difficulties of internal transport and communications. Sarawak, for example, had a mere 736 kilometres of roads, mostly gravel or unmetalled, in 1947 and this had increased to only 1363 kilometres by 1962 (Porritt, 1997, Table 13.1).

In Malaya economic projects ranked next after infrastructure. These ranged from the rejuvenation of the rubber industry through replanting with high-yielding trees, improvements to rice cultivation, and diversification into new crops (mainly oil palms), new land development schemes and pioneer industrialisation aimed at import-substitution. It is notable that the latter, which was to assume increasing importance from the 1960s onwards, received very small allocations of only just over 1 per cent of funds in the First and Second Malaya Plans. Both North Borneo and Sarawak started from a much lower base in all these respects. The colonial governments had to commission basic surveys to determine the actual nature and extent of the economic resources of these territories, such as surveys of soils and mineral deposits. There was also a need to foster diversification to lessen dependence on rubber, pepper and sago and to increase domestic rice production.

Social services occupied quite a high priority in the early postwar years but, except in Sarawak, these declined in relative importance by the later 1950s. Malaya already possessed a comparatively good level of adult literacy among males: for example, 83 per cent in the 15–19 age group, though much lower (at 54 per cent) for women (Lim Chong Yah, 1967, Table 10.9). There was a strong demand from all races for improved access to education. In absolute terms government expenditure rose from around $16 million in 1947 to $224 million in 1962, with a major emphasis on the primary level. Here again North Borneo and Sarawak started from low bases. In public health there was a marked improvement throughout Malaysia as hospitals and clinics were built. The Malayan death rate for all races more than halved between 1947 and 1961.

The capital for public investment came from a variety of sources, but in general Malaya relied primarily on domestic resources. The Korean War boom increased export earnings so greatly that the total expenditure estimates for the Draft Development Plan were raised from $215 million to $856 million. In the First and Second Plans foreign loans and grants constituted only 28 per cent and 13 per cent respectively of the total financial commitment. The balance came from government surpluses and domestic borrowing from, for example, the Employees' Provident Fund and the Post Office Savings Bank. North Borneo and Sarawak were less well-endowed, and required more external assistance. This came mainly from Britain through the Colonial Development and Welfare Fund, although North Borneo's timber boom was generating much more domestic revenue by the 1959–64 Plan. All Malaysian states had substantial, though not unmanageably large, public debts by the early 1960s. The public sector share of total consumption rose from 9.2 to 16 per cent. The amplitude of Malaya's domestic resources is evident from the fact that between 1948 and 1960 the proportion of national income saved was 17.6 per cent against capital formation at 10.7 per cent. As a proportion of annual GDP (at 1959 prices), Gross Domestic Capital Formation averaged 7.6 per cent from 1947 to 1958, rising to 13 per cent from 1959 onwards (S.A. Lee, 1974, 16, 145; Bhanoji Rao, 1980, Table 10; Gudgeon, 1981, 210–11; Porritt, 1997, 179).

Exactly comparable data for the Borneo territories are not available for this period, but the general composition and trend was the same as for Malaya: that is, a sharp rise in levels of investment by the early 1960s and an increasing share for the public sector, with an emphasis on buildings/construction followed by machinery/vehicles (Silcock, 1956; Sarawak Government, 1961; IBRD, 1963; Wilson and Grey, 1966, a, b; Bugo, 1984).

However, it was one thing to compile plans with estimates of expenditure and the accompanying sectoral allocations, and quite another to achieve the targets in full. There was a general shortage throughout the Malaysian territories of officials with required levels of skills and practical experience. In Malaya there was the additional factor of the Emergency which not only placed strains on the administrative structure, but also rendered operations dangerous in the rural areas when the armed threat was at its peak in the early 1950s. Thus, the Draft Development Plan achieved overall only about 80 per cent of planned expenditure. Agricultural projects fared best at 82 per cent, but education at 65 per cent fell well short of rising demand. The Plan was 'little more than a collection of [543] disconnected departmental schemes' (Rudner, 1972, 66). The First and Second Malaya Plans performed distinctly better at 88 per cent and 123 per cent of target, though social services (health in particular) still lagged badly at 25 per cent and 70 per cent. These were underpinned by a more sophisticated planning apparatus and a bureaucracy which grew approximately threefold between 1948 and 1959. The advent of Malayan independence in 1957 'imbued the [plans] with politics of decolonization' (Rudner, 1979, 817). The National Operations Room in Kuala Lumpur, and the energetic role of Tun Abdul Razak as Minister for Rural Development in the early 1960s were held up as a model for developing countries.

North Borneo and Sarawak had similar difficulties in fulfilling targets. The latter could only achieve 70 per cent of projected expenditure in 1956, but the situation improved in the later 1950s with appointments to key posts such as Director of Public Works. Not all expenditure was developmental. In North Borneo $8.7 million (nearly a quarter of the total public debt) was paid out to timber companies, notably the BBTC, as compensation for the surrender of monopoly rights.

Though the colonial governments and the independent Malayan state adopted a more *dirigiste* policy towards the economy in the postwar years, this was confined largely to the public sector. The stance towards the private sector was for the most part *laissez-faire*, though there were some initiatives in the introduction of new crops and technology, land development and industrialisation which had broad implications for private enterprise.

The principal source of growth in the Malaysian economy remained the agricultural sector (tin exports stagnated at between 30–40 000 tonnes in the 1950s, with export restriction reintroduced in 1956). Data on the area cultivated and output of major crops are given in Table 9.4.

Table 9.4   Malaysia: area and production of major crops, 1950–60

Year	Rice	Rubber	Oil Palm	Coconuts	Cocoa	Pepper	Sago
(a) *Area (000 hectares) Malaya (M), North Borneo (NB), Sarawak (S)*							
1950 M	273	1437	96[a]	194	n.a.	–	–
NB	30	48		18	18	–	–
S				n.a.			
1955 M	291	1483	111[a]	208		–	–
NB	28	40		18		–	–
S				n.a.			
1960 M	321	1549	135[a]	–	–	–	–
NB	31	69	–	20	1	–	–
S	–	143	–	–	–	–	–
(b) *Production (000 tonnes)*							
1950 M	436	704	53		–	–	–
NB	25	24		24[b]	–	–	–
S	n.a.	56	–	–	–	–	23
1955 M	636	647	57	–	–	–	–
NB	47	20	–	35[b]	–	–	–
S	–	40	–	–	–	20	20
1960 M	860	718	90	–	–	–	–
NB	50	22	–	80[b]	–	–	–
S	n.a.	54	–	–	–	8	18

n.a. = not available.
[a] Average in production.
[b] Copra

Sources: Rice: D. Lim, (1973), Table 11.11; Lim Chong Yah. (1967), appendix 6.1; Rubber: Barlow (1978), Appendix 3.2; Gudgeon (1981), Table 9, 219; Oil Palm: D. Lim, (1973), Table 11.7; Lim Chong Yah (1967), Appendix 5.2; Coconuts: Gudgeon (1981), Table 9; Cocoa: Gudgeon (1981), Table 9; Pepper, Sago, Timber: *ABS*, North Borneo, Sarawak; Bugo (1984).

In the export sector the rubber area and output stagnated, too, during this decade. The growing obsolescence of most of the existing planted area was, by then, inescapable. In Malaya about half the estate area and up to two-thirds on smallholdings had trees 30 or more years old (the assumed economic life). The situation in the Borneo territories was similar. Average yields were low and falling. Intensification of production by planting with new types of trees capable of double or triple the current yields per hectare offered the only means of lowering unit costs and meeting competition from synthetic rubber as well from low-cost competitors such as Indonesia.

The Mudie Commission Report (1954) concluded that accelerated replanting was the last opportunity for the rubber industry to '[set] its house in order' (cited in Barlow, 1978, 85). This necessitated financial assistance. Government in Malaya had already made a start in 1951 by imposing a special replanting cess (export duty), the proceeds from which were used to recompense owners who could furnish proof of replanting their property with approved types of high-yielding trees up to 21 per cent of the area (estates), and one-third (smallholdings). Post-Mudie, the subsidies were raised to $988 and $1478 per hectare respectively. The Borneo territories were ahead of Malaya, with Sarawak having started a Rubber Development Scheme in 1947, and North Borneo in 1950.

The initial results of these programmes were modest, particularly on smallholdings where the smallest owners (two hectares or less) could not, even with assistance, afford the loss of income for up to seven years which cutting out old trees entailed. However, in the later 1950s improved levels of assistance boosted the rate and by 1965 half the Malayan smallholding area had been replanted. In North Borneo nearly half the aggregate area, which grew by 92 per cent between 1951 and 1962/3, was under high-yielding trees, but Sarawak, with a 54 per cent increase in area, still lagged badly at only 18 per cent (Gudgeon, 1981; Cramb, 1988, 120).

Besides the rejuvenation of the existing cultivated area, the question of the development of new land came to the fore, given greater urgency by the rapidly burgeoning population which, in conjunction with the Muslim law of inheritance that required division among all the heirs, was increasing pressure on land. This was evident in the more developed west-coast states of Malaya (Perak, Selangor). In 1956, as one of its last major acts, the colonial government created the Federal Land Development Authority (FELDA) to open large blocks of virgin land in less-developed areas, such as Pahang. These were sub-divided into 3–4 hectare blocks for allotment to families, mainly Malay, from overcrowded areas. Financial assistance was provided, plus housing and planting materials (usually rubber in the early schemes) and technical advice to bring the crop to maturity, after which the loans were to be repaid out of the settler's income (targeted at $400 per month). Besides FELDA, state governments opened land for distribution to

small farmers who could furnish capital and remain in their existing locations (*in situ* schemes). Such schemes together constituted the main source
of land development under the Second Malaya Plan.

Neither North Borneo or Sarawak sought to implement large-scale land
development schemes along the Malayan pattern prior to federation in
1963. Government's prime concern was to encourage permanent settlement with crops such as rubber. In Sarawak the Land Code of 1958 sought
to restrict the creation of further native customary rights over land in order
to contain the spread of shifting cultivation, regarded as uneconomic.
There were five categories of land: mixed zone, native area, native customary, reserved, and interior area land. Non-natives could occupy land only in
the first of these, the mixed zone, which constituted a mere 7.9 per cent of
the total and was mostly situated in the towns and coastal areas. This
restrained expansionary activities in the interior, especially by the Foochow
Chinese (Hong, 1987,45–7; Leigh, 1988, 183).

With rubber undergoing rejuvenation, the major new source of growth
in agriculture was the oil palm (though this had been taken up by some
European estates as early as the 1920s). It was now seen to offer quicker
(maturity after three years) and better returns than rubber, and also had
been recommended by the IBRD Mission as a suitable crop for smallholders. Again, Malaya took the lead at this stage (Table 9.4), with rubber
estates turning over some of their land to oil palms and increasing use on
FELDA schemes. This development is highly significant as it marked the
effective commencement of competition between crops for land. By the
early 1960s Malaya supplied 20 per cent of world demand for palm oil. In
North Borneo several estates took up the crop, and a 3000 hectare scheme
for smallholders was started in the Beaufort/Klias Peninsula area (Gudgeon,
1981, 235).

Statistics on other crops are very patchy (Table 9.4). Output of coconuts,
pepper and sago flour showed fluctuating patterns. Rice remained largely a
subsistence crop, and the industry showed signs of growth only in Malaya
where government continued the programmes started in the 1930s aimed
at improving existing land and bringing further areas under cultivation.
Major initiatives in the 1950s included the later show-piece irrigated
schemes in Kedah (Muda) and Kelantan (Kemubu). Another line of action
was to encourage farmers to grow a second crop in the off-season, but this
did not really pick up until the mid-1960s (see below). This extensification
was coupled with measures to assist more intensive cultivation (fertiliser
subsidies, access to improved seeds, training with small tractors and so on).
From 1949 government maintained a generous guaranteed minimum price.
The results are evident in the growth of the area planted (Table 9.4), and a
marked rise in yields per hectare. The extent of Malayan self-sufficiency
stood at nearly 63 per cent in 1960 against just over 40 per cent in the
1930s (Cheng, 1973, Appendix 9; Amarjit Kaur, 1992, Table 1).

Similar policies were pursued in the Borneo territories, but in North Borneo the cultivated area stagnated up to 1960. Increased funding for agriculture in the 1959–64 plan added about 8000 hectares, but output was highly susceptible to the weather. Production met 60 per cent of needs in a poor year, and 70–80 per cent in a good one (Gudgeon, 1981, 207, 220, 234). For Sarawak the picture is one of declining self-sufficiency in this period. Despite an Assistance to Padi Farmers Scheme (1958), only 36 per cent of rice farmers produced enough for their own needs. As farmers switched to rubber in the 1950s, there was a concomitant shortage of land for hill-*padi*. Imports to make up the shortfall rose steeply from around 20 000 tonnes in 1950 to 60 000 tonnes (50–60 per cent of total consumption) by the early 1960s (Solhee, 1988, 88–9; readings from graph in Cramb, 1988, 119; *AR Sarawak*, 1962; Sarawak Government, 1984, 67).

Apart from cultivated crops, the main product in the primary sector to show notable growth was timber, principally from North Borneo which passed rubber as the chief export earner in 1958. Timber exports from Sarawak also showed quite respectable growth, but lagged increasingly behind from the mid-1950s. In the former state the stimulus came from the revocation, with compensation, of BBTC's monopoly in 1952. There were now three other foreign concessionaires, two British and one American, as well as some annual licensees, mostly Chinese and former sub-licensees of the BBTC. Like their predecessors in the late nineteenth-century Malayan tin industry, the latter made a quick start by exploiting the most accessible areas by labour-intensive methods. Between 1953 and 1955 their output was over twice that of the concessionaires who concentrated on mechanisation (tractors) which initially met problems (E. Lee, 1976, 20). After this initial burst of activity government imposed an annual *coupe* (or cut) for each annual licensee, but these operators proved difficult to restrain. By 1960 seven had obtained the Special Licence as a prerequisite to gaining a full concession. In Sarawak the Foochow Chinese, who had profited substantially from the rubber boom in 1950–1, used these resources to play a leading role in logging developments (Leigh, 1988, 183).

The 1950s and early 1960s were a period in which the agricultural sector, though it did not deliver major rises in productivity, was revitalised and the basis laid for substantial gains once the activity in rubber, oil palms and land development schemes came to fruition. Oshima (1987, 245) identifies the large investment in this sector (at a time when neighbouring countries such as Burma, Thailand and Indonesia were unsuccessfully pursuing domestic industrialisation) as the 'key' to Malaysia's later industrial transition.

In addition to diversification in the primary sector, the IBRD Mission had recommended moves to build up secondary industries of various kinds in Malaya to cater for a larger portion of the domestic market for manufactured goods (i.e., import-substitution: IBRD, 1955, 85). As we have seen

(Chapter 8.4), industrialisation thus far had been related mainly to the processing of raw materials and production of items enjoying the protection of distance (e.g., bricks, cement). In 1955 manufacturing and construction accounted for 5.3 per cent of Malayan GDP and roughly 10 per cent of the labour force. Most (80–90 per cent) was in Chinese ownership, the balance Indian, and the typical firm was small and privately-owned. Eighty-seven per cent had less than 20 workers, but accounted for only 23 per cent of gross sales (Wheelwright, 1963, Tables 10.1, 10.3, 10.12).

However, the IBRD did not consider that Malaya possessed any comparative advantages here which could be readily exploited. Whilst most firms appeared to be efficiently operated, there was a lack of 'the complex of basic raw materials usually associated with advanced industrial development' (IBRD, 1955, 84). Wages were relatively high due to competition for labour from the major export industries and commerce. Lacking, too, were domestic sources of cheap power and fuel. There was a need to increase average firm size, adopt best managerial practices and technology. 'All these factors militated against the spontaneous development of a significant manufacturing sector' (Snodgrass, 1980, 207). An initiative to help break these constraints was needed from outside the sector, namely from government.

Thus, the newly-independent Malayan government passed a Pioneer Industries Ordinance in 1958 which offered inducements such as tax holidays up to five years, guarantees (to foreign firms) on freedom to remit profits and repatriate capital, and so on. A modest level of tariff protection, averaging about 15 per cent, was given. Between 1958 and mid-1962 a total of 73 firms were granted pioneer status. The total called-up capital was $69 million of which the bulk (nearly 53 per cent) was from overseas: 28.4 per cent from Singapore alone, and the balance of nearly 19 per cent from within Malaya. Among the overseas investors Britain led with $16 million, followed by the Bahamas ($5 million), Hong Kong ($4.3 million), USA and Canada ($5.4 million), Australia ($2.7 million), Japan ($1.3 million) (Wheelwright, 1965, 47). Pioneer firms were predominantly consumer-goods oriented (80 per cent of output in 1959 falling to 66 per cent by 1963) (D. Lim, 1973, Table 12.4). They were mainly located along the west coast of the Peninsula. Selangor alone had 54 per cent of value-added (Snodgrass, 1980, 208), and was the site of the first industrial estate (Petaling Jaya) set up by government to provide fully serviced sites for companies.

In the light of Chinese predominance in the Malayan manufacturing sector at independence in 1957 we may ask why entrepreneurs from this group did not play a more prominent role in the pioneer industries programme from 1958? Perhaps the major reason lay in the new, public corporate-type of manufacturing venture being established: for example, batteries, paint, electric cables, pharmaceuticals, tyres and tubes, petroleum products. The British agency houses figured among investors here (Drabble and Drake, 1981). It was not that Chinese absolutely lacked capital: rather that for the most part they retained a longstanding preference for smaller private companies or partnerships, and for investment in areas they understood well, notably commerce. 'There was very little mobility of Chinese-owned capital from industry to industry at the end of the 1950s' (Mackie, 1992, 168). The facility to tap directly into local sources of private capital only began to widen with the formation of the Malayan Stock Exchange (10 out of the initial 19 member firms were in Singapore) in 1960 (Drake, 1969, 210).

The infant industrial sector, though still only 6 per cent of GDP by 1961, was the most dynamic part of the Malayan economy in the late 1950s and early 1960s, averaging 10 per cent growth annually. Producer goods industries (chemicals, non-metallic minerals, basic metals, transport equipment), though the smaller part of the sector, averaged 32 per cent a year from 1959–1963 and had stronger linkage effects on the rest of the economy (D. Lim, 1973, Tables 12.2, 12.3). This latter reflected the general impetus from the development programmes of the period, which were starting to come to fruition by the early 1960s and helped to produce the more stable growth rate in GDP of 6.4 per cent a year from 1959 onwards (Table 9.1). This development is also significant in that for the first time a Malayan government was able effectively to set the conditions under which foreign capital could enter the country.

The Borneo territories remained largely untouched by import-substitution industrialisation at this time. The existing industries were primarily of the processing type: for example, in 1962 sawmills and other timber-related works constituted 56 out of 129 factory establishments in Sarawak. The next largest group (16 units) was miscellaneous food manufactures (Sarawak Government, 1970, Table 14.3).

Taken together, the surge in public and private investment which we have reviewed constituted the largest boom since the first two decades of the century. An important difference, though, was that in Malaya this:

> tended to favour long-lived assets [buildings etc.] over short-lived but more immediately productive investments ... [This] undoubtedly helped to create capacity upon which the Malayan economy [could] draw for some time into the future [but] two important types of social risk are inherent ... the problem of terms of trade fluctuations ... [and] mounting popular expectations [of] the benefits to be provided by economic development ... within a reasonable period of time.
>
> (Snodgrass, 1966, 84–5)

As we have seen in earlier chapters, levels of capital investment in the Borneo territories were far below Malaya. Silcock (1956, 77–8) attempted a rough calculation for Sarawak which put private capital formation in 1955 at $33 million, and public at $17 million, together equivalent to just over 13 per cent of GDP. The sectoral distribution was very similar to Malaya with building/construction at 63 per cent, and machinery/vehicles 34 per cent, but agricultural investment was only a small residual at 3 per cent. Government expenditure accounted for less than 6 per cent of the total (Sarawak Government, 1961, 45–6). The next two years saw a sharp increase to an annual average of $105 million, or 20 per cent of GDP, with a much enlarged government share at 28 per cent (calculated from Bugo, 1984, Appendix 1–2).

Data on North Borneo are even more sparse. The earliest estimate of national income (GNP) is $300 million for 1961, with fixed capital formation of $60 million, two-thirds private, one-third public. Investment was thus 20 per cent of GNP, and was estimated at 18 per cent for the following year (IBRD, 1963, 3, Table V). A large part of the private investment was going into the timber industry, ranging from $9 million to just over $15 million between 1959 and 1961, then accelerating sharply to $18 million in 1962 and $21.5 million in 1963 (Wilson and Grey, 1966a, Table 16).

Improvements to transport facilities retained a high priority in both private and government investment in these territories. In Sarawak the 1950s saw substantial improvements in water transport with large increases in the numbers of powered coastal and river craft, together with imports of outboard motors (up by nearly 200 per cent between 1950 and 1955 alone: (Silcock, 1956, Table 1).

Between 1947 and 1962 the Malayan workforce grew from 1.875 million to 2.306 million, or a fairly modest annual rate of about 1.4 per cent against population growth approaching 3 per cent (Table 6.1 above). With immigration no longer a significant component, it was this natural increase which provided the main source of additional labour. The bulk was absorbed outside the agricultural sector which grew marginally in absolute terms (1.288 to 1.308 million), but fell sharply from about 66 per cent to 55 per cent of the total workforce during this period. The share of manufacturing increased from 0.126 to 0.157 million (approximately 25 per cent), and very slightly from 6.7 to 6.8 per cent of the workforce. By far the largest growth came in the tertiary sector, up from 23.9 to 34.6 per cent of the total, with commerce and services absorbing 335 000 out of the aggregate increase of 431 000 (D. Lim, 1973, Table 7.8). This reflected the rising tempo of domestic economic activity generated by the development plans.

These figures do not suggest any significant intersectoral transfers of labour from agriculture to industry. The additional workers, particularly in manufacturing and various service occupations, came increasingly after 1957 from urban Chinese women under the age of 40. Chinese men were more prominent in construction and commerce. Snodgrass observes that 'the Chinese had the most modernized [i.e., non-agricultural] employment structure .. [and] .. supplied most of the rather modest skilled and educated labour inputs' (1980, 88, 92). In agriculture the census data indicate a substantial influx of Malay women of all ages. For Indians, women and men, the evidence shows a heavy drop in employment totalling 12 000 and 23 000 respectively by 1967, as estates began to reduce their total workforce after 1960 (Snodgrass, 1980, Table 4.18; Hirschman and Aghajanian, 1980). The division of labour along ethnic lines was still the outstanding characteristic.

In terms of nominal wages, labour obtained a fluctuating, though generally rising, share of Malayan GDP at current prices: e.g. 39.7 per cent in 1955, 44.3 per cent in 1958 and 43.5 per cent in 1963. In particular industries, such as rubber, nominal monthly earnings for tappers increased much faster than productivity. A strong push factor here came from the amalgamation of labour unions in the various Peninsular states into the National Union of Plantation Workers (NUPW) in 1954, which undertook collective bargaining with employers, achieving increases in wages as well as ancillary benefits (such as housing, medical care). For real wages Table 9.5 shows that after an upward surge during the Korean War boom, both food and retail prices dropped back to remain fairly steady for the rest of the 1950s and early 1960s, which suggests some improvement in living conditions.

Against these improvements, the growth in employment proved increasingly unable to absorb the increase in population of working age. We have noted the generally capital-intensive nature of the import-substitution industries, and the trend to decreased employment on estates. Officially the unemployment rate was put at 2 per cent in 1957 rising to 6 per cent by 1962, but this left out of account the 'passively unemployed': that is, those who wished to work but who for various reasons – such as poor nutritional levels, inability to shift domicile, institutional or other barriers – were not actively seeking a job. If these were included the unemployment rate could have approached as much as 9 per cent by the early 1960s. Because of this under-estimation, the Second Malaya Plan (1961–5) target of 340 000 new jobs fell well short of the numbers actually entering the labour market, conservatively put at around 500 000 (D. Lim, 1973, 143–7).

In contrast to Malaya, North Borneo faced a continuation of the tight labour supply situation inherited from before the war. Between 1947 and 1962 the absolute numbers of Chinese altered little. However, substantial immigration from Indonesia boosted their numbers nearly sixfold (Wilson and Grey, 1966a, Tables 7, 9). Underlying these figures was a shift by Chinese out of wage-earning jobs into self-employed work in towns or in rubber planting (as this sector expanded in the 1950s). It seems that Indonesians replaced indigenous workers with the larger employers (estates and timber cutting), owing to a superiority in skills. Daily wage rates

Table 9.5   Malaya: price indices, selected years, 1947–73 (1959 = 100)

Year	Food prices[a]	Retail prices[b]
1947	89.7	89
1950	90.6	85
1952	131.6	113
1955	104.4	99
1960	101.6	100
1965	104.8	102
1967	116.3	108
1973	147.5	127

[a] Six food items.
[b] Official prices index for food, clothing, household goods, fuel, power, services, rent.
Source: Adapted from Barlow (1978), Appendix Table 1.2.

for unskilled labour stood at $2.00 in 1948 (four times the prewar level), $3.50 for semi-skilled and up to $5 skilled. These rose to $3.50, $7 and $12 respectively in the Korean War boom, and then remained unchanged up to the mid-1950s. These represent increases of 75, 100 and 140 per cent. Against these the daily budgets of Chinese and indigenous workers rose by 44.5 per cent and 80 per cent respectively (calculated from data in Baker, 1962, 90). Thus Chinese workers, who constituted the majority of the semi- and skilled groups, did relatively well, whilst the predominantly unskilled indigenous labourers did not keep pace. Trade union activity was negligible.

Sarawak presents a similar picture in terms of the composition and distribution of its labour force. Two contrasting tendencies emerged at this time. Labour scarcities could develop in certain sectors of agriculture since a high market price for a particular crop drew workers away from other occupations (a marked superiority in flexibility over Malayan agriculture: Royal Institute of International Affairs, 1957). But this seems to have resulted in a mismatch of distribution and needs. By the early 1960s substantial under-employment was reported in rural areas, and unemployment (though only at about 2 per cent) in the urban areas. The great bulk of the workforce, some 58 per cent, was concentrated in rice cultivation which had the lowest net output value per head. Employment in the higher value sectors (mining, manufacturing, building, utilities and transport) accounted for only 7.6 per cent of workers (Wilson and Grey, 1966b, Table 2). In both the Borneo territories the pressures towards major structural changes in the labour force were as yet muted.

The 1950s and early 1960s saw a process of economic and social differentiation gathering impetus among the Malay peasantry, generating the beginnings of a rural entrepreneurial class. A microcosm of this trend can be seen in Mukim Mawar (a pseudonym) in Selangor, where the main benefactors were those with best access to rubber land and government assistance (replanting grants). These were the village 'official-cum-elite' class, the district and village heads, schoolteachers, contractors and so on. These were tied in with the inception of political activities resulting from the formation of political parties postwar (Shamsul, 1986, 68–71).

Active steps to upgrade the economic status of Peninsular Malays had begun with the establishment of the Rural and Industrial Development Authority (RIDA) in 1950. RIDA became engaged in a wide range of activities from village-based projects to improve rice production, livestock, rubber processing and sales, to bus transport and boat-building companies. However, this mission proved beyond the resources allotted to RIDA, which became marginalised politically by the mid-1950s (after the resignation of its first Director, Datuk Onn bin Jaafar) though continuing more limited tasks until superseded by MARA (*Majlis Amanah Rakyat*) in 1965. The major tasks of rubber planting and land development were passed to other new organisations such as FELDA (1956) which continued after Independence (D. Lim, 1973, 191). There were thus strong elements of continuity.

Postwar British governments, though they wished to see British economic interests in Malaya generally conserved, were not especially responsive to the demands of capitalist business there. The Colonial Office supported the state-initiated schemes for replanting rubber smallholdings despite objections from British rubber interests that this bolstered 'inefficient' producers. These same interests (together with tin companies) failed to persuade the national Malayan government to continue the appointment of nominated commercial members (as had been the case in the FMS Federal Council prewar) to the post-Independence legislature (White, 1994, 259–60).

A step which arose directly out of independence was the setting up of a Central Bank in Malaya (*Bank Negara Tanah Melayu*) in 1959, again following a recommendation from the IBRD Mission. It was thought that the Malayan economy had matured sufficiently to make independent control of the money supply possible, though in practice the Bank's functions were initially constrained by the existing strong integration with the British monetary system through British banks operating in Malaya, and the need to maintain a fixed exchange rate with sterling. 'For Malayan ministers, a central bank was overwhelmingly a political symbol rather than an instrument to wield real economic independence' (Schenk, 1993, 427). Initially, the Bank was not empowered to issue a separate Malayan currency as this would have involved withdrawal from the Currency Board which covered Malaya, Singapore and the British Borneo territories. The Board was not finally dissolved until June 1967, by which time Singapore had left the Federation.

The Central Bank's early focus was on regulating and encouraging the activities of commercial banks in Malaya, in particular to expand their role as lenders to domestic borrowers. This it did so successfully that total loans and advances grew by nearly 84 per cent from 1960 to 1963 (Edwards, 1970, Table 42). Government also entered this sector by subscribing capital (along with several commercial banks and the Colonial Development Corporation) to the Malayan Industrial Development Finance Ltd (MIDFL) set up in 1960 to assist projects with longer gestation periods. A subsidiary, Malayan Industrial Estates Ltd (MIEL) developed the serviced areas, such as Petaling Jaya, referred to earlier (Snodgrass, 1980, 209).

Important institutional developments in the Borneo territories during the 1950s were the setting up of Executive and Legislative Councils in North Borneo (1950), with increased representation for commercial interests. A similar expansion took place in the Council Negeri in Sarawak. There was a general growth in the machinery of local government.

A vital area of government activity, education, was common to all these territories. The major goal under both the colonial and national Malayan governments was the attainment of universal primary education, to be accompanied in the latter instance by a unified national system. For the time being, though, the system had to be built around distinct language streams: Malay, Chinese (Mandarin), Tamil and English (the three latter with some instruction in Malay). After 1957 the political issue of the primacy of the national language, Bahasa Malaysia, and the promotion of a 'Malayan consciousness', took precedence over the economic contribution of education to nation building. In North Borneo and Sarawak the continuing use of English as the first medium of instruction was an important issue in the lead-up to federation. Throughout Malaysia primary school enrolments soared during these years, with a knock-on effect into secondary education and, in the Peninsula, the first tertiary institution, the University of Malaya in Kuala Lumpur (1959).

Looking overall at the sources of economic growth, increase in capital stock emerges as by far the most important, accounting, in Malaya, for 70 per cent of the growth in GDP, followed at a great distance by additional labour inputs (17 per cent), and the balance (13 per cent) from improvements to technology, education and organisation (Bhanoji Rao, 1980, 25). This fits the general pattern from about 1950 onwards in developing countries with large primary sectors in which an enlarged capital base was the essential precursor of technical progress.

9.4   The Malaysian economy at federation

The data in Table 9.6 show that structural change, notably a relative decline in the share of agriculture in GDP and an increase in the industrial share, had begun in the Malayan economy from around 1955. A comparable time series for the Borneo territories is not available but in 1961, just prior to federation, the structure of GDP in North Borneo and Sarawak showed a considerably larger primary sector and a smaller secondary sector. The tertiary sector was roughly similar in size to that in Malaya. Approximately 61 per cent of the economically active population in Malaya worked in the primary sector against 80 per cent in Borneo, with 6.4 per cent and just under 4 per cent respectively in manufacturing industry (IBRD, 1953, Table IV).

Even though the growth of import-substitution manufacturing in Malaya was apparent by the early 1960s, the condition of the Malaysian economy continued to be determined principally by the external demand for primary commodities for which the barter terms of trade showed a falling trend after the Korean War. However, the development plans constituted a platform for rejuvenation and diversification from which the sector could regain growth momentum.

As part of the process leading to federation an IBRD mission in early 1963 evaluated the economic position and the feasibility of 'closer economic cooperation between the prospective Malaysia[n] territories'. The report recapitulated the cautionary assessment by the earlier mission to Malaya in 1955, focusing on the uncertain prospects for the main primary products, and the entrepot trade of Singapore and Penang which faced slower growth or even decline as neighbouring countries, principally Indonesia, promoted direct shipments to their markets. The mission concluded that, except for the booming timber exports from North Borneo, incomes and employment in the near future were likely to fall behind population growth. Coupled with rising current expenditure by government, this implied smaller surpluses for investment in economic and social development. Merger into a federation, in the Mission's view, would result in a larger and more diverse economy which would soon become 'substantially stronger than the sum of its present parts'. This strength would manifest itself through greater overall stability due to the potential for the transfer of incomes and employment between the territories (IBRD, 1963, 1–9).

Table 9.6   Malaysia: sectoral composition of GDP, selected years, 1947–63

Year	Primary	Secondary	Tertiary
Malaya (percentage at 1959 factor cost)			
1947	49.7	6.7	43.6
1955	53.2	10.4	36.4
1960	50.9	11.7	37.4
1963	45.5	12.6	41.9
North Borneo/Sarawak (factor cost)			
1961	50.5	9.5	40.0

Source: Malaya calculated from Bhanoji Rao (1974), Table C.2. North Borneo/Sarawak from Bhanoji Rao (1980), Table 15.

It was recommended that priority be given to the setting up of a common market in a Malaysian Federation, so that goods could move freely internally with external tariffs set at about the current Malayan levels. The existing entrepot trade could be maintained by the establishment of Free Trade Zones in the various ports. A common market should stimulate the growth of manufacturing industry, but a cautionary note was sounded that whilst industrial growth rates might well differ initially between territories, in the longer term the aim should be growth on 'a well balanced regional basis [but] if a tendency towards excessive industrial concentration ... should develop ... a policy of differential incentives might then be justified' (IBRD, 1963, ch. III). Overall, the Mission found no evidence of overlapping or potential conflicts of economic interest among the territories.

On the basis of this report the economic case for the formation of the Malaysian federation does not appear as urgent or as strong as the politico-strategic one (see section 9.2 above). The needs of the constituent governments to find some kind of *modus vivendi* among themselves, and with neighbouring governments, with the arrival of independence was a more urgent imperative. Plainly, the Mission hoped that the merger would generate a stronger momentum of collective economic growth than the individual territories could attain by themselves. But it also seems that the two more advanced units, Singapore and Malaya, were expected to play the leading role in development.

Part III

Towards a Newly-Industrialised Country (1963–90)

10
The Economy in Review 1963–90

The 37 years between the formation of the Federation of Malaysia in 1963 and the formal conclusion of the NEP in 1990 were a period of unprecedentedly rapid economic growth and change. The purpose of this chapter is to present an overview of the international economic environment during this period, the rate of growth and pattern of structural transformation in the Malaysian economy, and finally a discussion of the role of the state in the process.

10.1   The international environment

Since the 1960s a New International Division of Labour has replaced the Old International Division of Labour which had underpinned global trade since the late nineteenth century. The basis moved away from an exchange of primary products, largely from the southern hemisphere, for manufactured goods, mostly from the northern hemisphere, towards a much more complex multilateral network in which countries around the globe have sought to industrialise both as a means of import-substitution (ISI), and to exploit comparative advantage in export markets (EOI). For many LDCs the major impetus in industrialisation came from the latter source. Between 1960 and 1988 world exports grew fourfold against a threefold rise in world output (Dixon and Drakakis-Smith, 1993, 23).

This was achieved through a process of 'globalisation', characterised by high mobility of industrial capital seeking out locations (increasingly in LDCs) where resources of land, labour and services were relatively cheap, and where governments offered reasonable political stability along with attractive inducements such as tax holidays, assurances of no nationalisation, and so on. Movements of capital were accompanied by transfers of technology, and a revival of international migration of labour, the latter mostly from LDCs (e.g., South Asia, Indonesia, the Philippines). The leaders in globalisation were the multinational corporations (MNCs), headquartered mainly in the developed countries but with operations that increasingly transcended national boundaries.

Overall, these conditions presented what might be termed a 'window of opportunity' for LDCs to embark on the transition from predominantly primary-producing to industrialised economies. However, the rate of progress was uneven over time and between countries. The first decade or so of the period saw a continuation of the 'golden age' of international trade (1950–73) noted in Chapter 9.3. Most parts of the world experienced high rates of growth of real GDP (Table 10.1). The expansion of international trade at 7–8 per cent a year (O'Brien, 1997, 110) was facilitated by a lowering of barriers under the General Agreement on Tariffs and Trade (GATT).

A watershed in the international economy occurred in 1973 in the form of the first of two 'oil shocks' (the second came in 1979) in which the price of oil jumped from US$2.50 per barrel to nearly US$11 in 1975 and then to US$35 in 1979, causing major balance of payments problems for fuel-importing countries. A second factor was a rise in inflation from 1971 following the US government's severance of the dollar-gold link. International exchange rates became volatile. OECD governments switched from policies aimed at full employment and general economic development to control of inflation and avoidance of balance of payments deficits. There was, however, no immediate shift to trade protectionist policies, and neither were international capital flows adversely affected, at least until the early 1980s. Growth rates in LDCs were little affected, with Asia and Latin America even improving slightly (Table 10.1)

In the 1980s the world economy experienced a severe downturn, particularly in the middle years of the decade. The industrialised countries, already growing less quickly than LDCs since 1965, slowed still further (Table 10.1). This downturn was not merely a reaction to the 1979 oil shock, but was also a reflection of longer-term trends, principally the declining performance of

Table 10.1   World comparative economic performance, 1960–89 (% compound annual growth)

	1965–80	*1980–89*
Real GDP		
Industrialised countries	3.7	3.0
All LDCS	5.9	4.3
LDCs (E. Asia)	7.3	8.4
Real GDP per capita		
Industrialised countries	2.8	2.5
All LDCs	3.4	2.3
LDCs (E. Asia)	4.8	6.7

Source: World Bank (1990), Table 1.3.

industrialised countries whose economies were experiencing structural problems (the decline of older industries such as textiles, coal, steel). Manufactured goods from LDCs faced increased difficulty of access to these markets due to the imposition of tariff protection, import quotas and so on. However, the Asian region as a whole proved resilient and actually improved its growth rate. This was due largely to the outstanding performance of the East Asian NICs, South Korea, Hong Kong and Taiwan, together with Singapore (dubbed the Four Tigers: see Table 10.2).

In the latter part of the 1980s general growth rates recovered under strong demand in export markets, though there was a general trend towards the formation of regional economic groupings, coupled with non-tariff barriers to trade, such as Voluntary Export Restraints (VERs), and Orderly Marketing Agreements (OMAs).

The high Asian growth rates just noted (and which continued beyond our period up to the massive regional crash in 1997–8) have been labelled a 'miracle' (see *Business Review Weekly*, Sydney, 5 Feb. 1996). The unprecedented nature of this performance was to achieve the transition from largely primary producing economies (excepting Hong Kong and Singapore which historically were mainly service economies) to ones with substantial industrial sectors within the space of two to three decades. This was most evident in the Four Tigers and the ASEAN-4 (Malaysia, Thailand, Indonesia and the Philippines). Real incomes rose and 'succeeded in defying the vicious circle of poverty in the post-World War II era' (Chow and Kellerman, 1993, 3).

Table 10.2   Growth of real GDP in Asia-Pacific region, 1960–90 (annual average %)

	1960–9	1971–80	1981–89	1990[a]
Japan	10.9[b]	5.0[c]	4.0[d]	n.a.
NICs				
Hong Kong	10.0	9.5	7.2	3.0
South Korea	8.5	8.7	9.3	6.3
Singapore	8.9	9.0	6.9	7.5
Taiwan	11.6	9.7	8.1	7.2
ASEAN-4				
Indonesia	3.5	7.9	5.2	6.4
Malaysia	6.5	8.0	5.4	7.0 (6.7)[e]
Philippines	4.9	6.2	1.7	5.0
Thailand	8.3	9.9	7.1	9.9

[a] Projected.
[b] 1960–70.
[c] 1971–80.
[d] 1981–90.
[e] Average 1960–90.
Sources: Ariff (1991), Table 5.3; Dixon and Drakakis-Smith (1993), Tables 1.1, 3.1; Malaysian Government (1991a), Table 2.2.

During these years the countries around the Pacific Rim, in particular East and Southeast Asia and North America, emerged as the new epicentre of the world economy. The regional share of total world exports rose from approximately 35 per cent in 1970 to nearly 38 per cent in 1987, with a roughly similar share of world imports. The striking feature here was that much of this increased trade was intra-regional: up from about 54 per cent to 66 per cent of exports, and from 59 per cent to 64 per cent of imports (Ariff, 1991, Tables 5.4, 5.5). On the basis of this exchange of goods, coupled with inter-country flows of investment capital and technology, there developed a regional dynamism. Japan was the leader, or spearhead, for much of this period, with neighbouring countries (the four Tigers) being drawn into the growth process in the 1960s and 1970s followed by the ASEAN-4 in the 1970s and 1980s. This progressively widening swathe has been compared to a V-shaped 'flying geese pattern' (Chen, 1989, 20). From the historical experience of these countries emerged a sequence of stages of industrialisation, each with a specific combination of capital. labour, technology and product-mix, as follows (drawn from Chen, 1989, 21):

1 Early stage – a low capital and technological threshold; labour-intensive production of consumer goods (foodstuffs, textiles, etc.).
2 Middle stage – mid-level technology; a mix of consumer and intermediate goods (non-metallic minerals, rubber and wood products, chemicals, petroleum refining).
3 Late stage – capital-intensive production (consumer durables, intermediate and capital goods).
4 High technology – industries based on information technology, materials sciences.

Whilst these stages might suggest a linear pattern of progress, the concept of a 'technological ladder' of structural change (Tan, 1993, 149) in the region is more appropriate. The method of ascent has been that as a country at, say, the early (labour-intensive) stage neared the production frontier real wages rose, lessening comparative advantage in export markets, so that industries moved to another country with lower wage levels and the original host country had to attempt a move to a higher level. There was, of course, nothing inevitable about the ascent. At all stages the availability of capital and technology from more advanced countries was crucial.

Numerous factors have been suggested to account for Asia's outstanding growth performance. These include: favourable geographical location and resource endowments, openness to exogenous influences, competitiveness in export products, high rates of domestic savings, a net inflow of foreign capital as the export surpluses of the colonial period turned into trade deficits, low starting points for growth well inside the production frontier, large inputs of labour of generally good quality (education), positive work ethics (e.g, the Confucian ideal) and, pre-eminently, the leading role played by the state. The latter provided political stability and followed pragmatic, outward-looking policies, with conservative macro-economic management (monetary and fiscal policy, balance of payments, trade protection, foreign borrowing). Further factors were the emergence of new national elites, in particular an indigenous capitalist class and, in general, an absence of extreme inequalities in incomes and wealth (Hill, 1993; Maddison, 1993, 21–4). In the remainder of this book we shall examine the importance of these in the Malaysian context.

10.2   The Malaysian economy

The starting point

By the early 1960s the Malaysian territories had achieved relatively high levels of per capita GDP based on exports of primary commodities. The overall average (at current prices) was $860, probably about twice the level in Thailand and the Philippines, both of which had significantly larger manufacturing industrial sectors. Within Malaysia there were substantial differences in per capita GDP with Singapore (which had the bulk of the manufacturing capacity) at about $1300, and Malaya, North Borneo (now Sabah) and Sarawak closer together at approximately $800, $700 and $550 respectively (IBRD, 1963, 2, 26). As we saw in Chapter 9, Malaya and the Borneo territories had begun to rejuvenate the principal primary industry, rubber, in the 1950s and thus had the prospect of much higher productivity in the near future. Plans for diversification into oil palms were in hand. Whilst land development thus far was more extensive in Malaya, reserves were by no means exhausted and the entry of Sabah and Sarawak into the Federation gave scope for extending the frontiers of cultivation much further. The natural resource base was also being extended into timber extraction on a much enlarged scale, and the search was on for fresh deposits of oil. Whilst Malaysia had a consistent trade deficit in services, merchandise exports brought in a surplus sufficient to keep the balance of payments positive in most years.

The transition to independence in each of the territories had been smooth, with the departing British leaving a generally efficient administrative system and bureaucracy. Domestically the Malayan Emergency had officially ended in 1960, and hostilities with Indonesia (Confrontation 1963–5) over the formation of the federation affected principally the entrepot trade of Singapore and Penang. A much more important event for the economy was Singapore's forced withdrawal from the federation in 1965 which removed the wealthiest section of the domestic market together with much industrial capacity. As a result 'much of the resource comple-mentarity and development inducing potential of Malaysia was lost' (Lai, 1975, 406). This put far greater emphasis on the programme of import-sub-stitution industrialisation which had been under way in Malaya since 1958. Despite this loss in membership Malaysia was in a relatively good position to launch a drive for rapid economic growth.

The rate and pattern of growth

The average annual rates of growth of Malaysian real GDP can be seen from Table 10.3. The main impetus came from exports of primary products in the 1960s as the early development plans (rejuvenation of the rubber industry, oil palms and so on), together with the boom in timber production, began to pay off. This continued into the 1970s, with the unit values of most primary exports steadily rising particularly in the latter part of the decade. However, at this stage manufacturing output became increasingly important, growing at 11.8 per cent a year against 10.9 per cent in the 1960s (Amsden, 1997, Table 1). The slow-down in the early part of the 1980s reflected the depression in the global economy, followed by recovery at the end of that decade led by export-oriented industrialisation in manufactures.

It is also clear from Table 10.3 that growth rates differed between the Malaysian territories. Sarawak was the slowest grower until the early 1980s, but the more fluctuating rates for the East Malaysian states reflected their greater dependence on primary products which, as always, were subject to heavy year-to-year price fluctuations. As an example, Sabah's GDP (at 1970 prices) grew by some 23 per cent in 1972–3, but then barely changed over the next two years (calculated from *ABS* Sabah) due largely to sharp changes in the export values of sawn logs. The economies of Peninsular Malaysia and Sabah/Sarawak were marching to a different beat, with the former being increasingly driven by manufacturing industry and the latter continuing a dependence upon primary production. For Malaysia as a whole, however, the possession of primary and secondary sectors both capable of responding to the demands of world markets was something of an insurance. Malaysian GDP per capita grew at an annual average of approximately 4 per cent between 1970 and 1990 (calculated from Malaysian Government, 1991b, 37).

Structural change was the outstanding characteristic in these decades. The changing composition of GDP is set out in Table 10.4. Not all figures are directly comparable owing to differences in official categories over time, but the process of change was clearly well under way in the Peninsula in the 1960s with agriculture down to about 27 per cent by 1970, slowing markedly in the 1970s and then falling to 16 per cent by 1990. Forestry and mining came to the forefront in East Malaysia in the 1970s and 1980s. Services showed the least degree of change in share, though in absolute terms the sector expanded greatly.

Table 10.3   Malaysia: growth of GDP, 1961–90

Year	Per cent per annum (constant prices)			
	Peninsular Malaysia[a]	Sabah	Sarawak	Malaysia
1961–65[b]	4.7	n.a.	n.a.	–
1966–70[b]	5.0	n.a.	n.a.	5.3
1971–75[c]	7.3	7.2	4.3	7.3
1976–80[c]	8.6	3.8[d]	4.5[d]	8.6
1981–85[e]	4.8	5.1	7.4	5.1
1986–90[e]	6.9	5.2	4.4	6.7

[a] Separate data unavailable from 1971. Calculated as residual after deducting Sabah/Sarawak figures from Malaysian GDP.
[b] 1959 prices.
[c] 1970 prices.
[d] 1976–9.
[e] 1978 prices.
Sources: Bhanoji Rao (1974) Table B8; Jomo (1990a), Table 3.1; Wee (1995), Table 3.1; *ABS*; Sabah, Sarawak, Malaysia, various years; *Mid-Term Review Third Malaysia Plan, Table 5–1; Fourth Malaysia Plan, Table 5–3; Fifth Malaysia Plan, Table 2–2.*

During this period the total Malaysian workforce doubled from about 3.2 million to 6.4 million, a growth rate of 3.5 per cent a year. The structural changes (Table 10.5), followed the familiar pattern of a declining share for the primary sector, and a corresponding increase in the secondary sector (manufacturing in particular), though differing classifications make the Sabah data for 1970 and 1980/90 non-comparable. The tertiary sector, already large in 1970, showed the smallest amount of relative growth. Again, there were significant regional differences, with Peninsular Malaysia experiencing the biggest shift from primary to secondary activity, though it is worth noting that absolute numbers in the primary sector there did not begin to fall until the 1980s.

Whilst development of agriculture and resource-based industries remained important throughout the period, Malaysia looked increasingly to manufacturing industry to fuel the pace of economic growth. Policy passed through several phases, each defined by a dominant strategy.

1958–70	First round of import-substitution industrialisation (ISI)
1970–80	First round of export-oriented industrialisation (EOI)
1980–5	Second round of ISI
From 1986	Return to EOI

Underlying these phases were the successive five-year Malaysia Plans (numbers one to five in this period) from 1966 onwards, and the NEP from 1970–1990. The NEP is examined in detail in section 10.3.

Table 10.4 Malaysia: structural change in GDP, 1960–90

Year	Per cent share of GDP[a]				
	Agriculture[b]	Forestry	Mining	Industry[c]	Services[d]
1960					
Pen. Malaysia	40.5[e]	n.a.	6.1	8.6	50.0
Sabah	55.1[e]	n.a.	negl.	2.2	42.5
Sarawak	45.5[f]	n.a.	8.5	8.2	38.0
Malaysia[g]	47.0	n.a.	7.3	6.3	43.5
1970					
Pen. Malaysia	26.6	1.6	5.6	14.0	53.0
Sabah	19.8	34.9	negl.	2.4	42.9
Sarawak	22.7	16.2	3.7	9.4	48.0
Malaysia	30.8	17.6	6.3	13.4	51.3
1980					
Pen. Malaysia	25.2	n.a.	8.0	22.0	48.0
Sabah	14.7	20.4	21.3	4.0	39.8
Sarawak	14.5	13.1	30.3	7.6	41.0
Malaysia	22.8	n.a.	10.0	20.0	47.2
1990					
Pen. Malaysia	16.0[h]	n.a.	7.0	30.0	47.0
Sabah	26.2	10.4	20.0	7.0	35.9
Sarawak	9.4	14.4	32.9	12.8	31.4
Malaysia	19.4	n.a.	9.8	26.8	44.2

[a] Not all horizontal rows add to 100 per cent due to variations in source data.
[b] Includes fishing.
[c] Manufacturing only.
[d] Includes construction.
[e] 1967 (includes forestry/logging)
[f] 1962.
[g] Unweighted average.
[h] Includes forestry.
Sources: ABS for each territory, selected years; Malaysia: Ministry of Finance (1990/1), Table 3.1.

Malaysia's dependence on exports increased very substantially from 42 per cent of GDP in 1963 to 69 per cent in 1990 (calculated from IMF, 1991). However, the pattern of trade re-oriented itself away from traditional trading partners, notably the European Community countries, towards the booming Asia-Pacific region which took nearly 75 per cent of total exports in 1988 against 67 per cent in 1970, and was the source of 78 per cent of imports compared to 59 per cent. The USA remained the single largest market for Malaysian exports, but the emphasis shifted from primary products (of which roughly one-third now went to ASEAN countries) to manufactures, with the USA taking 36 per cent in 1988 (Ariff, 1991, Tables 3.1, 3.2, 3.5). By 1990 manufactures constituted some 60 per cent of

Table 10.5 Malaysia: composition of workforce, 1960–90 (%)

	1970	1980	1990
Primary Sector			
Pen. Malaysia	48.1[a]	38.1	22.7
Sabah	30.1[a]	36.0[a]	67.6
Sarawak	68.3	56.3	47.6
Secondary Sector			
Pen. Malaysia	8.1	19.2	28.7
Sabah	25.1[b]	39.9[b]	11.6
Sarawak	6.5	10.6	15.1
Tertiary Sector			
Pen. Malaysia	43.8	41.9	48.5
Sabah	44.8	24.5	20.8
Sarawak	25.2	33.1	37.3

[a] Excludes logging.
[b] Includes logging.
Source: Calculated from Wee (1995), Table 3.15.

Malaysian exports against only 12 per cent in 1970 (Malaysian Government, 1991b, 42). These gave a broader base to the economy than the earlier reliance on a few primary commodities, and whilst the economy remained vulnerable to external influences the degree of instability caused by export price fluctuations lessened. Another supportive factor here was the growth of a more resilient domestic economy (Ariff, 1991, 87). The net barter terms of trade did not favour Malaysia, showing a long-term decline (1959 = 100) to an index of 62 in 1974, recovering slightly to 78 in 1979 and then falling to a low of 48 in 1988 (Jomo, 1990a, Table 3.19). The trade regime was generally liberal, and the levels of tariff protection not high by international standards, though incentives tended to be biased against exports and in favour of producers catering for the domestic market (D. Lim, 1992; Alavi, 1996).

Population growth and urbanisation

Between 1960 and 1990 the total Malaysian population increased from approximately 8.2 million to 17.8 million, an annual rate of 2.6 per cent (Table 6.1 above). However, whilst Peninsular Malaysia averaged a steady 2.5 per cent, the East Malaysian states showed higher growth rates: 4 per cent for Sabah, and 2.7 per cent for Sarawak. Immigration (discussed below) was a major factor here.

The prime impetus continued to be natural population growth. Both the crude birth rate (CBR) and crude death rate (CDR) fell substantially in the Peninsula, the CBR by 10 per cent and the CDR by about 23 per cent between 1970 and 1983/4. However, there were marked differences between ethnic groups with the Malay CDR falling by 30 per cent (with improvements in rural health services) against 17 per cent for Chinese and 14 per cent for Indians (calculated from Tan. *et al.*, 1987, Table 1; Saw, 1988, Table 3.2).Decreases in CBR reflected a general decline in fertility, and here the positions were reversed with Malays registering a 12 per cent drop, Chinese 33 per cent and Indians 29 per cent (calculated from Leete and Kwok, 1986, Table 12).

These changes in fertility have been ascribed to a variety of causes: improved levels of education among women, wider use of contraception and a generally later age of marriage, especially among Chinese whose reproduction rate was approaching bare replacement level by the 1980s. Interestingly, though, fertility among Malay women showed a slight increase in the late 1970s, which was maintained up to the mid-1980s and then levelled off but was still well above that of other ethnic groups. Contributory factors here were a switch in 1982 from the anti-natalist policy (followed since 1965) to a pro-natalist stance with the announcement of a long-term target population for Malaysia of 70 million by 2100. Around the same time a rise in Islamic fundamentalism emphasised traditional values and lessened the use of modern contraception. Moreover, larger families were less of a financial strain for *bumiputeras* because of favourable treatment (such as education scholarships) under the NEP. Thus, whilst the non-*bumiputera* population followed the conventional demographic transition trend (from high to low fertility), the *bumiputera* groups, were less affected due to the differential impact of modernisation, cultural and religious factors (Leete, 1996, 174–5).

Sabah and Sarawak showed broadly similar trends, though in both states fertility levels among indigenous groups have remained higher than those in the Peninsula (Leete, 1996, 146).

The main consequence of falling fertility for Malaysia's economic growth was a gradual tightening in the domestic supply of labour which became marked by the 1980s. There was a resumption of immigration on a scale reminiscent of the early decades of the century, only in this instance the main sources were Indonesia and the Philippines. Indonesians totalled an estimated 500 000 in the Peninsula by the mid-1980s (8–10 per cent of the labour force), with a further 140 000 in Sabah and 10 000 in Sarawak. Filipinos, many illegal, were concentrated in Sabah (Table 10.6). Altogether the Malaysian population was boosted by around one million people (*Far Eastern Economic Review, or FEER*, 29 April 1993). None the less, Malaysia remained one of the most sparsely populated countries in the region with a density of only 51 per square kilometre in 1988 compared to Indonesia (91), Thailand (107) and the Philippines (196) (calculated from Ariff, 1991, Table 5.1). This growth in population has been associated with changes in the proportions of the respective ethnic groups in the total population (Table 10.6).

There were also marked shifts in geographical distribution as between rural and urban areas, and also in regional terms due to internal migration. Each of these aspects carried strong political and economic implications for the relationship between *bumiputeras* and non-*bumiputeras*.

Internal migration has been a constant process in Malaysia since the Second World War, with economic and work-related reasons figuring prominently. These factors were strengthened under the NEP by government's inclusion of population redistribution as one means of rectifying economic imbalances between the ethnic groups. In the Peninsula the Chinese were for a while the most mobile group, but since 1970 Malays have predominated, accounting for roughly two-thirds of migrants between 1970 and 1990 (Chan, 1994, Figure 3). The major movements of population occurred on the west coast, with Penang, Selangor and Johor being the largest gainers as manufacturing industries concentrated in the Penang Free-Trade Zone, the Kelang valley and around Johor Bahru. On the east coast large land development schemes in Pahang in the 1970s, and the discovery of oil and natural gas off the coast of Terengganu in the 1980s drew both inter- and intra-state migrants. Those states experiencing outflows were Perak, as the tin mining industry declined in the 1980s (see Chapter 12.1), Perlis, Kedah, Melaka and Negeri Sembilan as rice farming and other forms of agriculture became less attractive (UN, 1986; Chan, 1994).

In East Malaysia population distribution had remained fairly stable up to 1960. As in the Peninsula the bulk was situated in the westernmost regions (west coast in Sabah and the First Division in Sarawak). The main historical reason that could be offered for this was doubtless the economic orientation towards the Singapore entrepot from the nineteenth century. From 1960 the

Table 10.6   Malaysia: population by ethnic group, selected years (%)

	Bumiputera	Chinese	Indians	Others
Pen. Malaysia				
1957	50	37	11	2
1991	58	29	10	3
Sabah				
1960	76	23		1
1991	61	12		27[a]
Sarawak				
1960	68	31		1
1991	70	28		2[a]

[a] Includes non-Malaysian citizens.
Source: Adapted from Leete (1996), Tables 1.3, 6.1.

balance shifted: in Sabah from the west coast and the central zone to the east coast as timber and other primary industries expanded, and in Sarawak to the Third Division (see Maps 3 and 4), again due to growing primary production both in agriculture and mining (UN, 1986, Tables 33, 34).

With regard to urbanisation, it should be recalled here that in Chapter 5.2 the argument was put forward that the hierarchy which developed in the Malay Peninsula during the colonial period centred on two 'urban circuits', the northern based on Penang (Georgetown) and the southern on Melaka, with the latter largely displaced by Kuala Lumpur by 1900. These circuits were driven principally by the tin and rubber industries. These remained the basic stimuli up to the 1960s. After a peak annual rate of 5.8 per cent from 1947 to 1957, urban population growth slowed to 3.2 per cent from 1957 to 1970 (Table 10.7), which was largely due to more towns achieving an urban classification than an actual shift in population location (Evers, 1983, 331). In East Malaysia the decade 1960–70 saw rapid growth at 5.3 per cent, comparable to the Malayan peak rate in 1947–57. Much of this occurred in Sarawak (which had 58 per cent of the urban population in these states) in the largest size group, Kuching, Sibu, Miri (towns of more than 20 000 inhabitants), and in the smaller units (2000–10 000) (UN, 1982, Table 19).

From the 1960s, and particularly after the commencement of the NEP in 1970, new elements entered the situation. For Peninsular Malaysia, Evers (1983, 332) suggests three factors: the commercialisation of peasant agriculture, industrialisation and the growth of the bureaucracy. The first

Table 10.7   Malaysia: urbanisation, 1957–85 (% of total population)[a]

	1957		1970		1985
Pen. Malaysia	26.6		28.7		41.0
Growth rate p.a.		3.2		5.0	
No. urban centres	36		49		58
Sabah	12.9[b]		16.5		22.6[c]
Growth rate p.a.		5.3		6.5	
No. urban centres	3		3		5[c]
Sarawak	12.6		15.5		19.2[c]
Growth rate p.a.		5.3		4.3	
No. urban centres	3		3		4
Malaysia	n.a.		26.7		37.4

[a] Gazetted areas of 10 000 people and above.
[b] 1960.
[c] 1985.
Sources: UN Economic and Social Commission for Asia and the Pacific (ESCAP), 1982, Tables 10, 19, 20; McGee (1986), Table 2.6; Cho (1990), Tables 4.2, 4.3, fig. 4.2; Masing (1988), Table 5.1; Mohd Yaakub et al. (1989), Table 3.

of these involved a drive for maximum self-sufficiency in rice production (Chapter 11.2), together with the opening of land for commercial crops in previously undeveloped regions where new towns were started. The second involved the setting-up of industrial concentrations near already-established towns, and the creation of new towns for industrial estates. The third led to further large growth of the bureaucracy from about 140 000 in 1970 to 522 000 in 1983 (Zakaria, 1993, 156), with a concomitant need for urban dwellings and buildings for new ministries and so on. These factors also applied, though in lesser degree, to the East Malaysian states.

As a result of these developments, whilst marked regional differences in development still persisted, the former northern and southern circuits in the Peninsula became intermingled. The urban hierarchy was much more complex by 1990, and links between rural and urban areas stronger. At the upper levels of the hierarchy a number of 'boom' towns developed. The outstanding example is Kuala Lumpur, the federal capital and, since 1974, a district (*Wilayah Persekutuan*) separate from surrounding Selangor state, which has become a 'primate city' (Evers, 1983, 332), though not so dominant as Bangkok or Manila. Penang, though declining in its share of population, developed as the centre of an industrial area including Butterworth on the mainland. In Selangor a process of more or less continuous suburbanisation linked Kuala Lumpur through Petaling Jaya, Subang Jaya and Shah Alam to Port Kelang (formerly Port Swettenham). In the 1980s Melaka was revived as a centre of light industry, and in southern Johor, Johor Bahru and adjacent districts along the coast have similarly attracted a range of industries.

At the lower levels of the urban hierarchy the important role accorded to urban development under the NEP led to the building of new towns to serve as administrative and economic centres in areas of major rural development schemes. By 1987 Peninsular Malaysia had a total of 41 new towns in four such regions: the Jengka Triangle and Pahang Tenggara (DARA), Terengganu Tengah (KETENGAH), and Johor Tenggara (KEJORA), with a total population of nearly 196 000. However, these towns had limited success as stimuli to regional development. Their economic base was narrow, they faced competition for industrial investment from established towns, the linkages with rural hinterlands were weak, planning was faulty, and so on.

As evident in earlier chapters, urbanisation in East Malaysia has been very slow to develop any marked momentum. Since the Second World War the level of urbanisation has remained consistently around half that of Peninsular Malaysia (Table 10.7). From this low starting point, however, the annual growth rates, particularly in Sabah, compared well with those in the Peninsula. There is evidence to indicate some degree of concentration of population, with towns in the range 25 000–74 999 increasing their share from 9.1 per cent in 1970 to 13.5 per cent in 1980. These were Kota Kinabalu, Sandakan and Tawau in Sabah, Kuching, Miri and Sibu in Sarawak. There was a reverse trend in the 10 000–24 000 range, decreasing from 3.8 to 1.4 per cent, but the smaller towns (2000–4999 and 5000–9999) showed a significant increase from 1.2 to 2.8 per cent, and 0.9 to 2.2 per cent respectively (UN, 1982, Table 19).

As in the Peninsula, the policy of establishing new towns to act as regional growth centres in Sabah and Sarawak had not been very successful by the time of the Fourth Malaysia Plan (1981–5). Whilst older towns were emerging as important regional centres, such as Sibu in Sarawak and Semporna in Sabah (see Sutlive, 1978; Sather, 1997), an interactive urban hierarchy was slow to develop, due primarily to the still relatively poor state of transport and communications which hindered inter-urban communications. In Sabah, for example, only Kota Kinabalu possessed a 'semblance of a coherent hierarchy in relation to its hinterland' (Mohd Yaakub and Sidhu, 1989, 159).

A feature common to all the Malaysian territories was the sharp acceleration of urbanisation among Peninsular Malays and the indigenous peoples of Sabah and Sarawak after 1970. In Sarawak the fastest expanding urban group were the Melanau who went from under 7 per cent in 1970 to 14 per cent of their total in 1980, whilst Iban and Bidayuh increased from 0.6 per cent to nearly 5 per cent (Masing, 1988, Table 5.1). In the case of the Melanau a major factor behind this shift was probably the increasing mechanisation of the sago production process after 1945 with the mills largely in Chinese hands (Morris, 1991, 258), leading to underemployment in the villages.

10.3 The role of the state

The nature and effects of state intervention in the economies of East and Southeast Asia have been among the most extensively debated aspects of development in recent decades. Throughout much of the region 'the state [has been] the senior partner in the relationship between the public and private sector' (McCawley, n.d., 3). A central issue is whether a direct correlation can be established between the rate of economic growth and the type of government in power, with the most consistently successful cases being those moving to liberal democratic regimes and, at the other extreme, authoritarian ones attaining least success. A paradigm for a shift from authoritarian rule towards liberal democracy is that economic growth brings more complex structures which the bureaucracy by itself becomes less able to manage efficiently to maintain that growth. New social groups, notably a middle class, emerge which press for a more liberal regime through which they can exert more influence. Decision-making power has to be devolved increasingly to private interests whose actions are based 'at least in part, [on] the determination of the market' (Crouch and Morley in Morley, 1993, 281). In this model political change is driven by economic and social pressures.

As with most general models a close 'fit' in particular cases proves elusive. Whilst Japan provides perhaps the best example of a broadly democratic regime allied with rapid economic growth, other countries in the region have moved from authoritarian (including military) to democratic governments and back again whilst maintaining rapid economic growth: for example, Thailand. In Malaysia's case there exists 'ambiguity in the impact of economic growth' in these terms. The constitution installed at independence was democratic but, as we shall see, government moved from a largely *laissez-faire* stance in the 1960s to more authoritarian modes in the 1970s and 1980s whilst the growth rate accelerated, except for the mid-1980s downturn (Table 10.3). 'Rapid economic growth has provided an important justification for an increase in state power [but] on the other hand [it] has also had the opposite effect, strengthening ... those forces that seek to restrain state power and enliven the democratic process' (Zakaria, 1993, 144). A categorisation which attempts to capture this ambiguity in the Malaysian regime is 'quasi-democratic' (Crouch and Morley in Morley, 1993, 288): that is, a mixture of parliamentary democracy and authoritarianism, such as the power to detain without trial under the Internal Security Act (ISA) of 1960 in cases deemed to threaten national security.

The federal government of Malaysia was modelled on the preceding Malayan Federation, with strong centralist characteristics. The Alliance system of ethnically-based political parties, with Malay paramountcy mediated through UMNO at its centre (see Chapter 9.2), was progressively generalised, becoming the National Front (*Barisan Nasional*) in 1974. However, in East Malaysia the ethnic composition of political parties was more fluid than those in the Peninsula, and the local political process was a series of shifting alliances resembling 'a game of musical chairs' (Means, 1991, 38).

In contrast with most neighbouring countries the outstanding characteristic of the National Front regime has been its stability in both the earlier, more open, and later authoritarian modes. Throughout the period under review the overriding priority for the state was the maintenance of harmony in ethnic relations. 'Race is the *leitmotiv*' of Malaysian politics (Zakaria, 1993, 146, italics added), with inevitable profound effects upon economic activity. Government intervention in the economy had two main purposes, (i) to increase the size of the national 'pie' through rapid economic growth to meet popular expectations of higher living standards, and (ii) to restructure the economy to redistribute ownership of wealth and the pattern of employment so as to reduce the large differentials in income between ethnic groups. In this section we shall look primarily at (ii), and discuss (i) in Chapters 11–13.

From 1966 the Five-Year Plans for Malaya, Sabah and Sarawak were amalgamated into a single plan for the whole federation. The allocations of funds are shown in Table 10.8. Under the First Plan (1966–70) the major vehicles continued to be large land development schemes, agricultural diversification and infrastructure projects. Whilst annual economic growth averaged around 5 per cent (Table 10.3), there was growing discontent among Peninsular Malays over the widening gap in incomes with non-Malays (see Chapter 13). The perception was that, except for a few who had benefited from government contracts, for instance in rural development projects, Malays had not received a proportionate share in the general economic progress, particularly in the expanding non-rural sector. In ownership of corporate wealth 63 per cent was in foreign hands, 35 per cent other Malaysians (predominantly Chinese), and a mere 2 per cent with Malays. Non-Malays, for their part, were critical of Malay special rights and political privileges. Tensions boiled over in May 1969 when, following elections in which (predominantly Chinese) opposition parties performed unexpectedly strongly, severe racial rioting broke out in Kuala Lumpur. Parliamentary government was suspended for eighteen months and replaced by a National Operations Council.

This episode led to a marked shift in government towards a more authoritarian and interventionist role, especially in the economic sphere. It was clear that if the largely *laissez-faire* policies of the 1960s were con-

Table 10.8   Malaysia: development plan expenditure by sector, 1966–90 (% of total)[a]

	1 MP[b] 1966–70	2 MP 1971–5	3 MP 1976–80	4 MP 1981–5	5 MP 1986–90
Economic Sector					
Agriculture	26.3	21.7	22.1	11.8	16.0
Industry	3.3	16.5	15.3	27.3	17.0
Infrastructure	33.7	34.1	26.6	36.2	43.2
Social Sector					
Education	7.8	6.9	7.3	5.8	12.6
Health	3.5	1.8	1.4	0.9	1.5
Housing	4.9	2.4	6.1	4.9	2.2
Other	1.6	2.7	2.3	0.8	1.0
General					
Administration	3.3	3.6	2.2	1.0	1.6
Security	15.7	10.4	16.6	9.3	5.0

[a] Based on actual expenditure, except for 1986–90. Rounded to nearest 0.1 per cent.
[b] MP = Malaysia Plan.
Source: Calculated from Jomo (1990a), Table 5.2.

tinued the mass of *bumiputeras* could not hope, unassisted, to narrow the differentials in wealth, income and employment. The outcome was the announcement of the NEP to cover the 20 years from 1970 to 1990. The NEP had two principal aims, (i) the restructuring of the economy and society in order to eliminate the close identity between race and economic function inherited from the colonial period, and (ii) the eradication of poverty irrespective of race. The first was to be achieved by a restructuring of employment to reflect the ethnic composition of the population and the second through a redistribution of shares in national corporate wealth. There was not to be an arbitrary division of existing assets but rather a redistribution of the much larger national 'cake' expected to result from continued economic growth so that no group would be worse off in absolute terms. The *bumiputera* share of corporate wealth was to rise from 2 per cent to 30 per cent, that of other Malaysians from 35 per cent to 40 per cent, with foreign ownership falling from 63 per cent to 30 per cent (Jomo, 1990a, Table 7.3). In employment the proportion of *bumiputeras* was to decrease in the primary sector and rise sharply in the secondary and tertiary sectors (see Table 10.9).

The NEP targets were to be attained under the Second to the Fifth Malaysia Plans (1971–90). The major areas of activity were (i) continued rural development, principally through land schemes, to commercialise peasant agriculture, (ii) the promotion of manufacturing industry, especially export-oriented industrialisation, (iii) regional development (including new towns) to even out the large disparities between different areas (e.g., the east and west coasts of the Peninsula), (iv) ancillary policies involving, for instance, preferential treatment for *bumiputeras* in access to higher education and government employment to enable them to move into the mainstream of the economy as administrators, professionals, entrepreneurs and so on.

The bases of the NEP, strong economic growth combined with redistribution, contained a potential conflict, since the first required a high degree of allocative efficiency with resources moving according to the dictates of the market, and the second a distribution of wealth and employment according to non-market (political and social) criteria, which could slow growth. Moreover, though the NEP applied to Malaysia as a whole, it was primarily a response to the situation in the Peninsula, and indeed has been described as a 'form of Malay economic nationalism' (Shamsul, 1997, 251). There was a call for a *revolusi mental* (mental revolution) among Malays in their attitude towards commercial activity, to be accompanied by the emergence of a 'new' urban-based class alongside the 'old' rural-based groupings of this community (Lubeck, 1992, 191; Shamsul, 1997, 251–3).

The first decade of the NEP saw a much increased rate of economic growth (discussed in section 10.2). However, by the mid-1970s there was concern in government circles that wealth redistribution was falling behind

Table 10.9   Restructuring under the NEP, 1970–90

(a) Ownership

| | *(Percentage of share capital at par value)* | | | |
	1970	1980	1985	1990
Bumiputeras				
(a) Individuals	1.6	5.8	11.7	20.3
(b) Trust agencies	0.8	6.7	7.4	
Other Malaysians				
Chinese	27.2	⎫	33.4	44.9
Indians	1.1	⎬ 44.6	1.2	1.0
Other	–	⎮	1.3	0.3
Nominee Companies	6.0	⎭		8.4
Foreigners	63.4	42.9	26.0	25.1

Sources: 1970–85, Jomo (1990a), Table 7.3; 1990, Hara (1991), Table 1.

(b) Employment (i)

| | *(Percentage of total in each sector)* | | |
	1970	1990 (target)	1990 (achieved)
Primary			
Bumiputera	67.6	61.4	71.2
Non-*bumiputera*	32.4	38.6	28.8
Secondary			
Bumiputera	30.8	51.9	48.0
Non-*bumiputera*	69.2	48.1	52.0
Tertiary			
Bumiputera	37.9	48.4	51.0
Non-*bumiputera*	62.1	51.6	49.0

(c) Employment (ii)

| | *(Percentage employed as proportion of ethnic group)*[a] | | | | | |
| | 1970 | | | 1990 | | |
	Bumiputera	*Chinese*	*Indian*	*Bumiputera*	*Chinese*	*Indian*
Primary	61.0	25.4	51.2	36.7	13.5	21.8
Secondary	14.6	37.7	18.9	26.3	36.5	39.8
Tertiary	24.4	36.8	29.9	36.9	49.9	38.3

[a] Peninsular Malaysia only.
Sources: Jomo (1985), Table 5, (1990a), Table 7.3; Hara (1991), Table 1; Onozawa (1991),
Table III; Malaysian Government (1991b), Table 2.

target, and that private *bumiputera* entrepreneurs were not emerging in the hoped-for numbers. In 1975 the NEP was given a cutting edge sharper than simply specifying long-term target ratios. The Industrial Coordination Act (ICA) made compliance with requirements for *bumiputera* share ownership and employment quotas mandatory for the issue of an operating licence to companies with over $100 000 in shareholder funds and more than 25 workers. The Act drew adverse criticism from foreign and domestic (principally Chinese) investors, and despite some modifications in 1977 and 1979 the latter scaled down investment from around 67 per cent of the total in 1971 to between 12 and 30 per cent from 1976 to 1985 (Jesudason, 1989, Figure 5.1).

To offset the slow growth of *bumiputera* private enterprise the state extended involvement in the operation of the economy by creating institutions which would generate assets or acquire investments to be held in trust for that group (Mehmet, 1986). The basic funding lay outside the annual budget expenditure, thus categorising these institutions as 'off-budget enterprises', and later as 'non-financial public enterprises', with, effectively, unlimited supplies of interest free finance (Horii, 1991a, 294). Examples were the Urban Development Authority (UDA), Pernas [National Trading Corporation], Permodalan Nasional Berhad (PNB) [National Equity Corporation], and State Economic Development Corporations (SEDCs). The directors and managers were drawn respectively from the Malay elite (royalty, politicians, retired officials) and seconded civil servants. Ultimately there were 1188 such enterprises with aggregate paid-up capital of 24 billion *ringgit* (formerly dollars) of which nearly 17 billion, or 70 per cent, came from government (Horii, 1991a, Tables IV, V). Funding on this scale was possible only because of a large rise in revenue between the mid-1970s and early-1980s, mainly from petroleum exports. Despite these large investments, by 1980 (the halfway mark in the NEP) the redistribution of wealth was still lagging behind the pro-rata target (Table 10.9a). One significant advance, made possible by government's ample funds, was the purchase (by Permodalan Nasional) of controlling interests in the flagship companies of British enterprise in Malaysian commerce and primary production (tin, rubber, oil palms), such as the Guthrie Corporation (1981) costing 1.2 billion *ringgit*, and Harrisons & Crosfield (1982) and other leading agency houses for 800 million ringgit (Zainal Yusoff, 1990, 370). A similar process led to London Tin, one of the largest British groups, becoming the Malaysian Mining Corporation, giving *bumiputeras* ownership of 34 per cent of that industry's capital by 1982. The transfer of the official domicile of these companies to Malaysia largely completed the 'localization of the principal colonial investments in the country's primary products sector' (Saruwatari, 1991, 384).

In addition to government-funded *bumiputera* agencies, the major political parties became increasingly involved in economic activity through investment arms. UMNO led the way, setting up Fleet Holdings (later the Fleet Group) in 1972, which acquired investments spread over a wide range including publishing, television broadcasting, property development and so on. (Gomez, 1990, Table 3). The main motives were to gain control over influential sections of the media, and to generate sources of funds independent from non-*bumiputera* (principally Chinese) finance. In 1975 the Malayan Chinese Association established Multi-Purpose Holdings Berhad to pool Chinese resources as a counterweight to *bumiputera* interests, and finally in 1984 the Malayan Indian Congress set up Maika Holdings for similar reasons.

The early 1980s saw several major shifts in state policy. These changes were in large measure initiatives taken by Malaysia's new leader, Datuk Seri Dr Mahathir Mohamad, whose premiership commenced in 1981. Medically trained, and meritocratic in outlook, he represented a decisive break with previous leaders (Tengku Abdul Rahman, Tun Razak, Tun Hussein Onn) who came from the ranks of the Malay aristocracy, and has come to be widely regarded as the most important personal force shaping Malaysian life since that time (see Khoo Boo Teik, 1995).

In the early 1980s economic growth slowed, particularly in the Peninsula (Table 10.3), as world conditions deteriorated. Inspired by the examples of Japan and South Korea, Mahathir initiated a return to import-substitution industrialisation, only this time based on the establishment of heavy industries (iron, steel, cement, cars), which were to produce intermediate goods, consumer durables, and to generate linkages within the domestic economy. The investment came from a combination of public funds through the Heavy Industries Corporation of Malaysia (HICOM), Petronas, and private foreign capital (Mitsubishi, Honda). The allocation to industry under the Fourth Plan (1981–5) rose sharply to about 27 per cent (Table 10.8). Mahathir's leadership also formulated a 'Look East' policy advocating the adoption of work practices (discipline, group loyalty, high productivity, quality control and so on) based on those in East Asia, Japan in particular (Bowie, 1991, 115–7). These policies achieved only mixed success in the Malaysian context (see Chapter 12).

As the 1980s progressed, a combination of circumstances contributed to yet another change in policy orientation. The deepening world depression resulted in slower growth, even a negative one (–1 per cent in GDP) in 1985. Substantially raised levels of expenditure, on both recurrent costs and development, placed increasing strain on government revenue. Many of the non-financial public enterprises were operating unprofitably due to inefficient, and in some cases corrupt, management. For example, State Economic Development Corporation subsidiaries had accumulated losses totalling some 163 million *ringgit* by 1980 (Horii, 1991a, 308). In Sabah such institutions were increasingly plagued by irregularities and inefficiencies so that the state's finances were in an 'absolute mess'

(*Star*, 21 May 1985, cited in Loh, 1992, 237). Private domestic investment was not running strongly; an estimated US$12 billion (much of it Chinese capital) was estimated to have flowed out of Malaysia between 1976 and 1985 (Khoo Boo Teik, 1995, 137).

Prime Minister Mahathir became concerned that thus far the NEP had induced a 'get-rich quick' mentality which, instead of fostering extensive growth of competitive *bumiputera* entrepreneurs, had merely produced a small middle class, highly dependent on state patronage for contracts, employment and so on. He was also unhappy that the public sector had become so extensively involved in the operation of the economy, particularly with the increasing demands now made on limited government funds. The mainstay of a switch in policy was privatisation, announced in 1983 and implemented from 1984. This covered a range of measures: sale of state-owned companies in entirety or in part, sale or lease of physical assets, private financing of a state project on a 'build-and-operate' basis, contracting out services to private firms, and the introduction of competition into areas of state monopoly, such as a third television channel. 'In principle the privatization of state enterprises, assets, services and corporate equity ... was the material basis for a new vanguard – a "Malay-state–Malay-capital" alliance leading non-Malay capital' (Khoo Boo Teik, 1995, 134–5). This was the reverse of the previous 'Ali-Baba' situation in which Malays (Ali), lacking capital of their own, had lent their names to non-Malay, notably Chinese (Baba), capitalists who actually operated the business. Concurrently government announced the concept of 'Malaysia Incorporated', which depicted public and private enterprise not as mutually exclusive but as partners working to increase national prosperity.

Privatisation gathered pace throughout the 1980s and into the 1990s. By mid-1992 thirteen state enterprises had been privatised (to varying degrees) with a market capitalisation of some 201 billion *ringgit*, including lotteries, television, telecommunications, highway construction and operation, shipping, the national airline (MAS), electricity. The manner in which these enterprises were allotted to private interests attracted much criticism. The process did not involve an open process of competitive tenders to select the successful bidder; instead the method was a 'nebulous "first come, first served" principle' (Jomo, 1995, 8) which resulted in transfers to politically well-connected businessmen, mainly Malays but also some non-Malays, at relatively low valuations. Similarly, major contracts were awarded on criteria influenced strongly by political connections rather than the strict economic merits of the bid: for example, the contract to build the North–South Highway down the Peninsula west coast in 1987 (Jomo, 1995, 46).

In principle the rationale for privatisation was that dispersal of ownership would lead to faster capital accumulation, competition and greater effiency in the use of resources. In practice it served largely to intensify the growth of 'money politics', a phenomenon which had been on the increase in Malaysia since the 1960s. The prime financial benefits were restricted to a select group of *bumiputera* interests with access to political patronage, and a few non-*bumiputeras* who were similarly well connected. Because of their favoured treatment by government, the new entrepreneurs were seen as rent-seekers rather than as genuine innovators with most, though not all, disbursing their abnormally high gains in nonproductive activities such as real estate deals and corporate manoeuvring (Gomez and Jomo, 1997, 179).

Whilst the *bumiputera* individuals' share of corporate wealth showed a marked increase by the mid-1980s (Table 10.9a), it was becoming increasingly doubtful whether the NEP targets could be achieved by 1990, though there was evidence that in some sectors, such as agriculture and mining, banking and insurance, the ratio was already substantially in excess of 30 per cent (Table 10.10). At this juncture government faced a choice between whether to pursue redistribution unabated, or attempt to restore the momentum of growth to the economy. Mahathir chose the latter option, announcing in 1986 that the NEP restructuring process would be held 'in abeyance'. The main reliance for a quickening of growth was placed on increased investment. The ICA of 1975 was further modified by raising the levels of capital and workforce size at which the NEP quotas became applicable to a company. The Promotion of Investment Act (1986) was accompanied by improved tax allowances and export credit facilities. These were to some extent designed to mollify Chinese interests, but the strongest incentives were offered to foreign investors who were exempted from NEP quotas and limits on the proportion of equity which they could own provided more than 50 per cent of output was exported or sold to a company in a Free Trade Zone (FTZ), and the workforce was above a certain size.

The implications of this course of action for the NEP were reflected in a division of opinion among Malays in the late 1980s. A 'pro-growth' faction preferred less state regulation, whilst a 'pro-distribution' faction wanted the restructuring process kept as the first priority. Factionalism within UMNO became much intensified, culminating in a clash in 1987 over elections for the top posts of President and Vice-President, in which the 'pro-growth' faction (led by Mahathir) emerged victorious but so narrowly that a challenge over alleged irregularities in the election led to the deregistration of UMNO. In the ensuing race to register a successor party the 'pro-growth' faction won with the establishment of UMNO Baru (New UMNO), whilst the 'pro-distribution' faction set up Semangat '46 (Spirit of 1946) in opposition (Khoo Boo Teik, 1995, 106, 264, 323–6).

The fruits of this policy switch came from 1988 onwards as the international economy picked up. Real GDP accelerated from a very modest 1.2 per cent growth in 1986 to 8.9, 8.8 and 9.8 per cent in the three years 1988–90 (Alavi, 1996, Table 2.10). The leading role played by FDI is clear from the data on participation in the equity of approved manufacturing

Table 10.10 Bumiputera shares in publicly listed companies in Peninsular Malaysia: selected years (%)

	1970[a]	1984[b]
Agriculture/Mining	1.6	35.7[c]
Industry/Construction	4.7	24.5[d]
Transport/Communications	13.5	n.a.
Commerce	0.8	n.a.
Banking/Insurance	3.3	43.5
Other	2.0	49.7[e]
Average	1.9	32.2

n.a. = not available.
[a] As percentage of share capital of all limited companies.
[b] As percentage of total paid-up capital.
[c] Arithmetical average of oil palm (42.2 per cent), rubber (24.6 per cent) and mining (40.3 per cent).
[d] Industry only.
[e] Arithmetical average of properties (44 per cent), hotels (55.3 per cent).
Sources: 1970, adapted from Hirschman (1989); 1984, adapted from Horii (1991a), Table XII.

projects. From 1975–1986 this had ranged between about 18 per cent and 40 per cent, but leapt to approximately 49 per cent in 1987 and a peak of 74 per cent in 1989. The balance was split between *bumiputeras* 10 per cent, other Malaysians 13 per cent and public enterprises 3 per cent (Gomez and Jomo, 1997, Table 3.10). When the NEP came to a formal conclusion in 1990, official figures credited *bumiputera* individuals and agencies with just over 20 per cent of corporate equity, well short of the target of 30 per cent. Other Malaysians had some 45 per cent and foreigners 25 per cent, respectively about 5 per cent over and under target. Among the employment targets, the proportion of *bumiputeras* in the primary sector had fallen sharply (Table 10.9c), but had actually risen as a share of total employment (Table 10.9b).

Thus far we have been considering the Malaysian state at the federal level, and the main points to emerge are the progressive centralisation of power after 1965, and the predominance of Peninsular Malaysian concerns in the NEP. At the inter-state level the period witnessed considerable rivalry. It will be recalled that the economic rationale for federation included a more balanced regional distribution of development, especially in the location of manufacturing industries (Chapter 9.4). Inherent in this was the notion that there would be a net transfer of development funds to the less-well endowed Malaysian states, notably Sabah and Sarawak.

Almost from the outset of federation state leaders such as Donald (later Fuad) Stephens in Sabah were apprehensive that the initial guarantees, the Twenty Points (see Chapter 9.2), might not prove effective in delivering the benefits expected. The history of the East Malaysian states since 1963, and some in the Peninsula such as Kelantan, shows that those leaders who were supportive of the federal government, in which the National Front dominated, obtained relatively favourable treatment in the allocation of federal development funds. Conversely, when centre–periphery political relations deteriorated as, for example, they did between the Sabah and federal governments in the later 1980s over the role of a new multi-racial party, Parti Bersatu Sabah (PBS), funds were withheld (Crouch, 1996, 52). Other sources of tension were the designation of Labuan Island (part of Sabah) as a Federal Territory in 1984 without any compensation, with-holding of approval for a local television station and university, and the small proportion of indigenous Sabahans in the civil service.

A recent study calculates that both Sabah and Sarawak received net transfers of funds from the federal government up to the mid-1970s, but thereafter Sabah suffered a cumulative net outgoing of approximately $935 million *ringgit* up to 1988, and Sarawak $5322 million *ringgit* up to 1989 (Wee, 1995, 44). The main cause was that the state governments were allowed to retain a royalty of only 5 per cent of the value of petroleum products which boomed in the 1970s and 1980s. The federal government took the same proportion, but in addition received substantial dividends and tax payments from Petronas, a federal agency, in which ownership and control of these resources was vested in 1974. Commerce and industry received relatively small allocations of development funds over the five Malaysia Plan periods, averaging 3.3 per cent in Sabah, and 4.2 per cent in Sarawak against 9.7 per cent in Peninsular Malaysia (calculated from Wee, 1995, Table 2.12).

The same intimate links between political connections and business emerged in the East Malaysian states as in the Peninsula. As timber prices picked up in the early 1970s, the political leadership in both Sabah and Sarawak controlled the distribution of forest concessions and licenses to cut to attract and hold supporters as well as generating cash flows on which to found family fortunes. Concessions were also granted to institutions such as the Sabah and Sarawak Foundations and the State Economic Development Corporations to provide sources of funds for their operations. The favouring of ethnic groups close to the leadership underlay much of the political manoeuvring in these years.

In the foregoing survey we have seen the Malaysian state playing a decisive role in setting the overall direction of the economy through initiating structural changes, such as ISI and EOI, and in the redistribution of the gains in wealth, employment and so on from economic growth.

To return to the paradigm set out at the beginning of this section, to what extent were the state's actions in this period independent of, or alternatively driven by, pressures from interest groups in Malaysian society? The record was mixed. Prior to 1969 the government relied on the *Merdeka* political 'bargain', together with the assumed trickle-down effects of economic growth, to start the elimination of the ethnic division of wealth and labour inherited from the colonial period. When it did not, the first decade of the NEP saw the implementation, in response to *bumiputera* discontent, of politically determined economic policies to achieve these objects. The second decade brought contrasting trends. On the one hand, there was a marked extension of the authority of the executive branch of government at the expense of the residual powers of the sultans, and the independence of the judiciary (Crouch, 1996, 137–48). The HICOM programme and the switch to privatisation were undertaken largely independently of interest group pressures. On the other hand, in face of the impact of the global downturn, there was a substantial reduction in government's direct involvement in the economy. The relaxation of the ICA, in particular towards foreign investors, implied a recognition that market forces could not be subjugated to political considerations indefinitely.

In general, social groups do not appear as a major source of pressure on the state throughout this period. The emerging middle class, or 'classes' (Kahn, 1996), had as yet little more than a statistical identity. *Bumiputeras* 'acted ... not as a class pursuing common interests, but as individuals fighting for survival' (Crouch, 1996, 218). The Chinese were largely powerless to resist what was seen as overfulfilment of the NEP targets for wealth redistribution (see Table 10.10). 'Many ... [were] unconvinced that their ethnic group [was] receiving even a 30 per cent share from privatisation' (Milne, 1992, 18). The Indian community remained a minor partner in the Alliance system of government and received few, if any, overall gains from wealth redistribution (Table 10.9a). The trade union movement, kept firmly in check by government, accounted for only about 25 per cent of wage-earners in 1980, down to 17 per cent by 1990, and could muster little political influence as the loyalties of its members were divided along ethnic lines (Crouch, 1996, 90). Overall, then, the pre-eminent desire of the state to maintain political stability, together with the successful performance of the economy throughout much of this period and the continuing polarisation of society along racial lines combined to mute any pressures for a move from 'quasi-' to full democracy.

A final question to be addressed is whether state intervention had a retarding effect on the growth of the economy. A recent study argues that in Malaysia 'resource costs arising from rent-seeking activities have always been minimal by developing country standards ...[whilst] direct redistributional policies [were] not a major drag on growth because of the key role played by FDI flows and rapid export expansion in augmenting the domestic resource base' (Athukorala and Menon, 1996, 180). Against this view a leading critic of government intervention in Asian economies contends that this has been generally of low quality, resulting in an *ersatz* (or inferior) form of capitalism 'with massive inefficiency in the economy and a large number of rent-seekers'. The latter include 'strange breeds of capital-ists such as crony capitalists ... bureaucratic capitalists ... political leaders, their sons and relatives ... royal families' (Yoshihara, 1988, 3, 130). The problem with such general characterisations is that they imply that countries are locked into a static situation, whereas the situation in Malaysia (as elsewhere in the region) has been a dynamic one. As we have seen, by the 1980s *bumiputeras* were dividing into pro-development and pro-distributionist groups. By the end of the NEP small numbers of *bumiputera* entrepreneurs were starting to emerge who did not owe their initial success to political patronage, and who were forging links with non-*bumiputera* capitalists (Searle, 1999). Several scholars point out that the impressive performance of NICs in Asia in competitive export markets is at odds with Yoshihara's negative assessment (Mackie, 1989; Hill, 1993, 27). Whilst the prevalence of 'money politics' and state patronage led to some inefficient allocation of financial resources between 1970 and 1990, and probably retarded the development of a more numerous class of domestic entrepreneurs (*bumiputeras* and others), much of the expansion in exports, manufactures especially, came from foreign investment (Chapter 12.2) which was less affected by such constraints, particularly after the easing of the NEP from 1986.

11
The Primary Sector

At federation the primary sector of the Malaysian economy encompassed a very diverse collection of activities. These ranged from shifting agriculture through a continuum of sedentary non-capitalistic small farmers to capitalistic monocultural estates of 40 to several thousand hectares in size, together with extractive industries, notably timber, petroleum, tin, copper and so on. Foreign enterprise predominated in estates and the mining industries.

The development imperatives faced by government were, first, the upgrading and progressive commercialisation of food crop (principally rice) production in order to reduce dependence on imported supplies and economise on foreign exchange. Second, the rejuvenation of the older export industries such as rubber, had to be continued whilst encouraging diversification into oil palms and cocoa. At the same time the extractive industries (apart from tin) experienced explosive growth. Third, the primary sector had to provide much of the financial and employment underpinning for the economy whilst the nascent manufacturing industrial sector was growing. In agriculture and forestry government had to balance modernisation of the structure and methods of production against the political imperative to meet the rising material expectations of the 'traditional', largely *bumiputera*, rural sector. This involved questions of access, ownership and management of land, technical and financial support and, in East Malaysia particularly, ongoing tensions between native landowners and the competition from expanding official development schemes and private commercial interests (notably logging and hydro-electric schemes). Overall, the thrust of official policy has been to extend capitalistic, commercialised agriculture at the expense of subsistence, household labour-based production.

11.1   A review of agricultural production

Between 1963 and 1990 Malaysian agriculture showed the effects of the extensive investment in land development, technical innovations to raise

Table 11.1   Malaysia: area of major crops, 1965–90 (to nearest, 000 hectares)

Year	Rice	Rubber	Oil Palm	Coconut	Cocoa
1965	472	2043	97	277	
1970	571	2020	301	309	4
1975	624[a]	1991	642	n.a.	10
1980	711	2005	1021	248	124
1985	659	1949	1431	328	258
1990	654[b]	1837	1786[b]	n.a.	n.a.

n.a. = not available.
[a] 1978.
[b] 1988.
Sources: Malaysia, Sabah, Sarawak, *ASB*, various years; Fong (1989), Table 4.5; King and Parnwell (1990), Table 3.4; Jomo (1990a), Table 3.14; Mustapha (1989), Table 5.

yields, crop diversification and infrastructural supports begun in the 1950s. Actual expenditure on the agricultural sector over this period aggregated some $25 billion, or about 15 per cent of the total outlay on development (calculated from Jomo, 1990a, Table 5.1). The trends in planted area, production, yields per hectare, output growth rates, and changes in the structure of production are set out in Tables 11.1–11.4.

Market conditions for the major commodities were as follows. The Malaysian market for domestically grown rice expanded substantially as a result of the rapid population growth (Table 6.1) and the policy aimed at achieving full self-sufficiency in this basic foodstuff. Natural rubber continued to fluctuate heavily in price, but values improved significantly in the late 1970s and 1980s as this product became more competitive with petroleum-based synthetic rubber whose costs rose as a result of the 'oil shocks' (see Chapter 10.1). Malaysia, however, gradually relinquished its dominant position, declining from 37.5 per cent of world rubber supply in 1960 to 24.8 per cent in 1990, followed closely by Indonesia (24.2 per cent) and Thailand (24.4 per cent), with the latter taking the lead in 1991 (calculated from Barlow, Jayasuriya and Tan, 1994, Table 2.3). The declining momentum of the industry in Malaysia is reflected in the planted area and output, both of which peaked in 1980 (Tables 11.1 and 11.2a). During the 1980s, however, Malaysia became a major manufacturer of rubber goods, such as gloves, condoms, tyres, footwear, and so on (UN, 1991, 75), thus gaining some of the value-added production which had previously gone to other countries.

The question of active intervention in the market to try to lessen price fluctuations for rubber had been in abeyance since the prewar IRRA (see section 8.2). However, in 1970 the major producers formed the Association of Natural Rubber Producing Countries (ANRPC) to coordinate production and marketing. Demand conditions fluctuated strongly during the 1970s and

Table 11.2   Malaysia: production of major crops, 1965–90

(a) Output (nearest 000 tonnes)

Year	Rice	Rubber	Palm Oil	Pepper	Copra	Cocoa
1965	802	902	148	18	161	
1970	1072	1249	424	29	185	
1975	1268	1436	1239	30	156	
1980	1242	1530	2576	n/a	117	19[a]
1985	1190	1469	4133	19	97	51
1990	1269	1291	6095	32	64	151

[a] *Estates only.*

(b) Yield per Hectare

Year	Rice[a]	Rubber[b]	Palm Oil[a]	Copra[c]	Cocoa[a]
1970	2.8	1157 (E) 763 (S)			
1975	2.9	1272 (E) 972 (S)			
1980	2.9	1428 (E) 964 (S)	17.63 13.20[d]	7705	0.89 (E)
1985	3.0	1418 (E) 933 (S)	20.0 20.0	7230	0.51
1990	3.1	1335 (E) n.a. (S)	18.53 n.a.	6823	0.77

E = Estates: S = Smallholdings
[a] Tonnes.
[b] Kg.
[c] Nuts
[d] Group smallholdings (Peninsular Malaysia).
Sources: Rice, Fong (1989), Table 4.6; Rubber, Fong (1989), Table 4.3; Palm Oil, Malek bin Mansor and Barlow (1988), Table 2.6; Malaysia, *ABS*, 1990.

1980s. In 1981 virtually all producers joined the First International Natural Rubber Agreement (INRA 1), renewed as INRA 2 in 1988, the main object of which was to build up a large buffer stock with which to smooth out price swings (Barlow, 1978, 110; Barlow, Jayasuriya and Tan, 1994, 56).

  World output of palm oil grew at 10 per cent a year, enlarging its market share to 9 per cent against the principal competitor, soy-bean oil, with over one-fifth. Malaysia's share of total production increased from 25 per cent in 1970 to nearly 62 per cent in 1982 (Barlow, 1985b, Table 1). Among the lesser commercial crops coconuts showed a decline in the 1980s, but cocoa proved a highly attractive alternative (especially for smallholders).

Table 11.3   Malaysia: growth of agricultural output, 1966–90 (annual percentage)

Crop	1966–70	1971–5	1976–80	1981–5	1986–90
Rubber	6.0	3.1	1.6	0.06	n.a.
Palm Oil	24.1	24.3	15.5	49.3	n.a.
Rice	6.0	3.7	2.2	–13.6	n.a.
Fish	11.0	9.8	9.8	–10.4	n.a.
All Crops	8.0	5.6	5.9	4.0	3.86[a]

n.a. = not available.
[a] Arithmetical, not compound average.
Sources: 1966–70, adapted from Mustapha (1989), Table 4; 1986–90, calculated from Asian Development Bank (1990).

The rates of growth of agricultural output (Table 11.3) showed the strongest gains in the First Plan period (1966–70) as the use of high-yielding rubber trees, diversification into oil palms, cocoa and intensification of rice production paid off. Growth slowed over the next two planning periods, particularly in rubber and rice as returns and yields began to level off (see next section). Only oil palms retained, and from 1981–5 onwards increased, their momentum, though here again yield per hectare declined slightly by 1990 (see Table 11.2b). Overall Malaysian agriculture was showing signs of stagnation in the 1980s, facing problems of labour shortages in many areas. The

Table 11.4   Malaysia: organisational changes in commercial agriculture, 1960–80

	(Per cent of planted area of each crop)					
	Estates			*Smallholdings*		
	Pen. Malaysia	*Sabah*	*Sarawak*	*Pen. Malaysia*	*Sabah*	*Sarawak*
(a) 1960						
Rubber	50	42	2.	50	58	98
Oil-palm	87	negl.	n.a.	13	negl.	n.a.
Coconut	5	nil	n.a.	85	100	n.a.
Cocoa		n.a.			n.a.	
(b) 1980						
Rubber	22	9	2	78	91[a]	98
Oil-palm	55	52	15[b]	41	48	85[b]
Coconut	9	8	n.a.	91	92	n.a.
Cocoa	98	73	31	2	2 7	69

n.a. = not available.
[a] 1986,
[b] 1982.
Sources: Fong (1989), Table 4.5; Kitingan and Ongkili (1989), 91; *ABS*, various years.

sector contributed only 1 per cent of national growth during the NEP period, compared to 2.1 per cent from manufacturing and 3 per cent from services (Malaysian Government, 1991b, Table 3.2).

In terms of the structure of production the NEP period saw major changes. Among the most notable was the shift in the shares of estates and smallholdings in the planted area (Table 11.4), which saw the latter assuming a predominant position in rubber in Peninsular Malaysia and Sabah. In oil palms the position was more balanced, though smallholders gained ground as a result of the widespread adoption of this crop in land development schemes. In Sarawak the smallholdings continued as the dominant unit of production. There was little change in coconuts, but in the newest crop, cocoa, estates took the lead in the Peninsula and Sabah.

Estates continued to operate with hierarchies of management and labour, and levels of technical inputs designed to minimise unit costs of production. The important change for smallholders was that under official development policy they too were expected to apply similar principles; in other words, to operate more like estates. As many individual owners lacked the skills and resources to do this, government stepped in through agencies which opened up virgin areas, or which grouped together existing holdings for purposes of centralised management and marketing of produce. 'The establishment of the Federal Land Development Authority (Felda) in 1956, marked the on-set of guided agricultural development to eradicate the dualistic structure of the sector' (Fong, 1989, 127). Though many owners remained independent, increasing numbers came into the category of 'organised' or 'managed' smallholders.

11.2 Rice: the goal of self-sufficiency

Although, as Fujimoto (1991, 431) notes in relation to Peninsular Malaysia, the rice industry 'represents a rather minor segment of the national economy' in terms of its share of total output, it is economically and culturally central in the lives of rural people, largely *bumiputeras*, throughout the territories and therefore politically highly sensitive. Rice production expanded substantially by 4.7 per cent a year between 1965 and 1975 (Table 11.2), and fluctuated thereafter in the region of 1.2 million tonnes a year (short-term swings took it down to 925 000 tonnes in 1987 and back to 1 148 000 tonnes the next year). The Peninsular share was well in excess of four-fifths (84 per cent in 1964, 89 per cent in 1990).

Government policy towards the industry up to 1983 was 'protective' (Fujimoto, 1991, 431), having the objectives of (i) achieving the highest possible degree of national self-sufficiency through land development and technological innovation, (ii) increasing the incomes of farmers and (iii) supplying rice to consumers at reasonable prices.

Taking these points in turn, in the late 1960s Peninsular Malaysia aimed at total self-sufficiency. Despite the emphasis on technical progress, the bulk of the output increase came from expansion in the planted area: up by just over 50 per cent in 1965–80 (Table 11.1). Bray (1986, Table 2.2) calculates about two-thirds of the increase in yield between 1955 and 1973 came from this source. The most notable extensions were two major irrigation schemes initiated in the 1960s: Muda in Kedah (100 000 hectares), and Kemubu, Kelantan (20 000 hectares). Self-sufficiency was most nearly achieved at 95 per cent in 1975, dropping to 82 per cent in 1980 after which the target was reduced to 80–90 per cent in the face of growing doubts over the economic justification for the original aim.

The main technical measures were the use of high-yielding seed varieties, coupled with chemical fertilisers, pesticides and water control methods to enable double-cropping. Farmers received support under the guaranteed minimum price scheme, increased from $16 to $28–30 per picul in 1974 and obtainable by selling direct to the National Padi and Rice Board (LPN) set up in 1971. The Malaysian Agricultural Research and Development Institute (MARDI), created in 1969, carried out basic research, whilst the Farmers' Organisation Authority (1973) provided a composite package of low interest loans and credit, subsidised inputs such as fertilisers, and so on (Fujimoto, 1991, 432–3).

From the mid-1950s to the mid-1980s public expenditure on the rice industry in the Peninsula totalled cumulatively some $1250 million (Amarjit Kaur, 1992, Figure 2). The main effect on yields of *padi* was evident by the early 1970s. Between 1957/8 and 1974/5 the yield rose from 2.2 to 2.9 tonnes per hectare, an increase of nearly 32 per cent or 1.64 per cent per annum. By 1980 it was still 2.9 tonnes, and in 1984/5 had only reached 3 tonnes (Fong, 1989, Table 4.6), a rise of about 0.75 per cent per annum. These plainly represented diminishing returns for heavy investment, and by this time it was clear that even 80–90 per cent self-sufficiency was uneconomic. Peninsular Malaysia's production cost was nearly twice that of Thailand, and an estimated 500 000 tonnes of Thai rice, or 30 per cent of consumption, was smuggled annually from 1981–5 (Fujimoto, 1991, 442). World rice prices had fallen by well over 50 per cent from 1974 to 1986, and even with price support (offset by rising costs of inputs) increasing numbers of Malaysian rice farmers left the industry, their numbers contracting by 20 per cent in just four years, 1980–4. The planted area shrank (see Table 11.1), and unworked or abandoned land became an increasing problem. A 1981 survey found 40 per cent of Peninsular rice land idle, with 18 per cent thus for over three years. Many turned to off-farm employment in manufacturing and construction. This was particularly marked along the east coast where small farm sizes and stagnating yields led to 60–67 per cent of families in some areas engaging in non-agricultural work (Shand, 1986, 6; Fong, 1989, 143; Fujimoto, 1991, 438).

In the face of these circumstances government formulated the New Agricultural Policy (NAP) in 1984. There was a shift in emphasis from the generally protective attitude of the NEP towards rice farmers to a focus on developing a more efficient and commercialised industry in eight 'rice bowl' areas, all on the west coast (e.g. Muda, Krian, Seberang Prai) except for Kemubu, which together produced 55–60 per cent of the total. Farmers outside these areas were to be encouraged to turn to non-rice crops such as coffee, maize or groundnuts. The degree of rice self-sufficiency was lowered to a 'floating target' of 60–65 per cent. The NAP envisaged structural changes to try to overcome the problem of uneconomically-sized holdings, such as consolidation (no more large-scale, individualistic, development schemes), group farming, mini-estates, centralised management, mechanisation and so on (Fujimoto, 1991, 443–7). The later 1980s saw a reduction in the payment of subsidies to rice producers. Price subsidies alone represented 69 per cent of farmers' annual net income in 1984. Fertiliser subsidies totalled $430 million between 1981 and 1985 (Pletcher, 1989, 373–4), which government could ill afford in the economic depression at that time.

Rice policies since 1963 have certainly brought income benefits to farmers (see Chapter 13), particularly to those in the most-favoured 'rice bowl' areas. Overall, the incidence of poverty fell from 88 per cent of households in 1970 to approximately 50 per cent in 1990, but was still well above the rural average of 22.4 per cent (Courtenay, 1995, Table 7.1). The NAP improved the average yield per hectare by approximately 18 per cent between 1985 and 1990 (unweighted average of main and off-season crop, *ABS* Malaysia, 1992). However, these measures, by themselves, did not prove adequate to remedy some of the main structural problems of the industry, most notably the average farm size which in the Peninsula showed a continual decline in the postwar period. By the early 1980s, in the Muda region, 61.8 per cent of owners had less than the 1.1 hectares minimum necessary for a bare subsistence income. A main cause was the Muslim law of inheritance (*faraid*) which was broadly interpreted as requiring division into fractional shares among all the heirs (Amriah Buang, 1991), with the exception of FELDA schemes where only one heir could inherit. A study of the Muda district concluded that 'there must be a substantial movement of small farmers off the land or ... a more equal distribution ... if holding sizes are not to decline further' (T.G. Lim, 1989, 200, 202).

The problems of incompatibility between small farm size and technical innovation were difficult enough for mono-crop rice farmers who had received the bulk of government assistance. An even more numerous group, located mostly outside the 'rice bowl' areas and combining rice-growing with other crops such as rubber, coffee and sugar cane, faced a 'dilemma' in the face of modernisation. Their very lack of specialisation put them outside the scope of most government programmes, leaving them 'in an anomalous position in relation to existing development strategies ... the persistence of traditional agricultural practices is the result of the absence of options to change rather than ... an inherent attitude of not wanting change' (Zaharah Mahmud, 1980, 71). Average farm size in Johor, Negeri Sembilan, Melaka and Pahang is only 0.53–0.81 hectares (Muhammad Ikmal Said, 1990, 60). Farmers thus faced a choice similar to their predecessors at the advent of rubber at the beginning of the century: namely, whether to abandon the cultivation of rice, which at least assured them of subsistence, to concentrate on commercial crops open to the vagaries of the market, or quit agriculture for employment outside the sector. Increasingly the second option has been taken, especially in the developed states of Selangor, Perak and Penang where other employment has been readily available. In the Muda region, on the other hand, a growing number of farmers have amassed sufficient capital to acquire more land, hire workers, and buy (jointly with other households) combine harvesters/tractors which are rented out. In short they have begun to operate as capitalist farmers.

The East Malaysian territories had only about 25 per cent of the total rice area in 1980, and of this three-quarters lay in Sarawak (ABS, Malaysia, 1982). In the mid-1960s Sabah was about 60 per cent self-sufficient, and Sarawak only 40 per cent (Burrough and Burrough, 1974, 39; Solhee, 1988, 89). In broad terms the picture presented by this industry in both territories was quite similar to that in the Peninsula, namely expansion in area, output and yields especially in the 1960s and 1970s, but a slowing down thereafter. However, account has to be taken of marked differences in the composition of this sector, with hill (or dry) rice produced under shifting cultivation forming a much more substantial part. In Sarawak it still accounted for just over 50 per cent of the total in the early 1980s, though the proportion had declined significantly from 61 per cent in 1960 (calculated from Cramb, 1989a, Table 7) owing to a shift to *sawah*.

The general thrust of official policy followed that in Peninsular Malaysia: introduction of high-yielding varieties, fertilisers, irrigation, double-cropping and so on. The notable differences which emerged, though, were that the opening of fresh land, use of technical inputs and the spread of double-cropping fell well short of target. For Sarawak it has been argued that despite the Assistance to Padi Planters Scheme (operating since 1958), expenditure has been driven primarily by considerations of political patronage. Thus politicians have pursued popular support by distributing benefits too widely rather than concentrating it in those areas most likely to give the best economic returns (Solhee, 1988, 91–2). Other factors which have inhibited the spread of change have been the slow erosion of customary attitudes which (not without good reason from the viewpoint of security) considered rice cultivation a subsistence rather than a commercial activity. Thus, 'farmers' response to double-cropping [etc.] was to reduce the farm size, so that total production per household was more or less sustained at the subsistence level' (Solhee, 1988, 98). Extensive rather than intensive cultivation remained widespread. In 1982 a mere 35–40 per cent of the total irrigated area was double-cropped, and in 1984 about 40 per cent of the improved area was left unplanted (Solhee, 1988, 98). Similar constraints operated in Sabah where double-cropping was thought to offend the *padi* spirit (Burrough and Burrough, 1974, 41).

Sarawak did not undergo a 'Green Revolution' (Cramb, 1989a, 9), particularly in the hill-rice areas, and the same may be said of Sabah. On balance Sabah achieved higher yields per hectare in wet-rice, peaking at 2.8 tonnes (*padi*) per hectare in 1983 but then declining to 2.4 tonnes in 1990. Sarawak's best performance came between 1960 and 80, improving from 1.07 to nearly 2 tonnes, slowing to 2.3 tonnes in 1987 and falling sharply to 1.59 tonnes in 1990, compared to 3.45 tonnes in Peninsular Malaysia in the latter year (*ABS*, Malaysia, 1984, 1988, 1992). Hill-rice yields in Sarawak showed no particular trend and remained less than half those from wet-rice cultivation. The increasing density of the Iban population by the 1970s/80s put pressure on land reserves, decreasing rice self-sufficiency and pushing farmers towards, though not irrevocably, cash crops (Cramb, 1988, 129).

In terms of self-sufficiency neither state was able to approach the level achieved in the Peninsula. For Sarawak, Solhee (1988, 98) estimates that 'at best' domestic production during the 1970s and 1980s met only 60 per cent of needs, but Cramb (1989a, 28), who takes a slightly more positive view of the achievement, puts it at between 55 and 65 per cent. Sabah in the 1960s and 1970s stayed steady at around 60 per cent (calculated from *ABS*, Sabah, various years).

As against this general picture, it is useful to note the findings of several studies which illustrate conditions in various regions of the Borneo interior. Common features are that agricultural production, rice especially, was increasingly affected by external factors in the 1970s and 1980s. There were periods of heavy out- and return-migration of men from villages governed by the availability of employment in the timber and petroleum industries, government agencies and so on. Returnees placed sudden strains on food supplies, the division of labour between men and women, and access to land. A Sabah Padi Board Scheme to plant 2000 hectares of rice failed in the early 1980s due to poor land preparation. Overall, the trend was towards intensification of land use, which involved food crops as well as switches between cash crops (notably rubber, pepper) according to fluctuating returns, but technical innovation was limited. Access to improved transport facilities was a vital factor underlying change. The innovation of daily public launch services on the Rajang and Balleh rivers after 1970 greatly improved the situation in the Kapit district.

The completion of a road to Sandakan in 1983 opened up new land in the lower Labuk valley which, against the trend noted above, enabled an extensification of agriculture. New roads in the Layar, Bengoh and Krokong districts of Sarawak increased the output of export crops (rubber) as well as foodstuffs for local consumption. As in the Peninsula, off-farm employment became increasingly important. In 1990 the off-farm sector absorbed over a quarter of the available adult male labour force in the Kemena Basin, Sarawak, though the incidence was very uneven. There were no such workers in 30 per cent of the households surveyed, and only one in 44 per cent (survey based on Grijpstra, 1978; Schwenk, 1978; Whinfrey-Koepping, 1988; Cramb, 1990; Morrison, 1993; Windle, 1996).

11.3   The export crops

Prior to about 1960 the leading export, rubber (55 per cent of total export value in that year), had relatively little competition from other commercial crops for the use of land and labour. During the next three decades this situation changed radically. As Tables 11.1 and 11.2a show, oil palm cultivation expanded rapidly to overtake rubber in terms of output, and nearly in planted area, by the 1980s. As a proportion of total export value in 1990 the two crops accounted, respectively, for 5.5 per cent and 3.8 per cent (calculated from IMF, 1991); in rubber's case a stark illustration of the shifts in sectoral weights within the Malaysian economy. Another crop which came to prominence was cocoa.

For purposes of analysis we shall divide the agricultural sector into two: large-scale units (estates), and small-scale units (smallholdings) although, as we shall see, the land development schemes and other official policies, whilst directed at smallholdings, aimed to approximate them to estates in terms of management styles and technology. The structural shift giving smallholdings much larger shares in planted area and output has already been noted.

Estates

The estate sector underwent a major alteration in ethnic ownership. In Peninsular Malaysia this process had its beginnings with the sale and subsequent sub-division into smallholdings of foreign-owned rubber estates totalling some 146 000 hectares between the late 1950s and 1972. Many buyers were Chinese, mostly urban-based, who let the holdings to tenants leading to criticisms of displacement of the (largely Indian) workforce, and inefficient working. None the less, up to the NEP foreign capital continued to dominate the estate sector, constituting 52 per cent overall in 1973 (D. Lim, 1973, 196; Barlow, 1978, Table 6, 91–2). However, during the early 1970s Chinese–Malaysian capital took a large step into this sector through the activities of Lee Loy Seng, from an Ipoh mining family, who rapidly built up ownership of some 25 000 hectares of rubber land and 22 000 hectares of oil palms by 1974 through the purchase of British-owned companies (Fong, 1989, Table 4.11). By 1989 this group totalled 70 000 hectares, and had been joined by two others, Industrial Oxygen Incorporated Bhd (55 500 hectares) and Asiatic Development Bhd (27 200 hectares) (Hara, 1991, Table IV).

However, over the same period Western and Chinese-Malaysian capital in the plantation sector was overtaken by the growth of *bumiputera* interests, represented principally by organisations established and financed by government. This movement gathered pace in the late 1970s and early 1980s when the second oil shock generated ample revenue. The leading bodies were Pernas, Permodalan Nasional Bhd (PNB) and its subsidiary Amanah Saham Nasional Bhd (ASNB). By the mid-1980s the major British agency groups, accounting for over 60 per cent of estate capital, had passed into *bumiputera* control (Fong, 1989, 146–8; Hara, 1991, 358). At the same time some former British-owned companies diversified into fields quite removed from the primary production which had been their exclusive focus for so long: for example, property investment and development, furniture making, investment dealing and rubber manufacturing. (Barlow, Jayasuriya and Tan, 1994, Table 7.2). This horizontal shift in investment was one indication that the Peninsula was breaking away from the path dependency on rubber and tin which had been set up at the beginning of the century (see Chapter 4).

For the most part the estate sector continued to operate with the same managerial and supervisory systems as previously, but with Malaysian personnel now progressively replacing expatriates in executive positions. The period saw the general adoption of 'second stratum' technology by rubber estates: that is complete replanting with high-yielding trees capable of three to four times the yield per hectare of the original unselected varieties. These were accompanied by a range of costlier inputs (fertilisers, pesticides, yield stimulants, and so on). As labour costs rose, it became necessary to utilise workers more economically. The general development of the economy, manufacturing industry especially, in the 1970s and 1980s impacted upon rubber estates forcing them to compete for resources through a move to a 'third stratum' of technology consisting of further elaboration of the techniques and organisational changes originating in the second stratum (Barlow and Jayasuriya, 1986). Oil palm estates, too, had similarly to look for the most economic methods of production.

Starting with rubber replanting, we have seen (Chapter 9.3) that estates with their superior financial resources made much faster progress than smallholders. Up to 1969 nearly 60 per cent of replanting grants in the Peninsula went to estates (Shamsul, 1986, 86). By 1973 just over 90 per cent of their planted area was under high-yielding trees, with the process virtually complete at 98 per cent by the later 1980s. The average yield stood at 1418 kg per hectare in 1985 against 933 kg on smallholdings (Table 11.2b). At the same time the estate workforce (excluding illegal migrants) declined substantially from a peak of 285 000 in 1960 to 167 000 by 1980, a drop of over 40 per cent. As a result annual productivity per worker doubled from 1.5 to 3.0 tonnes, or 100 per cent, over the same period (Barlow, 1990, Tables 2.1, 2.3). The decline in the workforce reflected not only greater efficiency on estates, but also a 'pull' effect from other industries, notably the rising palm oil sector. In the 1980s a shortage of labour developed on Peninsular Malaysian estates in general. Normally this would have forced up wage rates in order to retain or attract back workers, but the shortage was largely offset by an inflow of migrant workers, many illegal, from neighbouring Indonesia and southern Thailand. They received below-award wages, and no benefits such as provident fund contributions or social security payments (Nayagam, 1990, 40–1).Thus a potential bottleneck in supply was eased. Average wages for rubber tappers rose on average 1.73 per cent a year between 1974 and 1989, and 2.02 per cent for oil palm harvesters, compared to 3.55 per cent for production workers in the electronics industry (Ramachandran, 1994, Table 5.21).

Apart from improved varieties of planting material, the technology of rubber production saw advances in systems of tapping, yield stimulation, latex collection, tree and soil maintenance (fertilisers, pesticides and so on). Processing prior to export was greatly improved by the introduction of a 'Standard Malaysian Rubber Scheme' (SMR) in 1965 which prescribed exact criteria of quality for premium grades in order to conform more closely to buyer needs. By 1973 there were six such grades (Barlow, 1978, 172).

The attraction of oil palms for investors was a shorter period of immaturity, and significantly higher annual returns, averaging between 20 and 30 per cent (1965–85) against under 10 per cent from rubber (Nayagam, 1990, 16). Estate growth has to a large extent come from the transfer of land formerly under rubber. Expansion was extremely rapid both in terms of planted area and yield (Tables 11.1, 11.2b), and also in labour productivity which grew by nearly 200 per cent between 1960 and 1982 (calculated from Barlow *et al.*, 1986, Table 2), far outstripping rubber.

Estate-type production had mixed fortunes in East Malaysia. In Sabah rubber estates underwent a relative decline even more marked than in Peninsular Malaysia (Table 11.4). In absolute terms the planted area fell from a peak of some 46 000 hectares in 1968 to a mere 5000 hectares in 1990. This crop lost its attraction to investors as, increasingly, estates were simply abandoned. Replanting with high-yielding trees proceeded slowly and had only reached 86 per cent by 1990. The situation in oil palms was exactly the reverse with the number of estates (many government schemes) nearly tripling from 72 in 1966 to 209 in 1990, and the planted area increasing from 36 000 to 133 000 hectares (Malaysia, *ABS*, 1973, 1992). In

Sarawak, as in the colonial period, the private estate area under both these crops remained minor.

As part of the process of agricultural diversification cocoa enjoyed a boom in the late 1970s due to civil war in Ghana, the world's major supplier. Sabah, where suitable land was in greatest supply (mainly in Tawau and Sandakan Residencies), raced ahead from 9000 hectares in 1975 to around 183 000 hectares in 1986, of which 73 per cent was on estates. The latter were mainly privately financed, as the government share was only 12 per cent (Kitingan and Ongkili, 1989, 91). In the Peninsula the crop was principally an intercrop with smallholder coconuts, and in Sarawak it was of minor importance on both estates and land schemes. The momentum of growth fell away in the later 1980s as expansion approached the limits of land, and the market proved highly unstable (Tate, 1996, 585–6; Amarjit Kaur, 1998; Malaysia, *ABS*, various years).

Smallholdings

Following independence smallholders became the focus of many government programmes to raise rural productivity and incomes, in order to reduce the incidence of poverty. These programmes operated through a multiplicity of institutions related to land and agricultural development. As in the rice industry, government policy passed through two phases: a generally 'protective' phase up to the NAP (1984), followed by a move to a more focused approach, with particular attention to a commercial evaluation of policies, and improving the linkages between agriculture and other sectors of the Malaysian economy (Zulkifly, 1988, 62). However, throughout both phases ran a common thread of bureaucratic management and control over smallholder production.

Land development schemes took two forms. One undertook improvements *in situ* for the rehabilitation of land within existing settled areas, while the other was designed to open up new areas to which settlers would move from districts experiencing pressure on land, where holdings were uneconomically small (say under 2 hectares), to blocks averaging 4 hectares. In Peninsular Malaysia the leading agencies were, respectively, FELCRA (Federal Land Consolidation and Rehabilitation Authority, and FELDA. These had counterparts in Sabah and Sarawak but, from the late 1970s, were also invited to operate in those states. By the mid-1980s a total of approximately 3.6 million acres of land had been rehabilitated or newly developed in the Peninsula (Fong, 1989, 136). The areas involved in East Malaysia were much smaller. In Sabah, the least densely populated state, the major settlement schemes covered only just under 50 000 hectares by 1990 (Sabah, *ABS*, 1990).

The aspects of development common to all states in Malaysia which will be examined are: the location of schemes, crops, titles to land, bureaucratic controls and political affiliations, the supply of technical and financial assistance, and the attitudes of participant farmers.

In terms of geographical location, the general principle under the NEP was to use the schemes to spread commercial activities to regions which had not been drawn into the export economy in the colonial period, and in particular to those with concentrations of *bumiputera* population. Thus, in the Peninsula the regional development authorities were set up in southeast Johor and Pahang (KEJORA and DARA), mid-Terengganu (KETENGAH), south Kelantan (KESEDAR). *In situ* schemes included west Johor and Trans-Perak (Fong, 1989, 136). In Sabah development centred on the east coast Residencies of Tawau and Sandakan, and to the west, interior districts such as Keningau and Nabawan/Pensiangan (Chandler, 1989; Hewgill and Cramb, 1994).

However, the economics of location were accompanied, and in some cases outweighed, by political considerations. At the local level the various forms of government assistance constituted a package of material largesse which the political elites found extremely useful as a means of dispensing patronage to supporters. Some villages in Selangor, for example, whose leaders had ties with UMNO gained access to replanting programmes in the 1960s much earlier than neighbours who supported Parti Islam SeMalaysia (Shamsul, 1986, 87). In East Malaysia, whilst development expenditure had broadly similar economic and political dimensions, it also reflected the particular conditions there such as the much more widely dispersed populations. In Sabah in the 1960s and 1970s the land development programme, which received between 7.5 and 12.6 per cent of total public development expenditure, was 'an attempt to restructure a diverse and dispersed population into cohesive agricultural communities to serve administrative and political ends' (Hewgill and Cramb, 1994, 3). An instance of this during the 1960s was the scheme at Nabawan which planned to move Muruts to an area where they would be more readily accessible to administrative controls. In Sarawak large schemes sought to concentrate resources in a particular area to which settlers would then be brought (Windle, 1996). An important contrast between East and Peninsular Malaysia which made the implementation of schemes in the former region more problematic was that attachment to shifting cultivation was still strong.

The principal export crops chosen for both *in situ* and new area development schemes were rubber and oil palms, with cocoa, pepper, coconuts, tea, coffee and tobacco as minor products. Rubber involved the replanting of old areas, and new plantings in the land schemes. In replanting, smallholders in the Peninsula continued to lag behind estates until the 1970s, despite successive increases in the level of financial grants. Following the establishment of the Rubber Industry Smallholders Development Authority (RISDA) in 1973, dissemination of the newest types of planting material was speeded up. RISDA pursued a collective approach, paying replanting grants to groups of owners and then, from 1979, promoting 'mini-estates' in which participating owners signed a contract giving the agency (which placed a *caveat*, or constraint on sale, over the land) the management of replanting and subsequent production and sale of crops for at least twelve years (Horii, 1991b). No precise figure is available for the proportion of smallholdings replanted by the late 1980s,but it was probably in excess of 90 per cent compared to 98 per cent on estates (Barlow, Jarasuriya and Tan, 1994, Table 2.4; estimate from data in Joseph, 1988). Sabah smallholders achieved slightly less replanting at 86 per cent, whilst Sarawak performed relatively poorly with barely half (51.5 per cent) by the mid-1980s (Malaysia, *ABS*, 1985, 1990). In the latter case this most probably reflects a declining interest in rubber and a switch to pepper growing among Dayak farmers in this period (Cramb, 1989a).

In both East and Peninsular Malaysia the smallholders were heavily dependent upon government for the supply of inputs (planting materials, fertilisers, pesticides) and advice on improved techniques of cultivation, and general management. One avenue for distributing these was through Group Processing Centres (GPCs) set up by the Malaysian Rubber Development Corporation (MARDEC) primarily for collective handling of crops such as rubber to strengthen the bargaining position of producers *vis-à-vis* middlemen. In Peninsular Malaysia there were already about 800 (government-owned) of these centres by 1973, and a further 350 private (mainly Chinese-owned) ones (Barlow, 1978, 321–2). The various agencies involved constituted in total a heavy demand on the resources of trained personnel available at any given time.

Right from the 1960s the rural development policies in Malaysia were regarded as a model for the Third World, in particular the land development schemes. By 1992 FELDA had developed 475 schemes in the Peninsula, resettling nearly 119 000 families (654 000 persons). A study of one of the earliest schemes, Kemendor (Melaka) established in 1958, revealed that over the next 30 years or so the majority of the settlers repaid their loans, achieved incomes above the FELDA target of $300 per month, and acquired material possessions (car, motor cycle, television, washing machine and so on). Most were satisfied with the level of social amenities provided (health, education, retail shops, electricity, telephones). In the mid-1980s replanting began, with 60 per cent of settlers taking the option to switch from rubber to oil palms (Tunku Shamsul Bahrin and Khadijah Muhamed, 1992, 80).

Not all schemes in the Peninsula were so successful and, as we shall see, the attempt to base land development in East Malaysia on similar principles and institutions encountered many problems. Perhaps the single most important issue in the minds of settlers in all parts of Malaysia concerned the question of title to land. The preference was for titles unencumbered by any restrictions as to sale, mortage, sub-division and so on. FELDA initially gave full title once the loan had been repaid, but this carried a *caveat* against the Muslim law of inheritance requiring division among the heirs. Land on FELCRA schemes could not be owned by individuals. From 1970 farmers held shares carrying the right to use the land and its products, and in the 1970s and 1980s similar forms of tenure were introduced on FELDA schemes (Horii, 1991b). Delays in issuing title were a frequent source of grievance among settlers, who interpreted this as a means of prolonging bureaucratic controls.

Land matters were especially contentious in East Malaysia because of the various categories of ownership. In Sarawak, for instance, there were four categories of land (see pp. 141–2 above). Development schemes affected mainly Native Customary Right lands, whose owners were generally reluctant to surrender land over which they held customary communal rights to government agencies, which would convert these into estates or individual smallholdings for commercial crops. When the Sarawak Land Development Board (SLDB), following the FELDA model, took over seven rubber schemes (some 7000 hectares) catering largely to Iban settlers, five were found to be on Native Customary Right land. Settlers were reluctant to give the schemes prime loyalty, absenteeism was high, rubber was sold privately and in 1981, with only 20 per cent of settlers having cleared their loans, the Board was instructed to withdraw completely from management of these schemes (Cramb, 1989b). Resettlement also encountered reluctance to move to other areas. In northeast Sarawak the SLDB established large oil palm and cocoa schemes on unencumbered state land to resettle Dayaks from more densely populated central and southwest areas. Conditions were so unattractive that many returned to their original districts. The schemes were turned into conventional estates operated largely by migrant Indonesian labourers. SLDB was incurring losses around $20 million a year by the mid-1980s, with corruption a major factor. Management of the estates was handed over to a commercial company, Sime Darby, from 1987. This reflected a new policy direction towards privatisation (Cramb and Reece, 1988, 16). Sarawak Land Consolidation and Rehabilitation Authority (SALCRA) had better success with *in situ* development schemes which involved land already owned, but the Land Custody and Development Authority (LCDA) (deemed 'native' for purposes of dealing in land) still met strong resistance to transfers of land rights in return for shares in an estate (Cramb, 1993a).

Similar conditions obtained in Sabah where each native living on the land was entitled to 6 hectares (15 acres). Few actually held title and, on moving to a scheme, most had still not received titles after waits of up to 30 years. The process was only speeded up in the late 1980s after the Sabah Land Development Board (SLDB) adopted a *berdikari* (self-reliance) policy (Hewgill and Cramb, 1994).

Did the large expenditure on development *in situ* and in new areas under the NEP produce commensurate benefits? As we saw in the case of the FELDA scheme at Kemendor (Melaka) income levels rose (this will be discussed further in Chapter 13.5), and the same was true of many other schemes, though by no means all, elsewhere in Malaysia. Settlers were able to afford consumables, and received relatively good social services. Some, as in Sabah, became minor *towkays* (business owners) living in nearby towns and employing Indonesians to work on their scheme holdings (Hewgill and Cramb, 1994). But, as Table 11.2b shows, despite considerable technological progress major crop yields on smallholdings were substantially below those on private estates. This was widely thought to reflect simply an immutable aversion among traditional farmers towards any changes. Instances of active resistance to innovation were by no means infrequent in both East and Peninsular Malaysia. An example was refusal by some Peninsular Malays to rehabilitate uncultivated land, and an insistence on planting crops (such as cocoa) unsuited to local conditions (Amriah Buang, 1991, 109). However, empirical research has illuminated a much wider range of factors. Whilst the basic obstacles in the way of participation in development projects were the uneconomic size of the smallest holdings and the correspondingly limited financial resources of owners, it appears that the quality of resources and information reaching smallholders was not uniformly good.

Why was this so? Basically because 'these changes, which essentially involve a more intensive use of resources, presuppose for their success both the presence of good management and the availability of capital to buy the resources needed' (Barlow, 1978, 308). In order to obtain optimum returns the new types of trees had to be accompanied by a range of inputs which were both expensive and required specialised knowledge (fertilisers, stimulants, herbicides), the ability to experiment with different production systems and so on. However, owners in Selangor complained that low yields from newly replanted rubber trees were due to the supply of inferior seedlings, fertilisers and pesticides by RISDA. Political pressures on agency officers to favour the constituencies of particular politicians affected the location and timing of development projects (Shamsul, 1986, 104). In Sabah 'the concept of a regimented estate discipline is foreign ... where little hierarchical structure prevails in traditional society' (Hewgill and Cramb, 1994, 6). A similar situation existed in Sarawak where farmers showed a rational attitude in their reluctance to participate in development schemes when it was not certain that resettlement would deliver the promised benefits (Cramb, 1990, 31–2).

Though the proportion of smallholders brought within the new forms of organisation and management increased substantially under the NEP, the majority remained 'traditional' or 'independent' operators. In Peninsular Malaysia the proportion in the managed category rose from 1 per cent in 1960 to 33 per cent in 1980 (calculated from Horii, 1991b, Table III). It is plain that the aim of government was to try to have it both ways: that is, to maintain or protect the position of the independent smallholder (certainly up to the NAP in 1984) whilst at the same securing cost and other management benefits through treating farmers on a collective or 'organised' basis. As Horii points out, 'the question ... arises as to whether ... government ... is not contradicting itself by undermining the basis of smallholders as management units' (1991b, 429). At the same time, the development of the 'group smallholding mode of management ... has been a very costly one, largely made possible by subsidies drawn from taxes on petroleum and other booming sectors during the 1970s' (Barlow, 1985a, 210). The programme marked 'the complete cutting off of settlers from their traditional stance as basically independent farmers. They were now ... merely paid workers, albeit assured of a better cash income than they might have earned otherwise' (Barlow, 1978, 241).

Large-scale development schemes proved an increasingly expensive way of improving agricultural productivity and incomes of a minority of the rural population. In Sabah the cost of resettling a family was between $25 000 and 35 000 on SLDB schemes, and $90 000–100 000 on Sabah Rubber Fund Board (SRFB) schemes. The 60 or so major schemes undertaken since the 1950s generated only 12 000 settlement places (Hewgill and Cramb, 1994, 3). In Peninsular Malaysia the schemes absorbed only about a quarter of the increase in rural population from 1961 (Cramb, 1989b, 22n.). Whilst yields were raised, by the 1980s the impetus to growth was fading (see Table 11.3). The palm oil industry was the only bright spot. Without this, the overall annual growth rate of the agricultural sector between 1981 and 1985 was only 1.4 per cent (Muhammad Ikmal Said, 1990, 73). The earliest schemes were now ready for replanting, but smallholders (like estates) faced labour shortages as young people migrated to the towns. As Hewgill and Cramb perceptively remark, 'settlement schemes are a short-term strategy designed to serve *only one generation of settlers*' (1994, 5; italics added).

At the end of our period, whilst there had been some convergence between the estate and smallholder sectors in Malaysian agriculture in terms of organisation and technology, dualism remained a distinct feature. Convergence was most evident among smallholders on the managed land schemes in Peninsular Malaysia where yields, at least in oil palms, could equal those on estates by the mid-1980s (Table 11.2b). In Sabah the oil palm land schemes averaged only 12.8 tonnes per hectare in 1984 against 17.5 tonnes on estates (Malek bin Mansor and Barlow, 1988, Table 2.5). Dualism persisted most strongly in the independent smallholdings, in particular those under 2 hectares which, as we have seen, had to combat obstacles of uneconomic size, and unevenness of access to government assistance, which were far from being solved at the conclusion of the NEP.

11.4   Forestry

'The evolution of Malaysian forestry is a dramatic display of the intricate working of social, cultural, political and economic forces on the management of a renewable resource' (Kumar, 1986, 64–5). As we have seen in earlier chapters the exploitation of forests for commercial profit, in particular the extraction of timber, had begun in the Peninsula and the Borneo territories around the turn of the century. However, it is only since the 1960s and 1970s that this activity has come to the forefront. Between 1960 and 1981 Malaysia's share of world exports of saw-logs (unprocessed logs) rose from 17 to 47.5 per cent, from 13 to 25.5 per cent of sawn-wood (processed) products, and from 0.1 to 6.5 per cent of plywood (Kumar, 1986, Tables 3.3–3.5). By 1986–88 Malaysia was the source of 92 per cent of the saw-logs exported from the Southeast Asia-Pacific region (Ooi Jin Bee, 1990, Table 10). As a leading export industry under conditions of rapid expansion, it has brought to the forefront tensions over the distribution of concessions, access to profits, rates of cutting, impact on the environment and upon the economic, social and cultural situations of indigenous groups living in the interior.

The growth of the timber industry has given major boosts to the economies of Sabah and Sarawak which together accounted for between about 60 and 70 per cent of Malaysian saw-log production from 1960–1983. The Peninsula had a majority share in wood products, as high as 92 per cent of sawn-wood exports in 1979, and 92 per cent of plywood in 1976. Malaysia's total net foreign exchange earnings for forest products rose by 441 per cent over the period 1966–77, of which just over half ($1263 million out of $2327 million in 1977) went to Sabah. For government, the industry represented an extremely high return on expenditure. Again taking Sabah, in 1980 total forest revenue was approximately $1.1 billion against expenditure of $30 million (Kumar, 1986, Tables 1.3, 1.4, 6.2, 6.9, 6.11). In 1991 timber exports accounted for 7.5 per cent of Malaysia's foreign earnings, and 160 000 people were employed in the various sectors of the industry (*The Australian*, 31 Aug. 1994).

The principal impetus for this growth has come from markets in Asia (notably Japan, South Korea, Hong Kong, Taiwan) and to a lesser extent Australasia. This is particularly the case for East Malaysia which exported an average of some 82 per cent (Sarawak) and 89 per cent (Sabah) of saw-logs, but in Peninsular Malaysia nearly three-quarters went to meet domestic needs in construction (figures for 1960–76, Kumar, 1986, Table 6.4). The output of saw-logs has always shown considerable year-to-year fluctuations. In the 1960s the changes varied between a peak increase of 27.5 per cent in 1966, a decrease of 15.3 per cent in 1969 and a 37.4 increase in the following year. Generally speaking output grew less rapidly in the 1970s (except for a 37 per cent jump in 1976) and the 1980s, particularly during the international depression (Kumar, 1986, Table 6.2; UN, 1991, Table IV.16). Whilst efforts have been directed towards increasing the proportion of sawn-timber among exports, the volume stagnated at around the 5–6 million cubic-metre level for most of the 1980s (UN, 1991, Table IV.16).

As we saw in Chapter 9.3, the timber industry operated on the basis of concessions granted to individuals or companies with strong political connections. The duration of these concessions has been between one and forty years in most cases. The 1960s were a period of unrestrained growth in the timber industry with the giving out of concessions unrestrained by clear policy definitions. It was not until the early 1970s, partly due to the 1960s rush, that the Food and Agricultural Organisation (FAO) assessed the resources coupled with the compilation of forest inventories for the Peninsula and East Malaysia (Kumar, 1986, 19–20). By that time most of the readily accessible areas in the lowlands had been extensively logged. This period might be compared to the situation in Malaya in the late nineteenth century in which the tin miners 'picked the eyes' of a district by labour-intensive extraction from deposits close to the surface (Chapter 4.4). A large proportion of the profits was remitted overseas, much of it for investment in real estate, thus reducing the amount of domestic capital available (Amarjit Kaur, 1998, 194).

In the late 1960s the Sabah government gave a ten-year special licence covering 40 square miles of forest to the Sabah Foundation, the income from which was to be used to finance other activities such as educational projects. At the same time, in 1969, eleven long-term (up to 1984) concessions in private hands were not renewed (Gudgeon, 1981, 265). Slower rates of growth for saw-log production (around 2 per cent a year) were projected for the 1970s, but sudden jumps in international prices in 1973 and 1976 led to surges in output. In the first of these years export volume rose by 31 per cent and total value by 97 per cent. In 1976 prices rose by 60 per cent, output by 35 per cent and value by 100 per cent (Gudgeon, 1981, 288, 315).

Sarawak's timber industry experienced similar trends, in particular in the second half of the 1970s. The price rise in 1976 led to production of saw-logs going up to nearly 2 450 000 hoppus tons against 1 393 000 in the previous year, with a further rise to 2 707 000 hoppus tons in 1977. Total value leapt from some $64 million in 1975 to $255 million in 1977 (*ABS Sarawak*, 1977). This pattern has continued throughout the 1980s. In 1988 Sarawak earned $7.8 billion from log exports, more than from crude petroleum exports (UN, 1991, 92–3). The rates of excision continued to grow. Overall, from 1965 to 1989 the forested area in Sarawak was reduced by approximately one-third (Amarjit Kaur, 1998, 191–7). FAO figures for 1985 indicate that forests as a percentage of the total land area were down to about 54 per cent in the Peninsula, 63 per cent in Sabah, 64 per cent in Sarawak and 60 per cent overall (UN, 1991, Table IV.15). Among the timber exporting countries of Southeast Asia, Malaysia had the lowest rate of reafforestation at 25 000 hectares a year during the 1980s (Thailand managed 31 000 hectares and Indonesia 164 000).

Pressure on Malaysia, especially from international conservationist groups, to reduce the rate of exploitation and embark on reafforestation and plantation-type projects mounted during the 1980s. There were signs that expansion might be slowing. In 1990 the Sarawak government announced its intention to establish 1500 hectares of forest plantations, and 10 000 hectares annually throughout the 1990s. Peninsular Malaysia planned 42 000 hectares of this type over the period 1989–93, whilst the Sabah government had already planted 20 000 hectares by 1991. Sabah made a relatively early start with forest plantations. In 1973 Sabah Softwoods (a joint venture of the Sabah Foundation and the North Borneo Timber Company) was set up to cultivate fast-growing species for pulp-wood in the Tawau district. From 1976 Sabah Forest Development Authority (SAFODA) began similar developments which had reached 12 000 hectares by 1987. Sabah has also raised the export duty on saw- or round-log exports whilst lowering royalties on logs for local processing (UN, 1991, 93).

The spin-off from forestry in terms of ancillary industries has consisted, at the primary stage, of saw-milling and then downstream manufacturing facilities such as plywood and furniture. The majority of these are situated in Peninsular Malaysia, which thus benefits disproportionately from the value-added and employment effects. In 1982 sawmills in the Peninsula totalled 583 against 135 in Sarawak and 223 in Sabah; the corresponding figures for plywood mills were 35, 2 and 6 (Kumar, 1986, Table 6.1). In 1986 Sabah Forest Industries (SFI) constructed a pulp and paper mill at Sipitang (southwest Sabah) employing over 1000 people to process timber from its local concession area. Speaking specifically about the saw-milling sector, Kumar has this to say: 'Generally, the industry has grown up under the circumstances of a sellers' market and an abundant supply of logs. The complacency this generated has resulted in a large number of fragmented, under-used plants throughout the country' (1986, 101).

The fact that the owners of timber concessions, the sub-contractors who carry out the actual logging, and the operators in the wood-based industry are different persons has also contributed to a lack of integration overall. The pressure of external demand for saw-logs in the late 1980s created a situation in which domestic industries faced a bottleneck in supplies, which was intensified by an influx of furniture manufacturers from Taiwan (because of the rising value of the New Taiwan dollar: UN, 1991, 94); hence the measures to encourage domestic consumption noted above.

Logging operations have been among the most intrusive factors in the lives of the indigenous peoples of the interior, particularly in East Malaysia. Deforestation, whether in the course of logging as an end in itself, or as a preliminary for major land development programmes, engenders competition with shifting cultivators for access to cultivable land. The latter have been under continual pressure from governments to switch from extensive land-use (officially regarded as inefficient) to intensive methods of cultivation which involves a shift to sedentary agriculture. The first method allows cultivation for only two or three seasons of dry-rice, and perhaps cassava, followed by a long fallow (resting) period of up to 20 years to restore fertility. The second requires inputs such as fertilisers, cover crops and so on to maintain fertility and productivity year by year.

Chandler (1987) identifies four main areas of impact of logging on the Sabah economy: (i) new employment opportunities in the timber industry, (ii) timber camps as markets for surplus agricultural produce, (iii) environmental effects, (iv) building of roads. Research on the districts of Keningau and Nabawan/Pensiangan in southwest Sabah, in which the major ethnic groups are Kadazan (Dusun) and Murut, shows that up to the mid-1980s 'in many respects the timber industry has had little impact on the traditional way of life of those people living in the interior' (Chandler, 1987, 1).

In terms of employment the situation appears to have been similar to that in the Peninsula during the rubber boom in the early twentieth century. Kadazans and Muruts, like Malays, were reluctant to take permanent wage employment, preferring short periods of wage work to obtain cash for consumer goods, bride-price, and so on. The timber companies, for their part, regarded locals as rather unreliable workers, liable to sudden absences and generally low-skilled. They provided about 10 per cent of the workforce, with the balance made up of Indonesians and Filippinos (40 per cent each) and Chinese (10 per cent) (Chandler, 1987, 8–12).

Despite opportunities to earn additional cash by supplying foodstuffs (rice, vegetables) there was no evidence of any changes in shifting cultivation techniques aimed at producing a saleable surplus of rice. Similarly, the availability of meat, chickens, vegetables for disposal was only occasional. One reason adduced for this was that consistent production for sale would have required substantial extra inputs of labour with every likelihood that the market would disappear once logging operations moved elsewhere (Chandler, 1987, 12–14).

The clearest evidence of impact came from environmental changes, principally from the building of the roads essential for logging extraction and the movement of lorries, tractors and other equipment. The exposure of large areas of soil in a high rainfall climate resulted in heavy erosion into rivers, rendering water unfit for drinking and bathing as well as decimating the fish population. Generally logging operations have had an adverse effect on wildlife numbers, in turn affecting the subsistence base of the villagers. At the same time the roads have opened up remote areas and provided easier access and transport (e.g., 4-wheel drive vehicles) between villages and centres such as Keningau, but once logging moves on these roads quickly deteriorate and the issue of upkeep is a difficult one (Chandler, 1987, 14–22).

Chandler's work recognises that the situation remains fluid in many respects. Logging is itself a shifting activity. 'Indigenous people with greater access to non-traditional lifestyles have adjusted their way of life, where feasible, to produce surplus or cash crops [whilst] those in the more remote areas, cut off from those values, continue to produce sufficient to meet their own needs' (Chandler, 1987, 23). In the latter instance the advent of logging operations has brought modern and traditional lifestyles into confrontation, a well-publicised example being the Penan of Sarawak.

The Penan are primarily a hunter-gatherer society needing continuous access to large areas of primary forest. This conflicts with the plans of the state government which, as we have seen, include timber concessions, land and hydro-electric development schemes, and national parks (affecting other groups as well as the Penan). The official rationale is that the concentration of previously dispersed and isolated communities through resettlement will facilitate the provision of economic-sized holdings for subsistence and commercial crop production, together with basic social and welfare services, thereby leading to a higher standard of living. The grassroots reaction was a strong reluctance to abandon traditional lifestyles in familiar areas containing, for instance, ancestral gravesites. This has been compounded by a widespread perception that the promised benefits have to a large extent failed to materialise. In the case of the Batang Ai hydro-electric scheme (1985) in Sarawak, some 2800 Iban were resettled. Though substantial cash compensation was paid, the subsequent resettlement project was not successful. Among the most significant shortfalls were that the promised free housing, water and electricity have had to be paid for. The subsistence crop (wet-rice) proved unsuited to the locality, forcing settlers to take wage work for SALCRA whilst waiting for commercial crops (rubber, coffee) to mature (survey based on Hong, 1987; Colchester, 1989; Cleary and Eaton, 1992).

Tensions between indigenous peoples, such as the Penan, and logging interests led to violent confrontations in the 1980s, including the burning of company buildings, sabotage of machinery and barricading of logging roads. One of the most controversial large projects, a hydro-power dam at Bakun on the upper Rajang river involving flooding an area about the size of Singapore and displacing in excess of 5000 people, has been on and off the planning boards since the early 1980s (a start was made in the mid-1990s but work was halted by the recession in 1997–8).

The forestry industry in Malaysia, and the related range of uses for land, raised the issue of the private benefits and social costs of development with the former going predominantly to a relative few under the system of political patronage outlined in Chapter 10.3, whilst the social costs (especially in East Malaysia) were borne by indigenous groups still largely dependent on the land. These politically fragmented groups have found it difficult to organise sustained and effective responses. In Chapter 6.2

it was argued that since the nineteenth century such groups, confronted with external pressures to change, lacked the capacity for voluntary association shown by others, notably Chinese and Europeans. However, in the late 1980s 'Longhouse Associations' emerged in the Baram region of Sarawak, marking perhaps the weakening of traditional personal relationships and replacement with more institutionalised ties (Colchester, 1989, 65–6).

11.5   Mining

The mining sector since 1965 presents a picture of gradual decline in some areas (tin), and explosive development in others (petroleum, LNG, copper). As is evident from Table 10.4 this sector was of relatively small importance in GDP up to about 1970.

Tin

Malaysian output rose only slowly from approximately 59 000 tonnes in 1957 to just over 75 000 tonnes in 1971 (Fong, 1989, Table 5.1). Interestingly, from 1966 Chinese miners regained the leading position lost to European mines in 1929. This was due to a sharp increase in gravel pump mines, whilst the number of dredges operating underwent a slow decline (Jomo, 1990b, App. Tables 4, 7). Under the NEP the ownership structure underwent a change similar to that in the rubber industry. Between 1970 and 1982 *bumiputera* ownership increased from 1 per cent to 34 per cent. Pernas purchased a controlling interest in the London Tin Corporation, renamed Malaysia Mining Corporation (MMC), and an exchange of shares was arranged with Charter Consolidated Ltd, the other major British interest, making MMC the largest tin mining company in the world (Saruwatari, 1991, 379–80).

The principal factors affecting the market were restriction of exports under successive International Tin Agreements (ITAs) from 1956, essentially a continuation of the 1930s scheme: (see Chapter 8.2), and the periodic release of surplus stocks from the large US government stockpile. Tin faced competition from other base metals (copper, lead, aluminium). Furthermore the global depression in the early 1980s reduced demand for tin. In an effort to support the price level, the Malaysian government established Maminco, a subsidiary of MMC and a joint venture with a Swiss metal trader, to conduct buying operations on the London Tin Market from 1981 in what became an attempt to corner the market. This venture came to a disastrous end in 1985 when, in the face of a continuing surplus of supply, the International Tin Council withdrew price support, leading to a collapse from $29 600 to $13 600 a tonne. The Malaysian government's estimated losses amounted to $660 million (Fong, 1989, 159–61; Jomo, 1990b).

Following the crash many of the higher-cost gravel pump mines closed, which accounted for most of the massive drop in the labour force from 24 000 in 1984 to 12 000 in 1986 (Jomo, 1990b, Table 3). There was something of a revival in the later 1980s, but the international prospects for the tin industry remained very limited. Few major new uses for the metal were in prospect. Within Malaysia the best alluvial deposits have been mined out, the industry is subjected to heavy taxation and the incentives to prospect for new ore deposits are weak (Fong, 1989, 169–72). Government has given some assistance such as a 25 per cent reduction in power tariffs, and about $70 million in 'soft' loans. The best prospects appear to lie in the development of domestic uses for tin (UN, 1991, 97–9).

Iron Ore, et cetera

Among Malaysia's other metal-mining industries, mostly located in the Peninsula, the leaders were iron ore and bauxite. However, neither was of prime importance. The first showed a marked fall in output from 6.85 million tonnes in 1965 to only 344 000 tonnes in 1990. Bauxite too had a declining trend, from just over 1 million tonnes in the early 1970s to 376 000 tonnes in 1990. A new line of enterprise, copper mining, made its appearance during the 1970s: for example, the Mamut mine near Mount Kinabalu in Sabah, the single largest mining venture in Malaysia (Voon and Teh, 1992). Among precious metals, gold production in the Peninsula was as high as 4500 troy ounces in 1971 and 2700 troy ounces in Sarawak in 1968, but the size of both seemed fairly static (Malaysia, *ABS*).

Petroleum, gas

In previous chapters we saw that this industry provided Sarawak with a boost to export earnings around the First World War and in the 1920s, with production from the Miri field declining from 1929 onwards. In 1967 Sarawak exported only some 45 000 tonnes of crude oil, but the discovery of new deposits the following year boosted output over fourfold to 199 000 tonnes, and by the time of the first 'oil shock' in 1973, to 4.27 million tonnes. Shortly thereafter discoveries were made off Sabah's coast, giving exports of nearly 3.5 million tonnes by 1977 (Malaysia, *ABS*, various years). Sarawak obtained 53 per cent of its export earnings from oil in 1972 rising to 62 per cent by 1982 (*Sarawak Report*, 1983, 58–9). For Sabah the proportion went from a negligible 0.6 per cent in 1970 to 40 per cent in 1980 (Wee, 1995, Table 4.3). Malaysia's exports of crude oil in 1990 totalled nearly 30 million tonnes (Malaysia, *ABS*, 1992). At peak values, in 1982, petroleum and LNG accounted for practically 29 per cent of Malaysian export earnings, but by 1988 had fallen to around 18 per cent (Fong, 1989,Table 5.4; Jomo, 1990a, Table 3.10).

In addition to oil, large deposits of natural gas were discovered off-shore from Bintulu, Sarawak, in 1971. At that stage private interests were driving development, and the Shell Oil Company together with Mitsubishi Corporation of Japan, proposed a joint venture for an LNG Plant at Bintulu. The scale of this development prompted the federal government to set up the National Petroleum Development Corporation (Petronas) in 1974 to coordinate progress for the whole industry. This was done principally through production-sharing agreements (70:30 in favour of Petronas), of which there were seven by the early 1980s. The terms were made more flexible to attract foreign investors following the general change in the government's policy in the mid-1980s (Chapter 10.3). At that time Malaysia's oil reserves were estimated at about 20 years, with gas reserves for several centuries. (Fong, 1989, 172ff). In total 44 oil fields and 47 gas fields had been identified, with an investment of $2.9 billion by 1984 (Fong, 1989, 175).

Peninsular Malaysia was able to participate in the boom from the late 1970s due to discoveries of oil and natural gas off-shore from Terengganu, which contained 57.2 per cent and 51.6 per cent respectively of Malaysia's total reserves as at 1985. However, due to the greater diversity of the Peninsular economy, petroleum and gas exports only reached just over 15 per cent of total exports in 1980 (Wee, 1995, Table 4.3). A case study of the oil/natural gas complex at Kerteh, Terengganu (Voon and Khoo, 1986), provides valuable insights into the effects of these industries on the economy of the surrounding area. In common with much of the east coast, that state had lagged far behind the west coast of the Peninsula in development since the turn of the century. The incidence of poverty in 1976 was three times that of Selangor and the Kuala Lumpur Federal Territory. From the late 1970s, projects initiated by Petronas, the State Economic Development Corporation, HICOM, and Esso Production Malaysia resulted in the construction of a 50 kilometre 'petroleum belt' along the coast with investments totalling over $4 billion. These include a refinery, gas plant, support bases (sea terminal, airfield), housing projects, schools, health and sport facilities, along with the Paka power station and Perwaja Steel Mill (see Chapter 12).

All these facilities were constructed within a decade, and produced two quite separate communities, one of 'petroleum' employees (not unlike the west-coast tin mining camps of the late nineteenth century), and the other of 'native' households. The new facilities were 'fenced and guarded entities with an architecture, function and population largely imported … in stark contrast to the traditional kampung setting … in their midst or as their backdrop' (Voon and Khoo, 1986, 52). The petroleum workers were essentially transients, often with families elsewhere. The reaction of the local Malay population was similar in many respects to that against logging in Sabah: 'The links [with] the local economy are few and ineffective … the kampung inhabitants consider themselves largely excluded [and] had not taken full advantage of the demand for labour even during the height of the construction phase' (Voon and Khoo, 1986, 56). Locals possessed lower levels of education and skills, whilst immigrants (Filippino, Thai, Indonesian) were available at lower rates of pay for unskilled jobs. Costs of living, rents and so on escalated. Multiplier effects from the power station and steel mill were few in employment terms.

At the state level, too, the benefits have been more apparent than real. Whilst per capita GDP in Terengganu in 1990 was 1.36 times the Malaysian average, the incidence of poverty at 31.2 per cent was second only to Sabah (Wee, 1995, Table 5.9). As in East Malaysia the state government could retain only 5 per cent of the gross value of production. However, in the broader Malaysian context the operations of Petronas did generate some spin-off in terms of upstream and downstream facilities, principally the construction of drilling platforms, pipelines and refining capacity at various locations: Lutong (Sarawak), Port Dickson (Negeri Sembilan), Tangga Batu (Melaka) and Kerteh (Terengganu). Petronas was also a major consumer of a wide range of services (food, engineering, transport, communications, and so on). Besides being exported in liquid form, natural gas also began to be used domestically as a part substitute for oil. In 1982 Petronas launched the Peninsular Gas Utilisation Project of which the first phase, completed in 1985, comprised collection, processing and distribution facilities at Kerteh. Local customers were a Tenaga Nasional power station, and the Perwaja steel mill. Subsequent construction began on a 725 kilometre pipeline to serve other parts of the Peninsula. In Sarawak the $3000 million LNG plant at Bintulu started exports in 1983, as well as supplying local customers including an ASEAN fertiliser plant and the Duyong Gas Complex on Labuan Island. By 1990, however, linkages with other domestic sectors, in particular petro-chemical industries had yet to develop to any great extent (Fong, 1989, 176ff; UN, 1991, 120).

11.6 Overview

Participants in a seminar at Universiti Pertanian Malaysia (Malaysian Agricultural University) in 1988 concluded that in spite of the high rates of agricultural growth from 1966–1980 (Table 11.3), a 37 per cent increase in total cropped acreage from 1960–1983 and raised expenditure on research and development, the sector had not reached a 'turning point' at which it could provide a powerful stimulus to Malaysia's industrialisation through the supply of raw materials and a source of effective demand for the products of industry. Particular problems identified included: persistent low levels of productivity, technological innovation and per capita incomes, and hence low purchasing power, especially among the independent or 'unorganised' smallholders. These operated uneconomic-sized holdings, for which the 'production possibility curve has invariably been almost reached and is impossible [*sic*] to be extended further unless land consolidation or reform is introduced' (Mohamed Ghazali and Abdul Aziz in Fatimah Arshad *et al.*, 1989, 284).

Agriculture had a 'product-mix' of crops still largely export-oriented and, being long-cycle perennials (rubber, palm oil), difficult to modify in the shorter term. By comparison agriculture in Taiwan and Japan was based largely on an annual crop, rice, from which diversification into higher value crops (fruits, vegetables) was achievable more rapidly. Malaysia, the seminar concluded, could benefit from a better balance between food and non-food, annual and perennial, crops and animal production, which could offer more protection against fluctuations in prices as well as assisting the establishment of more agro-based industries. Stronger linkages between agriculture and domestic industry were needed in the provision of intermediate and capital goods as Malaysia was still heavily dependent on imports of these items (Fatimah Arshad *et al.*, 1989).

The mining and forestry sectors were mainstays of the Malaysian economy, at least until the rapid expansion of manufacturing industry in the late 1980s. By that time tin production was stagnating, and exports of crude petroleum, LNG and saw-logs were levelling out. All faced the problem of exhaustion in the relatively short term, although timber resources could be renewed through reafforestation (a slow process).

The pace of expansion and ambitious development schemes was slowing by the late 1980s. As Brookfield remarked about Peninsular Malaysia, the 'gold rush' approach to the use of resources was over and the economy 'now has to move into a less exploitative and more conservationist mode' (1994, 93–4). Much the same could be said of Sabah and Sarawak, although official recognition of this need, and its translation into action, were only in the earliest stages up to 1990. Because of the much smaller degree of industrialisation (see next chapter) these states remained in danger of being caught in the staple trap (see Chapter 1.1).

12
Industrialisation

12.1   Pattern and process of growth

At this point the reader is invited to refer to the review in Chapter 10.1 of the 'ladder' of technological change in the Asian region. We saw in Chapter 9.3 the beginnings of this transition in Peninsular Malaysia from 1958 with the pioneer industries programme aimed at import-substitution (ISI). The bulk of industry at that stage was concerned with processing primary products (tin, timber, rubber) and consumables such as pineapples, vegetable oil, biscuit manufacture, beverages and rubber goods. In 1959 these industries accounted for approximately 73 per cent of the total value-added, and 53 per cent of the industrial labour force (calculated from Fong, 1989, Table 6.2). In many respects the pioneer industries programme achieved its aims. The number of firms granted pioneer status rose from 18 in 1959 to to 246 in 1971. By 1968, when the programme was reviewed, such firms contributed around a third of value-added but in certain industries (textiles, petroleum products, basic metals and electrical goods) the proportion was three-quarters or more (Bhanoji Rao, 1980, 229).

The results were evident in the composition of imports in which consumption goods dropped from about 47 per cent in 1961 to 26 per cent in 1972, whilst intermediate goods increased from 28 per cent to just over 36 per cent, and investment goods from 17 to 33 per cent (Bhanoji Rao, 1980, Table 56). By 1973 about 90 per cent of durable and non-durable consumer goods and intermediate goods were produced domestically (UN, 1991, 16). This emphasis on consumption goods is reflected in the composition of industrial output (Table 12.1).

For much of this period Malaysia was fortunate in that generally good prices for primary products enabled balance of payment problems from the continuing high level of imports to be avoided (Fong, 1989, 201).

At the same time a number of drawbacks emerged. The procedure required to obtain pioneer status was bureaucratically protracted. There was a lack of consistency in the criteria on which pioneer status was granted,

Table 12.1   Structural change in Malaysian manufacturing industries: selected years (as percentage of gross output value)[a]

	Primary[b] processing	Consumption[c] goods	Consumer[d] durables	Intermediate[e] goods	Capital[f] goods
Pen. Malaysia					
1959	51.5	21.9	12.6[g]	8.2[g]	1.3
1971	15.5	31.2	24.1	24.8	3.6
1989	–[h]	26.1	44.2	24.8	4.2
Sabah					
1969	n.a.	72.8	16.7	2.3	7.6
1989	n.a.	34.3	38.3	21.4	5.9
Sarawak					
1970	4.5	6.6	30.3	56.2	2.6
1990	n.a	8.9	12.1	77.7	1.0

n.a. = not available.
[a] Cross-addition does not always total 100 due to omission of miscellaneous industries.
[b] Processing of agricultural products off-estates.
[c] Foodstuffs, beverages, tobacco, paper/paper products.
[d] Textiles, footwear, wood products, rattan, furniture, printing, leather, rubber, electrical machinery etc.
[e] Chemicals/chemical products, petroleum and coal products, non-metallic mineral, basic metals, metal products, machinery (excluding electrical).
[f] Transport equipment.
[g] Data incomplete.
[h] From 1976 included in food and rubber products categories
Sources: Calculated from Hoffman and Tan (1980), Table 11.4; Wee (1995), Table 3.4; *ABS*, Sabah and Sarawak, 1971, 1973, 1990.

and no attempt by government to plan industrial development, with the result that some fields of production (e.g. dairy products, paints, plastics) were over-supplied with firms relative to market-size (D. Lim, 1973, 257–8). Only limited use was made of domestic raw materials. The capital-intensive nature of much investment meant that less labour was absorbed than had been hoped for.

The relatively quick saturation of the domestic market's capacity to absorb manufactures meant that the pioneer industries, if they were to expand further, needed to look to export markets. Manufactures as a proportion of total West Malaysian exports had certainly grown substantially from approximately 14 per cent in 1958 to 27 per cent in 1969 (D. Lim, 1973, Table 7.18), but few of these industries, apart from wood products, gave much promise at this stage of being able to penetrate overseas markets to any major extent.

Manufacturing industry in East Malaysia was also extremely limited in its range at this time. In Sabah most firms were connected with timber, hemp and coconut-oil milling, but there was some growth in the 1960s in light manufacturing of consumables (soap, foodstuffs, furniture) (Gudgeon, 1981, 238). Sarawak seems to have got off to a very slow start. In the three years 1968–70 only 10 new industrial projects were approved representing a total investment of approximately $15.5 million (Sarawak Government, 1984, 83).

By the late 1960s the limitations of industrialisation based on ISI were becoming clear, and there was also a demonstration effect from the East Asian 'Tiger' economies which were pursuing export-oriented industrialisation (EOI). In 1968 the Malaysian government attempted to improve the situation through the Investment Incentives Act which widened the range of industries eligible for inducements such as deductions for overseas promotional campaigns, exemption from payroll tax for companies exporting more than 20 per cent of total production and so on (D. Lim, 1973, 266–7).

Under the EOI regime the pace of industrialisation picked up in the 1970s (Table 12.2) particularly in Peninsular Malaysia. The fastest-growing industries (1969 = 100) were electrical and electronic machinery/appliances (487), transport equipment (853), and 'Other manufacturing', principally professional and scientific instruments and supplies (a 'phenomenal' 1706). However, the textiles, electrical and transport equipment industries were as yet of small weight in the economy. The trend towards the production of consumer durables, intermediate and capital goods, which is evident from Table 12.1, continued.

The 1970s also saw a quickening of the pace of industrialisation in East Malaysia, though this did not greatly affect the share of manufacturing in GDP; indeed, in Sarawak it had fallen slightly by 1980 (see Table 10.4). The number of new projects approved in Sarawak totalled 258 between 1971 and 1981, bringing investment of $3170 million; $2658 million of this sum came in a single year, 1979, much of it associated with an LNG plant constructed at Bintulu, with an output capacity of at least 6 million tonnes

Table 12.2   Malaysia: growth rate of manufactured exports and value-added 1971–89 (annual percentage)

Year	Value-added	Exports
1971–5	11.6	27.6
1977–80	13.5	24.9
1981–5	4.9	14.3
1986–9[a]	12.9	31.0

[a] Calculated from source data.
Source: Jomo and Edwards (1993), Table 1.2.

a year. *Bumiputera* participation, at 60 per cent, was well above the NEP target due to this project and also the ASEAN fertiliser project. The other major categories were, as might be expected, wood products (22 per cent) followed by foods (20 per cent) and a range of consumer durables and non-durables (*Sarawak Report*, 1984, 83; Bakar, 1990, 189). In Sabah the industrial structure followed a pattern similar to Sarawak, led by wood and food products, comprising some 34 per cent and 21 per cent respectively of projects undertaken between 1968 and 1983, and chemicals (14 per cent) (Zulkifly, 1986, Table 1).

The global depression of the early 1980s substantially slowed the growth of Malaysian manufacturing (Table 12.2). It was at this stage, with a slowing in private investment and decreased ability on the part of government to maintain large-scale public funding of projects, that Dr Mahathir introduced the policy changes of 'Look East', the introduction of heavy industries (HICOM), and the beginnings of the swing towards privatisation ('Malaysia Incorporated': see Chapter 10.3). The industries selected for investment were principally cement, steel, petro-chemicals, shipbuilding and a car assembly plant, which have been described as 'a second round of import substitution' (Jomo, 1993, 28) and 'premature heavy industrialisation' (D. Lim, 1992, 95). The industries were set up at a time when world economic conditions were adverse, namely stiff international competition requiring the Malaysian industries to be given heavy tariff protection. The steel project, Perwaja Terengganu Sdn Bhd (a joint venture with Nippon Steel Corporation), quickly ran into severe technical problems though it finally became profitable in 1989. Two cement plants faced a decline in demand and operated at below optimum capacity, raising production costs. The Malaysian national car (Proton Saga), a joint venture in car-assembly with Mitsubishi, had early difficulties in achieving sales targets, despite substantial tariff protection (Jomo, 1990a, 128–34), but again achieved profitability in the late 1980s.

A further aspect of the 'Look East' policy was a government-backed drive to form Malaysian equivalents of Japanese *sogoshoshas* (super-large trading corporations) to assist in promoting sales in export markets, help Malaysian manufacturers cope with large overseas orders and so on. There were about six of these by the mid-1980s, but the model proved un-transplantable and in any case largely unnecessary. By 1990 most were either defunct or operating at a low level (Chee and Gomez, 1994).

The general recovery of the manufacturing sector in the later 1980s, as world conditions improved, was very rapid (Table 12.2). The index of production (1981 = 100) jumped from 126 in 1986 to nearly 186 in 1989. Leading performers were electrical/electronic goods (192 to 345), rubber products (124 to 325), basic metals/metal products (117 to 184) and transport equipment (72 to 140) (UN, 1991, Table II.1). This expansion was largely export-oriented, though there was some import-substitution in, for example, rubber goods production.

In terms of the 'ladder' of structural change, Malaysia had largely moved through the first, labour-intensive, stage by the end of the 1970s, and into the middle-to-late stages during the 1980s. However, towards the end of this decade the process showed signs of slowing: for example, the relative position of electrical/electronic goods as the leading manufactured exports was virtually unchanged at approximately 57 per cent in 1989 against 54.5 per cent in 1983. The other leading industries, though far behind in weight, were still in more or less the same order of magnitude. This analysis pertains primarily to Peninsular Malaysia, but the same picture applies broadly to East Malaysia, although in Sarawak's case the industrial structure was skewed heavily towards intermediate goods (Table 12.1) by the LNG and ASEAN fertiliser plants, both at Bintulu.

Between the commencement of the ISI programme in 1958 and the end of our period, Malaysian industry developed a dualistic structure. There were the larger-scale EOI ventures with few linkages to the domestic economy, and an ISI sector, medium to small scale, catering to the domestic market and requiring some tariff protection (Fong, 1989, 230; Jomo, 1993, 38) Even within the closely related textile (basic cloth production) and garment industries this same dualism was observable. 'Whereas the textile industry has been attuned to the domestic market under relatively high effective protection, the garment industry has developed predominantly as an enclave industry for exports, with local labour the only major domestic input' (UN, 1991, 34).

It should not be forgotten that manufacturing industry in Malaysia was not confined to the urban areas. Manufacturing played a significant, though not the largest, role among the range of rural non-farm activities (RNAs) which formed an increasingly vital component in the incomes of rural dwellers, of whom an estimated 25 per cent were primarily dependent on these sources in the mid- to late 1970s. Of this proportion some 38 per cent were providers of services, followed by manufacturing at just over 21 per cent. The leading manufacturing activity, by far, was food, beverage and tobacco production (62 per cent of that group), followed by wood, cane and bamboo products (about 22 per cent), with simple machinery, equipment and metal products (e.g. agricultural implements) making up the balance (Mukhopadhyay and Chee Peng Lim, 1985, 8–11). Whilst the government included the promotion of *bumiputera* RNAs as a whole among the aims of the NEP (e.g., the development of traditional handicrafts), official policy did not specifically focus on RNA manufacturing as a means of assisting ISI. Indeed, the priority given to assisting larger, more capital-intensive and largely urban-based industries in practice fostered competition which RNA producers found difficult to meet, for example, in soap, shoes, domestic utensils, which suffered a decline. Rural consumers thus lost a source of relatively cheap goods. No incentives were offered to large-scale firms to forge links with RNAs as sub-contractors, or suppliers of semi-processed materials (Mukhopadhyay and Chee, 1985, 24, 476ff, 487).

12.2 Sources of growth: supply side

Capital

We can begin by saying in broad terms that whilst the bulk of capital investment over this period came from domestic sources (public and private), the timing and volume of FDI were, as before in Malaysian history, crucial determinants of the pattern and rate of growth. Table 12.3 shows that between 1961 and 1990 the level of gross domestic savings fell short of the level of gross domestic investment in the early 1960s (the ISI surge), early 1970s (NEP introduction), and early 1980s (HICOM programme). There was also a shortfall of some 4 per cent in 1990.

Why was FDI such an important component in Malaysia's industrialisation? We shall see that the main reason, from the Malaysian side, was political. The NEP, with its emphasis on increasing the *bumiputera* share in investment and in particular the ICA (1975), inhibited the readiness of the principal domestic savers, the Chinese, to sink substantial funds into fixed and relatively illiquid assets such as industrial plant and equipment. Foreign capital was, for the government, the main means of offsetting this reluctance. It was also easier for the state to manage by setting the terms of entry and operation, and was readily available as a joint partner with public investment, which assumed prominence in the later 1970s and early 1980s. FDI could contribute to a favourable balance of payments, and also generate new employment and import technology. From the viewpoint of foreign investors, particularly Japan and the East Asian NICs, capital was driven off-shore by factors such as rising domestic wage levels and appreciation in the international value of currencies (notably the yen after 1985) making their exports more expensive, together with a desire to gain direct access to markets in developing countries, thus avoiding trade barriers (Phongpaichit, 1993). Malaysia as a host country was attractive for its political stability, initially low wages and developed infrastructure, particularly in the Peninsula.

Table 12.3 Malaysia: Gross Domestic Savings (GDS) and Investment (GDI) as proportions of GNP, 1961–90 (%)

Year	GDS	GDI	Surplus/deficit
1961–65	17.9	18.9	–1.0
1966–70	18.2	16.5	+1.7
1971–75	21.1	24.9	–3.8
1976–80	30.3	28.1	+2.2
1981–85	27.6	36.1	–8.5
1986–90	31.3	29.8	+1.5

Source: S.Y. Lin (1992), Table 3.1.

There are no accurate, comprehensive collections of data on stocks and flows of FDI for Malaysia, or indeed for any of the ASEAN countries. The figures in Table 12.4 are for Peninsular Malaysia and represent only the proposed capitalisation of projects approved, of which possibly 20–25 per cent were never actually implemented (Anuwar and Wong, 1993, 81). Table 12.4a shows that nearly three-quarters of FDI had its origins in the 1980s, with one-third coming in the three years 1988–90. A more detailed breakdown shows that in the first decade of the NEP foreign equity in approved projects accounted for about one-third. This dropped to just over one-quarter as FDI slackened in the first half of the 1980s, but recovered sharply to about 49 per cent in 1987 and was running at 58 per cent in the first months of 1988 (Anuwar and Wong, 1993, Table 3.1.).

Table 12.4b shows that the principal investor countries also shifted in relative importance. The USA and Europe lost prominence whilst Japan came to the forefront with two 'waves' of investment (see below). Among the Asian NICs Singapore led the way, providing 13 per cent between 1982 and 1987, but in the last two years Taiwan leapt to prominence from a mere 0.6 per cent in 1986 to 25 per cent in 1989 and 35.9 per cent in 1990 (Chia, 1993, Tables 4, 5). The largest accumulation of investment by a single country was held by Japan with approximately 44 per cent of paid-up capital and loans, and 26 per cent of fixed assets at the end of 1986

Table 12.4   Net FDI in Malaysia,[a] 1961–90

(a) Total Investment Approvals (US$ millions)

Years	*Amount*
1961–80	4 453
1981–90	11 850
(1988–90)	5 523
1961–90	16 303

(b) Principal Investors 1982–90 (per cent)

	1982–7	*1988–90[b]*
USA	6.7	5.96
Europe[c]	20.8	5.90[d]
Japan	22.8	26.70
Asian NICs[e]	14.9	32.70

[a] Peninsular Malaysia only.
[b] Annual average, calculated from source data.
[c] France, West Germany, Netherlands, UK.
[d] UK only.
[e] South Korea, Taiwan, Hong Kong, Singapore.
Source: Abstracted from Chia (1993), Tables 2, 4, 5.

(Anuwar and Wong, 1993, Table 3.8). A further general shift occurred in the main object of FDI from resource-based manufacturing in the 1960s and early 1970s to consumer durables and intermediate products (as evident from Table 12.1). In sum, Malaysia received nearly 28 per cent of the total FDI entering the ASEAN region between 1961 and 1990, second only to Singapore (43 per cent) (Chia, 1993, Table 2).

As Table 12.5 shows, capital investment was the largest contributor to the growth of industrial output between 1961 and 1988. This capital deepening was much in line with the early stages of industrialisation in developing countries as a whole, for which the average share between 1960 and 1987 was around 65 per cent (D. Lim, 1994, Table 1).

What little investment in secondary industry existed at the time of Malayan independence (1957) came predominantly from the Chinese section of the community. Foreign capital was concentrated in primary production and processing, and the services (overseas trade) sector. It was highly unlikely that either of these interest groups would have moved into major import-substitution industrialisation of their own volition. Chinese entrepreneurs could only raise capital on a relatively small scale, whilst foreign (principally British) capital was tied up in the existing structure of the primary export economy. The impetus came from the Malayan government in the form of the Pioneer Industries Ordinance (1958), examined in Chapter 9.3.

The British agency houses in Malaysia, keen to comply with the new political rationale for investment, and discerning the market opportunities which the general development of the economy presented, were among those best placed to move into manufacturing. Investments covered a range from agricultural inputs (chemicals, machinery), consumables (matches, tobacco, confectionery, pharmaceuticals), durables (sanitary ware, wood products, electronic components, cars, precision instruments), and intermediate and capital goods (processed rubber latex and palm oil, transport equipment, cast iron). The inflow eased off in the later 1960s due to various factors including the devaluation of the pound sterling in 1967, the civil disturbances in Malaysia in 1969, and a shift in the attention of

Table 12.5   Malaysia: contributions to output growth, 1961–88

| | Annual growth (per cent) | | | |
	1961–7	*1968–74*	*1975–81*	*1982–88*
Capital	1.65	2.63	3.41	2.89
Labour	1.51	1.62	1.86	−2.29
TFPG[a]	2.93	2.72	1.90	−0.78

[a] Total Factor Productivity Growth.
Source: Abstracted from Fry (1991), Table 1.

British investors towards the European Economic Community (Saham, 1980, Tables 2.7, 5.2, 5.3, 25–6).

The vehicles for such enterprises were increasingly private and public limited liability companies which grew, respectively, from 38.5 per cent and 6.95 per cent of establishments in 1959 to 54.76 and 23.7 per cent in 1971. By contrast the once-preferred forms of ownership by individuals or private partnerships fell from a combined 52 per cent to about 20 per cent over the same period (Hoffman and Tan, 1980, Table 11.2; figures for Peninsular Malaysia only).

Japanese investment in Malaysia during this period, as in other countries, was of the 'old wave' type, focusing on resource-based and ISI ventures producing for the domestic market (Phongpaichit, 1993, 100). Some of these were joint ventures with Chinese Malaysian interests, such as Malayan Sugar (Jesudason, 1989, 61).

During the 1960s the Chinese community was able to take advantage of the growth of the economy mainly in the areas of construction (property development), with a lucrative field in government contracts, and in banking where the number of local banks in the Peninsula doubled, all substantially controlled by Chinese with the exception of Bank Bumiputra (1965). Some leading families (e.g. the Kuok and Loy families), used capital accumulated in rubber, tin, trading and so on to set up substantial manufacturing ventures, but the majority of Chinese businessmen in the Peninsula lacked the capital, technical and managerial skills to enter this sector on a scale comparable to foreign interests. Their industrial ventures continued to be small in scale, labour-intensive and at low levels of technology (Jesudason, 1989, 60–4).

In East Malaysia too, which received comparatively less FDI, the largest groups of entrepreneurs were Chinese. In Sabah the leaders were the 'timber *towkays*' who were accumulating fortunes in the 1950s and early 1960s (E. Lee, 1976). In Sarawak the Foochow community played a leading role, more than doubling in size between 1947 and 1970 and spreading to most districts but especially towns such as Sibu, Miri and Kuching. An industrial classification in 1970 showed the Foochow to be prominent in manufactures such as wood and rattan furniture, building materials, bakeries, as well as in property, finance and general trade (Leigh, 1988). The scale of business remained small, averaging only $250 000 in paid-up capital in projects approved between 1968 and 1982 (Sarawak Government, 1984, 82).

Private *bumiputera* capital in Malaysia showed few signs at this stage of being able to develop outside areas such as traditional cottage handicrafts, timber, transport and contracting. Government soon started to take initiatives to persuade Malays to pool their resources, such as a National Investment Company (1961) to buy shares in industrial companies with pioneer status. Progress was slow. By 1964 the company held only

$3.2 million of shares out of a possible $15.1 million allotted to *bumiputeras* (Jesudason, 1989, 64–5). The RIDA, inherited from the colonial government, failed to provide much assistance to Malays, and in 1966 was succeeded by the Majlis Amanah Ra'ayat (MARA). These measures were not sufficient to enable Malays to break into areas of the economy, notably manufacturing industry, where foreign and domestic non-Malay capital was strongly entrenched.

The total capital stock in the economy from all sources grew rapidly during these years. A study by Abraham and Gill (1969) shows that between 1959 and 1966 the aggregate for Peninsular Malaysia (at 1964 prices) rose from $7612 million to $12 931 million, or by 70 per cent. Three important characteristics should be noted: first, that new buildings and construction overtook perennial crops (dominant since the First World War) as the prime area of capital formation; second, machinery and equipment grew fastest (130 per cent); and third (a portent for the future), public investment expanded from about one-quarter to one-third of the total, growing twice as fast as private investment.

The introduction of the NEP from 1970 meant that industrialisation had to serve the concurrent tasks of (i) maintaining economic growth, and (ii) spearheading the redistribution of wealth and employment (see Chapter 10.3). Since it was clear that government remained firmly in control of the country following the 1969 disturbances, the impact on FDI was not adverse. Major transnationals made investments at this time. Some, such as Motorola, Intel and Hitachi set up electronic components plants oriented wholly to exports. Monsanto, Nippon Steel Glass, Ericsson and BHP, on the other hand, produced chemicals, glass, telecommunications equipment and steel roofing mainly for the domestic market (Anuwar and Wong, 1993, Tables 3.1, 3.17).

The ICA of 1975 had a depressing effect on investment because it required firms with over $100 000 in shareholders' funds and more than 25 workers to obtain an operating licence. To obtain this Malaysian firms had to reserve at least 30 per cent of equity for *bumiputera* interests while foreign firms producing for the domestic market were limited to 30 per cent equity and those exporting could own up to 100 per cent depending on usage of local materials and the proportion exported. After protests from Malaysian (principally Chinese) and foreign interests the Act was modified to some degree in 1977, but none the less there was a marked fall in projects submitted for approval in the late 1970s. The average share of equity fell below 30 per cent for Chinese (against 70 per cent in 1971), and fluctuated between about 25 and 40 per cent for FDI (Jesudason, 1989, Tables 5.1, 5.2).

Concern that flagging private investment might affect the achievement of NEP aims led government to take a much-expanded role for the public sector. Capital formation here was aided by a surge in official revenues, from petroleum in particular through royalties, company taxes and export duties. Total federal revenue climbed from $2400 million in 1970 to nearly $14 000 million in 1980 and $21 000 million by 1985, or from 20 per cent to 29 per cent of GNP (Jomo, 1990, Table 8.4). Public investment reached a peak of 55 per cent of total investment by 1985 (UN, 1991, 39). Allocations of public funds to the 'off-budget enterprises', such as Permodalan Nasional, under the Second, Third and Fourth Malaysia Plans totalled $7688 million (calculated from Jesudason, 1989, Table 4.3). In addition, these organisations could raise government-backed commercial loans. Permodalan Nasional alone had investments aggregating $6.2. billion by 1985. However, 'State enterprise expansion, at best, was an enormous exchange of assets in which the state paid out cash for existing assets built up by the foreign and Chinese sectors. There was little net increase in production and employment' (Jesudason, 1989, 84). State investment contributed to a relative decline in the proportion of foreign-owned fixed assets (Table 12.6).

The attitude of the government towards FDI in the 1970s was that it was one among various sources of investment, and was required to comply with the requirements of the NEP. By the late 1970s, however, there was growing official concern that the long-term NEP targets for wealth shares might not be attained. For political reasons government could not be seen to be actively encouraging Chinese investment, thus FDI became the more attractive option. This was particularly the case with Japanese investment which was targeted under the 'Look East' policy adopted in the early 1980s.

FDI was coopted into the second round of ISI which focused on heavy industries. HICOM, set up in 1980, established several joint ventures in steel, motor-cycle engines, a national car (the Proton), petrochemicals and cement, with various Japanese companies as minority shareholders. Their performance is examined in the section on technology below. Most of this investment went to Peninsular Malaysia, and relatively little to East

Table 12.6 Malaysia: foreign share in fixed assets of manufacturing firms, selected years (average per centage)[a]

Category[b]	1968	1980	1988
Consumables	50.0	44.0	46.5
Consumer durables	48.0	31.0	34.2
Intermediate	61.5	48.0	31.0
Capital	74.0	39.0	35.0
Overall	61.0	39.0	39.0

[a] unweighted.
[b] Categories as per Table 12.1 notes.
Source: Calculated from data in Rajah Rasiah (1992), Table 1.

Malaysia: for instance, Mitsubishi took a 17.5 per cent share in the LNG plant at Bintulu (Sarawak).

The slump of the early 1980s intensified the slow-down in capital investment, both domestic and foreign. Domestic savings, while running at a high level (Table 12.3), continued to prefer high-return/low-risk assets such as government securities (UN, 1991, 12). In 1985–6 the government relaxed the terms of the ICA in relation to NEP requirements, and passed a Promotion of Investments Act which enabled foreign investors to own up to 100 per cent equity if only 50 per cent of output were exported or sold to FTZs or Licensed Manufacturing Warehouses (Jesudason, 1989, 188–9). In the remaining four years of the NEP, in concert with a general recovery in the world economy, EOI in Malaysia became the main driving force in industrial growth (Table 12.7 below), with FDI accounting for 49.1 per cent of approved equity in 1987, and 58.2 per cent in the first months of 1988. The leading investors were Japan, with the rise in the value of the yen pushing companies to relocate off-shore in a 'new wave'. Other Asian NICs, notably Taiwan, greatly increased their foreign investments in developing countries such as Malaysia because their very economic success had lost them privileged access to markets under the US Generalized System of Tariff Preferences (Chia, 1993, 84).

FDI had a mixed impact on the Malaysian economy. In the first round of ISI (see Chapter 10.2) growth in new employment was limited, and some domestic firms were displaced by foreign-owned ventures. Balance of payment effects were probably negative as imports of equipment (and so on) tended to offset capital inflows. EOI expansion was more beneficial in most of these respects, particularly in job creation for women from the rural areas. The increased foreign exchange earnings, especially in the later 1980s, helped to pay for associated imports, thus assisting balance of payments. Against this the net outflow of money representing repatriated profits and, in the 1980s, increasingly foreign debt-servicing was averaging $4.8 billion annually from 1983–1988 (Jomo, 1990a, Table 3.20).

Labour

Between 1970 and 1990 Malaysia's total labour force doubled from approximately 3.2 million to 6.4 million, or an average annual growth rate of 3.53 per cent (against 2.7 per cent for population growth). The numbers in manufacturing grew practically sixfold from 225 000 to just over 1.3 million, or about 9.2 per cent a year, (calculated from Wee, 1995, Table 3.15). Out of the total in 1990, some 1.23 million (95 per cent) were in Peninsular Malaysia. As a proportion of the total Malaysian workforce the share in manufacturing went from 11.4 per cent in 1970 to 19.5 per cent in 1990 (Jomo and Edwards, 1993, Table 1.1). The growth rates for the various regions can be seen in Table 12.7, which shows Peninsular Malaysia generally outpacing Sabah and Sarawak.

Table 12.7 Malaysia: growth rate of manufacturing labour force, 1970–90
(% per annum)

	1970–80	*1980–90*	*1970–90*
Pen. Malaysia	10.7	8.4	9.6
Sabah	8.6	5.4	7.0
Sarawak	4.3	8.7	6.5
Malaysia	9.9	8.7	9.3

Source: Calculated from Wee (1995), Table 3.15; Malaysia, *ABS*, 1991.

Expansion was relatively slow in the ISI phase in the 1960s due to the capital-intensive character of many pioneer industrial companies. However, in the early 1970s when EOI was getting under way the labour force grew very rapidly continuing into the 1980s until the slump struck and only starting to pick up again in 1988–90. Thus the situation was generally one of over-supply of workers in the 1960s, rapid absorption in the 1970s turning into over-supply again for much of the 1980s. This was reflected in unemployment rates around 7.5 per cent in 1970, falling to 4.7 per cent by the early 1980s, rising again to an estimated 9.5 per cent in 1987. However, as the economy recovered in the late 1980s unemployment dropped quickly to 6 per cent in 1990 (Jomo, 1990a, Table 4.3; Malaysian Government, 1991b, Table 4.3; UN, 1991, 26).

What were the principal sources of this greatly increased supply of labour for industry, and what were the factors which attracted workers into this sector? Any augmentation of the labour supply must come from among four sources: (i) a redistribution of the existing workforce between economic sectors, (ii) entry into the workforce of previously unused or little-used sections of the population, such as women and children, (iii) natural population growth, and (iv) immigration.

In the fully industrialised countries an inter-sectoral shift of surplus labour (whose marginal productivity is at or near zero) from the primary to the secondary and tertiary sectors was one of the major historical constituents in growth. They could leave that sector without causing a significant reduction in output, and in the early stages of industrialisation become available to employers without the need to raise wage levels. As long as workers remained available under these conditions the supply of unskilled labour was effectively unlimited, but once the primary sector shed all surplus labour a 'turning point' was reached beyond which manufacturers had to raise wages in order to attract further labour. The resultant competition for workers caused a general rise in real wages (Lewis, 1954).

Empirically, doubt has been cast on the existence of substantial surplus labour in Asian rice-growing economies in general (Oshima, 1981). In the

Malaysian case, as we have seen in earlier chapters, rice cultivation constituted a relatively small sector in the Peninsula, though it had more
weight in the Borneo territories. By the 1970s and 1980s off-farm activities
were absorbing a growing share of the work-time of small farmers. Primary
export production (rubber, palm oil and so on) required year-round work
from wage labour on estates, smallholdings and mines. Thus, it appears
unlikely that any major surplus of labour existed in the Malaysian primary
sector when industrialisation got under way. Indeed, the expansion in the
cultivated area, notably oil palms (Table 11.1), required a larger rather
than a smaller workforce. Total employment in the primary sector
rose from 1.7. million in 1970 to 2 million in 1982, but thereafter declined
to approximately 1.8. million by 1990 (Barlow et al., 1986, Table 1;
Malaysian Government, 1987; Wee, 1995, Table 3.15). Clearly, whilst this
sector did shed some labour, largely in Peninsular Malaysia, just how
much was surplus is doubtful. As we saw in Chapter 11, estates, land
schemes, independent smallholdings and rice farms experienced labour
shortages in the 1980s. It will be shown below that immigrants made good
much of this deficit.

The second, and largely new, source of industrial labour consisted of
women, many from the rural areas. Between 1957 and 1987 the labour force
participation rate for women rose from around 30 per cent to 46 per cent in
Peninsular Malaysia. In Sabah the comparable rates were 31 per cent and
43.8 per cent. No earlier figure is available for Sarawak, but the level in 1987
was considerably higher at nearly 64 per cent. From 1980 to 1986/7 women in
this sector took 95 per cent of the new jobs created, pushing their cumulative
share from 38.3 to 45.1 per cent (ABS, Sabah, 1960; Malaysian Government,
1987, Table 7.1; L. Lim, 1993, Tables 6.2; 6.3, 6.9).

Women were mainly employed in a few industries: electronics, textiles
('the two most feminised industries'), foodstuffs, footwear, chemicals,
rubber and plastics, where the prime attributes required were manual dex-
terity coupled with easy manageability. These jobs carried the lowest wage
rates and were highly vulnerable to retrenchments in times of economic
downturn, notably the mid-1980s. None the less, this work offered attractive opportunities to young rural (mainly Malay) women to move to the
towns, as well as to non-Malay women already there who preferred the
greater independence it provided over domestic service. The effects of this
structural change were most evident in Peninsular Malaysia where women
as a proportion of the primary sector workforce fell from 50 per cent to just
over 27 per cent between 1975 and 1986.

Increasing numbers of women, especially Chinese Malaysians, sought
work outside Malaysia (e.g. in Singapore and Taiwan), but at the same time
there has been a return flow into both Peninsular and East Malaysia of
Taiwanese, South Korean and Filippino women for work in domestic
service, restaurants and entertainment (L. Lim, 1993, 193).

The rapid natural population growth after the Second World War led to a sharp increase in the population of working age (15–64 years) at 3.5 per cent annually in the 1970s and early 1980s, slackening to 3.1 per cent by 1985 as the declining fertility took effect (see Chapter 10, section 10.2). In absolute terms the total working population nearly doubled from about 4.8 million in 1965 to 9.25 million in 1985, making it the main source of additional workers (Oshima, 1988, 4–5).

Increasingly in the 1970s and 1980s, for the second time in its history, Malaysia turned to foreign workers to obviate what could otherwise have developed into a bottleneck situation. For the most part migrant workers went to the agricultural, construction and services sectors which, by 1991, drew an estimated 30 per cent, 70 per cent and 10 per cent respectively of their workforce from overseas (principally Indonesia, the Philippines, Bangladesh). Manufacturing absorbed only some 41 000 (3 per cent) of the total (Hugo, 1993, Table 3). A substantial proportion of these, perhaps around one-third, were expatriate professional, managerial and skilled workers coming from the leading investing countries (Japan, South Korea, Taiwan, USA, Britain: Pillai, 1995, 226).

In aggregate terms Sabah, a perennially labour-short region, felt the major impact with nearly 500 000 immigrants by 1988, which may well have practically doubled the size of the workforce (Malaysian Government, 1987, Table C3.7; Pillai, 1995, 229). In terms of the domestic migration of labour the eastern and Peninsular regions of Malaysia were largely selfcontained for much of this period. Thus, for example, the Sabah Migration Fund recruited only between about 1000 and 4000 workers a year from the Peninsula from 1970 to 1984 (Soenarno, 1986, Table 3). However, more recently there were signs of a more integrated labour market. Manufacturers in the Penang region, having mostly exhausted local supplies of labour, started to look towards East Malaysia as a potential source (Nooriah, Morshidi and Abibullah, 1995, 128).

The pattern of real wages in Malaysia did not fit the Lewis model of stability in the early stages of industrialisation. There was a drop in both agriculture and manufacturing industry, the latter falling by 1.2 per cent a year between 1963 and 1973, reflecting the capital-intensive nature of ISI. Both then moved upwards in the 1970s and early 1980s, manufacturing rising at 2 per cent a year, as demand for labour surged, and even more strongly at 3.5 per cent a year from 1980–1988 (Barlow *et al.*, 1986, Table 1; Rajah Rasiah, 1994, Table 10). The continued rise in the 1980s may seem surprising in face of the slump, but money wage rates were not depressed, at least for those in employment, though rates for new entrants dropped (Fong, 1989, 228), and annual inflation was a low 1.4 per cent.

By the late 1980s unit production costs in Malaysian manufacturing were high relative to neighbouring countries, having doubled between 1975 and 1983 in textiles and wearing apparel, rubber and food products, iron and steel.

In electrical machinery/appliances they had nearly tripled between 1975 and 1981. Attempts to reduce costs in the later 1980s by way of improved technology, for instance, had no apparent effects in textiles, iron or steel, but in electrical machinery the index (1981 = 100) fell substantially to around 66 by 1988 (UN, 1991, Table II.7). Wage levels throughout the 1970s and 1980s were determined mainly by market forces, with management in a stronger situation vis-à-vis labour unions whose position was heavily circumscribed by legislation limiting the right to strike, and so on. Workers in the new export industries, notably electrical, were prevented from forming in-house unions until 1988 (Jomo, 1990a, 87–8).

To summarise, rising real wages in the secondary and tertiary sectors since the 1970s have been a 'pull' factor, strengthened (in Peninsular Malaysia particularly) by 'push' factors such as pressure on land, changes in rural lifestyle and improved education. However, in one major respect there has been a recurrence of the distinctive pattern in the earlier tin and rubber booms, namely substantial inflows of migrant workers. Most of these, it is true, did not go into manufacturing industries, but their presence slowed the pace of structural change and probably delayed moves to economise on labour use. Labour was not used particularly efficiently in the early stages of industrialisation. Annual growth in productivity was negative (–0.19 per cent) from 1973–1980, but improved markedly to 4.07 per cent between 1980–1989 (Rajah Rasiah, 1994, Table 7). At the end of the 1980s the main labour constraints facing Malaysia lay in shortages in the professional and technical spheres (*FEER*, 6 Jan. 1994).

Structural change in the labour force advanced much further in Peninsular than in East Malaysia (see Table 10.5). In Sabah and Sarawak the movement of labour was more out of subsistence agriculture into primary export industries and services. The evidence from various localities in these two states indicates that, except in the most isolated areas, the population retained a footing in both the subsistence and commercialised sectors. Many villages experienced out- and in-migration according to the availability of jobs in forestry, mining, government services and the expanding urban centres such as Kota Kinabalu, Kuching, Sibu and Sandakan.

Technology

At this point it is helpful to recall Kuznets' view (see Chapter 1.1) that the central driving force in the onset of modern economic growth has been the progressive application of scientific methods to the production process through technological innovation (in combination, of course, with additional factor inputs of capital and labour).

On a global scale the trend since the Industrial Revolution has been for technological innovation to be dominated by the USA, Western Europe and Japan, and especially by multinational corporations originating from these countries. Since the early 1970s about two-thirds of the international supply of 'disembodied proprietary technology' has been of US origin, and 80 per cent of 'measured international payments' for technology were generated by exchanges within multinational corporations (MNCs), again mostly of US origin. The major areas of innovation have been in micro-electronics, bio-technology, new materials (such as ceramics, polymers), renewable energies and automation which have a 'vast potential for unlocking new technological combinations' (Ernst and O'Connor, 1989, 22). The problem for developing countries such as the Asian NICs, and recently the ASEAN-4, has been how best to acquire modern technology given the MNC dominance over its generation and supply.

In Malaysia, prior to the commencement of pioneer industries from 1958, technological innovation was confined mainly to primary produc-tion (commercial agriculture and mining), along with the infrastructure (railways, power supplies, telephones) and medical services. Some innova-tions were imported, for example tin dredges, and some developed locally, like the techniques of rubber production (see Chapter 4). Research capacity was almost wholly represented by government departments and statutory bodies, such as the Rubber Research Institute.

In the first phase of ISI Malaysia was heavily dependent on imported technology. The paucity of domestic research resources here was com-pounded by the exemptions granted to the preponderantly foreign investors on imported capital equipment, which gave little incentive to engage in local research and development (R and D).

This pattern did not alter greatly during the NEP, indeed, in some respects import-dependency actually increased. Between 1970 and 1989 imports of intermediate goods for the manufacturing sector rose from 20.7 per cent to 32.9 per cent of total imports, whilst capital goods went from 26.6 to 34.3 per cent (Anuwar, 1992, Table 2.9). During the 1970s government took several initiatives towards creating an institutional framework to promote local science and technology. These included establishing the Standards and Industrial Research Institute of Malaysia (SIRIM), and the National Council for Research and Development, both in 1975, the Ministry of Science, Technology and the Environment (1976), the Coordinating Council for Industrial Technology Transfer (1982), and the Malaysian Institute of Micro-Electronic Systems (1985) (UN, 1991, 59–61). However, there remained a lack of central direction in local research, and a continuing emphasis on the agro-industries until the formulation of the Industrial Master Plan in 1986 (see section 12.3 below and Anuwar, 1992, 95–6).

Even so, R and D expenditure in Malaysia in 1988 was still a very low 0.8 of GDP (0.7 in the public sector and a near-negligible 0.1 per cent in the private sector) compared to 2 per cent in South Korea (0.8 and 1.2 per cent respectively) and from 2.4 to 2.7 per cent in several OECD countries (0.5 to

1.4 per cent, and 1.3 to 1.9 per cent respectively) (Anuwar, 1992, Table 7.1). A survey of the 800 member firms of the Federation of Malaysian Manufacturers in 1987 elicited only 67 replies, of which 48 per cent reported R and D expenditure averaging a mere $150 000 a firm (Fong, 1989, 224).

The principal sources of manufacturing technology for the private sector in Malaysia continued to be foreign, notably the leading investor countries. Between 1975 and 1989 a total of 1579 agreements received government approval. Japan accounted for 34 per cent, the United Kingdom 13 per cent and the USA 11 per cent. The bulk (some 49 per cent) involved the provision of technical assistance and know-how, 9 per cent management contracts, 11 per cent joint ventures and 14 per cent trade marks and patents. Only 1.7 were for turn-key (complete plant) projects. The electronics/ electrical, chemical and fabricated metal industries comprised some 42 per cent of the agreements. Since the mid-1970s Malaysia drew 35 to 40 per cent of its machinery requirements from Japan (Anuwar, 1992, Tables 5.1, 5.2).

A survey in 1979–81 of 300 Malaysian firms, or just over one-third of those in the five major sectors (electronics, textiles, veneers/plywood, iron/steel, petrochemicals and plastics) indicated that the level of technology, as measured by the capital/labour ratio, was significantly lower, especially where a firm had a foreign parent company. For example, a comparison of four electronic companies in Japan and their Malaysian subsidiaries showed the latter as having approximately one-third the capital per worker (Fong, 1986, Table 4.3). In this case it should be noted that the production functions in each country were quite different. The components of the integrated circuits (masks, and wafers or chips) were produced by highly capital-intensive methods in Japan and sent to Malaysia for the less capital-intensive assembly. The technology gap was reflected in a labour productivity in Japan roughly 2.7 times that in Malaysia (calculated from Fong, 1986, Table 4.3.). Corresponding data for the other industries in the survey showed broadly similar contrasts in levels of technology and productivity between most Malaysian and foreign-domiciled firms.

Based on the results of this survey the competitive strengths of the various export industries were assessed as good in the case of electronics assembly, fabric manufacturing and finished textile products, plastics, wood veneers and plywoods. These were, however, based on advantages which could be easily eroded, such as low labour costs and a cheap domestic supply of timber. Existing iron and steel plants were fairly competitive, but new plants, such as an integrated steel plant at Telok Kalong (Terengganu) and a sponge iron plant in Labuan incorporating the latest technology, were thought to have much better prospects. Man-made fibres and downstream petrochemicals were not competitive due to dependence on imported raw materials (Fong, 1989, Table 9.1).

The capital intensity of Malaysian industry underwent a substantial increase between 1981 and 1986. This was most notable in the heavy industries such as steel (up by 325 per cent), petroleum refining (223 per cent), and transport equipment (186 per cent) (Anuwar, 1993, Table 2.1).

The Malaysian experience with new technology during the 1980s was mixed. Perwaja Steel in Terengganu commenced operation in 1985, but the initial technology supplied from Japan proved defective and by 1987 losses and other liabilities amounted to $2 billion (*FEER*, 24 Feb. 1994). Rising labour costs led to the beginnings of automation in the fabric and garment-making industries, but at a rate slower than the national average (Rajah Rasiah, 1993, 13). In the leading manufacturing industry, electronics and electrical machinery (50 per cent of manufactured exports by 1985), automation began with the application of microprocessors and computerised machines to the assembly process. The earlier reliance upon unskilled and semi-skilled labour was replaced by a growing need for engineers and technicians to maintain the production equipment (O'Connor, 1993).

Overall, Malaysian industry had not gone far down the track towards high-technology industries by 1990. One measure of improved efficiency (the accuracy of which is still under debate) is Total Factor Productivity Growth (TFPG) which seeks, *inter alia*, to quantify the effects of the application of new technology. Studies of output growth in developed and developing countries between 1960 and the late 1980s have found that in general TFPG has made by far the largest contribution in the former (varying from 50 per cent in the USA to 87 per cent in West Germany). In the developing countries, however, new capital investment at around 65 per cent has been the main source, followed by labour (14 to 30 per cent), and TFPG (14 to 28 per cent) (D. Lim, 1994, Table 1). The evidence for Malaysia (Table 12.5 above) is mixed, with TFPG growing most rapidly from 1961 to 1974, but slowing substantially thereafter and becoming negative from 1982 to 1988. Capital inputs were clearly dominant from 1975, though accompanied by substantial growth in the labour force. Another study, covering the shorter period 1979–89, provides different figures but confirms the leading role of capital accounting for 80 per cent of growth, and labour and TFPG at 10 per cent each. When these aggregates are broken down by sector, capital was almost wholly responsible for growth in intermediate goods, where the TFPG was negative (–1 per cent), and just over half in consumer goods which had a positive TFPG of 2 per cent. Export-oriented industries had a TFPG rate of just over twice that of domestic-oriented ones (Alavi, 1996, Tables 5.5, 5.6, 5.8), reflecting pressure to remain competitive internationally.

The continuing regional imbalance in the location of secondary industry (section 12.4 below) meant that technological change was confined mainly to the western parts of the Peninsula. Such change started to penetrate the

East Malaysian territories only in the 1980s largely through projects with a high component of government funding, notably the Bintulu LNG plant and the ASEAN fertiliser plant.

12.3   Sources of growth: demand side

Markets

Table 12.8 sets out the sources of manufacturing output growth in Malaysia from 1959 to 1989 in terms of market demand. Very clearly the domestic market was the dominant force right up to the early 1980s. Import substitution was important up to the early 1970s. Domestic demand expansion (net growth in the domestic market) was a much greater stimulus, particularly in the first 15 years or so of the NEP. Export expansion, apart from a modest surge in the mid-1960s, was relatively weak until the later 1980s when, as we have seen, government encouraged private investment, FDI in particular.

When the impact of demand on the various categories of manufactured commodities is disaggregated, consumption goods enjoyed a period of predominance during the first round of ISI (1959–68). The scope for ISI was largely exploited by the early 1970s, and thereafter domestic demand expansion took over with an increasing shift to intermediate and capital goods as the Malaysian economy felt the impact of construction booms in the 1970s and early 1980s before the slump hit. Leading industries here were industrial and other chemicals, non-metallic minerals, iron and steel, and fabricated metal products. It was not until the revival of EOI from the mid-1980s that the major export industries (textiles, electrical/electronic goods) really came to the forefront (see Ariff, 1991, Table 2.4; D. Lim, 1992, Tables 6.7, 6.8).

Between 1970 and 1990 Malaysia's aggregate exports at current prices grew at an average of 14.65 per cent a year, and imports at 15.7 per cent. The index of export volume (1985 = 100) rose at 5.15 per cent a year

Table 12.8   Malaysia: market sources of manufacturing output growth, 1959–89 (%)

Year	Import substitution	Export expansion	Domestic demand expansion
1959–63	41.0	−1.0	60.0
1963–8	46.2	13.4	40.5
1968–71	38.5	6.1	55.4
1971–4	−49.7	1.7	148.0
1973–78	36.2	−79.7	143.5
1979–84	−26.0	25.0	101.0
1984–9	−27.0	53.0	74.0

Sources: Hoffman and Tan (1975), Table A.3, (1980), Table V.5; D. Lim (1992), Table 6.8; Alavi (1996), Table 2.11.

(calculated from IMF, 1991). The geographical distribution of external trade in this period is shown in Table 12.9. For both exports and imports the greatest change was the shift in focus towards the Pacific Rim region, in particular the newly industrialising economies and the USA, and away from the EC (European Community) countries. Whilst Malaysia had a longstanding trade connection with the USA, this had changed from the tin and rubber of the earlier part of the century to a wider range of manufactured products by the 1980s. Japan had become the biggest customer for Malaysia's primary exports, taking 28.4 per cent in 1987 (M. Ariff, 1991, 59). The bulk of Malaysia's imports came from the East Asian region.

What emerged in East Asia during this period was a growing interdependence in trade and investment which was of general benefit to the various regional economies. This interdependence 'was achieved without much by way of a formal integration framework' (Yamazawa, 1992, 1519), such as regional trading blocks. Malaysia, as one of the founding members of ASEAN (1967), participated in the early stages of such a framework in the form of preferential tariff arrangements (PTAs) for intra-ASEAN trade. Progress proceeded initially by voluntary product-by-product agreements but such concessions were slow in coming as members were reluctant to forgo any advantages. In 1980 an 'across the board' approach was adopted affecting all products up to a certain trade value, for instance a cut of 20 per cent in tariffs on goods up to US$1 million. Even so, these concessions did not have much stimulating effect on intra-ASEAN trade in general as this consisted largely (50 per cent) of trade in petroleum between Malaysia, Indonesia and Singapore, the major refining centre. It was not until 1989 that the third ASEAN Summit adopted a specific target to bring 50 per cent by value, or 90 per cent by number, of commodities under the PTAs within five years (Imada, 1991, 5–8).

Table 12.9   Malaysia: geographical distribution of foreign trade, selected years (%)[a]

	Exports		Imports	
	1970	1988	1970	1988
Japan	18.3	19.9	17.5	23.0
Asian NIEs[b]	27.0	30.5	10.9	22.1
ASEAN	25.4	24.4	22.5	18.8
USA	13.0	17.3	8.6	17.7
EC	20.3	14.4	23.4	13.3

[a] Columns do not total 100 due to some overlap (Singapore is in both the NIE and ASEAN groups).
[b] Newly-industrialising economies: Hong Kong, Singapore, South Korea, Taiwan.
Source: Adapted from Ariff (1991), Table 2.9.

The composition of Malaysian exports is shown in Table 12.10. The largest proportionate changes were a fall in the share of inedible crude materials (notably rubber), and rises in mineral fuel/lubricants, machinery and transport equipment. The last two categories were particularly important in exports from the Peninsula.

On the import side the main alterations were that both Sabah and Sarawak became increasingly dependent on imports of manufactures, machinery and transport equipment. A growing proportion of these supplies came from the Peninsula which exported 13 per cent of its manufactures to East Malaysia in 1990 against only 0.3 per cent in 1964. The respective export figures for machinery and transport equipment were 10 per cent and 4.9 per cent. In 1990 Sabah bought 57.8 per cent of its manufactures from Peninsular Malaysia (14.3 per cent in 1964), and Sarawak 67.6 per cent against 2.3 per cent (Wee, 1995, Tables 4.5, 4.9).

Under the terms of the domestic common market introduced after federation, Sabah and Sarawak had to bring their tariffs into line with those of Peninsular Malaysia, and thus could not give special protection to encourage ISI along the lines pursued in the Peninsula. Most of the manufactured imports from the latter source were up to 50 per cent more expensive than comparable goods from elsewhere (Wee, 1995, 93–6). In some cases (wood manufactures and petroleum products) the East Malaysian states were importing goods made from raw materials previously exported to Peninsular Malaysia, a classic case of lost value-added reminiscent of the export of raw rubber to the USA and its reimportation as rubber goods in the colonial period. Whilst both Sabah and Sarawak enjoyed favourable overall balances of visible trade in most years from the 1970s onwards, their trade with Peninsular Malaysia incurred an increasing deficit almost from the outset following federation. By 1990 this was running at about $4.5 billion, or 237 per cent of the value of their combined exports to the Peninsula (calculated from Wee, 1995, Table 4.7). There was very limited scope for bilateral trade between the two East Malaysian states as their economies were largely complementary.

12.4   Government policy

Planning

Prior to the mid-1980s policies related to industrialisation comprised a range of initiatives scattered over time. We have already looked at the legislative measures on pioneer industries (1958), investment incentives (1968) and industrial coordination (1975). Allocations of public expenditure to industrial development under the Five-Year Plans reflected government's growing involvement, rising from some 3 per cent under the First Plan to a peak of 27 per cent under the Fourth, falling back to 17 per cent under the Fifth Plan (Table 10.8) as the emphasis shifted back to private enterprise. The bulk of this expenditure was in Peninsular Malaysia. In East Malaysia outlays were relatively small at under 1 per cent in the First Plan, peaking at 5.5 per cent in Sabah (Fourth Plan) and 6.5 per cent in Sarawak (Third Plan) (calculated from Wee, 1995, Table 2.12).

The sluggish performance of private investment, both domestic and foreign, in industry in the early 1980s, combined with falling official revenues, led to the formulation of plans specifically focused on this sector. The first of these, the major planning instrument for Malaysia as a whole, was the Industrial Master Plan (IMP) announced in 1986. It proved difficult, however, to produce an overall strategy which catered equally for the needs of all the Malaysian territories, and this was followed by the Sabah Action Blueprint (SAB) in 1987.

The Industrial Master Plan concluded that the ISI sector had not developed behind tariff protection to the level where industries were competitive internationally, and that the EOI sector was still narrowly based on two major industries, electronics/electrical machinery and textiles, which accounted for 65 per cent of manufactured exports in 1983. The first of these was in turn dominated by the assembly of semiconductors from components of which 90 per cent or more were imported, thus generating few linkages to domestic industries. Other drawbacks included dependence on foreign technology, only limited amounts of which were transferred, a lack of skilled workers and inadequate incentives to expand exports: (Jomo, 1990a, 134–42).

On the basis of this analysis twelve industries were identified as a core group for cohesive policies to develop their production potential in the period to 1995. Seven were resource-based (products from rubber, palm-oil, wood, chemicals/petrochemicals, non-ferrous metals, non-metallic minerals and foodstuffs), and five non-resource-based (electronics/electrical

Table 12.10   Composition of Malaysian exports, selected years (%)

	Sabah		Sarawak		Pen. Malaysia	
SITC[a]	1963	1990	1963	1990	1963	1990
Foods	2.2	5.1	8.0	2.2	4.2	5.0
Drinks/Tobacco	15.6	negl.	–	negl.	negl.	0.8
Inedible Crude Materials	74.9	26.2	34.4	29.1	62.4	8.0
Min. Fuel/Lubricants	0.7	26.6	53.6	55.5	0.5	10.5
Animal/Veg. Oils, Fats	–	4.6	0.5	0.7	3.4	7.9
Chemicals	–	19.7	0.3	1.7	0.1	2.3
Manufactures	1.8	9.3	0.9	3.1	26.3	21.8
Machinery/Transport Eqpt	1.5	8.3	0.3	7.6	1.9	43.0

[a] Standard International Trade Classification.
Source: Adapted from Wee (1995), Table 4.3.

machinery, transport equipment, machinery and engineering products, iron and steel, textiles/wearing apparel). The main focus points were to be a renewal of export orientation, and a more liberal trade regime (lessening of tariff protection). Backward linkages between the resource-based industries and domestic raw material producers were to be strengthened. The heavy industries in the non-resource-based group (e.g. iron and steel) should aim at achieving a competitive position in the domestic market closely linked to the engineering and machinery industry. Other points included the development of domestic technological capability (UN, 1991, 53–6).

In previous sections we have noted the relatively low rate of structural change towards industrialisation in the economies of Sabah and Sarawak. By the 1980s there was a growing feeling in those states that a more determined drive to speed up this process was needed, and one which, moreover, took account of the special local circumstances such as geographical location, inadequate infrastructure and highly dispersed populations.

In Sabah the government announced the SAB in September 1987. The main points were as follows (D. Lim, 1991):

1 To diversify all sectors of the economy and enhance the amount of value-added to the various primary products.
2 To identify and develop the 'competitiveness factors' which would give Sabah a comparative advantage. These were appropriate technology, a skilled workforce, flexible investment capital, adequate infrastructure, entrepreneurship, a strong institutional structure for problem-solving, and marketing strategies.
3 To enhance the participation of private enterprise as an offset against the hitherto dominant role of government in many areas of production.
4 To establish an administrative structure to oversee implementation, headed by the existing State Development Planning Committee supported by several ministerial committees.

This was thus a very general plan, rather than one specifically directed at industrialisation, but as far as the latter was concerned the implication was clearly that natural resource-based industries were the prime aim. 'To have argued for a plan which emphasize[d] manufacturing [alone] would have been to build the house on sand' (D. Lim, 1991, 10). In other words, Sabah leadership did not at this stage envisage trying to duplicate the range of manufacturing industries which had developed in West Malaysia.

In implementation, however, the SAB fell far short of the desired aims. The principal reasons, apart from internal shortcomings within the plan, were that the twelve ministerial committees worked without any budgetary and timescale framework, and for the most part met very infrequently

(D. Lim, 1991). Critics also pointed to fundamental problems, such as Sabah's relative geographical isolation, in attracting external investment. Unless the federal government approved special incentives for Sabah 'it [would be] difficult to compete on an equal footing with the Peninsula for investors' (Ongkili and Pang, 1992, 17).

Whilst the Sarawak economy faced similar problems, there does not seem to have been anything formal corresponding to the SAB. However, in October 1988 a seminar was held in Kuching to discuss the formulation of strategies for socio-economic development to take the state into the 1990s. The discussion on industrialisation had a rationale similar to the SAB, namely the need to develop resource-based industries to facilitate 'down-stream processing' of primary products, with private capital urged to take a more prominent part (Zainal Abidin Sulong in Abdul Majid Mat Salleh, Solhee and Kasim, 1990).

Tariffs

The industrial objects of Malaysian trade policy since 1958 were (i) to reduce dependence on imports through a programme of import-substitution industrialisation, and (ii) to promote the export of manufactured goods. In the succeeding three decades there were three phases of trade regime (D. Lim, 1992, 94–5):

1   1958–69 – 'nascent protection'. Government opted for the imposition of selective tariff protection for ISI firms, but the rates were low by international standards.
2   1970–80 – 'protection'. Tariffs rose to medium levels, and protection was extended to selected EOI firms. Rates dropped for some products in the late 1970s.
3   1980s – 'premature heavy industrialisation'. High protection given to heavy industries under the HICOM programme (second round of ISI).

Tariff rates generally rose in the 1960s and early 1970s, and declined in the late 1970s. The 1980s can be divided into two sub-periods: 1980–6 up to the announcement of the Industrial Master Plan, when rates rose, and 1986 onwards during which the trade regime (along with the policy on FDI) was liberalised and tariffs generally lowered (Alavi, 1996, 176). Import duty as a proportion of total import value fell from just under 9 per cent in 1985 to around 4.5 per cent in 1990–1 (Okamoto, 1991, Figure 1).

Right up to the late 1980s consumer goods received more tariff protection than intermediate or capital goods. For example, in 1963/5 the effective rates of protection (ERPs) were respectively 42, 25 and 5 per cent. In 1974 they stood at 50, 37 and 28 per cent. However, by 1987 the ERP on consumer goods stood at 9 per cent against 65 per cent on intermediate goods. Further analysis indicates that export-oriented industries consistently received lower levels of protection than domestic-oriented industries: in 1987 ERPs were 23 per cent and 37 per cent respectively (D. Lim, 1992, Table 6.3; Alavi, 1996, Table 3.15).

The above figures reflect the changing rationale underlying government tariff policy. Overall, this was used as a tool to assist infant industries to become established. However, in implementation the policy was flawed in several respects. Protection was granted on a blanket basis, and whilst levels of ERP varied over time, the basic case for continuing protection was not reviewed in the light of the actual performance of individual industries. Thus, whilst there is no evidence to suggest that tariffs retarded growth in productivity, once granted these have tended to become a fixed feature rather than one which, by means of regular review, might have been used in a carrot-and-stick fashion to push more industries to reach international competitiveness within a given time frame. ISI and EOI industries were treated as separate categories with protection favouring the former, which did not help Malaysia to move up the technological ladder from labour-intensive to high-technology industries with strong export-competitiveness (Alavi, 1996, 52, 168–9, 173–6).

Monetary and fiscal policy

The principal aim of government in this area was to maintain the stability of the economy, with particular targets being to keep inflation at the lowest level possible and maintain a sound balance of payments position. In general the governments of the East Asian region achieved a 'superior policy framework' (Thomas and Yan, 1996, 273) in these respects over the three decades from 1960–1990. This success was reflected in relatively low levels of inflation. A sample of seven Asian countries had an average annual inflation rate of 15.1 per cent (1965–80), and 11.4 per cent (1980–6). Within this group Malaysia stood out with annual inflation at 4.9 per cent in the first sub-period, and 1.4 per cent in the second. Only briefly, in 1973–4, did inflation reach double figures at 10.4 per cent and 17.4 per cent (Semudram, 1987, Table 4.2).

Apart from the surge in inflation in 1973–4, which arose largely from external factors such as a sharp rise prices of imported commodities (Semudram, 1987, 84), the decades of the 1960s and 1970s did not pose any major problems of stabilisation for the Malaysian government. The federal budget ran at a consistent and rising deficit, due mainly to increased public expenditure on development which government was able to finance by domestic borrowing. Both monetary and fiscal policy followed a counter-cyclical pattern to dampen the effects of trade fluctuations (principally export earnings) on the domestic economy.

There were no serious balance of payments problems during these two decades. The net deficit on invisibles (services) account rose steadily, due notably to payments for freight and insurance, but the high rate of growth of commodity exports (boosted by oil in the later 1970s) was sufficient to underpin both this and a large expansion in imports (mainly intermediate and capital goods) (Jomo, 1990a, Table 3.18).

However, the situation deteriorated in the early 1980s as the global slump took hold. Between 1980 and 1986 the unit prices for Malaysian primary exports declined by 40 per cent whilst import prices fell by only about 7 per cent, with a resultant deficit on visible trade account of $105 million in 1981 and $753 million in 1982 (IMF, 1991), an unprecedented event in Malaysian economic history. The barter terms of trade, which had been in long-term decline since 1959 (= 100) slumped from 71 in 1980 to 53 in 1982, recovered slightly to 60 in 1984 and then dropped to a record low of 48 in 1986, discouraging private investment. The deficit on invisibles, meanwhile, ballooned to well over $10 billion annually in 1984–5 (Jomo, 1990, Tables 3.19, 3.20). The overall result was a series of deficits on current account in seven successive years, 1980–6, reaching at its peak the equivalent of 13 per cent of GNP in 1982 (Semudram, 1987, 100).

As previously, the Malaysian government took counter-cyclical measures (though critics in Malaysia argued that the downturn was structural rather than cyclical in nature) (see Khor, 1987). As we saw in section 12.1 above, the HICOM investment programme commenced, financed by public expenditure which came from funds borrowed externally (from Japan in particular). The total foreign debt increased from about $15.4 billion in 1981 to $50.7 billion in 1986, the latter equivalent to approximately 76 per cent of GNP, far above the average for LDCs of 47.9 per cent. The annual cost of servicing this debt stood at 8.6 per cent of GNP. Fiscal policy was very expansive. Government revenue nearly doubled from about $11 billion in 1979 to $21 billion in 1985. Both recurrent operating and development expenditure increased in roughly the same proportion. This was deficit financing on a large scale, the gap reaching nearly 67 per cent of revenue in 1982 (calculated from Jomo, 1990, Table 8.2). Between 1980 and 1984 the international exchange rate of the Malaysian *ringgit* appreciated in real terms by 9.75 per cent (calculated from Alavi, 1996, Table 2.6), thus lowering the competitiveness of exports. In order to assist export-oriented industries the government remodelled the Export Credit Refinancing facilities to allow more exporters improved access to low-interest credit (4 per cent) either prior to or at the time of shipment of goods.

At the same time the large outflows of currency needed to service external debts caused a weakening in the value of the *ringgit* so that the real effective exchange rate fell by some 37 per cent between 1984 and 1990 (calculated from Alavi, 1996, Table 2.6), cheapening exports whilst making imports dearer. The effects were immediate. The US$ value of manufactured exports rose by 15 per cent from 1985 to 1987, whilst manufactured imports increased by only 6 per cent. The visible trade balance returned to a substantial surplus by 1987 to the extent of 8 per cent of GNP. This was more than sufficient to offset the deficit on invisibles and restore a positive balance of payments on current account in the late 1980s. The federal budget continued in deficit, but with a reduction of more than half compared with the peaks of the early 1980s (Jomo, 1990a, Table 8.6).

Malaysia's foreign indebtedness reached a high point in 1987 at 77 per cent of GNP, with the interest absorbing 16.2 per cent of annual export earnings. Thereafter there was a decline as government drew back from further overseas borrowings, and by 1989 the total debt had been reduced to just under $42 billion, with a debt-service ratio of 9.3 per cent (Jomo, 1990a, 195; UN, 1991, 3). The economic recovery from the late 1980s was financed mainly by an increased flow of FDI.

Thus far we have viewed the situation at the federal level. Data on the state finances of Sabah and Sarawak reveal much the same pattern in government expenditure: that is, deficit financing throughout much of the period since the mid-1960s, with the size of the deficit increasing. There were two components in revenue: state and federal funds. State revenue came principally from sources with a limited life, forestry and petroleum, together accounting for about 60 per cent in the late 1980s. Allocations of federal funds provided a declining proportion of the total over time, falling from 52 per cent to 51 per cent between 1966/70 and 1986/90 in Sarawak, and from 47 per cent to 33 per cent in Sabah (Wee, 1995, Tables 2.3, 2.4). The latter reflected the surrender of all but 5 per cent of petroleum royalties from the mid-1970s, and Sabah's worsening political relationship with the federal government in the 1980s (see Chapter 10.4).

In addition, under the special arrangements for joining Malaysia, both states received grants of various types from the federal government (e.g., for roads). Whilst the absolute size of these grants compared favourably with those to most states in Peninsular Malaysia, the annual average rate of increase between 1976 and 1990 at around 13 per cent was among the lowest. Moreover, the spending power of these funds was considerably less in East Malaysia due to higher price levels there, averaging an additional 27.3 per cent (1976–86), and still 15 per cent in 1991 (Wee, 1995, Tables 2.5, 2.6). Both state governments had anticipated a consistent net transfer of funds from federal revenue to aid in development. Such net transfers did occur up to the mid-1970s, but thereafter the flow turned in the reverse direction again largely due to the surrender of petroleum royalties (Wee, 1995, 44).

Overall, the Malaysian government succeeded in maintaining monetary and fiscal stability, together with low inflation throughout this period by a combination of pragmatic and moderate policies. These counteracted the periodic fluctuations arising out of the country's exceptional openness to the international economy, and accelerated the recovery in export values after the slump of the mid-1980s. A composite index of distortion in the pricings of three variables (foreign exchange, factors of production and products) in the 1970s puts Malaysia in the low to medium range, comparable to South Korea (D. Lim, 1994, Table 5).

Regional development

It was noted in Chapter 9.4 that the IBRD Report (1963) on the economic aspects of a federation advocated a balanced distribution of industry throughout Malaysia. However, it was not until the early 1970s that regional development became an important part of government policy. The need to spread industry more widely also gained urgency as a means of reducing the high rates of unemployment in the 1960s, and of assisting the NEP aim of generating employment outside the agricultural sector for *bumiputeras*.

A start in establishing new locations for industry had commenced soon after the Pioneer Industries Ordinance (1958) with the construction of industrial estates providing facilities (roads, buildings, power) to attract new firms. Those sites built during the 1960s were near major urban centres such as Petaling Jaya, a satellite town of Kuala Lumpur. These did not alter the existing concentration of industry. In 1971 four states in the Peninsula (Perak, Selangor, Negeri Sembilan, Johor) accounted for 75 per cent of employment and output in manufacturing (Cho, 1990, 207).

In 1971 an amendment to the Investment Incentives Act of 1968 made provision for tax rebates differentiated according to the location of a project (Spinanger, 1986, 39). By 1987 a total of 103 industrial estates had been established in Peninsular Malaysia, but the main concentrations continued to be along the west coast with 51 in Penang, Perak, Selangor and Negeri Sembilan against 23 in the northern states (Terengganu, Kelantan, Kedah, Perlis) and 29 in the south (Pahang, Melaka and Johor) (calculated from UN, 1991, Appendix J). Industrial estates in East Malaysia were relatively few: for example, in Sabah a total of 10 were opened between 1970 and 1981 mostly around Kota Kinabalu (Zulkifly, 1986, 369). More were planned in the late 1980s (nine each for Sabah and Sarawak) but high costs deterred investors. Taking land as an illustration, the average price per square metre in these estates in 1987 was $33 in Peninsular Malaysia, $65 in Sarawak and $80 in Sabah (UN, 1991, Appendix I, J).

One category of industrial estate of particular interest was the Free Trade Zone (FTZ), pioneered in countries such as South Korea and Taiwan. The FTZs were aimed principally at attracting foreign investors with a package of incentives which included duty-free imports of raw materials and capital equipment, tax concessions and simplified customs proceedures. From the government viewpoint '[these] were seen as offering a way of achieving greater development of efficient export industries without some of the political costs that a general liberalisation of trade policy would entail – namely contraction of inefficient but politically entrenched protected industries' (Warr, 1986, 179). The main condition was that a firm should export (again free of duty) at least 80 per cent of output. FTZs were set up mainly in Penang, Selangor and Melaka. Penang was the first (1972) and most successful with five zones (three at Bayan Lepas on the Island and two at Prai on the mainland). Bayan Lepas was 'the birthplace of the electronics industry in Malaysia' (Nesadurai, 1991, 106).

The FTZs had positive and negative effects on the Malaysian economy. In the first category, they gave a quick stimulus to investment and employment. The 53 firms in the Penang FTZs averaged a paid-up capital of $6.2 million, nearly two-and-a-half times that in non-FTZ firms, and 842 jobs per firm against 148. Penang's unemployment rate had dropped from 15 per cent in 1970 to 5.7 per cent in 1983 (Nesadurai, 1991, Tables 3, 6). A cost-benefit analysis concludes that from FTZs as a whole by the early 1980s 'the net benefits to Malaysia … had already exceeded the net costs incurred in establishing the zones' (Warr, 1986, 205). Net benefits included jobs created, gains from foreign exchange, local purchases of raw materials and electricity.

These were the short-term gains. The potential long-term gains were in the areas of technology transfer, the upgrading of the skills of Malaysian workers and management, and the development of linkages with the local economy. Here the balance in the period under review was less favourable. We have seen (section 12.2) that imported technology was generally of a lower level, especially where Malaysian firms had overseas parents. The preponderance of simple assembly work in production did not give much opportunity for labour to upgrade skills. The concentration of export production in the FTZs tended to create enclaves separate from non-FTZ firms producing primarily for the domestic economy, thus fostering a dualistic industrial structure (Alavi, 1996, 41). Linkages were weak. In a sample of 86 companies spanning all manufacturing sectors, two-thirds imported all their machinery. Goods produced for final consumption, mainly food and drinks, and rubber products, drew on local materials but, by definition, had no forward or 'downstream' linkages (O'Brien, 1993).

An analysis of the Penang FTZs showed that intra-industry linkages were rather stronger *within* the zones. In 1982, for example, firms purchased 13.2 per cent of raw materials and intermediate inputs from within the zone and only 3.6 per cent within the Malaysian customs area (the balance of 83.2 per cent was imported). None the less, the beginnings of local linkages were evident with 35 firms as ancillary suppliers to electronics producers (Nesadurai, 1991, Table 12, 129).

Despite the incentives offered from the early 1970s to even out the distribution of industries by locating new ventures in the less-developed regions, the efforts under the Second, Third and Fourth Malaysia Plans (1970–85) were not successful in reducing substantially the heavy concentration along the west coast of the Peninsula, and in particular the 'national core region' consisting mainly of the Federal Territory of Kuala

Lumpur and environs, and the Kelang Valley region of Selangor which, in 1985, still accounted for some 41 per cent of manufacturing value-added, with a further 42 per cent coming from Penang, Perak, Negeri Sembilan and Johor. Of the total projects approved between 1974 and 1983, only 4.8 per cent were sanctioned on the basis of locational incentives (Santokh Singh, 1987, 1, 12, 18).

In the late 1980s, as the economy recovered from the depression, regional development regained momentum, but with a significant new dimension: the 'growth triangle'. Such projects have a trans-border rationale, seeking to develop areas in adjacent countries by linking their resources in a complementary fashion. In Asia the concept had already been pioneered in the early 1980s linking Hong Kong with Shenzhen Special Economic Zone and Guangdong province in South China. The first in the ASEAN region was initiated in 1989–90 by the governments of Singapore, Malaysia and Indonesia to exploit the combined resources of the Island (organisational skills, domestic and international capital and so on), southern Johor and the Riau islands, notably Batam and Bintan (land and relatively cheap labour). It was given the acronym SiJoRi. For Singapore the triangle represented a step forward in the drive to strengthen the Island's pivotal economic role in the region, and though this gave rise to reservations on the part of the Indonesian and Malaysian governments. The latter was already keen to develop southern Johor as an alternative entrepot centre to Singapore, and from the late 1970s established the Pasir Gudang industrial estate and Johor port, which did not, however, succeed in diverting away the bulk of container traffic (Guinness, 1992, 36–8).

The SiJoRi triangle capitalised on the close historical connections between Johor and Singapore. Johor benefited greatly from a shift of labour-intensive industries from Singapore where costs were rising. The relationship, initially at least, tended to be complementary rather than competitive, giving Johor one of the lowest poverty ratios in Malaysia and a foremost reputation among foreign investors (Drabble and Mills, 1992). 'Growth triangles' as a development device have since gained further popularity in the surrounding region. Though it lies beyond our period we might note that in 1993 a 'northern triangle' (Penang, Perak, Kedah, Perlis, north Sumatra and southern Thailand) was established, and more recently (1994) an East ASEAN triangle comprising Sabah, Sarawak, Brunei, Kalimantan, north Sulawesi and the southern Philippines (Hasnah Ali, 1996).

Another concept aimed at regional development in the late 1980s was that of the 'urban industrial corridor'. This developed out of a recognition in the Industrial Master Plan that the earlier efforts to distribute industries more evenly had failed. It involved acceptance that, initially at least, industries were best sited in close relation to major urban centres which already enjoyed 'good infrastructure, well developed communications, ancillary services and skilled manpower' (Santokh Singh, 1987, 23). This would result in the growth of 'elongated' concentrations of industries between major centres, such as that between Kuala Lumpur and Port Kelang in Selangor. Over time, as the infrastructure improved, industries would push into the currently less-developed regions and towards the smaller towns, forming 'mini-corridors' branching off from the major ones and ultimately helping to reduce geographical disparities in levels of development.

Though this concept was only beginning to be put into practice at the end of our period, it is clear that initially the dominance of the west-coast states of the Peninsula would be reinforced. The 'western corridor', containing 33 out of 53 urban centres with populations in excess of 10 000 in 1980, would link three prime industrial regions, the northern (Penang, Butterworth, Sungei Patani, Kulim), the central (Kuala Lumpur, Kelang, Seremban, Port Dickson), and the southern (Johor Bahru northwestwards to Segamat). On the east coast a mini-corridor would link Kota Bharu, Kuala Terengganu and Kuantan, and in East Malaysia the Industrial Master Plan proposed a 'loosely-defined enclave concept' around Kuching, Sibu, Bintulu, Kota Kinabalu, Sandakan, Tawau and Labuan (Santokh Singh, 1987, 25–8).

12.5   Infrastructure

We have seen in previous chapters that the Malaysian territories came to independence with vastly differing levels of physical infrastructure (roads, railways, ports, telecommunications, power supplies). By far the best-served regions were those along the west coast of the Peninsula, contrasting markedly with conditions on the east coast and in the Borneo territories. In 1965, for example, Sarawak had a total of 904 kilometres of state-maintained roads, of which only 224 kilometers (25 per cent) were metalled (Sarawak, *ABS*, 1977).

The general expansion of the economy, manufacturing industry in particular, created a strong demand for improved transport facilities to permit the smooth flow of goods and materials to and from ports and within the country, together with adequate utilities (water and power). Expenditure on infrastructure development over the first five Malaysia Plans (1966–90) averaged some 35 per cent of the total (see Table 10.8). By far the largest proportion went to transport, followed by communications and energy. The balance went on water supplies and sewerage/urban drainage. In East Malaysia transport, communications and utilities were the prime targets. In Sabah an average of 51 per cent of total development expenditure in Plans One to Four (1966–85) went on these facilities (calculated from Kitingan and Ongkili, 1989, Table 16) and in Sarawak 39.8 per cent (1966–90) (calculated from Wee, 1995, Tables 2.11, 2.12).

Of all forms of transport, roads and bridges received the greatest attention. In Peninsular Malaysia the largest road projects initiated in the 1980s were the trans-Peninsular East–West Highway linking Kelantan and Perak, and the North–South Highway (largely following the existing trunk route down the west coast built around the turn of the century) from Penang to Johor Bahru. New networks of feeder roads to service the regional land development schemes, plus new and upgraded rural roads to give villagers better access to towns and markets, were constructed (Fong, 1989, 244). In Sarawak priority was given to building a system of trunk roads linking major towns (for instance, Kuching–Miri, a distance of nearly 1100 kilometres) and regional centres, with the focus shifting to rural roads under the Third Plan (Sarawak Government, 1984). In Sabah a comparable project was a continuous road link from Sandakan to Kota Kinabalu. Probably the largest long-term project was the Trans-Borneo highway to connect Sabah, Sarawak and Brunei. Overall, these developments enabled, and at the same time were driven by, a substantial growth in motor vehicles in Malaysia, which increased from 26 per 1000 population in 1970 to 89 in 1985 (Fong, 1989, 245).

Despite this progress Sabah and Sarawak still lagged far behind Peninsular Malaysia in 1990. The latter had a total of some 41 000 kilometres of roads (82 per cent paved) against 8675 kilometres (31.4 per cent paved) in Sabah, with Sarawak poorly served with only 4456 kilometres (30 per cent paved) (calculated from Wee, 1995, Table 2.7).

As the main alternative to road transport, the railways in the Peninsula and Sabah have had a struggle to achieve profitability without any extensions to the existing networks. Privatisation was on the horizon for Malayan Railways (KTM) in the late 1980s. Given the importance of external trade, the expansion of ports in all parts of Malaysia was vital. Penang and Port Kelang continued to dominate in the Peninsula, with Johor Port emerging in competition with Singapore. In East Malaysia Bintulu was developed as a specialised port for oil and LNG shipments. In the mid-1970s the Malaysian International Shipping Corporation was set up to lessen foreign dominance in the export and import trades. With the geographical separation of the Malaysian territories, civil aviation assumed importance both for passenger travel and air cargo with Malaysian Airline System (1973) operating domestically and internationally (Fong, 1989, 246–51). As an example Sabah experienced an annual growth of 13.1 per cent in total aircraft passengers and 15.3 per cent in air freight from 1963 to 1986 (Kitingan and Ongkili, 1989, Table 17).

Energy supplies were one area in which the Malaysian economy was hard pressed to keep up with rapidly expanding demand, especially during the 1980s with consumption growing at around 7 per cent a year. Between 1980 and 1990 the manufacturing sector constituted the largest source of demand, rising from 32.8 per cent to 34 per cent with transport and communications between about 15.5 and 17.5 per cent (UN, 1991, Table IV.28). Electricity generation was carried out by the National Electricity Board (NEB, later Tenaga Nasional) in the Peninsula, with similar bodies in Sabah and Sarawak. The principal fuels used were oil and petroleum products (over 60 per cent). Natural gas came to prominence in the 1980s, supplying 18 per cent of fuel in 1985 (UN, 1991, Table IV.28). Hydro-power, coal and coke, firewood and so on were relatively minor sources for much of the period. Coal production in Malaysia had ceased in 1960.

Due to the abundance of resources domestically Malaysia had a declining need to import fuels, with energy imports falling from 11 per cent of merchandise exports in 1965 to 4 per cent in 1987 (UN, 1991, 117). However, the heavy dependence on a depleting asset, petroleum, led to the adoption in the 1980s of a 'Four Fuel Strategy' which aimed at an energy-base spanning petroleum, natural gas, coal and hydro-power in more balanced proportions by the 1990s. Considerable expenditure went into developing the second and third of these. In 1982 Petronas launched the Peninsular Gas Utilisation Project to convey supplies from the source off-shore at Terengganu initially to a petrochemical plant, steel mill, power generating station and other users in that state, and later to other parts of the Peninsula via a cross-country pipeline. It proved difficult, though, for Petronas and major consumers such as Tenaga Nasional to agree on the supply price for the gas (Tate, 1991, 312–24; UN, 1991, 120).

Hydro-power is an energy source with vast potential, but its distribution is ill-matched with the centres of population and production. Peninsular Malaysia, with 82 per cent of the population, has only 1 per cent of the potential, whereas Sarawak has 9 per cent of population but a massive 71 per cent of the potential power. In the latter state a major hydro-power project at Batang Ai helped to increase generating capacity by some 98 per cent between 1980 and 1985 (Fong, 1989, 257). But, for this hydro-power to become available to the Peninsula economy a link needed to be built involving about 800 kilometres of cable of which 620 would be undersea; a dauntingly large cost and technical problem. The power supply was to come from another, even more massive, hydro-power scheme requiring the construction of a dam at Bakun on the Rajang river covering 18 000 hectares, displacing many thousands of people. The cost was estimated at $15 billion (*FEER*, 10 Mar. 1994). This project was alternately pursued and shelved during the 1980s and early 1990s, but was finally put on hold after the economy deteriorated in 1997. The ecological ramifications of these projects are examined in Chapter 13.4.

The period of the NEP thus saw very large expansion of the physical infrastructure in Malaysia for many classes of user: urban, rural, industrial and domestic. Rural electrification schemes were a priority under the Fourth Plan (1981–5) benefiting nearly 450 000 households (of which 86 per cent were in the Peninsula) (Fong, 1989, 257). None the less it became clear in the 1980s that the infrastructure was barely up to the demands placed on it and might well retard future industrial growth. Power failures ('brown outs') were frequent in industrial centres such as Kelang valley, Penang and Melaka. A UN study predicted that Malaysia's road and highway systems, water and electricity supplies would reach capacity limits by 1993 (UN, 1991, 123).

12.6 Overview

To what extent had Malaysia undergone an 'industrial revolution' between about 1960 and 1990? In broad terms the structural changes followed the conventional pattern of a relative decline in the share of primary industries and an increase in that of secondary industries. In the late 1980s manufactures overtook agriculture as a contributor to GDP. The economy had moved through the early and middle stages of industrialisation and into the late stage (see Chapter 10.2). The urbanised proportion of the population was approaching 40 per cent (Table 10.7). The physical and institutional infrastructure had been substantially improved.

It can certainly be said, therefore, that by 1990 Malaysia was well down the track towards industrialisation: however, at that date the process still had some considerable way to go before it could be considered 'indigenised'. This term is not used with any ethnic connotations, but rather in the sense of pervading the entire fabric of the Malaysian economy. An analogous process was the introduction of rubber in the 1870s, requiring the best part of half a century to take root (quite literally) as the leading sector of the economy. In the case of manufacturing industry, despite some 30 years of rapid growth, the roots were still relatively shallow.

In this chapter we have surveyed the contributions of capital, labour and technology to the industrial growth process. In the case of each of these factors although there was some degree of intermingling – for example between foreign and domestic capital, and within domestic capital itself (Chinese and *bumiputera* capital) – none the less there remained quite a strong degree of segmentation. Continuing with the example of capital, FDI was confined largely to the export sector and in particular to the FTZs. The 'footloose' character of much of this investment was crucial in the migration of industries to Malaysia in the early ISI and EOI stages, where they were able to start up with few links to pre-existing industries (Garnaut, Grilli and Riedel, 1995, 33). However, they possessed the potential to leave the country relatively quickly if conditions deteriorated. Domestic capital, too, could and did take flight in the late 1970s/early 1980s.

In the labour market there was some inter-sectoral mobility, with *bumiputeras* in particular moving from rural areas to towns and employment in government, industry, the professions and so on. However, the economy could not have achieved a rapid rate of growth had not foreign workers come in to relieve the shortages in agriculture and construction. Internal labour migration occurred largely within Peninsular and East Malaysia, with little movement between the two regions.

Among all the factors, dependence on foreign technology gave most cause for concern. A UN report in 1985 detected 'complacency, probably derived from easy access to the foreign partners, [which] has hindered the formation of any coherent ... policy designed to develop indigenous industrial technology ... [T]here is no synergistic effect ... between government policies and the activities of the private sector' (cited in Jesudason, 1989, 160).

13

The Distribution of the Benefits

Per capita GDP in Malaysia rose from $1828 in 1950 to $3088 (1985 international dollars) in 1973, the period in which the foundations of rapid development were laid, and then to $5775 in 1990. The annual rate of growth in these two periods was 2.2 per cent and 3.8 per cent respectively. In the first period the performance was relatively modest, surpassed easily in Southeast Asia by Singapore (7.1 per cent) and Thailand (3.8 per cent), with Indonesia and the Philippines only slightly better (2.4 per cent). In the second period, however, only Singapore (6 per cent) and Thailand (5.2 per cent) achieved faster growth (Table 7.2 above).

The distribution of these much enhanced levels of income between and within the various ethnic groups, between urban and rural dwellers, and between the various states in the Malaysian Federation, has been a contentious issue. Marked differences also appeared in the distribution of services (notably education and health), and also in the impact of rapid development on the physical environment. Before examining these various aspects, it will assist the reader to have an outline of the pattern of social change in Malaysia since the mid-1960s, in order to show the increasing complexity of the social order as reflected in the proliferation of income-producing occupations.

13.1   Outline of social change

'Malaysia's rapid economic growth … since independence transformed its class structure. The most striking changes have been the rapid growth of the urban middle class and the decline in rural occupations' (Crouch, 1996, 181). Tables 13.1 and 13.2 show the distribution of employment in terms of occupation and ethnicity in selected years.

From the first of these tables we can see the growth in each of the categories 1–5 (see key to Table 13.1). Analysts usually take the first four of these as containing the bulk of 'middle-class' occupations. The services sector (5) does contain some managerial posts but is excluded from the present analysis following Crouch (1996, 181–2). On this basis Table 13.1 shows the middle class doubling proportionately in Peninsular Malaysia from approximately 16 per cent in 1960 to 32 per cent in 1988. In Sabah, with its less developed employment structure, the proportions were smaller at 7.6 per cent and 26.3 per cent respectively, though the difference had narrowed by 1988. The increase in Sarawak was similar from 7.9 per cent in 1960 to 22.3 per cent in 1988. There was a general decline in the rural sector (6), greatest in the Peninsula which also took the lead in new production and transport jobs.

As an example of the effects of industrialisation on the expansion in middle-class job categories, the electronics industry in the 1970s and 1980s saw the emergence of a 'middle stratum of skilled workers, computer scientists and engineers ... located somewhere between the unskilled worker on the shop floor and the, often expatriate, general management' (Kahn, 1996, 63).

In ethnic terms Table 13.2 reflects the progressive weakening of the links between race and economic function. Peninsular Malays recorded major gains in all middle-class categories, especially (2), (3) and (4), and became predominant in the professions (1), clerical (3), services (5) and production (7). The Chinese and Indian share fell in all categories, though the general growth in employment meant that in absolute terms more were absorbed except in agriculture. In East Malaysia the Sabah figures for 1960 are not

Table 13.1   Distribution of employed persons by occupation, 1960 and 1988 (%)

				Category (see key)			
	(1)	*(2)*	*(3)*	*(4)*	*(5)*	*(6)*	*(7)*
Pen. M'ysia							
1960[a]	3.1	1.2	2.9	8.6	8.6	56.7	19.0
1988	7.6	2.2	9.7	12.5	12.5	26.9	28.6
Sabah							
1960[a]	1.8	0.4	2.0	3.4	3.2	77.3	11.9
1988	6.2	1.9	9.2	9.0	9.6	44.7	19.5
Sarawak							
1960	2.1	0.3	1.5	4.0	2.3	81.5	8.3
1988	6.3	1.1	6.4	8.5	7.9	52.0	17.9

[a] 1957.

Key: (1) Professional, Technical and Related; (2) Administrative and Managerial; (3) Clerical and Related; (4) Sales and Related; (5) Services; (6) Agriculture, Husbandry, Forestry, Fishermen, Hunters; (7) Production, Transport Equipment Operators.

Sources: 1960, calculated from Snodgrass (1980), Table 4.17; Colclough, Table 6 in Abdul Majid Mat Salleh, Solhee and Kasim (1990); *ABS*, Sabah, 1972, Table 3.6; 1988 calculated from Malaysian Government (1990), Tables 1.12, 1.13, 1.14.

Table 13.2 Malaysia: distribution of employed persons by occupation and ethnic group, 1960 and 1988 (%)

Year[a]	(1)		(2)		(3)		Category (4)		(5)		(6)		(7)	
	1960	1988	1960	1988	1960	1988	1960	1988	1960	1988	1960	1988	1960	1988
Pen. M'ysia														
Bumiputera	41	58	17	35	27	54	16	36	40	59	62	70	27	46
Chinese	39	33	67	55	46	37	66	56	36	27	24	19	54	41
Indian	11	8	12	6	19	9	17	7	13	12	13	11	19	12
Sabah[b]														
Bumiputera	1	77	1	32	1	66	1	51	2	82	91	96	6	74
Chinese	5	22	1	65	7	33	15	46	9	16	35	3	28	25
Sarawak [1960 data n.a.]														
Bumiputera.		51		15		53		30		64		90		53
Chinese		42		80		46		69		31		9		46

n.a. = not available.

[a] 1957 for Peninsular Malaysia.

[b] Figures for 1960 not directly comparable with 1988, or with Pen.Malaysia for 1957. For Pen.Malaysia they represent percentage of total employment in each category. For Sabah they are proportions of the total workforce in each ethnic group. For 1988 both regions are on the same basis.

Key: (1) Professional, Technical and Related; (2) Administrative and Managerial; (3) Clerical and Related; (4) Sales and Related; (5) Services; (6) Agriculture, Husbandry, Forestry, Fishermen, Hunters; (7) Production, Transport Equipment Operators.

Sources: Snodgrass (1980), Table 4.17; Malaysian Government (1990)Tables B3.7; C3.7, D3.7; Sabah, *Statistical Handbook* 1972, Table 3.6.

comparable with 1988, though they indicate the very low *bumiputera* involvement in the modern sector at the first date. By the latter date this group predominated in all sectors except for administrative/managerial (2). Sarawak data for 1960 are unobtainable, but the 1988 figures show the Chinese more strongly represented in categories (2) and (4).

The data in Table 13.2 do not permit a precise calculation of the middle-class component within each ethnic group, but another study gives this for Malaysia as a whole as approximately 27 per cent each for *bumiputeras* and Indians, and 43 per cent for Chinese in 1990 against roughly 13 per cent, 23 per cent and 29 per cent respectively in 1970 (Crouch, 1996, Table 4). It is not surprising that under the NEP the *bumiputera* middle class showed the largest proportionate growth, followed by Chinese, but the Indians showed relatively little increase (a mere 4 per cent). Whilst the latter were comparatively well-represented in certain professions such as law and medicine (approximately 29 per cent and 36 per cent receptively of the totals in the Peninsula), this group experienced most difficulty in breaking away from earlier employment patterns. In the late 1980s plantation workers, mostly rubber, still accounted for 63 per cent of all Indian households (*FEER*, 7 June 1990)

Table 13.2 shows a substantial relative decline in agricultural employment (6) in the Peninsula among non-*bumiputeras,* but a contrary upward trend for *bumiputeras.* None the less, the rural development programmes created new employment and income-earning categories. The promotion of *bumiputera* enterprise under the NEP meant that this group was able to break away from the colonial pattern in which most jobs outside the production of rice, rubber and so on had been held by non-indigenes. The trend to off-farm employment can be illustrated by a field study of a village in Upper Perak in the late 1970s in which the occupational structure of 70 non-agricultural household heads had, as major categories, 53 per cent business-men, petty traders and white-collar government employees, a further 17 per cent government blue-collar workers, and 16 per cent timber workers (Wan Hashim, 1988, Table 8.2).

In Selangor NEP rural development projects generated a profusion of lucrative contracts which local politicians used as the means of dispensing patronage, enriching supporters, bypassing their opponents, and helping to produce a new class of *bumiputera* small capitalist entrepreneurs in the villages (Shamsul, 1986, 241–5). At the general level, government intervention in the rural economy through development schemes involving corporate institutions (e.g., FELDA, FELCRA, smallholder cooperatives) promoted social differentiation by advancing the system of production beyond the '[simple] household form' (Muhammad Ikmal Said, 1990, 74) which had reached its peak during the colonial period.

Similar changes were also taking place in East Malaysia, but the impact was intensified by the pressures of modernisation on the indigenous groups there. These may be illustrated with the case of the Sarawak Iban who, in the nineteenth and much of the twentieth century:

> were secure in their position at the centre of their universe. Structurally and ritually, the longhouse was the focal point ... All this has [by the 1970s] changed ... The Iban are no longer secure .... many are anxious about what they perceive as their marginality ... they are now expanding into urban areas and being brought within the sphere of modern cultures.

> (Sutlive, 1978, 171)

In recent decades the town of Sibu 'has emerged as a new niche with an important resource – cash' to act as an exchange centre for the 'scores of Iban traders' who have set up businesses in the surrounding rural areas (Sutlive, 1978, 156). Using our criteria for middle-class occupations, approximately 38 out of 168 (22.6 per cent) in a sample of economically active Iban in Sibu in 1970 could be classified in this group (calculated from Sutlive, 1978, Table 7–3). The Sarawak coastal town of Bintulu, with its burgeoning industrial and port facilities, performed a similar function in attracting people from the surrounding Kemena Basin into off-farm employment (Morrison, 1993).

13.2   Income distribution and poverty eradication

The pattern of income distribution has implications for a country's standard of living, level of savings (and thereby investment and the rate of economic growth), as well as overall political and social stability. The degree of equality/inequality is usually measured in terms of the Gini coefficient on a scale from 0 (complete equality) to 1 (complete inequality). Empirical values normally fall in the range between 0.3 and 0.6 (Snodgrass, 1980, 103n.7). Over the period from the mid-1960s to the late 1980s the countries of East and Southeast Asia were generally successful in decreasing income inequality along with the incidence of poverty. In 1990 the Gini values for Singapore (0.42), and the ASEAN-4, Malaysia (0.48), Thailand (0.47), the Philippines (0.45) and Indonesia (0.31) (Drakakis-Smith, 1993, Table 3) all fall in the lower half of the scale.

In Malaysia's case the importance of income distribution and poverty reduction was heightened by the issue of inequality between and within the various ethnic groups. This has attracted a considerable volume of research, most of which focuses on the Peninsula. Data on the East Malaysian states did not become available until the 1970s. The accuracy of the official statistics, in particular the calculation of the poverty line income (PLI) and the resultant proportion of poor households, has been critically assessed as tending to underestimation (see Jomo, 1990a, 145–51).

The existence of substantial inter-ethnic income inequality in the Peninsula was evident in the early postwar years (Table 9.2 above). The first thirteen years of independence (1957–70) saw a further growth in disparity as indicated by the rise in the Gini coefficient from 0.412 to 0.513 (Table 13.3), and the rise in the ratio of incomes, especially Chinese against Malay (Table 13.4). Just over half (52.5 per cent) of income growth in this period went to Chinese, with 37.8 per cent to Malays and only 9.4 per cent to Indians (Perumal, 1992, Table 4). Hirschman (1975a) found that the mean incomes of the top 20 per cent rose by 39 per cent, whilst those of the bottom 20 per cent fell by 14 per cent. The urban:rural income ratio moved in favour of the former, easily explainable by the expansion of import-substitution industrialisation during this period and slower growth of productivity in the agricultural sector, especially among rice growers and rubber smallholders. These groups contained the highest proportions of poor households at 88.1 per cent and 64.7 per cent respectively in 1970 (Jomo, 1990a, Table 7.1).

Inequality continued to increase in Peninsular Malaysia during the early years of the NEP up to 1976 with the Gini coefficient going from 0.513 to

Table 13.3   Peninsular Malaysia: household income by ethnic group, 1957–84 ($1959 prices)

	1957/8	1970	1976	1984
Malay				
Mean	134	170	234	380
	1.24[a]	1.43	1.48	1.47
Median	108	119	158	258
Chinese				
Mean	288	390	533	669
	1.35[a]	1.47	1.64	1.47
Median	214	265	325	456
Indian				
Mean	228	300	364	488
	–	1.56[a]	1.50	1.42
Median	228	192	243	343
All Races				
Mean	207	261	348	488
	1.38[a]	1.59	1.64	1.52
Median	150	164	212	322
Gini Coefficient	0.412	0.513	0.567	0.480

[a] Mean divided by median, author's calculation. A rise means increasing inequality, and a fall the reverse.
Source: Perumal (1989), Table 2.

0.567 (Table 13.3), though the annual rates of growth of household incomes for all ethnic groups were substantially above those in the previous period, with Malays in the lead at 5.47 per cent, Chinese 5.34 per cent and Indians 3.28 per cent (calculated from Table 13.3). In terms of the ratio of incomes, however, Malays made only a very marginal gain against the Chinese though rather more against the Indians (Table 13.4). Income inequality increased in the urban areas, due most probably to the wider variety of types of employment and differentials in rates of pay. The rural–urban income differential narrowed slightly (Table 13.4) as the numbers and scope of development projects directed at *bumiputera* improvement increased under the NEP. The scattered data for East Malaysia (Tables 13.4, 13.5) show much wider income differentials and incidences of poverty, indicating that the bulk of benefit from development was going to urban-based interests (Leigh, 1979).

The next eight years (1976–84) saw a marked diminution in income inequality throughout Malaysia. Peninsular Malay mean incomes grew at 6.25 per cent a year, faster than before, whilst those of the Chinese and Indians slowed markedly to 2.88 per cent and 3.73 per cent respectively (calculated from Table 13.3). The Gini coefficient fell appreciably from 0.567 to 0.480. Income ratios (Table 13.4) tell a similar story, with the Chinese:Malay ratio now substantially more favourable to the latter than in 1957/8. During these years the Malay share of income growth was between

Table 13.4 Malaysia: income differentials by race and location, 1957/8–89

Ratio of mean incomes	1957/8	1970	1976	1984	1989
Peninsular Malaysia[a]					
Chinese:Malay	2.15	2.29	2.28	1.76	1.70[b]
Indian:Malay	1.70	1.76	1.56	1.28	1.29
Chinese:Indian	1.26	1.30	1.46	1.37	1.32
Urban:Rural	1.85	2.14	2.11	1.87	1.72
Sabah					
Chinese:*Bumiputera*	n.a.	n.a.	3.46[c]	2.70[b]	2.50[b]
Urban:Rural	n.a.	2.74[c]	n.a	1.90[d]	1.62[d]
Sarawak					
Chinese:*Bumiputera*	n.a.	n.a.	3.40[c]	1.87[d]	1.88[d]
Urban:Rural	n.a.	2.70[c]	n.a.	2.22[d]	1.77[d]

n.a. = not available.
[a] 1957/8–84 at 1959 prices.
[b] 1979 prices.
[c] Current prices.
[d] 1978 prices.
Sources: Perumal (1989), Table 4; calculated from Wee (1995), Table 5.3; Malaysian Government (1991a), Table 10.1. and (1991b), Table 2.5.

Table 13.5   Malaysia: incidence of poverty by ethnic group, 1970, 1976, 1990 (%)

	1970	1976	1990
Pen. M'ysia			
Bumiputera	65.0	n.a.	20.8
Chinese	26.0	n.a.	5.7
Indian	39.0	n.a.	8.0
Overall	49.3	n.a.	15.0
Sabah			
Bumiputera	n.a.	67.1	41.2
Chinese	n.a.	22.2	4.0
Overall	n.a.	58.3	34.3
Sarawak			
Bumiputera	n.a.	68.7	28.5
Chinese	n.a.	29.6	4.4
Overall	n.a.	56.5	21.0
Malaysia			
Overall	n.a.	42.4	17.1

n.a. = not available.
Source: Malaysian Government (1991b), Table 2.6.

about 47 and 52 per cent against 34 to 45 per cent (Chinese), and some 8 to 12.5 per cent (Indians) (Perumal, 1992, Table 4). The position of Indians relative to Malays (1.28 against 1.70) had deteriorated, but was little altered against Chinese. The urban:rural ratio had practically returned to its 1957/8 level.

Trends were similar in East Malaysia, though the incidence of poverty was still considerably higher (Tables 13.4, 13.5). Rural monthly incomes grew very rapidly. From 1970 to 1984 these rose by about 92 per cent in Sabah and 119 per cent in Sarawak (1978 prices), but could not match the massive near-200 per cent surge in the Peninsula (calculated from Wee, 1995, Table 5.3). This suggests that rural development schemes had more positive effects in Peninsular Malaysia.

The major driving forces behind the rapid growth of incomes in this period were the expansion of export-oriented industrialisation, especially in the west-coast states of the Peninsula, and the booming primary export industries in East Malaysia. Rural development in general created the new forms of employment noted in the previous section. It should be remembered that government activity in the economy was at its height during this time, financed in large part with revenue from primary exports, notably petroleum. This public expenditure constituted a substantial transfer payment in the process of redistribution of incomes, which in general benefited *bumiputeras* over non-*bumiputeras,* and among the former, the better-off groups more than the poorer ones. Fiscal policy on taxation also tended to favour *bumiputeras,* and possibly had a regressive effect on income distribution within that group although the findings of various studies are at variance on this point (Jomo, 1990a, 95–100).

During the slump from 1984 to 1987 urban incomes throughout Malaysia were most severely affected, falling by nearly 15 per cent in Sabah and 7–8 per cent in Sarawak and Peninsular Malaysia (calculated from Wee, 1995, Table 5.3). This reflected the depressed state of manufacturing industry. Rural incomes, on the other hand, showed barely any change. In the economic recovery which began in the late 1980s income ratios again narrowed in all states, though least so in Sabah where Chinese incomes were still 2.5 times those of *bumiputeras* in 1989 (Table 13.4). The rates of poverty reduction slowed and in Sabah even increased slightly, giving that state the highest rural and urban levels in the federation (Table 13.5).

Despite some 20 years of redistributive policies a number of points stood out in the late 1980s. First, the inter-ethnic income ratios, though considerably narrowed, still favoured non-*bumiputeras* quite substantially (Table 13.4). Second, intra-ethnic income inequality as measured by the Gini coefficient among Peninsular Malays was higher in 1987 (0.477) than in 1970 (0.466), but lower among Chinese (0.430 against 0.455) and Indians (0.402 against 0.463) (Ishak and Ragayah, 1990, Table 2). Comparable information for East Malaysia was not obtainable. In terms of household income shares for Malaysia overall, the top 20 per cent and middle 40 per cent lost a little ground to the bottom 40 per cent over the period of the NEP. Taking rural households, the respective averages were 50, 35 and 15 per cent in 1990 against 53, 36 and 12 per cent in 1970 (calculated from Wee, 1995, Figures 5.2–5.4).

Third, it can be said that in general the NEP had led to few large shifts in the regional relativities of national income (in terms of per capita GDP) and incidence of poverty. For those states with the heaviest concentrations of manufacturing industries (the Peninsula west coast) the relationship was inverse: that is, higher per capita incomes were associated with lower incidence of poverty. Likewise, the poorer, less-industrialised, Peninsula states (for instance, Kedah and Kelantan) had high poverty levels. However, in several primary-product dependent states both income per capita and the poverty levels were relatively high. Terengganu leapt from twelfth to first place in income per capita following the oil and gas discoveries, but still had 31.2 per cent poverty (the second highest) in 1990. Sabah and Sarawak ranked fourth and sixth highest respectively in income in 1990 (against second and eighth in 1970) and first and fifth in poverty levels (fifth and sixth in 1976) (Wee, 1995, Tables 3.11, 5.9). Table 13.6 shows that by 1980 both Sabah and Sarawak had lost considerable ground to Peninsular Malaysia in terms of their proportions of average Malaysian

GDP per capita, recovering by 1990 (though in Sabah's case well short of the 1970 relativity and for Sarawak no net gain).

What were the factors which produced and maintained this geographical pattern of income distribution and incidence of poverty? One analysis explains the situation in terms of 'dominant core' regions (such as Selangor and the Federal Capital Territory) and 'peripheral' regions (north and east in the Peninsula, Sabah, Sarawak). The former had better access to material resources, notably infrastructure, and – very importantly – more weight in the process of political decision-making. The latter 'have little say in where and in what manner resources are to be used ... they tend to be the objects of development ... rather than being agents and active participants' (King and Parnwell, 1990, 2).

Let us look at some examples of this dichotomy. With few exceptions those states which were able to attract the new export industries achieved the largest decreases in the poverty ratio. Among these industries manufacturing, with its relatively strong demand for labour, appears as the major contributor. On the other hand, the burgeoning primary industries, notably timber, petroleum and natural gas, did not have such extensive demand linkages. Logging is a constantly shifting industry, which brings only short-term income and employment benefits to a particular locality. Timber contractors tended to employ contract workers brought in from outside an area, leaving only the lowest paid jobs for local labourers. The prime benefits were concentrated in a few hands (Lian, 1990, 124–6), namely the concession holders and contractors. Natural gas and petroleum industries were of the enclave variety with relatively few points of contact with the local economy such as the Lutong refinery and LNG plant at Bintulu. Moreover, a substantial proportion of the export earnings (the federal petroleum royalty) was removed from these states and therefore did not benefit the generality of the people.

Table 13.6   Malaysia: per capita GDP by region, selected years ($1978 prices)

	1970	1980	1990
Pen. M'ysia	875[a]	2955	3996
	(90)[b]	(92)	(98)
Sabah	1177	3066	4500
	(118)[b]	(95)	(102)
Sarawak	881	2292	3883
	(89)[b]	(71)	(88)
Malaysia	994	3221	4392

[a] Unweighted average of all Peninsular states.
[b] Bracketed figures show percentage of Malaysian average.
Sources: Calculated from Wee (1995), Table 3.11; Malaysian Government (1991b), Table 2.8.

Those localities with some particular advantage such as a good infrastructure of transport and communications or proximity to ports were best placed to take advantage of opportunities for development. Often these advantages had long historical roots. In Peninsular Malaysia the Kuala Lumpur/Kelang valley region had been a centre of rubber and tin production since the late nineteenth century, and was a natural focus for the growth of an industrial conurbation stretching from the federal capital to Port Kelang in the 1970s and 1980s (Aiken *et al.*, 1982; Lee Boon Thong, 1994). The district of Kuala Langat (Selangor), populated largely by Javanese migrants from the late nineteenth century, had a continuous history of commercial smallholder agriculture (coffee, rubber, oil palms, cocoa). The people possessed a strong work ethic, a good spirit of cooperation and self-help (*gotong royong*), together with effective village leaders. Incomes in the 1980s were well above the average for this type of enterprise (Jali, 1990, 60–76).

Marked inequalities in income were on the whole a newer phenomenon in East Malaysia, and emerged in the process of opening up the country mainly through improved communications which exposed indigenous communities to external forces. For example, among the Bidayuh (Land Dayak) people of the Upper Sadong district in Sarawak the distribution of household resources had been fairly equal until postwar. Such inequalities as occurred tended to be accidental, and any deliberate attempt to accumulate material wealth ('prestige goods') attracted strong social disapproval. From the 1950s an 'indiscriminate' rush into cash crops (pepper and rubber) occurred in which some were more fortunate than others; incomes diverged and social controls weakened whilst desire for change strengthened, encouraged by official development projects. Fragmentation took place in village life, epitomised by the construction of detached houses by the more successful. Inequality appeared to have become entrenched (Grijpstra, 1976, Chapter 15).

Despite the efforts towards redistribution, the incidence of poverty in Malaysia towards the end of the NEP remained overwhelmingly rural. Rice farmers stood out in all regions, with approximately 79 per cent in Sabah, 56 per cent in Sarawak, and 40 per cent in Peninsular Malaysia below the poverty line income. Rubber smallholders were not far behind at 67 per cent, 62 per cent and 40 per cent respectively. Coconut smallholders and fishermen also had significant ratios, the former around 75 per cent in Sabah (approximate readings from Wee, 1995, Figure 5.6).

The explanation for these regional differences in residual or 'hard core' poverty lay primarily in the better response to land and agricultural development programmes in Peninsular Malaysia discussed in Chapter 11. Crop yields were generally lower in East Malaysia, and small farmers had progressed less far along the continuum from subsistence to largely commercialised operations: for example, the Iban in Sarawak had arrived at a 'diversified *semi*-commercial type of agriculture supplemented by off-farm employment' (Cramb, 1988, 130).

The urban–rural divide has remained quite distinct over the last two or three decades. Town dwellers experienced the largest gains, with a transformed physical environment of high-rise offices, public and private housing estates, shopping centres, and all manner of service facilities. Whilst some rural dwellers benefited greatly, for many the changes swept aside traditional ways of living and this, together with an increasing need for cash, has brought new insecurities and sources of resentment. We have seen the impact on the less-developed communities in East Malaysia. Poorer farmers in the rice bowl areas of Peninsular Malaysia, such as the Muda region, have developed a resistance to changes such as the introduction of mechanised harvesting (see Scott, 1985). As younger people, men and women, move out of the villages to seek employment in industry, the armed forces or the services sector, the money they send back has created a dependence on remittances among the older family members who remain, especially those who have derived the least direct benefits from development programmes.

> From the standpoint of the rural scene, it could be argued that the development policies pursued since Independence ... may together have succeeded too well ... In the longer term ... the commercialisation of rural production has [created] a growing need for state intervention to replace the 'safety net' of both the old rural social system and the essentially transitory remittance economy that is taking its place.
>
> (Brookfield, 1994, 79–80)

This comment was made in relation to Peninsular Malaysia, but has much relevance to East Malaysia as well.

Whilst the official figures permitted government to argue that the NEP target for poverty eradication by 1990 (16.7 per cent in the Peninsula; none was specified for East Malaysia) had been surpassed at 15 per cent (Malaysian Government 1991b, Table 2.6), the impact of income redistribution on the growth of the economy is difficult to assess in detail. Kuznets has theorised that in the early stages of modern economic growth income inequality first increases and then later decreases (represented by an inverted U-shaped curve). This is caused by the movement of labour from the agricultural sector, where inequality is less pronounced, to the industrial sector where productivity and incomes are higher. Once the agricultural labour surplus has been transferred, a similar rise in wages occurs in that sector and inter-sectoral inequality decreases (Dowling, Ifzal Ali and Soo, 1985).

There has been considerable discussion as to whether a trend of this type has emerged in Malaysia since independence The data in Tables 13.3 and

13.4 offer some support, but the general view seems to be that a firm judgement would be premature. The period involved, some three decades, is relatively short, whilst Kuznets based his conclusions on more than a century of growth in now fully-developed countries. The Malaysian data do not include items such as undistributed company earnings and capital gains which would favour the higher-income groups (see Ishak and Ragayah, 1990, 112; Randolph, 1990). Moreover, as we have seen (Chapter 12.2), Malaysian economic growth was not based principally on a transfer of surplus labour out of agriculture but rather additional sources of labour, such as women and immigrant workers. It is clear, though, that without some intervention such as the NEP in 1970 to tackle the problems of income inequality and poverty, increasing inter-ethnic tensions (particularly in Peninsular Malaysia) would in all probability have had adverse effects on the general climate for continued rapid economic growth in subsequent years.

13.3 Social services

In this section attention will be focused on education, medical and other utilities (such as piped water). The importance of these in the economic development process is that improvements help to create a workforce which is physically healthier, more literate and numerate, which in turn facilitates increased productivity and adaptation to technological change. In education the implied rate of return on investment in developing countries is at least equal to if not better than that from non-human capital (D. Lim, 1996, ch. 6). A major feature of post-Independence Malaysia has been the greatly increased demand from all ethnic groups for education at all levels.

Education

The first priority lay with the expansion of primary and secondary education. This was facilitated as development projects improved the network of roads and communications, especially in the rural areas. Primary school effective enrolments (there was some backlog of over-age students at first) in Peninsular Malaysia leapt from 58 per cent of the eligible age group in 1955 to to 86 per cent in 1960, and stabilised around 91 per cent by the early 1970s. This represented an overall increase of 97 per cent in less than 20 years. In Sabah and Sarawak, starting from a lower base, the increase over the same period was even more startling at 217 per cent, gaining speed after federation (Rudner, 1994, ch. 12, Table 5). The enrolment rate in these states reached 90 per cent from the mid-1970s.

A significant feature of these sharply rising enrolment rates was the growing proportion of women. At the primary level only 44 per cent of the eligible female age group was enrolled in Malaya in 1953, as against 78 per cent of males. Again, expansion was extremely rapid, reaching 89 per cent of potential by the late 1960s, and bringing females to 49 per cent of total enrolments. Progress in this last respect was slower in East Malaysia, attaining 45 per cent by 1973. There was also a marked general improvement in school retention rates (Rudner, 1994, 321–2).

These developments had a knock-on effect on secondary school enrolments which in Peninsular Malaysia increased by nearly 73 per cent (1965–70), 86 per cent in the 1970s, and 56 per cent in the 1980s. Enrolment ratios by 1980 stood at about 75 per cent for lower secondary, and 41 per cent for upper secondary schools (Crouch, 1996, 186). Comparable ratios are not available for East Malaysia, but as an indication of the fast growth from a small base, secondary pupils in Sabah went from under 7000 in 1963 to nearly 110 000 in 1988 (Kitingan and Ongkili, 1989, 293), practically a 16-fold increase. For Malaysia as a whole, secondary education enrolments rose from 28 per cent to 59 per cent of potential between 1965 and 1987, with the proportion of female students going from 39 per cent to 58 per cent of potential between 1975 and 1991 (Jones in Ogawa, Jones and Williamson, 1993, Table 8.4; *FEER*, 19 May 1994).

Extensive development of tertiary education began towards the end of the 1960s, just prior to the NEP. The number of universities in Malaysia grew from one to seven by 1990, together with numerous colleges, technical and vocational schools. Total tertiary enrolments at government and government-aided institutions expanded from some 13 000 in 1965 to 194 000 in 1990, plus nearly 36 000 at private institutions and (in 1985) about 35 000 studying overseas (Crouch, 1996, 186). The age group enrolment ratio went from 2 per cent in 1965 to 7 per cent in 1987 (Jones in Ogawa, Jones and Williamson, 1993, Table 8.4).

The development plan allocations (actual expenditure achieved was usually somewhat lower) to education and training fluctuated over time (Table 13.7), but on average were slightly higher in East than in Peninsular Malaysia from 1966 to 1990, though there was a sharp increase for the latter region under the Fifth Malaysia Plan. In per capita terms Peninsular Malaysia allocated $828 for education and training (1966–90), against $758 in Sabah and $649 in Sarawak (Wee, 1995, Table 2.13). However, on the basis of estimated expenditure per student, East Malaysia came out well ahead: for example in 1984 in secondary education the respective figures were $694 against $1715 and $1279 (Institute of Strategic and International Studies, 1986, 114).

How well did this major expansion meet the needs of the nation? Education was expected to serve political and social aims, as well as economic ones. Under the NEP the national language, Bahasa Malaysia, was introduced progressively as the medium of instruction at all levels. A quota system of access to higher education boosted *bumiputera* enrolment shares in local tertiary institutions to 67 per cent in degree courses (1980), and approximately

Table 13.7   Development plan allocations by region: education, health, social and community services, 1966–90 (% of total)

	1MP[a]	2MP	3MP	4MP	5MP	1966–90
Education/Training						
Pen. M'ysia[b]	9.7	7.7	8.0	8.5	14.3	10.6
Sabah	9.1	5.6	14.8	13.6	11.7	12.0
Sarawak	11.5	7.6	11.9	9.7	12.0	10.9
Health						
Pen. M'ysia[b]	3.9	2.8	2.0	1.6	1.6	1.9
Sabah	6.1	3.9	1.7	3.1	1.8	2.5
Sarawak	5.2	3.3	1.7	2.0	4.4	3.0
Social Services[c]						
Pen. M'ysia[b]	7.3	3.4	5.6	8.8	7.4	7.3
Sabah	5.7	9.9	3.4	4.3	2.3	3.9
Sarawak	5.0	8.5	6.0	3.7	3.5	4.5

[a] MP = Malaysia Plan.
[b] Separate figure not available. Calculated as residual when Sabah/Sarawak deducted from Malaysian total.
[c] Includes Community Services.
Source: Calculated from Wee (1995), Table 2.12.

93 per cent in diploma and 70 per cent in certificate courses (1988) (Crouch, 1996, 188). This was a leading factor in the emergence of a *bumiputera* middle class (see section 13.1). At lower levels of the education system, as a proportion of youths aged 15, *bumiputeras* had already by 1972 achieved near parity of enrolments (45 per cent) with Chinese (47 per cent), and were better than Indians (39 per cent) (Snodgrass, 1980, Table 9.5). The latter, in particular the children of estate workers, remained educationally disadvantaged throughout the NEP period, as Tamil schools on estates suffered from inadequate numbers and poor training of teachers, proportionately low enrolment ratios coupled with high student drop-out rates and so on (Ramachandran, 1995).

The system was also intended to foster national solidarity through a common language and ideology (*rukunegara*), but was less successful here. The Director-General of Education observed in the mid-1980s that the continuing segregation of primary and some secondary schools along ethnic lines fostered significant differences in learning experience, together with ethnic polarisation, low levels of aspiration and competitive spirit. Educational levels in East Malaysia were below those in the Peninsula, with a slower growth of tertiary institutions, particularly at university level.

In economic terms, whilst the workforce became generally more literate and numerate, by the 1980s a situation of 'education-occupation mismatch' was developing. The slump of the mid-1980s saw estimated unemployment at 15–19 per cent among graduates, nearly 90 per cent of whom were *bumiputeras* (Jones in Ogawa, Jones and Williamson, 1993, 255). Many aimed at a job in government or related fields on which a recruitment freeze was imposed. When conditions of rapid economic growth returned after 1988 unemployment declined, but the educational system was found to be producing far too few graduates in certain fields, notably engineers. By the early 1990s there was a shortfall of some 4000 engineers a year, which necessitated recruitment from India and the Philippines (*FEER*, 29 Sept. 1994). The Malaysian ratio of R and D scientists and technicians was 3.7 per 10 000 people in 1985–9, well above ASEAN neighbours (Indonesia 1.7, Thailand 1.5, the Philippines 1.1), but far short of the East Asian newly industrialising economies such as South Korea with 21.6 (D. Lim, 1996, Table 6.9).

Health

There is no doubt that, overall, conditions of living in Malaysia improved very considerably in this period. Life expectancy increased from 61.6 to 69 years for males, and from 65.6 to 73.5 years for females between 1970 and 1990. The infant mortality rate dropped by two-thirds (39.4 to 13.5 per 1000 live births). The ratio of doctors to population improved from 1:4302 to 1:2656. The daily calorie intake in 1988 was 2686 (119 per cent of requirements). Nearly 70 per cent of houses had a piped water supply, and just over 71 per cent had electricity in 1985 (Cho, 1990, Table 1.7; Malaysian Government, 1991b, Table 2.4; D. Lim, 1996, Table 6.5). Table 13.7 indicates that in proportionate terms development plan allocations for health declined almost continuously, but picked up in Sarawak under the Fifth Plan. On a per capita basis the East Malaysian states received higher allocations than the Peninsula except for Sabah in the Fifth Plan (Wee, 1995, Figure 5.7). As a share of GDP Malaysian health expenditure was 6.4 per cent in 1981, by far the highest in the Asian region (Singapore was next at 4.8 per cent) (D. Lim, 1996, Table 6.10).

However, there were wide regional variations in health conditions, access to water, electricity, clinics, hospitals and so on. The west-coast states in the Peninsula were served the best, facilitated of course by the relatively good communications infrastructure. Ninety per cent of the population in the Peninsula lived within 3.2–4.8 kilometres of a government clinic. Roughly 80–90 per cent of west-coast households had piped water and electricity by 1985. The east-coast states and the Borneo territories faced major problems here, with between 30 to 70 per cent of households with these amenities. In Sabah, for instance, approximately 43–45 per cent of the rural population had safe water and sanitary facilities in-house or nearby (Kitingan and Ongkili, 1989, 245; Cho, 1990. Table 1.7; Wee, 1995, 119).

Levels of 'diseases of underdevelopment' (such as malaria, tuberculosis, dysentery, typhoid) were significantly higher than those in the Peninsula.

For example, 10.2 per cent of in-patients treated and new admissions at government hospitals and dispensaries in Sabah from 1976–1984 were for malaria compared to 0.6 per cent in the Peninsula. Sarawak had a very low incidence of this disease (0.4), but more tuberculosis cases (2.7 per cent against 1.2 per cent) (Wee, 1995, Table 5.18). However, the trend in many diseases in East Malaysia, notably dysentery, typhoid, pneumonia (less so in Sarawak), was markedly downwards compared to earlier periods. Surveys in Sarawak just postwar showed disease rates in the 80–90 per cent range among rural people. By contrast, in the NEP period remote areas such as the Belaga district (upper Rajang river, Sarawak) gained static and travelling dispensaries, upriver dresser stations and a flying doctor service for those beyond the reach of clinics. None the less, 'while the population as a whole is [now] reasonably fit and healthy, symptoms of undernourishment … are common' (Alexander and Alexander, 1993, 258).

13.4   The environment

The environmental impacts of the growth of both primary and secondary industries was felt most strongly in the sphere of land use: for example, expansion in the cultivated area (see Table 11.1), accelerated deforestation through commercial logging and land development schemes, urbanisation, new infrastructure (ports, highways, dams). Peninsular and East Malaysia came to federation with experiences in land use similar in essence but differing in degree. The problem common to both regions following the development of export production from the late nineteenth century had been a tension between the expanding frontier of commercial land usage and the subsistence needs of the indigenous communities. The differences in degree lie in the policies which were pursued, especially since federation, some of which exacerbated rather than resolved this tension.

In the Peninsula, as we saw in Chapter 4.3, the colonial government acted relatively quickly to distinguish between agricultural production for export (mainly rubber) from subsistence production (rice, coconuts, vegetables) and the 'traditional' village lifestyle. The principal device was the FMS Malay Reservations Enactment (1913), a blanket device which failed to prevent large numbers of Malays from taking up commercial rubber production but which, in the longer term, imposed restrictive conditions on land use and exchange. After independence Malay farmers were encouraged to become commercially oriented, whilst the main thrust in land use shifted to the large, publicly-funded, schemes such as FELDA. The extensive areas of virgin forest cleared for such schemes were in sparsely populated regions, such as central and southeast Pahang, and thus did not require substantial displacement of existing Malay communities. Commercial logging in these areas also rapidly extended deforestation.

Between 1966 and 1978 the area of primary forest in the Peninsula decreased by some 15 per cent (Cho, 1990, 106).

These changes had a major impact on the communities of *orang asli*, affecting the basis of their traditional lifestyle of shifting cultivation and hunting/gathering. Government policy since 1980 promoted the regrouping of *orang asli* in designated Central Areas, involving a switch to sedentary commercial farming. Thirteen such projects were scheduled under the Fourth Plan (1981–5), but of these only eight were operational by 1988. Numerous practical problems, coupled with a widespread reluctance among *orang asli* to give up traditional ways of living, slowed progress and delivery of the promised material benefits of higher living standards (Zahid Emby, 1990, 94–109).

A similar situation, but of much wider incidence, emerged in East Malaysia where logging and land development schemes impinged increasingly on many indigenous tribal groups. In Sarawak an estimated 30 per cent of the forest area was denuded by logging between 1963 and 1986, and in Sabah commercial forests were reduced by two-thirds from 1972 to 1985 (Cleary and Eaton, 1992, 137). The situation regarding land ownership was considerably more complicated than in the Peninsula. In Sarawak, for example, the security of native customary land among the various categories (mixed zone, reserved, interior area and so on) became increasingly tenuous as the pressure from politically well-connected interests for timber concessions intensified. Federal and state agencies pursued development schemes which further constricted native customary land, and involved resettlement that threatened to transform many of the indigenes into a wage labour force for estates. Hydro-electric development began with the Batang Ai scheme, opened in 1985, flooding 8400 hectares and entailing the resettlement (with major economic and social dislocation) of about 3000 Iban. This was dwarfed by a proposal to build a dam at Bakun on the upper Rajang flooding 73 000 hectares, displacing over 5000 people from 52 longhouses and submerging several schools and dispensaries (Hong, 1987, 170–90). Work on this project did not begin until the mid-1990s, and was shelved with the onset of the global economic crisis.

The net effects from all these changes were evident in the physical landscape of the East Malaysian states. Deforestation spread to the uplands. Timber felling and the accompanying infrastructure of logging roads, camps and so on led to denudation of forest cover, heavy losses of topsoil, and also silting-up of rivers, with concomitant damage to flora and fauna. In human terms there was widespread disruption of traditional patterns of settlement, shifting agriculture, food-gathering and general social/cultural relationships. Monetary compensation for loss of native customary land rights, housing and so on was often slow in materialising, and where paid, the sudden excess of cash above subsistence needs has often been quickly dissipated in unproductive ways (liquor, cockfighting, conspicuous consumption) (Hong, 1987; Colchester, 1989).

The tensions generated and popular reactions such as blockading access to timber concessions, involving armed confrontations on occasion, are well exemplified by the experience of the Penan (numbering around 10 000) in Sarawak. Pressures to abandon their hunter-gatherer existence and adopt a more settled lifestyle predate the timber boom, but have been vastly intensified by it. The extent to which groups of Penan have been able to adapt to changing conditions has varied. In Belaga district they 'live in isolated areas away from outside pressures [and] have been able to keep the pace of change and development to a level to which their society can adjust'. In Limbang district, on the other hand, they 'are not optimistic about their future. The ... land allocated to them is inadequate for them to survive on' (Langub, 1996, 113, 114).

Among the responses of government to the pressures on the environment have been the creation of national parks and wildlife sanctuaries (totalling just over 250 000 hectares in Sarawak by 1985: calculated from Colchester, 1989, Table 4), though these too have involved the resumption of native customary lands and extinguishment of traditional access to forest resources. Another line of policy has aimed at the development of 'eco-tourism' to capitalise on conservation of existing assets (for instance, the orang-utan, turtles, Mount Kinabalu in Sabah), and the building of special facilities such as wildlife centres where research, tourism and traditional ways of life could coexist (*FEER*, 1 July 1993), though perhaps somewhat uneasily.

A recent multi-disciplinary study concludes that in general the Malaysian government's approach to natural resource-use (land, forests, fisheries, water, mines) in this period emphasised maximum production and revenue-earning rather than management following principles of strict cost-benefit analysis (Vincent, Ali and Associates, 1997, 352–9).

13.5 Overview

In these decades of rapid change Malaysian society moved away from the situation in the colonial period in which membership of a particular ethnic group had been a major factor in determining a person's occupation, income-earning potential and general role in the process of economic growth. This does not mean that being of *bumiputera,* Chinese, Indian or other ethnic origin was by itself the crucial determinant for an *individual* in these respects, although the British tended to ascribe to individuals what they considered to be inherent general characteristics. Rather, the argument here is that these groups, through historical interaction over an extended period, had *collectively* produced a structure in which economic functions were distributed along ethnic lines.

The NEP had considerable success in altering this situation. However, it can be argued that the state, by operating through a process of affirmative action towards *bumiputeras*, had in fact helped in the emergence of another structure in which a person's ethnicity itself had come to play a definitive role affecting the distribution of occupation, wealth, education and so on. Again, this is not meant to imply anything about the intrinsic qualities of a particular ethnic group. What it did do between 1970 and 1990 was to subject distribution to criteria other than primarily economic ones, such as political patronage. It is clear, though, that as already noted, without some intervention such as the NEP to tackle the problems of income inequality, employment structure and incidence of poverty, it is unlikely that Malaysia's development experience would have been anywhere near as successful as we have seen.

14
The Perspective from History

There is general agreement among observers that the transformation in the Malaysian economy since about 1963 has been highly impressive. Descriptions such as 'phenomenal' (Athukorala and Menon, 1996, 2), and 'surprising in light of the experience of much of the rest of the developing world' (Vincent, Ali and Associates, 1997, xi) have been applied. These suggest that the unquestionably rapid economic growth post-Independence was due to some distinctively new formula discovered by Malaysia, in common with the other countries, collectively referred to as the 'Asian miracle'.

However, as our historical study shows, this growth and transformation had lengthy antecedents. Major changes in the volume and structure of production and trade were in progress, especially in the Peninsula, from *c.*1800. By that time these territories had already experienced some three centuries of spasmodic economic growth of the premodern type in which external stimuli had been the main driving force. At this stage the sparse population meant little pressure to stimulate production for domestic consumption. The predominant ethos, among both the indigenous elites and the foreign elements (Asian and European) was mercantilist: that is, the export of a range of primary products in return for imports, principally manufactures and foodstuffs. The rulers in the Malay sultanates in the Peninsula and Brunei exercised a patrimonial and personal control over the distribution of the gains from trade which was not very favourable to local accumulation of wealth by the elite or foreign merchants. Among the tribal groups in Borneo participation in the procurement of trade goods had elements of compulsion, or 'forced trade', due to competition among local elites for the power which control conferred. None the less, the basic elements of the later primary exporting economies were already present. The favourable geographical location of the Peninsula in relation to long-distance maritime trade routes was evident in the growth of port-polities, notably Melaka, Johor-Riau and Kuala Terengganu.

The economic history of Malaysia since 1800 can be viewed as a gradual filling-up of the natural resource-rich region with population and various forms of productive activity. British colonial rule brought an economic regime operating on principles of free trade which created new entrepots (Penang, Singapore) from which merchants conducted a network of transactions with minimum impositions from government. This helped to loosen traditional constraints on capitalist enterprise.

The first major spurt in growth (c.1870–1929) resulted from the rapid expansion of two staple commodities, tin and then rubber (the latter introduced on government initiative), both raw materials essential to the 'second industrial revolution' in the West. These brought in foreign capital (accompanied by corporate ownership) and immigrants on an unprecedented scale, as well as involving locally resident Asian merchants and substantial numbers of indigenous small farmers. They also helped to generate numerous ancillary activities (produce dealers, mercantile firms, transport, banking and shipping networks) creating geographical concentrations of export production such as the Kelang valley (Selangor) in the Peninsula which later provided focal points for industrialisation. However, at this early stage, apart from some competition for labour in the early 1900s and some mobility in Chinese capital, the staple industries did not interact with each other in competition for resources, and had only limited linkages with other local industries, mainly processing ones. The Borneo territories were less extensively affected because of their peripheral geographical position, poor infrastructure and governments with very limited financial resources.

The colonial state was not so much patrimonial along traditional lines as paternalistic in its dealings with the indigenous population. In the Peninsula, though many Malays took up commercial rubber cultivation against the wishes of officials, as a community they were left outside the mainstream of economic progress by devices such as Malay reservations. As in many tropical colonial countries, the government 'made more progress in creating administrative [rather] than entrepreneurial *elites*' (Lewis, 1970, 35) from among the indigenous peoples. In North Borneo and Sarawak the Chartered Company and the Brookes dealt with different situations. The indigenous populations, especially in the interior, were much more mobile and a good deal of official resources was expended in 'settling' the various groups in defined locations and heading off intergroup conflicts.

This long phase of export-led growth was one during which per capita incomes grew faster than those of any other country in the Asian region (Table 7.2). Insofar as Malaysia had an economic 'core', this lay in Singapore, though the concentration of export production along the west coast of the Peninsula, and the growth of Kuala Lumpur, presaged the rivalry which was to emerge post-Independence. As Fisher (1956, 309) has remarked in the context of Malaya and Singapore (but with equal applicability to Malaysia as a whole), 'prior to 1914 the effect of geography on politics is paramount; but ... since that time the influence of politics on geography is at least equally to the fore'.

For the quarter-century to 1950 the growth impetus weakened as the economy ran into problems of over-supply of tin and rubber against declining foreign demand. Government's resort to export control schemes for both these commodities retarded technological change, especially in rubber production. Although new primary industries (oil palms, iron ore) appeared, their scale was insufficient to have a major impact. Import-substitution industrialisation made little headway, due partly to prevailing attitudes and policies in the colonial government, and partly to the small, politically divided (SS, FMS, UMS) domestic market. The Pacific war and Japanese occupation period was wholly negative from the viewpoint of growth.

Postwar the Malaysian territories faced a changed situation. North Borneo and Sarawak, under direct colonial rule from London, started a more systematic exploitation of their economic potential (surveys, development plans and so on), but were still well behind Malaya. Whilst the primary export industries throughout the region, rubber and tin especially, had of necessity to be reconstructed, it was evident by the early 1950s that these could not provide a stable basis for long-term development. With the advent of independence it was clear, too, that general rural development was needed to raise the standard of living of the indigenous farmers and bring them into the mainstream of the economy. However, though inequality in incomes had created large concentrations of poverty along ethnic lines, income per capita overall was still one of the highest in Asia (see Table 7.2). Malaysia was not a poor country in either relative or absolute terms.

Post-Independence the state was the major initiator of development, creating an environment within which private capital would operate. The formula adopted was basically the same as that which had served well in the earlier period of growth: that is, an open economy with a leading role for foreign capital, coupled with new measures chosen pragmatically to meet Malaysia's need to maintain inter-ethnic harmony, principally the NEP. One difference from the tin and rubber boom, though, was that because of the reluctance of non-*bumiputera* Malaysians to invest in relatively illiquid industrial assets, foreign capital was a substitute for, rather than a complement to, domestic funds.

The NEP was the distinctively Malaysian solution to the need to combine rapid economic growth with a restructuring of wealth ownership, employment and a large reduction in the incidence of poverty. It illustrates an important requirement for a new national state, namely decisive and realistic political leadership. Under colonial rule there was little scope for independent action by (British) Malaysian officials. Broad policy issues, such as the commodity control schemes, were decided in London. After independence a new group of leading personalities, *bumiputeras* in particular, emerged to take control at state and federal level. The constant preoccupation of these leaders was maintenance of the political and social stability essential to underpin continued rapid economic growth. This was evidenced in sound macro-economic policies, administered by a generally efficient civil service, to operate an open economy increasingly linked to the dynamic East Asian region.

In this writer's view, these various factors are far more relevant to explaining Malaysia's economic success than that of a prevailing ideology (religious or philosophical) such as Confucianism, held by some commentators to be central to East Asian rapid progress. Here, as in so many areas, Malaysia showed such diversity that no one set of values was dominant in the economic sphere. We should not forget either that the attempt to import ideologies under the 'Look East' policy was not especially successful.

By 1990 Malaysia as a whole had dissolved the colonial economic structure and avoided the 'staple trap' (see Chapter 1.1) by grafting on industrial enterprise and technology largely from external sources rather than depending on industrialisation to develop from within the domestic economy. This meant, however, that dependency on a relatively narrow range of export products, notably electrical/electronic goods and textiles, remained strong.

For a variety of reasons, mainly geographical location, poor infrastructures, higher costs and peripheral position in federal politics, the economies of Sabah and Sarawak and some Peninsular states, notably Kelantan, encountered much more difficulty in getting started on a transition to industrialisation. Insofar as they remained dependent on a small range of primary commodities (timber, oil, natural gas) it can be argued that they are in a 'staple trap'. The patrimonial style of the federal government in the distribution of development funds to the states (reminiscent of precolonial rulers and their supporters), the surrender of the bulk of oil revenues, and the preferences of wealthy local elites for seeking profits from resource (timber) exploitation have been important factors retarding industrialisation, in addition to the factors mentioned above.

There is much in Malaysia's historical experience up to 1990 which is similar to neighbouring countries: for example Thailand and Indonesia developed primary exporting economies and industrialised rapidly. Both imported foreign capital and enterprise, but neither had the degree of openness possessed by Malaysia which enabled the country to fuel expansion with external resources of sufficient magnitude to exert an overall transforming effect on the economy.

14.1   Postscript

By 1990 Malaysia still had a considerable way to go to attain the top rung of the technological 'ladder' by moving into high-technology industries. The

NEP was replaced by the New Development Policy (NDP) planned to culminate in a fully developed (industrialised) economy by 2020. The national growth rate remained high, real GDP expanding at approximately 8.7 per cent a year from 1990 to 1996, whilst the incidence of poverty declined to around 8 per cent by 1995 (though per capita incomes remained lower in East Malaysia). Massive capital projects were planned, including a Multimedia Super Corridor just south of Kuala Lumpur at a planned cost of 50 billion *ringgit* to boost the country into the information technology sphere. A construction boom, including facilities for the 1998 Commonwealth Games, transformed the federal capital. Preparatory work began on the Bakun dam in Sarawak (*FEER*, 4 Sept. 1997). 'Money politics' and privatisation remained powerful influences on the operation of the economy.

This headlong advance was abruptly reversed from mid-1997 under the impact of the economic 'meltdown' in East and Southeast Asia which saw national currencies such as the *ringgit* lose much of their exchange value. The Malaysian economy contracted by an estimated 7 per cent in 1998. Under pressure of events Prime Minister Mahathir, a prominent critic of international currency speculators and the austere remedial policies favoured by agencies such as the IMF, announced from 1 October 1998 a fixed US$–*ringgit* exchange rate, a freeze on external dealing in the *ringgit*, and restrictions on remittance of foreign capital which had been in Malaysia less than twelve months. Concurrently, the dismissal of Anwar Ibrahim as Deputy Prime Minister, followed by his arrest and trial on various charges, have generated popular demand for *reformasi* (reform) in major areas of national life, not least in the conduct of the economy (*FEER*, 21/28 Jan. 1999).

These measures marked an abrupt move away from the longstanding open-economy policy but were, none the less, very much in line with the pragmatism which has characterised post-Independence Malaysian policy. Helen Hughes (1993, 5) has remarked that 'as soon as paradigms are deserted for reality it becomes evident that … at least five different "models" [of development] apply in developing East Asia'. This judgement could be extended to say that, with some broad similarities, each country in the region is constructing an individual path to an industrialised economy. From the perspective of history Malaysia's transition to modern economic growth, particularly in recent decades, cannot accurately be described as 'miraculous' but, nevertheless, with its distinctive combination of both foreign and domestic resources in the nineteenth and twentieth centuries, it has been thus far one of the smoothest and most successful in the developing world.

Bibliography

Note: for abbreviations of journal titles, please refer to list (pp. xvii–xviii above).

Abdul Aziz Abdul Rahman (1998), 'Economic Reforms and Agricultural Development in Malaysia', *ASEAN Economic Bulletin,* 15, 1, 59–76.

Abdullah Azmi bin Abdul Khalid (1981), 'The Trade of Malaya with special reference to the Federated Malay States 1900–40' (MA Hons, University of Sydney).

Abdul Majid Mat Salleh, Hatta Solhee and Mohd Yusof Kasim (eds) (1990), *Socio-Economic Development in Sarawak: Policies and Strategies for the 1990s,* Kuching: Angkatan Zaman Mansang (Azam).

Abraham W.I. and Gill, M.S. (1969), 'The Growth and Composition of Malaysia's Capital Stock', *MER,* xiv, No. 2, 44–53.

Abu Bakar, M., Amarjit Kaur and Ghazali, A.Z. (eds) (1984), *HISTORIA: Essays in Commemoration of the 25th Anniversary of the Department of History, University of Malaya,* Kuala Lumpur: Malaysian Historical Society.

Adelman, I. and Morris, C.T. (1997), 'Development History and Its Implications for Development Theory', *World Development,* 25, No. 6, 831–40.

Aiken, S.R., Leigh, C.H., Leinbach, T.R. and Moss, M.R. (1982), *Development and Environment in Peninsular Malaysia,* Singapore: McGraw-Hill.

Alavi, Rokiah (1996), *Industrialisation in Malaysia: Import Substitution and Infant Industry Performance,* London: Routledge.

Alexander, J. and Alexander, P. (1993), 'Economic Change and Public Health in a Remote Sarawak Community', *Sojourn,* 8, No. 2 (Aug.), 250–74.

Allen, G.C. and Donnithorne, A. (1954), *Western Enterprise in Indonesia and Malaya,* London: Geo. Allen & Unwin.

Amarjit Kaur (1985), *Bridge and Barrier: Transport and Communications in Colonial Malaya 1870–1957.* Kuala Lumpur: Oxford University Press.

Amarjit Kaur (1992), *Irrigation and Rice Cultivation in West Malaysia,* Centre for Southeast Asian Studies, University of Hull, Occasional Paper No. 21.

Amarjit Kaur (1998), *Economic Change in East Malaysia: Sabah and Sarawak since 1850,* London: Macmillan.

Ampalavanar, Rajeswary (1971/2), 'The Chettiars and British Policy in Malaya 1920–41', *Tamil Oli,* 9, 76–86.

Amriah Buang (1991), 'Behind the Un-economic Size of the Malay's Idle Agricultural Land', *MTJG,* 22, 2, 103–12.

Amsden, A. (1997), 'Bringing Production back in – Understanding Government's Economic role in Late Industrialisation', *World Development,* 25, 4, 469–80.

Andaya, B. (1983), 'Melaka under the Dutch 1641–1795', in Sandhu and Wheatley (1983).

Andaya, L.Y. (1992), 'Interactions with the Outside World and Adaptation in Southeast Asian Society', in Tarling, N. (ed.), *Cambridge History of Southeast Asia, I,* Cambridge: Cambridge University Press.

Andaya, L.Y. and Andaya, B. (1982), *A History of Malaysia,* London: Macmillan.

Anderson, J.N. and Vorster, W.T. (1983), 'Diversity and Inter-dependence in the Trade Hinterlands of Melaka', in Sandhu and Wheatley (1983).

Anuwar, Ali (1992), *Malaysia's Industrialisation: The Quest for Technology,* Singapore: Oxford University Press.

Anuwar, Ali (1993), 'Technological Transfer and the Malaysian Manufacturing Sector', in Jomo (1993).

Anuwar, Ali and Wong, P.K. (1993), 'Direct Foreign Investment in the Malaysian Industrial Sector', in Jomo (1993).

Appell, G.N. (1977), 'The Status of Social Science Research in Sarawak and its relevance for development', *Studies in Third World Societies,* No. 2.

Ariff, Mohamed (1991), *The Malaysian Economy: Pacific Connections,* Singapore: Oxford University Press.

Asian Development Bank (1990), *Key Indicators of Developing Asian and Pacific Countries,* Manila: Asian Development Bank.

Athukorala, P.C. and Menon, J. (1996), 'Export-Led Industrialisation, Employment and Equity: The Malaysian Case', Working Papers in Trade and Development 96/5, Dept of Economics, RSPAS, Canberra: Australian National University.

Bakar, Hamzah (1990), 'Opportunities in Petrochemical and Petroleum Related Industries in Sarawak', in Abdul Majid Mat Salleh *et al.* (1990).

Baker, M.H. (1962), *North Borneo: The First Ten Years 1946–56,* Singapore: MPH.

Baldwin, W.L. (1983), *The World Tin Market,* Durham, NC: Duke University Press.

Banuri, Tariq (ed.) (1991), *Economic Liberalization: No Panacea. The Experiences of Latin America and Asia,* Oxford: Clarendon Press.

Barlow, Colin (1978), *The Natural Rubber Industry: Its Development, Technology and Economy in Malaysia* (with Special Annex Tables), Kuala Lumpur: Oxford University Press.

Barlow, Colin (1985a), 'Institutional and Policy Implications of Economic Change: Malaysian Rubber 1950–85', *Kajian Ekonomi Malaysia,* XXII, No. 2, 57–76.

Barlow, Colin (1985b), 'The Oil Palm Industry', *Outlook on Agriculture,* 14, No. 4, 204–11.

Barlow, Colin (1990), 'Changes in the Economic Position of Workers on Rubber Estates and Smallholdings in Peninsular Malaysia 1910–85', in Rimmer and Allen (1990).

Barlow, Colin (1997), 'Growth, Structural Change and Plantation Tree Crops: The Case of Rubber', *World Development,* 25, 10, 1589–607.

Barlow, C. and Jayasuriya S.K. (1986), 'Stages of Development in Smallholder Tree Crop Agriculture', *Development and Change,* 17, 4, 635–58.

Barlow, C., Findlay, C., Forsyth, P. and Jayasuriya, S.K. (1986), 'The Impact of Malaysian Structural Change on Traditional Industries: The Case of Rubber', *SER* (Apr.), 18–32.

Barlow, C., Jayasuriya, S. and Tan, C. Suan (1994), *The World Rubber Industry,* London: Routledge.

Bassett, D.K. (1989), 'British Country Trade and Local Trade Networks in the Thai and Malay States', *MAS,* 23, 4, 625–43.

Bhanoji Rao, V.V. (1974), 'The Postwar Development Pattern and Policy of the Malaysian Economy', PhD, University of Singapore.

Bhanoji Rao, V.V. (1980), *Malaysia: Development Pattern and Policy, 1947–1971,* Singapore University Press.

Bhar, S. (1980), 'Sandakan 1879–1979', *JMBRAS,* LIII, Pt 1, 120–49.

Bilas, Richard A. (1963), 'The Growth of Physical Output in the Federation of Malaya 1930–60', *MER,* VIII, No. 2, 81–90.

Black, Ian (1983), *A Gambling Style of Government: The Establishment of the Chartered Company's Rule in Sabah 1878–1915,* Kuala Lumpur: Oxford University Press.

Booth, Anne (1990), 'The Economic Development of Southeast Asia 1870–1985', Working Paper No. 63, Centre of Southeast Asian Studies, Monash University.

Booth, Anne (1991), 'The Economic Development of Southeast Asia 1870–1985', *Australian Economic History Review*, XXXI, No. 1, 20- 52.

Bowie, A. (1991), *Crossing the Industrial Divide: State, Society and The Politics of Economic Transformation in Malaysia*, New York: Columbia University Press.

Bray, F. (1986), *The Rice Economies,* Oxford: Basil Blackwell.

Brookfield, H. (ed.) (1994), *Transformation with Industrialization in Peninsular Malaysia*, Kuala Lumpur: Oxford University Press.

Brown, D.E. (1970), *Brunei: The Structure and History of a Bornean Malay Sultanate,* Brunei Museums Journal, Monograph No. 2.

Brown, Ian (1993), 'Imperialism, Trade and Investment in the Late Nineteenth and Early Twentieth Centuries', in Butcher and Dick (1993).

Brown, Rajeswary A. (1994), *Capital and Entrepreneurship in South-East Asia*, New York: St Martin's Press.

Bugo, H. (1984), *The Economic Development of Sarawak: The Effects of Export Instability,* Kuching: Summer Times Publishing.

Burns, Peter (1982), 'Capitalism and the Malay States', in Alavi, H., Burns, P.L., Knight, G.R., Meyer, P. and McEachern, D. (eds), *Capitalism and Colonial Production*, London: Croom Helm.

Burrough, P.A. and Burrough, J.B. (1974), 'Sabah – 1963–73: Ten Years of Independence', *Review of Indonesian Malayan Affairs (RIMA),* 8, 2, 25–61.

Business Review Weekly, Sydney, 5 February 1996.

Butcher, John (1979), *The British in Malaya 1880–1941,* Kuala Lumpur: Oxford University Press.

Butcher, John (1993a), 'The Demise of the Revenue Farm System in the Federated Malay States' in Butcher and Dick (1993).

Butcher, John (1993b), 'Loke Yew', in Butcher and Dick (1993).

Butcher, John and Dick, Howard (eds) (1993), *The Rise and Fall of Revenue Farming: Business Elites and the Emergence of the Modern State in Southeast Asia*, New York: St Martin's Press.

Chai, Hon Chan (1964), *The Development of British Malaya 1876–1909*, Kuala Lumpur: Oxford University Press.

Chan, Kok Eng (1994), 'Internal Migration in a Rapidly Changing Country: The Case of Peninsular Malaysia', *MJTG*, 25, 2, 69–77.

Chanderbali, David S. (1983), 'Indian Indenture in the Straits Settlements 1872–1910: Policy and Practice in Province Wellesley', (PhD., Australian National University).

Chandler, Glen (1987), 'Confronting Change: Interaction Between the Timber Industry and Villagers in the Interior of Sabah', Malaysia Society *(ASAA)*-Malaysian Social Science Association Colloquium, Universiti Sains Malaysia, Penang.

Chandler, Glen (1989), 'Agricultural Development in Sabah', Occasional Paper No. 1, Development Studies Centre, Monash University.

Chaudhuri, K.N. (1990), *Asia Before Europe: Economy and Civilisation of the Indian Ocean from the rise of Islam to 1750*, Cambridge: Cambridge University Press.

Cheah, Boon Kheng (1994), 'Feudalism in Pre-Colonial Malaya: The Past as a Colonial Discourse', *JSEAS*, 25, 2 (Sept.), 243–69.

Chee, Peng Lim and Gomez E.T. (1994), 'Malaysian *sogoshoshas*: Superficial Cloning, Failed Emulation', in Jomo (1994).

Chee, Stephen (1990), 'The Political Economy of Governance: Why the Malaysian Government Has Grown', in Ambrin Buang (ed.), *The Malaysian Economy in Transition*, Kuala Lumpur: Institute of Public Administration.

Chen, Edward K.Y. (1989), 'East and Southeast Asia in the World Economy: Isssues, Problems and Prospects', in *Copenhagen Papers in East and Southeast Asian Studies, 4/89,* Centre for East and South-east Asian Studies, University of Copenhagen.

Cheng, Siok Hwa (1973), *The Rice Trade of Malaya,* Singapore University Education Press.

Chew, Daniel (1990), *Chinese Pioneers on the Sarawak Frontier 1841–1941,* Kuala Lumpur: Oxford University Press.

Chia, Siow Yue (1993), 'Foreign Direct Investment in ASEAN Economies, *Asian Development Review,* 11, 1, 60–102.

Chiang Hai Ding (1970), 'Sino-British Mercantile Relations in Singapore Entrepot Trade 1870–1915', in J. Ch'en and N. Tarling (eds), *Studies in the Social History of China and South-East Asia,* Cambridge: Cambridge University Press.

Chiang Hai Ding (1978), *A History of Straits Settlements Foreign Trade 1870–1915,* Singapore: National Museum.

Chin, John M. (1981), *The Sarawak Chinese,* Kuala Lumpur: Oxford University Press.

Cho, George (1990), *The Malaysian Economy: Spatial Perspectives,* London: Routledge.

Chow, P.C.Y. and Kellerman, M.H. (1993), *Trade – The Engine of Growth in Asia,* New York: Oxford University Press.

Christie, J.W. (1988), 'Iron Working in Sarawak', in J.W. Christie and V. King (eds), *Metal Working in Borneo: Essays on Iron- and Silver-Working in Sarawak,* Centre for S.E. Asian Studies, Hull University, Occasional Paper No. 15.

Cleary, M.C. (1996), 'Indigenous trade and European Economic Intervention in North-West Borneo c.1860–1930', *MAS,* 30, 2, 301–24.

Cleary, M.C. and Eaton, P. (1992), *Borneo: Change and Development,* Singapore: Oxford University Press.

Colchester, M. (1989), *Pirates, Squatters and Poachers: The Political Ecology of Dispossession of the Native Peoples of Sarawak,* London: Survival International.

Courtenay, P.P. (1972), *A Geography of Trade and Development in Malaya,* London: Bell.

Courtenay, P.P. (1995), *The Rice Sector of Peninsula Malaysia: A Rural Paradox,* Sydney: Allen & Unwin.

Cramb, R.A. (1988), 'The Commercialisation of Iban Agriculture', in Cramb and Reece (1988).

Cramb, R.A. (1989a), 'Smallholder Agricultural Development in a Land Surplus Economy; The Case of Sarawak, Malaysia 1963–88', Agricultural Economics Discussion Paper Series (2/89), Dept of Agriculture, University of Queensland.

Cramb, R.A. (1989b), 'Contradictions in State-sponsored Land Schemes for Peasant Farmers: The Case of Sarawak, East Malaysia 1963–88', Agricultural Economics Discussion Paper Series (3/89), Dept. of Agriculture, University of Queensland.

Cramb, R.A. (1990), 'The Changing Agricultural Economy of the Saribas', in Muhammad Ikmal Said and Savaranamuttu (1990).

Cramb, R.A. (1993a), 'The Evolution of Property Rights to Land in Sarawak: An Institutionalist Perspective', *Review of Marketing and Agricultural Economics,* 61, 2, Pt II, 289–300.

Cramb, R.A. (1993b), 'The Impact of the Japanese Occupation (1941–5) on Agricultural Development in Sarawak', Malaysia Society (ASAA) 8th Colloquium, University of Southern Queensland.

Cramb, R.A. and Reece, R.H.W. (eds) (1988), *Development in Sarawak,* Monash Paper on Southeast Asia, No. 17, Centre of Southeast Asian Studies, Monash University.

Crouch, Harold (1994), 'Industrialisation and Political Change' in H. Brookfield (1994).

Crouch, Harold (1996), *Government and Society in Malaysia*, Sydney: Allen & Unwin.

Crouch, H. and Morley, J.W. (1993), 'The Dynamics of Political Change', in James W. Morley (ed.), *Driven By Growth: Political Change in Asia-Pacific Region*, New York: M.E. Sharpe.

Cunyngham-Brown, S. (1971), *The Traders*, London: Newman Neame.

Curtin, P. (1984), *Cross-Cultural Trade in World History*, Cambridge: Cambridge University Press.

Cushman, Jennifer (1986), 'The Khaw Group: Chinese Business in Early Twentieth Century Penang', *JSEAS*, XVII, 1, 58–79.

Cushman, Jennifer (1991), [Edited by Craig J.Reynolds] *Family and State; The Formation of a Sino-Thai Tin-Mining Dynasty 1797–1932*, Singapore: Oxford University Press.

Denker, M.S. (1989), 'Japanese Economic Interests in Malaya and Japan–Malaya Relations in Historical Perspective', *ASIEN*, 33 (Oct.), 66–95.

Dick, H.W. (1996), 'The Emergence of a National Economy, 1808–1990s' in J.T. Lindblad (ed.), *Historical Foundations of a National Economy in Indonesia 1890s–1990s*, Amsterdam: North-Holland.

Dick, H.W. and Rimmer, P. (1989), 'Cities, Transport and Economic Integration: A Systems Approach to the Economic History of South-east Asia Since 1850', ECHOSEA Workshop, Canberra, Australian National University.

Dixon, C. and Drakakis-Smith, D. (1993), *Economic and Social Development in Pacific Asia*, London: Routledge.

Dodge, N. (1977), 'Mineral Production on the East Coast of Malaya in the Nineteenth Century', *JMBRAS*, 50, Pt 2, 89–110.

Dodge, N. (1980), 'Population Estimates for the Malay Peninsula in the Nineteenth Century with special reference to the East Coast States', *Population Studies*, XXXIV, No. 3 (Nov.), 437–73.

Dowling, J., Ifzal Ali and Soo, D. (1985), 'Income Distribution, Poverty and Economic Growth in Developing Asian Countries', *SER*, xxx, 1, 1–13.

Drabble, J.H. (1973), *Rubber in Malaya 1876–1922: The Genesis of the Industry*, Kuala Lumpur: Oxford University Press.

Drabble, J.H. (1979), 'Peasant Smallholders in the Malayan Economy, with special reference to the Rubber Industry', in J.C. Jackson and M. Rudner (eds), *Issues in Malaysian Development*, Singapore: Heinemann.

Drabble, J.H. (1983), 'The Rubber Industry in Melaka', in Sandhu and Wheatley (1983).

Drabble, J.H. (1984), 'Towards a General Economic History of Malaya: Some Preliminary Thoughts', in Abu Bakar, Amarjit Kaur and Ghazali (1984).

Drabble, J.H. (1989), 'The Emergence of the Modern Malayan Economy; The Impact of Foreign Trade in the Nineteenth Century', Monash University Centre for South East Asian Studies, Working Paper No. 54.

Drabble, J.H. (1990), 'Politics of Survival: European Reactions in Malaya to Rubber Smallholders in the Interwar Years', in Rimmer and Allen (1990).

Drabble, J.H. (1991), *Malayan Rubber: The Interwar Years*, London: Macmillan.

Drabble, J.H. and Drake P.J. (1974), 'More on the financing of Malayan rubber 1905–23', *Economic History Review*, 2nd Series, XXVII, No. 1 (Feb.), 108–20.

Drabble, J.H. and Drake, P.J. (1981), 'The British Agency Houses in Malaysia: Survival in a Changing World', *JSEAS*, XII, No. 2, 297–328.

Drabble, J.H. and Mills, J.A. (1991), 'Historical Roots of Economic Development in Malaysia: Eighteenth Century Aspects', 12th International Association of Historians of Asia (IAHA) Conference, Hong Kong.

Drabble, J.H. and Mills, J.A. (1992), 'Singapore, Riau, Johor: Some Historical Perspectives on the Growth Triangle of the 1990s', ECHOSEA workshop, Canberra, Australian National University.

Drakakis-Smith, D. (1993), 'That was then, this is now', *SJTG*, 14, 2, 88–96.

Drake, P.J. (1969), *Financial Development in Malaya and Singapore*, Canberra: Australian National University.

Drake, P.J. (1972), 'Natural Resources versus Foreign Borrowing', *Economic Journal*, 82 (Sept.), 951–62.

Drake, P.J. (1979), 'The Economic Development of British Malaya to 1914: An Essay in Historiography with some questions for Economic Historians', *JSEAS*, X, No. 2, 262–90.

Dunn, M. (1984), *Kampf um Malakka* [Struggle for Malacca], Wiesbaden: F. Steiner Verlag.

Dunn, F.L. (1975), *Rain-forest Collectors and Traders: A Study of Resource Utilisation in Modern and Ancient Malaya*, Monographs of the Malaysian Branch Royal Asiatic Society, No. 5.

Edwards, C.T. (1970), *Public Finance in Malaya and Singapore*, Canberra: Australian National University Press.

Emerson, R. (1937), *Malaysia*, Kuala Lumpur: University of Malaya Press (reprinted 1964).

Ernst, D. and O'Connor, D. (1989), *Technology and Global Competition The Challenge for Newly Industrialising Economies*, Paris: OECD Development Centre.

Evers, H.D. (1983), 'On the Evolution of Urban Society in Malaysia', in Sandhu and Wheatley (1983).

Falkus, Malcolm (1990), *The Blue Funnel Legend*, London: Macmillan.

Far Eastern Economic Review (FEER), Hong Kong, various issues.

Fatimah Mohd Arshad, Abdul Aziz Abd. Rahman, Wan, L.F. and Wong C.F. (eds) (1989), *Malaysian Agricultural Development Policy: Issues and Directions*, Centre for Agricultural Policies Studies, Serdang: Universiti Pertanian Malaysia.

Figart, David M. (1925), *Plantation Rubber in the Middle East*, Washington, DC: US Dept of Commerce.

Fisher, C.A. (1956), 'The Problem of Malayan Unity in its Geographical Setting' in C.A. Fisher *et al.* (eds), *Geographical Essays on British Tropical Lands*, London: Geo. Philip.

Fisher, C.A. (1963), 'The Geographical Setting of the Proposed Malaysian Federation', *Studies in the Geography of South-east Asia*, London: Geo. Philip.

Fisher, C.A. (1964), 'Some Comments on Population Growth in Southeast Asia since 1830', in C.D. Cowan (ed.), *The Economic Development of South-East Asia*, London: Allen & Unwin.

Fisk, E.K. and Osman-Rani, H. (1982), *The Political Economy of Malaysia*, Kuala Lumpur: Oxford University Press.

Fong, Chan Onn (1986), *Technological Leap: Malaysian Industry in Transition*, Singapore: Oxford University Press.

Fong, Chan Onn (1989), *The Malaysian Economic Challenge in the 1990s: Transformation for Growth*, Singapore: Longman.

Fredericks, L.J. (1973), 'The Impact of the Cooperative Movement in Colonial Malaya 1922–40', *JMBRAS*, 46, Pt 2, 151–68.

Fry, M.J. (1991), 'Domestic Resources Mobilization in Developing Asia', *Asian Development Review*, 9, 15–39.

Fryer, D.W. and Jackson, J.C. (1966), 'Peasant Producers or Urban Planters: The Chinese Rubber Smallholders of Ulu Selangor', *Pacific Viewpoint*, 7, No. 2, 198–228.

Fujimoto, A. (1991), 'Evolution of Rice Farming under the NEP', *The Developing Economies*, XXIX (Dec.), 431–53.

Garnaut., R, Grilli, E., and Riedel, J. (1995), *Sustaining Export-Oriented Development: Ideas from East Asia*, Cambridge: Cambridge University Press.

Golay, F. (1976), 'Southeast Asia: The Colonial Drain Revisited', in C.D. Cowan and O.W. Wolters (eds), *Southeast Asian History and Historiography: Essays Presented to D.G.E. Hall*, Ithaca, NY: Cornell University Press.

Gomez, E.T. (1990), *Politics in Business: UMNO's Corporate Investments*, Kuala Lumpur: Forum Books.

Gomez, E.T. and Jomo, K.S. (eds) (1997), *Malaysia's Political Economy: Politics, Patronage and Profits*, Cambridge: Cambridge University Press.

Grijpstra, B.G. (1976), *Common Efforts in the Development of Rural Sarawak, Malaysia*, Amsterdam: Van Gorcum.

Grijpstra, B.G. (1978), 'The Transition from Shifting Cultivation to Cash Crops: Changes in a Dayak Village', in M. Zamora, V. Sutlive and N. Altshuler (eds), *Studies in Third World Societies, No. 3*.

Gudgeon, P.S. (1981), 'Economic Development in Sabah 1881–1981', in A. Sullivan and C. Leong (eds), *A Commemorative History of Sabah 1881–1981*, Kota Kinabalu: Sabah State Government.

Guinness, P. (1992), *On the Margin of Capitalism: People and Development in Mukim Plentong, Johor, Malaysia*, Singapore: Oxford University Press.

Gullick, J.M. (1981), *Malaysia: Economic Expansion and National Unity*, London: Benn.

Gullick, J.M. (1985), 'Kedah in the Reign of Sultan Ahmad Tajuddin II (1852–79)', *JMBRAS*, LVIII, Pt 2, 107–34.

Gullick, J.M, (1989), *Malay Society in the Late Nineteenth Century*, Kuala Lumpur: Oxford University Press.

Gullick, J.M. (1990), 'The Growth of Kuala Lumpur and of the Malay Community in Selangor', *JMBRAS*, LXIII, Pt 1, 154–67.

Gullick, J.M. (1992), *Rulers and Residents: Influence and Power in the Malay States 1870–1920*, Singapore: Oxford University Press.

Gunawan, B., Raghavan, R. and Valenbreder, D. (1980), 'The Emergence of the Malay Business Class in West Malaysia', Centre for the Study of Anthropology and Sociology, Publ. No. 29, University of Amsterdam.

Hall, Kenneth R. (1985), 'The Opening of the Malay World to European Trade in the Sixteenth Century', *JMBRAS*, 58, Pt 2, 85–104.

Hanson, J.R. (1975), 'Exchange Rate Movements and Economic Development in the late Nineteenth Century: A Critique', *Journal of Political Economy*, 83, No. 4, 859–62.

Hanson, J.R. (1980), *Trade in Transition: Exports from the Third World 1840–1900*, New York: Academic Press.

Hara, F. (1991), 'Malaysia's New Economic Policy and the Chinese Business Community', *The Developing Economies*, XXIX, 4, 350–70.

Hashim, Muhammad Yusoff (1986), 'Perdagangan dan Perkapalan Melayu ... Melaka di Abad Ke-15/16', in Muhammad Yusoff Hashim *et al.* (eds), *Kapal dan Harta Karam* [Ships and Sunken Treasure], Kuala Lumpur: Muzium Negara.

Hasnah Ali (1996), 'Growth Triangles in the ASEAN Region: Issues Challenges and Prospects', ASAA 20th Anniversary Conference, La Trobe University.

Heng Pek Koon (1992), 'The Chinese Business Elites of Malaysia', in McVey (1992).

Hennart, J.F. (1986), 'Internalization in Practice: Early Direct Foreign Investment in Malaysian Tin Mining', *Journal of International Business Studies*, 16 (Summer), 131–43.

Hewgill, A.C. and Cramb, R.A. (1994), 'Land Settlement in Sabah: Politics, Problems and Prospects', ASAA 10th Conference, Murdoch University, Perth.

Hill, Hal (1993), 'Southeast Asian Economic Development: An Analytical Survey', Working Paper 93/4, Economics Division, RSPAS, Canberra: Australian National University.

Hill, Hal (1996a), 'Regional Development in Southeast Asia', Working Paper 96/1, Economics Division, RSPAS, Canberra: Australian National University.

Hill, Hal (1996b), 'Towards a Political Economy Explanation of Rapid Growth in Southeast Asia', Working Paper 96/2, Economics Division, RSPAS, Canberra: Australian National University.

Hill, R.D. (1977), *Rice in Malaya*, Kuala Lumpur: Oxford University Press.

Hill, R.D. (1982), *Agriculture in the Malaysian Region*, Budapest: Akademiai Kiado.

Hill, R.D. (1983), 'The History of Rice Cultivation in Melaka', in Sandhu and Wheatley (1983).

Hirschman, C. (1975a), 'Economic Progress in Malaysia: How widely has it been shared?', *United Malayan Banking Corporation Review*, 10, No. 2, 35–54.

Hirschman, C. (1975b), *Ethnic and Social Stratification in Peninsular Malaysia*, Washington DC: American Sociological Association.

Hirschman, C. (1989), 'Development and Inequality in Malaysia: From Puthucheary to Mehmet', *Pacific Affairs*, 62, 1, 72–81.

Hirschman, C. and Aghajanian, A. (1980), 'Women's Labour Force Participation and Socio-Economic Development: The Case of Peninsular Malaysia', *JSEAS*, XI (March), 30–49.

Hirschman, C. and Guest, P. (1990), 'The Emerging Demographic Transitions of Southeast Asia', *Population and Development Review*, 16, No. 1, 121–52.

Ho, Robert (1968), 'The Evolution of Agriculture and Land Ownership in Saiong Mukim', *MER*, 13, 81–102.

Hoffmann, L. and Tan, S.E. (1975), 'Patterns of Growth and Structural Change in West Malaysia's Manufacturing Industry 1959–68', in D. Lim (ed.), *Readings in Malaysian Economic Development*, Kuala Lumpur: Oxford University Press.

Hoffman, L. and Tan, S.E. (1980), *Industrial Growth, Employment and Foreign Investment in Peninsular Malaysia*, Kuala Lumpur: Oxford University Press.

Hong, Evelyne (1987), *Natives of Sarawak: Survival in Borneo's Vanishing Forests*, Penang: Institut Masyarakat Malaysia.

Horii, K. (1991a), 'Disintegration of the Colonial Economic Legacies and Social Restructuring in Malaysia', *The Developing Economies*, XXIX, 4, 281–313.

Horii, K. (1991b), 'Bumiputera Policy and Structural Changes in the Smallholder Economy: From Traditional to Organised Smallholder', *The Developing Economies*, XXIX, 4, 414–30.

Horner, L. (1973), 'Japanese Military Administration in Malaya and The Philippines', PhD, University of Arizona.

Houben, V.J. (1992), '"Menyang Tanah Sabrang": Javanese Coolie Migration In- and Outside Indonesia', ECHOSEA Workshop on Island Southeast Asia and the World Economy 1790s–1990s, Australian National University.

Huff, W.G. (1989), 'Bookkeeping, Barter, Money, Credit and Singapore in the International Rice Trade 1870–1939', *Explorations in Economic History*, 26, 161–89.

Huff, W.G. (unpublished), 'Finance, Banking and Economic Development in Southeast Asia since 1850', ECHOSEA Workshop Paper, Australian National University.

Huff, W.G. (1992), 'Sharecroppers, Risk, Management and Chinese Rubber Estate Development in Interwar British Malaya', *Economic Development and Cultural Change*, 40, No. 4, 743–75.

Huff, W.G. (1994), *The Economic Growth of Singapore: Trade and Development in the Twentieth Century*, Cambridge: Cambridge University Press.

Hughes, Helen (1993), 'East Asia: Is There an East Asian Model?' Working Paper 93/4, Economics Division, RSPAS, Canberra: Australian National University.

Hugo, G. (1993), 'Indonesian Labour Migration to Malaysia: Trends and Policy Implications', *Southeast Asian Journal of Social Science*, 21, No. 1, 36–70.

IBRD (1955), *The Economic Development of Malaya*, Singapore: Government Printer.

IBRD (1963), *Report on the Economic Aspects of Malaysia*, Kuala Lumpur: Government Printer.

Imada, P. (1991), 'Production and Trade Effects of an ASEAN Free Trade Area', *The Developing Economies*, XXXI, 1, 3–23.

IMF (1966/7), *International Financial Statistics, Supplement*, New York: IMF.

IMF (various years), *International Financial Statistics* New York: IMF.

Institute of Strategic and International Studies, (1986), *The Bonding of a Nation: Federalism and Territorial Integration in Malaysia*, Kuala Lumpur.

Ishak, Shari and Ragayah, Hji Mat Zin (1990), 'The Patterns and Trends of Income Distribution in Malaysia 1970–87', *SER*, XXV (Apr.), 102–23.

Jackson, James C. (1968a), *Planters and Speculators: European and Chinese Agricultural Enterprise in Malaya 1786–1921*, Kuala Lumpur: University of Malaya Press.

Jackson, James C. (1968b), *Sarawak: A Geographical Survey*, London University Press.

Jali, Nazaruddin M. (1990), 'The Javanese of Kuala Langat', in King and Parnwell (1990).

Jesudason, J.V. (1989), *Ethnicity and the Economy: The State, Chinese Business and Multinationals in Malaysia*, Singapore: Oxford University Press.

John, D.W. and Jackson, J.C. (1973), 'The Tobacco Industry of North Borneo', *JSEAS*, IV, No. 1, 88–106.

Jomo, K.S. (ed.) (1985), *Malaysia's New Economic Policies*, Kuala Lumpur: Malaysian Economic Association.

Jomo, K.S. (1988), *A Question of Class: Capital, the State and Uneven Development in Malaya*, New York: Monthly Review Press/Manila: Journal of Contemporary Asia.

Jomo, K.S. (1990a), *Growth and Structural Change in the Malaysian Economy*, London: Macmillan.

Jomo, K.S. (1990b), *Undermining Tin: The Decline of Malaysian Preeminence*, Sydney: Sydney University Transnational Corporations Research Project.

Jomo, K.S. (ed.) (1993), *Industrialising Malaysia: Policy, Performance, Prospects*, London: Routledge.

Jomo, K.S. (ed.) (1994), *Japan and Malaysian Development: In the Shadow of the Rising Sun*, London: Routledge.

Jomo, K.S. (ed.) (1995), *Privatising Malaysia: Rents, Rhetoric, Realities*, Boulder, CO: Westview Press.

Jomo, K.S. and Edwards, C. (1993), 'Malaysian Industrialisation in Historical Perspective', in Jomo (1993).

Jones, L.W. (1966), *The Population of Borneo*, London: London University Press.

Jones, Stephanie (1986), *Two Centuries of Overseas Trading: The Origins and Growth of the Inchcape Group*, London: Macmillan.

Joseph, K.T. (1988), 'The Rubber Smallholding Sector: Ethnic Perspectives and Policy Implications', in Manning Nash (ed.), *Economic Performance in Malaysia: The Insider's View*, New York: Professors' World Peace Academy.

Kahn, J.S. (1996), 'Growth, Economic Transformation, Culture and the Middle Classes in Malaysia', in R. Robison and D.S. Goodman (eds), *The New Rich in Asia*, London: Routledge.

Kathirithamby-Wells, J. (1993), 'Restraints on the Development of Merchant Capitalism in Southeast Asia before c.1800', in A.J.S. Reid (ed.), *Southeast Asia in the Early Modern Era*, Ithaca, NY: Cornell University Press.

Kathirithamby-Wells, J. and Villiers, J. (1990), *The Southeast Asian Port and Polity: Rise and Demise*, Singapore: Singapore University Press.

Kedit, P.M. (1980), *Modernization Among the Iban of Sarawak*, Kuala Lumpur: Dewan Bahasa dan Pustaka.

Khoo Boo Teik (1995), *Paradoxes of Mahathirism: An Intellectual Biography of Mahathir Mohamad*, Kuala Lumpur: Oxford University Press.

Khoo Kay Kim (1972), *The Western Malay States 1850–73: The Effects of Commercial Development on Malay Politics*, Kuala Lumpur: Oxford University Press.

Khoo Kay Kim (1974), 'Kuala Trengganu: International Trading Centre', *Malaysia in History*, (Dec.), 17–30.

Khoo Kay Kim (1988), 'Chinese Economic Activities in Malaya: An Historical Perspective', in Manning Nash (ed.), *Economic Performance in Malaysia: An Insider's View*, New York: Professors' World Peace Academy.

Khoo Kay Kim (1991), 'Taiping (Larut): The Early History of A Mining Settlement', *JMBRAS*, LXIV, Pt 1, 1–33.

Khor Kok Peng (1983), *The Malaysian Economy: Structures and Dependence*, Kuala Lumpur: Marican.

Khor Kok Peng (1987), *Malaysia's Economy in Decline*, Penang: Consumers' Association.

King, Victor T. (1978), *Essays on Borneo Societies*, Hull Monograph on S.E. Asia, No. 7, Oxford: Oxford University Press.

King, Victor T. and Parnwell, M.J. (eds) (1990), *Margins and Minorities: The Peripheral Areas and Peoples of Malaysia*, Hull: Hull University Press.

Kitingan, J.G. and Ongkili, M.J. (1989), *Sabah 25 Years Later, 1963–88*, Kota Kinabalu: Sabah Institute of Development Studies.

Koch, M. (1982), 'Malay Society in Temerloh, Pahang, under British Colonial Administration', PhD, Columbia.

Kratoska, Paul (1982), 'Rice Cultivation and the Ethnic Division of Labour in Malaya', *Comparative Studies in Society and History*, 24, No. 2, 280–314.

Kratoska, Paul (1983), 'Ends that We Cannot Foresee: Malay Reservations in British Malaya', *JSEAS*, XIV, No. 1, 149–68.

Kratoska, Paul (1988), 'The Post-1945 Food Shortage in British Malaya', *JSEAS*, XIX, No. 1, 27–47.

Kratoska, Paul (1990), 'The British Empire and the Southeast Asian Rice Crisis of 1919–21', *MAS*, 24, 1, 115–46.

Kumar, R. (1986), *The Rainforest Resources of Malaysia*, Singapore: Oxford University Press.

Kuznets, Simon (1959), *Six Lectures on Economic Growth*, London: Frank Cass.

Kuznets, Simon (1966), *Modern Economic Growth: Rate, Structure and Spread*, New Haven, Conn.: Yale University Press.

Lai, A.H. (1975), 'Problems of Federal finance in the Malaysian Plural Society', in D. Lim (ed.), *Readings on Malaysian Economic Development*, Kuala Lumpur: Oxford University Press.

Langub, J. (1996), 'Penan Response to Change and Development', in C. Padoch and N. Peluso (eds), *Borneo in Transition*, Kuala Lumpur: Oxford University Press.

Lee Boon Thong (1994), 'A Historical Analysis of Formative Settlement Patterning: A Background to the Klang Valley Dominance', *MJTG*, 25, 2, 107–14.

Lee, Edwin (1976), *The Towkays of Sabah*, Singapore: Singapore University Press.

Lee, Edwin (1991), 'Community, Family and Household', in E. Chew and E. Lee (eds), *A History of Singapore,* Singapore: Oxford University Press.

Lee Soo Ann (1974), *Economic Growth and the Public Sector in Malaya and Singapore 1948–60,* Singapore: Oxford University Press.

Lee, S.Y. (1974), *The Monetary and Banking Development of Malaysia and Singapore,* Singapore: Singapore University Press.

Lee, Y.L. (1962a), 'The Population of British Borneo', *Population Studies,* 15, 226–43.

Lee, Y.L. (1962b), 'The Port Towns of British Borneo', *Australian Geographer,* reprinted in Y.M. Yeung and C.P. Lee (eds), *Changing Southeast Asian Cities,* Kuala Lumpur: Oxford University Press.

Leete, R. (1996), *Malaysia's Demographic Transition,* Kuala Lumpur: Oxford University Press.

Leete, R. and Kwok, K.K. (1986), 'Demographic Changes in East Malaysia and their Relationship with those in the Peninsula 1960–80', *Population Studies,* 40, 83–100.

Leigh, Michael (1979), 'Is There Development in Sarawak?', in J.C. Jackson and M. Rudner (eds), *Issues in Malaysian Development,* Singapore: Heinemann.

Leigh, Michael (1988), 'The Spread of Foochow Commercial Power before the New Economic Policy', in R.A. Cramb and R.H. Reece (1988).

Leigh, Michael (1992), 'Politics, Bureaucracy, and Business in Malaysia', in A.J. Macintyre and K. Jayasuriya (eds), *The Dynamics of Economic Policy Reform in South-east Asia and the South-west Pacific,* Singapore: Oxford University Press.

Leinbach, Thomas (1972), 'The Spread of Modernization in Malaya 1895–1969', *Tijdschrift voor Econ. en Soc.Geografie, 63, 252–77.*

Levin, J. (1960), *The Export Economies,* Cambridge, MA: Harvard University Press.

Lewis, W.A. (1954), 'Economic Development with Unlimited Supplies of Labour', *The Manchester School of Economic and Social Studies,* 22, 131–91.

Lewis, W.A. (1966), *Economic Survey 1919–1939,* 8th edn, London: Allen & Unwin.

Lewis, W.A. (1969), *Aspects of Tropical Trade, 1883–1965,* Stockholm: Almquist & Wicksell.

Lewis, W.A. (1970), *Tropical Development 1880–1913: Studies in Economic Progress,* London: George Allen & Unwin.

Lewis, W.A. (1978), *The Evolution of the International Economic Order,* Princeton, NJ: Princeton University Press.

Li, Dun-jen (1982), *British Malaya: An Economic Analysis,* 2nd rev. edn, Kuala Lumpur: Institute for Social Analysis.

Lian, Francis Jana (1990), 'The Timber Industry and Economic Development in Sarawak', in Abdul Majid Mat Salleh, Solhee and Kasim (1990).

Lieberman, V. (1990), 'Wallerstein's System in the International Context of Early Modern Southeast Asian History', *Journal of Asian History,* 24, 1, 70–90.

Lim Chong Yah (1967), *Economic Development of Modern Malaya,* Kuala Lumpur: Oxford University Press.

Lim, David (1973), *Economic Growth and Development in West Malaysia 1947–70,* Kuala Lumpur: Oxford University Press.

Lim, David (1991), 'The Sabah Action Blueprint: A Development Plan in the Making', 7th Colloquium, Malaysia Society (ASAA), Melbourne University.

Lim, David (1992), 'The Dynamics of Economic Policy Making: A Study of Malaysian Trade Policies and Performance', in A.J. MacIntyre and K. Jayasuriya (eds), *The Dynamics of Policy Reform in South-east Asia and the South-west Pacific,* Singapore: Oxford University Press.

Lim, David (1993), 'Development Challenges and Opportunities for Sabah', Malaysia Society (ASAA) 8th Colloquium, University of South Queensland.

Lim, David (1994), 'Explaining the Growth Performances of Asian Developing Economies', *Economic Development and Cultural Change*, 42, No. 4 (July), 829–45.

Lim, David (1996), *Explaining Economic Growth: A New Analytical Framework*, London: Edward Elgar.

Lim Heng Kow (1978), *The Evolution of the Urban System in Malaya*, Kuala Lumpur: Penerbit Universiti Malaya.

Lim, J.S. and Shariffuddin, F.M. (1976), 'Brunei Brass: The Traditional Method of Casting', *Brunei Museums Journal*, 3, 4, 146–66.

Lim, Lin Lean (1993), 'The Feminization of Labour in the Asia-Pacific Rim Countries', in Ogawa, Jones, and Williamson (1993).

Lim Teck Ghee (1976), *Origins of a Colonial Economy: Land and Agriculture in Perak 1874–97*, Penang: Penerbit Universiti Sains Malaysia.

Lim Teck Ghee (1977), *Peasants and Their Agricultural Economy in Colonial Malaya 1874–1941*, Kuala Lumpur: Oxford University Press.

Lim Teck Ghee (1984), 'British Colonial Administration and the "Ethnic Division of Labour" in Malaya', *Kajian Malaysia*, 2, (Dec.), 28–66.

Lim Teck Ghee (1989), 'Reconstructing the Peasantry: Changes in the Landholding Structure in the Muda Irrigation Scheme', in G. Hart, A. Turton and B. White (eds) *Agrarian Transformations: Local Processes and the State in Southeast Asia*, Berkeley, CA: University of California Press.

Lim Teck Ghee and Muhammad Ikmal Said (1989), 'Malaysia: Rice, Peasants and Political Priorities in an Economy Undergoing Restructuring', in G. Hart, A. Turton, B. White, (eds), *Agrarian Transformations: Local Processes and the State in Southeast Asia*, Berkeley, CA: University of California Press.

Lin, S.Y. (1992), 'The Savings-Investment Gap', in H.Y. Teh and K.L. Goh (eds), *Malaysia's Economic Vision: Issues and Prospects*, Kuala Lumpur: Pelanduk Books.

Lingenfelter, Sherwood G. (ed.), (1990), *Social Organisation of Sabah Societies*, Sabah Museum and State Archives Dept.

Lockard, Craig A. (1976), 'The Early Development of Kuching 1820- 57', *JMBRAS*, XLIX, Pt 2, 107–26.

Lockard, Craig A. (1987), *From Kampung to City: A Social History of Kuching, Malaysia, 1827–1960*, Southeast Asia Series No. 75, Ohio University.

Loh, F. Kok Wah (1990), 'Tin Mine Coolies and Agricultural Squatters' in Rimmer and Allen (1990).

Loh, F. Kok Wah (1992), 'Modernisation, Cultural Revival and Counter-Hegemony: The Kadazans of Sabah in the 1980s' in J.S. Kahn and F. Loh Kok Wah (eds), *Fragmented Vision: Culture and Politics in Contemporary Malaysia*, Sydney: Allen & Unwin.

Lubeck, P. (1992), 'Malaysian Industrialisation, Ethnic Divisions and the NIC Model', in R.P. Appelbaum, and J. Henderson (eds), *States and Development in the Asia Pacific Rim Countries*, London: Sage Publishing.

Mackie, J.A.C. (1989), 'Ersatz Capitalism: A Review of *The Rise of Ersatz Capitalism in Southeast Asia*', *Asia-Pacific Economic Literature*, 3, 1 (Mar.), 103–5.

Mackie, J.A.C. (1992), 'Changing Patterns of Chinese Big Business in Southeast Asia', in McVey (1992).

Maddison, Angus (1989), *The World Economy in the Twentieth Century*, Paris: OECD Development Centre.

Maddison, Angus (1993), *Explaining the Economic Performance of Nations 1820–1989*, Working Paper in Economic History No. 174, Canberra: Australian National University.

Malaya (1930, 1939), *Average Prices, Declared Trade Values, Exchange, Currency and the Cost of Living*, Singapore: Dept of Statistics, SS and FMS.

Malaysia: Ministry of Finance (1990/1), *Economic Report*, Kuala Lumpur: Government Printer.

Malaysian Government (1966–90), *Malaysian Development Plans, 1–5,* Kuala Lumpur: Government Printer.

Malaysian Government (various years), *Annual Bulletin of Statistics (ABS)*, Kuala Lumpur: Government Printer.

Malaysian Government (1986), *State/District Data Bank, Selangor Dahrul Ehsan 1980–86*, Kuala Lumpur: Dept of Statistics.

Malaysian Government (1987), *Bank Data Negeri/Daerah*, Kuala Lumpur: Dept of Statistics.

Malaysian Government (1990), *Labour Force Survey Report 1987–8*, Kuala Lumpur: Dept of Statistics.

Malaysian Government (1991a), *Malaysia: Yearbook of Statistics*, Kuala Lumpur: Government Printer.

Malaysian Government (1991b), *The Second Outline Perspective Plan 1991–2000*, Kuala Lumpur: Government Printer.

Malek bin Mansor and Barlow, C. (1988), *The Production Structure of the Malaysian Oil Palm Industry … the Smallholder Sub-Sector*, Kuala Lumpur: Palm Oil Research Institute of Malaysia.

Manning, Chris (1995), 'Approaching the Turning Point?: Labour Market Change under Indonesia's New Order', *The Developing Economies*, XXXIII (Mar.), 52–81.

Masing, J. (1988), 'The Role of Resettlement in Rural Development', in Cramb and Reece (1988).

Maznah Mohamad (1995), 'The Origins of Weaving Centres in the Malay Peninsula' *JMBRAS*, LXVIII, Pt 1, 91–118.

Maznah Mohamad (1996), *The Malay Handloom Weavers: A Study of The Rise and Decline of Traditional Manufacture*, Singapore: Institute of South Asian Studies, Singapore (ISEAS).

McCawley, P. (n.d.), 'The Economic Role of Governments in ASEAN', Mimeo.

McFadyean, A. (1944), *The History of Rubber Regulation 1934–1943*, London, Geo. Allen & Unwin.

McFadzean, H.S. (1946), 'Report on Development in Sarawak', (CO 938/1/6).

McGee, T.G. (1986), 'Joining the Global Assembly Line: Malaysia's Role in the International Semi-conductor Industry', in T.G. McGee *et al.* (eds), *Industrialisation and Labour Force Processes: A Case Study of Peninsular Malaysia*, Canberra: Research School of Pacific Studies, Australian National University.

McRoberts, R. (1991), 'A Study of Growth: An Economic History of Melaka, 1400–1510', *JMBRAS*, LXIV, 2, 47–79.

McVey, R. (ed.) (1992), *Southeast Asian Capitalists*, Ithaca, NY: Cornell University Press.

Means, G.P. (1991), *Malaysian Politics: The Second Generation*, Singapore: Oxford University Press.

Mehmet, Ozay (1986), *Development in Malaysia: Poverty, Wealth and Trusteeship*, London: Croom Helm.

Milne, R.S. (1992), 'Privatization in the ASEAN States: Who Gets What, Why and With What Effect?', *Pacific Affairs*, 65, 1 (Spring), 7–29.

Milne, R.S. and Mauzy, D. (1978), *Politics and Government in Malaysia,* Singapore: Times Books International.

Milner, A.C. (1982), *Kerajaan*, Tucson: University of Arizona Press.

Missen, G. (1986), 'Wage Labour and the Political Economy in West Malaysia' in T.G. McGee *et al*. (eds) *Industrialisation and Labour Force Processes: A Case Study of Peninsular Malaysia*, Canberra: Research School of Pacific Studies, Australian National University.

Mitchell, B.R. (1982), *International Historical Statistics: Africa and Asia*, New York: New York University Press.

Mohd Yaakub Hj. Johari and Sidhu, Baldev. S. (1989), *Urbanisation and Development … Sabah Beyond 1990*, Kota Kinabalu: IDS, Sabah.

Morley, James W. (ed.) (1993), *Driven by Growth: Political Change in the Asia-Pacific Region*, New York: M.E. Sharpe.

Morris, H.S. (1978), 'The Coastal Melanau', in V.T. King (ed.), *Essays on Borneo Societies*, Oxford: Oxford University Press.

Morris, H.S. (1979), 'The Decline of Aristocracy: Economic and Political Change in Sarawak', in W.A. Shack and P.S. Cohen (eds), *Politics and Leadership: A Comparative Perspective*, Oxford: Oxford University Press.

Morris, H.S. (1991), *The Oya Melanau*, Kuching: Malaysian Historical Association (Sarawak Branch).

Morrison, Philip S. (1993), 'Transitions in Rural Sarawak: Off-Farm Employment in the Kemena Basin', *Pacific Viewpoint*, 34 (May), 45–68.

Muhammad Ikmal Said (1990), 'Capitalist Development and Changes in Forms of Production in Malaysian Agriculture' in Muhammad Ikmal Said and Savaranamuttu (1990).

Muhammad Ikmal Said and Savaranamuttu, J. (eds) (1990), *Images of Malaysia*, Kuala Lumpur: Persatuan Sains Sosial Malaysia.

Mukhopadhyay, S. and Chee Peng Lim (1985), *Development and Diversification of Rural Industries in Asia*, Kuala Lumpur: Asia and Pacific Development Centre.

Myint, Hla (1977), *The Economics of the Developing Countries*, 4th Rev. edn, London: Hutchinson.

Myint, Hla (1985), 'Organisational Dualism and Economic Development', *Asian Development Review*, 3, 1, 24–42.

Narsey, W. (1988), 'A Reinterpretation of the History and Theory of Colonial Currency Systems', PhD, University of Sussex.

Nayagam, James (1990), 'Technology Choice and Migrant Labour in the Malaysian Natural Rubber Industry' (unpublished paper, Rubber Research Institute of Malaysia).

Nesadurai, H.E.S. (1991), 'The Free Trade Zone in Penang, Malaysia: Performance and Prospects', *Southeast Asian Journal of Social Science*, 19, 1, 103–35.

Nonini, Donald M. (1992), *British Colonial Rule and the Resistance of the Malay Peasantry 1900–57*, Yale University, S.E.Asia Studies Monograph 38.

Nooriah, Y., Morshidi, S. and Abibullah, S. (1995), 'Regional Industrialisation, Labour Supply Problems and Manufacturers' Responses: The Penang Case', *MJTG*, 26, 2, 121–9.

North Borneo (various years), *Annual Report*, Jesselton, Government Printer.

North Borneo (various years), *Annual Report, Customs Dept*, Jesselton: Government Printer.

Nurkse, R. (1962), *Patterns of Trade and Development*, Oxford: Basil Blackwell.

O'Brien, L. (1993), 'Malaysian Manufacturing Sector Linkages', in Jomo (1993).

O'Brien, P.K. (1997), 'Intercontinental Trade and Development of the Third World since the Industrial Revolution', *Journal of World History*, 8, 1, 75–133.

O'Connor, David (1993), 'Electronics and Industrialisation' in Jomo (1993).

Office of Strategic Services, SEAC/R. and A. (1944), 'Shortages and Rationing in Malaya' (26 Oct.); 'Services and Labour in Malaya' (Dec.).

Ogawa, N., Jones, G.W. and Williamson, J.G. (eds) (1993), *Human Resources and Development Along the Asia-Pacific Rim*, Singapore: Oxford University Press.

Ogawa, N. and Tsuya, N. (1993), 'Demographic Change and Human Resource Development in the Asia-Pacific Region: Trends of the 1960s to 1980s and Future Prospects', in Ogawa, Jones and Williamson.

Okamoto, Y. (1991), 'Impact of Trade and FDI Liberalization Policies on the Malaysian Economy', *The Developing Economies*, XXXII, 4, 460–78.

Ongkili, J. (1986), *Nation-Building in Malaysia 1964–74*, Kuala Lumpur: Oxford University Press.

Ongkili, M.J. and Pang Teck Wai (1992), 'Industrialisation in the State of Sabah: Missing Links and Challenges', 9th ASAA Conference, University of New England, Armidale.

Onozawa, Jun (1991), 'Restructuring of Employment Patterns under the NEP', *The Developing Economies*, XXIX, 4, 314–29

Ooi Jin Bee (1990), 'The Tropical Rain Forest: Patterns of Exploitation and Trade', *SJTG*, II, 2, 117–42.

Ooi, K.G. (1994), 'Chinese Vernacular Education in Sarawak under Brooke Rule 1841–1946', *MAS*, 28, 3, 503–31.

Oshima, Harry (1981), 'A. Lewis' Dualistic Theory and it's [sic]Relevance for Postwar Asian Growth', *MER*, XXVI, 2, 1–26.

Oshima, Harry T. (1987), *Economic Growth in Monsoon Asia*, Tokyo: Tokyo University Press.

Oshima, Harry T. (1988), 'Malaysia's Labour Force Trends and Unemployment Problems in Comparative Perspective', *MJES*, XXV, No. 2 (Dec.), 1–17.

Overton, John (1989a), 'The State and Rice Production in Malaya in the Late Colonial Period', Malaysia Society (ASAA), 6th Colloquium, Sydney University.

Overton, John (1989b), 'Water, Water Everywhere ... The Krian Irrigation Scheme in Malaysia 1890–1988', Research Seminar, Canberra: Dept of Geography, Australian National University.

Pang Teck Wai (1989), 'Economic Growth and Development', in Kitingan and Ongkili (1989).

Parkinson, C.N. (1996), *The Guthrie Flagship; United Sua Betong*, Edited and Abridged by J.M. Gullick, Kuala Lumpur: MBRAS.

Parmer, J.N. (1960), *Colonial Labour Policy and Administration*, New York: J.J. Augustin.

Parmer, J.N. (1990), 'Estate Workers' Health in the FMS in the 1920s', in Rimmer and Allen (1990).

Perumal, M.C. (1989), 'Economic Growth and Income Inequality in Malaysia 1957–84', *SER*, XXXIV (Oct.), 33–46.

Perumal, M.C. (1991), 'Welfare and Economic Growth in Peninsular Malaysia 1957–90', 7th Colloquium, Malaysia Society, Melbourne University.

Perumal, M.C. (1992), 'Who Benefitted from Economic Development in Peninsular Malaysia 1957–87', *Asian Economic Journal*, VI, 2, 121–30.

Phongpaichit, P. (1993), *The New Wave of Japanese Investment in ASEAN*, Singapore: ISEAS.

Pillai, P. (1995), 'Malaysia', *ASEAN Economic Bulletin*, 12, 2, 221–7.

Pletcher, J. (1989), 'Rice and Padi Market Management in West Malaysia', *Journal of Developing Areas*, 23 (Apr.), 363–84.

Pongsupath, Chuleeporn (1991), 'The End of the Revenue Farm System in the Straits Settlements and its Effects on Investment Patterns of Penang Chinese 1900–20', 12th IAHA Conference, Hong Kong.

Porritt, V. (1997), *British Colonial Rule in Sarawak*, Kuala Lumpur: Oxford University Press.

Pridmore, J. (1956), 'Sarawak Currency', *Sarawak Museums Journal*, VII, No. 7, 111–21.

Pringle, R. (1970), *Rajahs and Rebels: The Iban of Sarawak under Brooke Rule 1841–1941*, London: Macmillan.

Pringle, R. (1971), 'The Brookes of Sarawak: Reformers in spite of themselves', *Sarawak Museums Journal (SMJ)*, XIX (Jul./Dec.), 53–70.

Puthucheary, J.J. (1960), *Ownership and Control in the Malayan Economy*, Singapore: Donald Moore.

Radcliffe, D. (1969), 'The Peopling of Ulu Langat', *Indonesia*, 8, 155–83.

Rajah Rasiah (1992), 'Foreign Manufacturing Investment in Malaysia' *United Nations Economic Bulletin for Asia and the Pacific*, XLIII, 1 (June), 63–77.

Rajah Rasiah (1993), 'Competition and Governance: Work in Malaysia's Textile and Garment Industries', *Journal of Contemporary Asia (JCA)*, 23, 1, 3–23.

Rajah, Rasiah (1994), 'Capitalist Industrialisation in ASEAN', JCA, 24(2), 197–215.

Ramachandran, S. (1994), *Indian Plantation Labour in Malaysia*, Kuala Lumpur: S. Abdul Majeed for INSAN.

Ramachandran, S. (1995), 'The Poverty of Education on the Malaysian Plantation Frontier', *MAS*, 29, 3, 619–35.

Randolph, S. (1990), 'The Kuznets Process in Malaysia', *The Journal of Developing Economies*, 25 (Oct.), 15–32.

Ranjit Singh (1984), 'The Structure of the Indigenous Economy in Sabah in the 1860s and 1870s', in Abu Bakar *et al.* (1984).

Reece, R.H.W. (1988), 'Economic Development Under the Brookes', in Cramb and Reece (1988).

Reid, Anthony (1988), *Southeast Asia in the Age of Commerce 1450–1680: Volume 1. The Lands Below the Winds*; (1993) *Volume 2: Expansion and Crisis*, New Haven, Conn.: Yale University Press.

Reid, A.J.S. (1992), 'Economic and Social Change, c.1400–1800', ch. 8 in Nicholas Tarling (ed.), *The Cambridge History of Southeast Asia*, vol. 1, Cambridge: Cambridge University Press.

Reid, A.J.S. (1993), 'The Origins of Revenue Farming in Southeast Asia' in Butcher and Dick (1993).

Reid, A.J.S. (1995), 'Humans and Forests in Pre-colonial Southeast Asia', *Environment and History*, I, 93–110.

Reid, A.J.S. (forthcoming), *Southeast Asia Before the Nation State: An Economic History*, London: Macmillan.

Reid, A.J.S. and Fernando, R. (1994), 'Shipping in Melaka and Singapore as an index of growth 1760–1840', 13th IAHA Conference, Tokyo.

Reynolds, Lloyd G. (1986), *Economic Growth in the Third World: An Introduction*, New Haven, Conn.: Economic Growth Center, Yale University.

Rimmer, P.J. and Allen, L. (eds) (1990), *The Underside of Malaysian History; Pullers, Prostitutes and Plantation Workers*, Singapore University Press.

Royal Institute of International Affairs (1957), 'Sarawak: Political and Economic Background', mimeo.

Rudner, M.R. (1970), 'Rubber Strategy for Post-War Malaya 1945–8', *JSEAS*, 1 (Mar.), 23–36.

Rudner, M.R. (1972), 'The Draft Development Plan of the Federation of Malaya 1950–55', *JSEAS*, III (Mar.), pp. 63–96.

Rudner, M.R. (1976), 'The Structure of Government in the Colonial Federation of Malaya', *Southeast Asian Studies* (Kyoto), 13, 4, 495–512.

Rudner, M.R. (1979), 'The Evolution of Development Planning in Malaysia', Proceedings of the 7th IAHA Conference, Bangkok, 813–44.

Rudner, M.R. (1994), *Malaysian Development: A Retrospective*, Ottawa: Carleton University Press.

Sabah Government of (various years, 1966–90), *Annual Bulletin of Statistics*, ABS, Kota Kinabalu: Dept of Statistics.

Sadka, Emily (1968), *The Protected Malay States 1874–95*, Kuala Lumpur: University of Malaya Press.

Saham, Junid (1980), *British Industrial Investment in Malaysia 1963–71*, Kuala Lumpur: Oxford University Press.

Sandhu, Kernial S. (1969), *Indians in Malaya 1786–1957*, Cambridge: Cambridge University Press.

Sandhu, Kernial S. and Wheatley, Paul (1983), *Melaka: The Transformation of a Malay Capital c.1400–1980*, 2 vols, Kuala Lumpur: Oxford University Press.

Santokh Singh, Mahinder (1987), 'The Corridor Concept in Malaysia's Industrial Master Plan', Malaysia Society (ASAA)-Malaysian Social Science Association Colloquium, Universiti Sains Malaysia, Penang.

Sarawak (various years), *Annual Report: Treasury, Posts, Shipping Office, Customs*, Kuching: Government Printer.

Sarawak (various years), *Annual Report: Dept of Customs and Trade*, Kuching: Government Printer.

Sarawak Government (1961), *Report on Gross Domestic Product and Capital Formation for 1961*, Kuching: Government Printer.

Sarawak Government of (1970), *Statistical Handbook*, Kuching: Dept of Statistics.

Sarawak Government (various years), *Annual Bulletin of Statistics*, ABS, Kuching: Dept of Statistics.

Sarawak Government of (1984), *Sarawak Report 1963–83*, Kuching: Government Printer.

Saruwatari, K. (1991), 'Malaysia's Localisation Policy and its Impact on British-Owned Enterprises', *The Developing Economies*, XXIX, 4 (Dec.), 371–85.

Sather, C. (1997), *The Bajau-Laut: Adaptation, History and Fate in a Maritime Fishing Society of South-Eastern Sabah*, Kuala Lumpur: Oxford University Press.

Saw Swee-hock (1988), *The Population of Peninsular Malaysia*, Singapore: Singapore University Press.

Schedvin, B. (1990), 'Staples and Regions of Pax Britannica', *Economic History Review*, 2nd Series, XLIII, 4, 533–59.

Schenk, C. (1993), 'The Origins of a Central Bank in Malaya and the Transition to Independence 1954–9', *Journal of Imperial and Commonwealth History*, 21, 2, 409–31.

Schwenk, R.L. (1978), 'Agricultural Development in the Upper Rejang Valley', in M. Zamora, V. Sutlive and N. Altshuler (eds), *Studies in Third World Societies*, No. 3, 91–111.

Scott, James C. (1985), *Weapons of the Weak: Everday Forms of Peasant Resistance*, New Haven, Conn.: Yale University Press.

Searle, Peter (1999), *The Riddle of Malaysian Capitalism: Rent-Seekers or Real Capitalists?*, Sydney: Allen & Unwin.

Seavoy, R. (1980), 'Population Pressure and Land Use Change in Northwestern Kalimantan', *SJTG*, 1, No. 2, 61–7.

Sellato, Bernard (1994), transl. S. Morgan, *Nomads of the Borneo Rain-Forest: The Economics, Politics and Ideology of Settling Down*, University of Hawaii Press.

Semudram, M. (1987), 'Economic Stabilization Policies in Malaysia', in P.B. Rana and F.A. Alburo (eds), *Economic Stabilization Policies in ASEAN Countries*, Field Report Series No.17, Asean Economic Research Unit, ISEAS.

Shaharuddin Maaruf (1988), *Malay Ideas on Development: From Feudal Lord to Capitalist*, Singapore: Times Books International.

Shamsul, A.B. (1986), *From British to Bumiputera Rule*, Singapore: ISEAS.

Shamsul, A.B. (1997), 'The Economic Dimension of Malay Nationalism', *The Developing Economies*, XXXV, 3, 240–61.

Shand, R.T. (ed.) (1986), *Off-Farm Employment in the Development of Rural Asia*, 2 vols, Canberra: Australian National University.

Sharom Ahmat (1984), *Change and Tradition in a Malay State: The Economic and Political Development of Kedah 1873–1923*, Kuala Lumpur: MBRAS Monograph 12.

Short, B.K. (1971), 'Indigenous Banking in an Early Period of Development: The Straits Settlements 1914–40', *MER*, 16, 1, 57–75.

Silcock, T.H. (1956), *Fiscal Survey Report of Sarawak 1956*, Kuching: Government Printer.

Silcock, T.H. (1959), *The Commonwealth Economy in Southeast Asia*, Cambridge: Cambridge University Press.

Silcock, T.H. (1963), *The Economy of Malaya*, Singapore: Donald Moore.

Silcock, T.H. and Fisk, E.K. (1963), *The Political Economy of Independent Malaya*, Berkeley, CA: University of California Press.

Smith, T.E. (1952), *Population Growth in Malaya: An Analyis of Recent Trends*, Oxford: Oxford University Press for Royal Institute of International Affairs.

Snodgrass, D. (1966), 'Capital Stock and Malayan Economic Growth: A Preliminary Analysis', *MER*, XI (Oct.), 63–85.

Snodgrass, D. (1980), *Inequality and Economic Development in Malaysia*, Kuala Lumpur: Oxford University Press.

Soenarno, Radin (1986), 'The Economic Dimension of Territorial Integration', in *The Bonding of a Nation: Federalism and Territorial Integration in Malaysia*, Kuala Lumpur: Institute of Strategic and International Studies.

Solhee, Hatta (1988), 'The Rice Self-Sufficiency Policy: Its Implementation in Sarawak', in Cramb and Reece (1988).

Soltow, Lee (1983), 'Long-Run Wealth Inequality in Malaysia', *SER*, XXVIII, No. 2, pp. 79–97.

Spinanger, D. (1986), *Industrialisation Policies and Regional Economic Development in Malaysia*, Singapore: Singapore University Press.

Statistical Abstract for the British Overseas Dominions (1926), No. 57, London.

Statistical Abstract for the British Empire, 1924–9, 1929–38, Nos 60, 68, 70, London.

Stenson, M. (1980), *Class, Race and Colonialism in West Malaysia: The Indian Case*, St Lucia: University of Queensland Press.

Stevenson, Rex (1975), *Cultivators and Administrators: British Educational Policy Towards the Malays 1875–1906*, Kuala Lumpur: Oxford University Press.

Straits Settlements (various years, 1870–1915), *Blue Book*, Singapore.

Straits Settlements Government (1926), *Average Prices and Declared Trade Values*, Singapore: Government Printer.

Stubbs, R. (1974), *Counter-Insurgency and the Economic Factor: The Impact of the Korean War Prices Boom on the Malayan Emergency*, Singapore, ISEAS Occasional Paper No. 17.

Sutherland, H. (1978), 'The Taming of the Trengganu elite' in R. McVey (ed.), *Southeast Asian Transitions*, New Haven, Conn.: Yale University Press.

Sutlive, V.H. (1978), *The Iban of Sarawak,* Arlington Heights, Ill.: AHM.

Talib, Shaharil (1984), *After Its Own Image: The Terengganu Experience 1881–1941,* Kuala Lumpur: Oxford University Press.

Talib, Shaharil (1990), 'The Port and Polity of Terengganu in the Nineteenth and Twentieth Century', in J. Kathirithamby-Wells and J. Villiers (1990).

Tan, Gerald (1993), *The Newly Industrialising Countries of Asia,* Singapore: Times Academic Press.

Tan, P.C., Kwok, K.K., Tan, B.A., Tey, N.P. and Zulkifli, S. (1987), 'Socio-Economic Development and Mortality Patterns and Trends in Malaysia', *Asia-Pacific Population Journal,* 2, No. 1, 3–20.

Tarling, N. (1974), 'Borneo and British Intervention in Malaya' *JSEAS,* V, 2, 159–65.

Tarling, N. (1992), 'Brooke Rule in Sarawak and its Principles', *JMBRAS,* LXV, Pt 1, 15–26.

Tate, D.J.M. (1979), *The Making of Modern Southeast Asia,* vol. 2, *Economic and Social Change,* Kuala Lumpur: Oxford University Press.

Tate, D.J.M. (1989, 1991), *Power Builds The Nation: The National Electricity Board of the States of Malaya and its Predecessors,* 2 vols, Kuala Lumpur: The National Electricity Board of the States of Malaya, and Tenaga Nasional Berhad.

Tate, D.J.M. (1996), *The RGA History of the Plantation Industry in the Malay Peninsula,* Kuala Lumpur: Oxford University Press.

Tham Seong Chee (1980), 'Rural and Urban as Categories in Malay Life', ASAA Third National Conference, Griffith University, Brisbane.

Thoburn, J.T. (1977), *Primary Commodity Exports and Economic Development … A Study of Malaysia,* London: J. Wiley.

Thomas, V. and Yan,Wang (1996), 'Distortions, Interventions and Productivity Growth: Is East Asia Different?', *EDCC,* 44, 2, 265–80.

Tregonning, K. (1965), *A History of Modern Sabah (North Borneo 1881–1963),* 2nd edn, Kuala Lumpur: University of Malaya Press.

Tregonning, K. (1967), *Home Port Singapore: A History of the Straits Steamship Company Ltd 1890–1965,* Singapore: University of Malaya Press.

Trocki, Carl A. (1979), *Prince of Pirates,* Singapore: Singapore University Press.

Trocki, Carl A. (1990), *Opium and Empire: Chinese Society in Colonial Singapore 1800–1910,* Ithaca, NY: Cornell University Press.

Tunku Shamsul Bahrin and Khadijah Mohamed (1992), 'Kemendor Revisited: A Study of a Land Settlement Scheme in Malaysia', *MJTG,* 23, 2, 79–92.

Turnbull, C.M. (1972), *The Straits Settlements 1826–67,* Singapore: Oxford University Press.

United Nationas (1948), *Statistical Yearbook,* New York: United Nations.

United Nations (1982), *Migration, Urbanization and Development in Malaysia,* New York: United Nations.

United Nations (1986), *Population of Malaysia,* Country Monograph Series No. 13, Bangkok: ESCAP.

United Nations (1991), *Malaysia: Sustaining Industrial Development Investment Momentum,* Oxford: Basil Blackwell.

Van der Eng, Pierre (1993), *The Silver Standard and Asia's Integration into the World Economy 1850–1914,* Working Papers in Economic History No. 175, Canberra: Australian National University.

Van der Eng, Pierre (1994), 'Assessing Economic Growth and the Standard of Living in Asia 1870–1990', Milan, Eleventh International Economic History Congress.

Vincent, J.R., Ali, R.M. and Associates (1997), *Environment and Development in a Resource-Rich Economy: Malaysia Under the New Economic Policy,* Cambridge, MA: Harvard University Press.

Voon, P.K. (1976), *Western Rubber Planting Enterprise in Southeast Asia 1876–1921*, Kuala Lumpur: University of Malaya Press.

Voon, P.K. (1987). 'Indebtedness and Land Use in Pre-War Malaya with Special Reference to the Indigenous Society', Tokyo: Institute of Developing Economies, Visiting Research Fellow Series, No.147.

Voon, P.K. and Khoo, S.H. (1986), 'An Overview of the Impact of the Oil Industry in Kerteh, Terengganu, Malaysia', *MJTG*, 13 (June), 46–59.

Voon, P.K. and Teh, T.S. (1992), 'Land Use and the Environment in the South Kinabalu Highlands, Malaysia', *MJTG*, 23, 2, 103–18.

Wan Hashim (1988), *Peasants Under Peripheral Capitalism*, Bangi: Penerbit Universiti Kebangsaan Malaysia.

Warr, P.G. (1986), 'Malaysia's Industrial Enclaves: Benefits and Costs', in T.G. McGee *et al.* (1986).

Warren, J.F. (1981), *The Sulu Zone 1768–1898*, Singapore: Singapore University Press.

Wee Chong Hui (1995), *Sabah and Sarawak in the Malaysian Economy*, Kuala Lumpur: S.Abdul Majeed for Institute of Social Analysis.

Wheelwright, E.L. (1963), 'Reflections on some problems of industrial development in Malaya', *MER*, VIII, 1, 66–80.

Wheelwright, E.L. (1965), *Industrialization in Malaysia*, Melbourne: Melbourne University Press.

Whinfrey-Koepping, E. (1988), 'The Family in a Changing Agricultural Economy: A Longitudinal Study of an East Sabah Village', Working Paper No. 47, Monash Centre of Southeast Asian Studies.

White, N.J. (1994), 'Government and Business Divided; Malaya 1945–57', *Journal of Imperial and Commonwealth History*, 22, No. 2 (May), 251–74.

Whittlesey, C.R. (1931), *Governmental Control of Crude Rubber: The Stevenson Scheme*, Princeton, NJ: Princeton University Press.

Wilson, J.R. and Grey, P. (1966a), 'The Economy of Sabah', Report prepared for the Committee for the Economic Development of Australia: mimeo.

Wilson, J.R. and Grey, P. (1966b), 'The Economy of Sarawak', Report prepared for the Committee for the Economic Development of Australia: mimeo.

Windle, Jill (1996), 'Economic Impacts of Rural Roads on Upland Farmers in Sarawak, Malaysia', ASAA 20th Anniversary Conference, La Trobe University.

Wong, K.B. (1974), 'The Structure of Trade and Economic Development in Sabah, Malaysia', MLitt, Glasgow.

Wong Lin Ken (1960), 'The Trade of Singapore 1819–69', *JMBRAS*, XXXIII, 4, 5–315.

Wong Lin Ken (1965a), 'The Economic History of Malaysia: A Bibliographic Essay', *Journal of Economic History*, XXV, (June), 244–62.

Wong Lin Ken (1965b), *The Malayan Tin Industry to 1914*, Tucson: University of Arizona Press.

Wong Lin Ken (1978), 'Singapore: Its Growth as an Entrepot Port 1819–1941', *JSEAS*, IX, No. 1, 50–84.

Wong Lin Ken (1979), 'Twentieth Century Malayan Economic History: A Select Bibliographic Survey', *JSEAS*, X, 1, 1–25.

World Bank (1989), *Malaysia: Matching Risks and Rewards in a Mixed Economy Program*, Washington, DC: World Bank.

World Bank (various years), *World Development Report*, New York. Oxford University Press for World Bank.

Yamazawa, I. (1992), 'On Pacific Economic Integration', *Economic Journal*, 102, 1519–29.

Yen Ching Hwang (1986), *A Social History of the Chinese in Singapore and Malaya 1800–1911*, Singapore: Oxford University Press.

Yip Yat Hoong (1969), *The Development of the Tin Mining Industry of Malaya,* Kuala Lumpur: University of Malaya Press.

Yoshihara, Kunio (1988), *The Rise of Ersatz Capitalism in South-East Asia,* Singapore: Oxford University Press.

Yuen Choy Leng (1974), 'Japanese Rubber and Iron Investments in Malaya 1900–41', *JSEAS,* V, No. 1, pp. 18–35.

Zaharah bt Hji Mahmud (1980), 'The Dilemma of Modernisation of the Dual-Cropping Peasantry of Peninsular Malaysia', *MJTG,* 1 (Sept.), 64–71.

Zaharah bt Hji Mahmud (1992), 'The Traditional Malay Ecumene of The Peninsula', in P.K. Voon and T.S. Bahrin (eds), *The View from Within: Geographical Essays on Malaysia and Southeast Asia,* Kuala Lumpur: Dept of Geography, University of Malaya.

Zahid Emby (1990), 'The Orang Asli Regrouping Scheme', in King and Parnwell (1990).

Zainal Aznam Yusoff (1990), 'Distributional Policies and Programmes The Malaysian Experience' in Lee, K.H. and Nagaraj, S. (eds), *The Malaysian Economy Beyond 1990,* Kuala Lumpur: Malaysian Economic Society.

Zakaria, Hji Ahmad (1993), 'Malaysia in an Uncertain Mode', in Morley (1993).

Zulkifly, Hji Mustapha (1986), 'Perindustrian dan Pembangunan: Industri Kilangan di Sabah' in Hairi Abdullah, Abdul Samad Hadi and Zulkifly Hji Mustapha (eds), *Sabah: Perubahan Dalam Pembangunan,* Bangi: Universiti Kebangsaan Malaysia/ Yayasan Sabah.

Zulkifly, Hji Mustapha (1989), 'The Evolution of Malaysian Agricultural Development Policy: Issues and Challenges', in Fatimah Mohd Arshad *et al.* (1989).

Zulkifly, Hj Mustapha (1990), 'Agricultural Transformation and Rural Development in East Malaysia ... Sabah', in King and Parnwell (1990).

Index